the promise
& perils of
postmodernism

truth *or* consequences

millard j.
erickson

InterVarsity Press
Downers Grove, Illinois

InterVarsity Press
P.O. Box 1400, Downers Grove, IL 60515-1426
World Wide Web: www.ivpress.com
E-mail: mail@ivpress.com

InterVarsity Press® is the book-publishing division of InterVarsity Christian Fellowship/USA®, a student movement active on campus at hundreds of universities, colleges and schools of nursing in the United States of America, and a member movement of the International Fellowship of Evangelical Students. For information about local and regional activities, write Public Relations Dept., InterVarsity Christian Fellowship/USA, 6400 Schroeder Rd., P.O. Box 7895, Madison, WI 53707-7895, or visit the IVCF website at < www.ivcf.org >.

ISBN 0-8308-2657-2

Printed in the United States of America ∞

Library of Congress Cataloging-in-Publication Data

Erickson, Millard J.
  Truth or consequences : the promise & perils of postmodernism / Millard J. Erickson.
    p. cm.
  Includes bibliographical references.
  ISBN 0-8308-2657-2 (paper : alk. paper)
    1. Postmodernism—Social aspects. I. Title: Promise & perils of postmodernism. II.
  Title: Promise and perils of postmodernism. III. Title.
  HM449 .E75 2001
  300′.1—dc21

          2001026464

23 22 21 20 19 18 17 16 15 14 13 12 11 10 9 8 7 6 5 4 3 2 1

20 19 18 17 16 15 14 13 12 11 10 09 08 07 06 05 04 03 02 01

To Dr. David S. Dockery
President, Union University
Discerning student of postmodernism
True friend, in good times and bad

CONTENTS

Preface

The word *postmodernism* has been so widely used in the past decade that it has become virtually a household word. The literature on it is immense, and it is the popular topic of discussions at many cocktail parties and coffee circles. Yet the discussion is sometimes poorly informed. In many cases, there is not a real acquaintance with what the sources of postmodern thought have actually said. Many of the commentaries upon and responses to postmodernism have been either uncritically accepting or strongly negative. As a corrective, we need to distinguish between postmodernism and postmodernity. Roughly, the former is the intellectual beliefs of a specific period, while the latter is the cultural phenomenon thereof.

This book is an attempt at an in-depth introduction to the movement known as postmodernism. To do this, I examine the background factors that preceded postmodernism, and the intellectual developments that have contributed to it. Early in my graduate study I was taught that one should let the best representatives, the most capable and influential members of the movement, speak for it. This is the aim of the first part of this book.

I have tried to acquaint readers with the content and even to some extent the style, of the intellectual leaders of postmodernism. I then attempt to evaluate postmodernism, both positively and negatively, before going on to offer a constructive approach that takes into account its strengths and undeniable insights, while avoiding its more problematic features. On the basis of the belief that postmodernism itself is not the final answer to the issues it attempts to address, I have sought to take the first steps toward a "postpostmodernism."

One immediate difficulty we encounter in attempting an effort of this type is the claim of postmodernism that there is no neutral ground to occupy in understanding and evaluating a given ideology, including itself. How, then, can I purport to perform such an analysis and evaluation?

It is at this point that I would ask any reader to ask carefully about the process of communication. How is it that postmodern authors can attempt to communicate and engage in dialogue with those whose thought is of a different paradigm and vice versa? The point I am raising and will ultimately press at some length is this: when two persons from different paradigms engage in discussion, what paradigm does their discussion utilize? Or, to put it differently, when we discuss modernism and postmodernism, what is the status of that discussion itself: is it modernist, postmodernist, or something entirely different? I once raised that question in a panel discussion on postmodernism, and received the response from one panel member, "I don't understand the question." That, however, is *the* question that must be asked.

It goes without saying that any conception should be able to apply its principles to itself. One reviewer of a secondary work on postmodernism complained that the author simply assumed modernism, failing to see that "every reading is a misreading." Unfortunately, the reviewer neglected to see or admit that on that principle, his own reading of the book he was reviewing was also a misreading. It is this predicament that calls for the last section of this book.

I wish to express my appreciation to all who have contributed to this volume. I am especially indebted to the students in my class on postmodernism and the Christian faith at Western Seminary, Portland, during the fall semester of 1998, and at Truett Seminary, Baylor University, in the January term, 1999, for their questions and comments. Several chapters of this book have been presented to learned societies: chapter twelve as a plenary paper before the southwestern regional meeting of the Evangelical Theological Society at New Orleans, Louisiana, March 26, 1999, and the far west regional, La Mirada, California, April 23, 1999. Chapter ten was presented at the annual national meeting of the Evangelical Theological Society, Orlando, Florida, November 19, 1998, and chapters fourteen and fifteen as a plenary address to the national annual meeting of the Evangelical Theological Society, Danvers, Massachusetts, November 18, 1999. The questions and comments offered on those occasions were very helpful to me in refining the material. I have also benefited greatly from numerous discussions with colleagues, students, and friends, on the topic of postmodernism. Maria den Boer has improved the style with her skillful copyediting. Finally, I wish to thank the editorial staff of InterVarsity Press, and especially Jim Hoover, for encouraging me in the completion of this manuscript and for publishing it.

part 1

backgrounds to
postmodernism

1

an introduction to postmodernism

three sketches

Postmodernism is both a popular and an intellectual movement, a sociological characteristic of much contemporary Western society and a sophisticated way of thinking. It is particularly the latter sense of postmodernism I am investigating here.

An immediate objection will be raised. How can we examine postmodernism as a system of thought, when by its very nature it decries any sort of systematization of thinking, any comprehensive understanding of life and reality? We need to note that there are different ways of thinking about and describing a particular set of ideas; these descriptions can be compared to different types of maps.

The National Oceanic and Atmospheric Administration publishes aeronautical charts that are used for Visual Flight Rules navigation. These charts are very precise in the depiction of topographical features of the country. They include indications of all towers and other potential obstructions, indicating their height in mean sea level and above ground level. Exact locations and elevations of all airports are given, together with considerable additional information about those airports.

There are also roadmaps published by professional cartographic companies, distributed by the American Automobile Association, and available for sale in various places. These maps are fairly accurate but show less detail than aeronautical charts. They indicate distances between points, rounded to the nearest mile. While sufficient for most road navigation, the information they provide is not extremely exact.

Finally, there are maps that direct persons to a given location, often drawn on scraps of paper, such as the back of an envelope. These depict the rough outline of the course to be followed, showing right and left turns, the intersection of roads, and pertinent landmarks, and give approximation of distances involved. They do not have a great deal of detail, and are seldom drawn to very exact scale. They do, however, enable a person to find her or his way from one point to another.

This analogy could be carried over to many different examples. One would be a rough drawing of a floor plan, versus the blueprints that a drafts-man might produce. Another would be the humming of a tune, versus the full symphonic score and production of a musical composition. Yet another would be the painstaking and detailed portrait a professional artist might make of a person, versus the relatively quick drawing that street artists do for a fee, or finally, a rough sketch; at its extreme, a stick-figure drawing.

I will attempt to describe postmodernism using such a rough map or sketch. There is no uniform, consistent, or thoroughly worked-out scheme of thought such that it could in any way be called a system, in which all details are developed, careful distinctions are drawn, and relationships among the elements of the system are precisely worked out. That is not the nature of postmodernism. If, however, we are to understand and describe at all, there must be some themes or motifs that can elaborated, or it is ques-tionable whether we are thinking at all, rather than simply feeling. What we will attempt to describe in this work is a collection of elements, loosely clus-tered, but nonetheless lending their character to the movement. It may be that some of the objection to "systematizing" postmodernism stems from a confusion between the various types of description.

Interestingly, John Caputo, one of the most sympathetic interpreters of the thought of Jacques Derrida, suggests something of this same analogy in his "map for the perplexed." He says:

> For a philosopher like Derrida, who is so much taken with aporias and im-passes, who thinks that you are really getting somewhere only when you are paralyzed and it is impossible to advance, only when there is no plannable, programmable way to proceed, there is a fitting irony in supplying a map, a lit-tle "Michelin's Guide to Jacques Derrida," which is something like giving the Cartesian coordinates to the Promised Land (*Foi*, 15). Still, a map gives the tourist and casual visitor to the country, who only has a few days to take in everything, a chance to see the major sights.[1]

---

[1]John D. Caputo, *The Prayers and Tears of Jacques Derrida: Religion Without Religion* (Bloom-ington: Indiana University Press, 1997), p. xxvii.

It is in this same sense—an overview of the ideas of several representatives of postmodernism—that I am presenting this work. In theory, if these ideas are really viable concepts others might adopt, then it ought to be possible to examine them. This is what an analytic philosopher, Samuel Wheeler, has attempted to do. He says, "These chapters discuss Derrida and other 'deconstructive' thinkers from the perspective of an analytic philosopher willing to treat deconstruction as philosophy, taking it seriously and looking for arguments. This attitude has often proved not to the liking of other analytic philosophers, who tend to view deconstruction and Derrida as enemies of rational thought rather than as interesting sources of new ideas."[2]

Before undertaking the actual detailed examination of several postmodern thinkers themselves, it may be helpful to look at several descriptions of postmodernism. This will help to illustrate the many different nuances of postmodernism and the variety of interpretations of it. These three sketches should not necessarily be thought of as postmodern treatises in themselves, or as primary sources of postmodernism. Rather, they are secondary works. Three varied approaches are the characterizations by Jean-François Lyotard; Alasdair MacIntyre; and James McClendon and Nancey Murphy.

Jean-François Lyotard

One of the earliest attempts to sketch the emerging postmodern ideology was Lyotard's *The Postmodern Condition: A Report on Knowledge*, which first appeared in French in 1979 and in English translation in 1984. As the title indicates, this is a study of the condition of knowledge, particularly in the most highly developed societies, and that condition is what Lyotard terms postmodernism. He contends that transformations have taken place which have altered the game rules for science, literature, and the arts. The context for this is the crisis of narratives.

The crisis can be seen in the problem that science, which has usually seen narratives as fables, has of legitimating itself. It does this using the discourse of philosophy. In the modern period this has been done with respect to some grand narrative. So, for example, in the Enlightenment model, truth is related to "a possible unanimity between rational minds." In the postmodern period, however, there is an incredulity about metanarratives.[3] In fact, this is Lyotard's definition of postmodernism. The conflict between science and its form of discourse and legitimation and the narra-

---

[2]Samuel C. Wheeler III, *Deconstruction as Analytic Philosophy* (Stanford, Calif.: Stanford University Press, 2000), p. 2.

[3]Jean-François Lyotard, *The Postmodern Condition: A Report on Knowledge* (Minneapolis: University of Minnesota Press, 1984), pp. xxiii-xxv.

tive approach comprises much of his discussion.

Lyotard's thesis is enunciated clearly: "the status of knowledge is altered as societies enter what is known as the postindustrial age and cultures enter what is known as the postmodern age."[4] This change has been going on since at least the end of the 1950s, and in Europe it is the completion of reconstruction. The pace of this transition varies from one country to another, and even within a given country, from one sector of activity to another.[5]

Lyotard chooses to expound this transition, not by an overall survey, but by examining in detail one area: science. He notes that for the preceding forty years the leading sciences and technologies have been concerned with language, whether in terms of linguistics, cybernetics, information storage and data banks, or several other types of problems. These technological transformations have a significant effect on knowledge and its two functions: research and the transmission of acquired learning. Genetics, with its cybernetic theoretical paradigm, is one example of the first function. In the second, the proliferation of information-processing machines is changing knowledge, particularly its dissemination.[6] Lyotard predicts that only such elements of the body of knowledge as can be translated into computer languages will be able to survive in this new world. Computers, however, bring with them a certain kind of logic, and thus, a determination of what constitutes acceptable "knowledge." This includes an exteriorization of knowledge to the knower. Whereas formerly the acquisition of knowledge was associated with the training of minds, that is becoming increasingly obsolete. More and more, knowledge is being treated as a commodity, produced in order to be sold.[7]

The information revolution is an indication of the changes that have taken place in the role of knowledge. In this postindustrial and postmodern age, knowledge is and will be a major factor in the worldwide competition for power. Whereas in previous ages war took place over territory, and then for raw materials and cheap labor, it is quite possible that in the future such a struggle will be concerned with the possession and control of information. Knowledge, however, has become commercialized, so that the state, which once had possession of education, has come to be viewed as a factor of opacity and noise, rather than of transparency. Learning will circulate along the same lines as money. As with money, there will be

---

[4]Ibid., p. 3.
[5]Ibid.
[6]Ibid., p. 4.
[7]Ibid.

"payment knowledge" and "investment knowledge."[8]

An important question is the problem of "legitimation." Science and technical knowledge is cumulative, but the debate is over whether that cumulation is regular, continuous, and unanimous, or periodic, discontinuous, and conflictual. Narrative knowledge has always existed alongside scientific knowledge, competing and conflicting with it. While it may never prevail over science, it has an advantage in terms of internal equilibrium and conviviality. The exteriorization and alienation found within science had a significant demoralizing effect among researchers and teachers in the 1960s.[9]

This demoralization affects the problem of legitimation. By this term Lyotard means something broader than the discussions of authority. In civil law, the question of legitimation authorizes a legislator to pass laws, and to set these up as norms. In the case of a scientific statement, there is a rule "that a statement must fulfill a given set of conditions in order to be accepted as scientific." In this case, legitimation is the process by which someone "is authorized to prescribe the stated conditions according to which a statement is to be included in that discourse for consideration by the scientific community."[10]

This question of legitimation leads Lyotard to a discussion of linguistic considerations, and particularly of "language games." He describes the differences among denotative statements, performative utterances and prescriptions, as well as questions, promises, literary descriptions, narrations and others. In Wittgenstein's language games, each of these types of utterance is considered a particular category of utterance governed by rules specifying its characteristics and uses. These are, in this realm, like the rules of a game such as chess, which specify the status of each piece and the ways they can be moved.[11] This is the nature of the observable social bond: a series of language game moves.

This leads Lyotard to a discussion of the nature of the social bond. Here he observes that there have been, in the past half-century, two major theories of the nature of society: that society is a functional whole, and that it consists of two opposed halves. The former has been especially expressed by Talcott Parsons, while the major form of the latter has been Marxism.

In the postmodern perspective on the nature of the social bond, much has been changed. Lyotard speaks of the breaking up of the grand narratives, which used to supply much of the basis of the social bond. Is the result

---

[8]Ibid., pp. 5-6.
[9]Ibid., pp. 7-8.
[10]Ibid., p. 8.
[11]Ibid., p. 10.

then the "dissolution of the social bond and the disintegration of social aggregates into a mass of individual atoms thrown into the absurdity of Brownian motion"? This is not the case, however, he maintains, and the dissolution scenario is a carryover of the concept of an "organic" society.[12] The idea that society is a collection of individual selves, each sufficient to itself, is based on too strong an understanding of the nature of the self. Rather, says Lyotard, "A *self* does not amount to much, but no self is an island; each exists in a fabric of relations that is now more complex and mobile than ever before."[13] While not claiming that the entirety of social relations is of the nature of language games, he is using language games as his general methodological approach. This does not require some fiction of social origins. Even before birth, the human child is already positioned within the web of language games by virtue of having been named.

This understanding of the social bond is not merely a matter of communication theory, however. With the emphasis now on cybernetics, communication restricts the understanding of language games to one particular variety, namely, the communication of information. The view Lyotard is developing is much more complex and varied. He especially emphasizes what he terms "agonistics." This is the concept of "moves," in which one linguistic move causes a displacement, requiring some change and response in the addressee. In a conversation, the partners change games from one utterance to another. An institution differs from a simple conversation in that it has rules, formal or informal, as to the bounds of admissible statements. These are not permanently fixed, but are provisional, and even such constraints are themselves the results of various language strategies. The boundaries themselves are stakes in the game, and only stabilize when they cease to be such stakes.[14]

A major element of Lyotard's essay is the distinction between scientific knowledge and narrative knowledge. In the modern period, there has been a tendency to reduce knowledge to science. This is too narrow an identification, however. Not only can knowledge not be reduced to science, it cannot even be reduced to learning. Learning is "the set of statements which, to the exclusion of all other statements, denote or describe objects and may be declared true or false." Science, then, is a subset of learning, a specialized form of learning. While it is composed of denotative statements, there are two additional conditions for the acceptability of such statements: the objects they refer to must be available for repeated access, and it must be

---

[12]Ibid., p. 15.
[13]Ibid.
[14]Ibid., pp. 16-17.

possible to determine whether a given statement is a case of the language the experts would deem relevant.[15]

Whereas scientists would limit knowledge in this way, it is not simply a collection of denotative statements. It must be understood broadly enough to include such matters as know-how, knowing how to live and how to listen. As a question of competence, it goes beyond merely the measure of the criterion of truth. It involves the criteria of efficiency, justice and/or happiness, and beauty. Knowledge is not only what enables someone to make "good" utterances in the area of the descriptive or denotative but also good prescriptive and evaluative utterances.[16]

While it is relatively clear on what basis the descriptive can be determined to be "good," what about these other kinds of knowledge? As with denotative knowledge they are judged good "because they conform to the relevant criteria (of justice, beauty, truth, and efficiency respectively) accepted in the social circle of the 'knower's interlocutors.'"[17] In other words, the criteria are those of the community, which are part of its culture. This is traditional or customary knowledge, which makes it possible to distinguish one who knows from those who do not, such as foreigners and children.

There have been many ethnological descriptions of this type of knowledge. All agree, however, in seeing narrative as the preeminent form of traditional knowledge. There are several ways in which narrative is the "quintessential form of customary knowledge."[18]

First, the popular stories recount what Lyotard refers to as "positive or negative apprenticeships." By this is meant the success or failure of the heroes of the stories. These stories enable the society in which they are told to define its criteria of competence, and thus evaluate what is done within it.

Second, the narrative form gives itself to a wide variety of language games: denotative, deontic, interrogative, evaluative.

Third, there are definite rules governing the transmission of narratives. There is a definite formula for introducing and concluding the story. These fixed patterns reveal certain characteristics of the phenomenon of storytelling. The only claim to competence that the narrator advances is having heard the story himself. The narratee could, by virtue of having been a narratee, also be able to become a narrator as well. Thus, the knowledge transmitted by the narratives is not limited to enunciation of content. It

---

[15]Ibid., p. 18.
[16]Ibid., pp. 18-19.
[17]Ibid., p. 19.
[18]Ibid.

determines "what one must say in order to be heard, what one must listen to in order to speak, and what role one must play (on the scene of diegetic reality) to be the object of a narrative."[19] There are speech acts performed not only by the speaker of the story, but also by the listener and any third party referred to. Thus, "what is transmitted through these narratives is the set of pragmatic rules that constitutes the social bond."[20]

Fourth, there is a definite effect of narrative knowledge on time. It follows a rhythm, involving a meter beating time in regular periods and accenting certain of those periods. This can be seen in nursery rhymes, for example. What happens is that time ceases to be a support for memory. Instead, there is an immemorial beating, which prevents the periods from being numbered. Even proverbs and maxims are splinters of potential narratives or molds of old ones.

What is striking about narrative form is that a culture that gives it precedence does not need any special procedures to authorize these narratives. Narratives both determine the criteria of competence and illustrate how they are to be applied. The question of authorization or legitimation is not dealt with in the same way as in the scientific approach: "They [the narratives] thus define what has the right to be said and done in the culture in question, and since they are themselves a part of that culture, they are legitimated by the simple fact that they do what they do."[21]

Scientific knowledge and its pragmatics are quite different. Citing as an example Copernicus's statement that the path of the planets is circular, Lyotard notes that such a statement brings with it certain tensions, which affect all three posts of the communication process: sender, addressee, and referent. These are classes of prescriptions that govern whether a statement can be admitted as "scientific." First, the senders should speak the truth about the referent. Second, the addressee should be able to give or refuse assent to the statement. Third, the speaker's description of the referent is supposed to conform to what is actually the case. This last prescription creates a problem, however. What one says is true because he proves it is, but what proof is there that the proof is true? Two rules are to be observed. The first is dialectical or rhetorical, namely, that although I cannot prove that reality is the way I say it is, as long as I can produce proof, it is acceptable to think that reality is as I say it is. The other is a metaphysical rule: the same reality cannot produce a plurality of inconsistent proofs. Stated differently, this means that God is not deceptive.[22]

---

[19] Ibid., p. 21.
[20] Ibid.
[21] Ibid., p. 23.
[22] Ibid., pp. 23-24.

These are the rules governing research. Research, however, has teaching as its necessary complement, since the scientist needs an addressee. This presupposes that the student does not know what the sender does, but can learn that, and that the student can become an expert with competence equal to that of the teacher, and in fact is even capable of exceeding the teacher. These requirements further presuppose that there are statements for which the exchange of arguments and the production of proof are believed to be sufficient so that they can be taught as they stand.[23]

Lyotard compares the pragmatics of science with that of narrative knowledge as follows:

1. Scientific knowledge concentrates on one language game, denotation, and excludes all others.

2. Scientific knowledge is not a direct and shared component of the social bond, being set apart from the language games that form it. It is indirectly part of it, because it gives rise to a profession and to institutions.

3. Within research, the competence required concerns only the sender, not the addressee or the referent.

4. Scientific statements are not validated by being reported. In pedagogy, a statement is taught only if it is still verifiable.

5. Science involves a diachronic temporality, that is, a memory and a project. That means that senders of statements should be familiar with previous statements about that referent, and only propose a new one if it is different from those earlier statements.[24]

It will be seen that there is an asymmetrical relationship between the two types of knowledge. Narrative knowledge is tolerant of scientific knowledge, because it does not give antecedent legitimation of its knowledge. It therefore regards scientific knowledge as a variant within the family of narrative cultures. The same is not true of scientific knowledge, however, because it questions the validity of narrative statements, concluding that they are not subject to argumentation or proof. This demand for legitimation is another form of imperialism, found in Western culture.[25]

Alasdair MacIntyre

Although not claiming to be postmodern himself, and without using the label of postmodernism, the philosopher Alasdair MacIntyre has sketched quite clearly the differences between modern and postmodern views. While the depictions are found in a number of his writings, he has stated the views

---

[23]Ibid., pp. 24-25.
[24]Ibid., pp. 25-26.
[25]Ibid., p. 27.

most clearly in *Three Rival Versions of Moral Enquiry*. The contrast between what he terms the "encyclopaedist" and the "genealogist" approaches sets forth the issues.

The encyclopaedist approach. Because the book comprises the lectures MacIntyre gave as the Gifford Lectures, he describes what he terms "Adam Gifford's Project in Context." The Gifford lecturers were to deal with natural theology, and Adam Gifford had written, "I wish the lecturers to treat their subject as a strictly natural science. . . . I wish it to be considered just as astronomy or chemistry is."[26] Two of the early Gifford lecturers posed the question of the definition or identification of a natural science and agreed that one mark is rational progress in inquiry. MacIntyre concedes that there has clearly been such progress in fields like chemistry and astronomy, but contends that this has not been the case in natural theology. In fact, he says, "Not only has there been no progress in respect of generally agreed results of such enquiries, but there is not even agreement as to what the standard of rational progress ought to be."[27] There was a considerable affinity between Gifford's view and that of the ninth edition of the *Encyclopaedia Britannica*. The editor of that work, Thomas Spencer Baynes, in his preface to the first volume, indicated that he expected his contributors not only to give detailed information about their assigned topic, but to do so within the framework of a particular architectonic of the sciences.[28]

What are the characteristics of a science, according to the *Encyclopaedia?* The difference in the sciences concerns their subject matter, rather than their method. The article on logic, by Robert Adamson, spells out these qualities of a science. Logic, as the author defines it, is "the critical theory of knowledge," or what we would term today epistemology. This is a science concerned with the methodology of the sciences, so that it can be defined irrespective of the subject matter. There are four constitutive elements of a science.[29] The first is the data or facts. Second, there are unifying conceptions, drawn from the facts by methodological reflection. If based on correct comprehension of the facts and done with sufficient inventiveness, these order the facts as exemplifying laws. Third, there are the methods used to move from the facts to the general conceptions, and then back to the facts for confirmation. Fourth, there is progress in the process, so that ever more adequate conceptions are formed, specifying increasingly more fundamental laws. What distinguishes science from prescientific and nonscientific

---

[26]Alasdair MacIntyre, *Three Rival Versions of Moral Enquiry: Encyclopaedia, Genealogy, and Tradition* (Notre Dame, Ind.: University of Notre Dame Press, 1990), p. 9.

[27]Ibid., p. 10.

[28]Ibid., p. 18.

[29]Ibid., p. 20.

thinking is a particular kind of history, namely, that of progress, which is relatively continuous.[30]

There is a certain universality about this ideal of science, as the editor and many contributors to the encyclopaedia saw it. They regarded both the details of each science and the overall conception of the structure of the sciences as essential characteristics of the educated person. In fact, the human sciences displayed an additional element beyond the sciences of nature. They were seen as revealing the elevation of the person in intellectual and moral progress.[31]

This application of the conception of science is carried to theology as well. A representative of this orientation is Robert Flint, who wrote the article "Theology" for the encyclopaedia. He attempted in this article to answer the question, "What . . . is truly scientific knowledge in Theology?" In his description of theology he therefore seeks to point out the presence of these same elements of science in this discipline. He begins with the data of theology, which includes both the data of nature, which forms the basis of natural theology, and the data of the Bible, which serves as the starting point for revealed theology. While the subject matter of theology is religion, that topic includes God. So the experience of God, who is the object of both religious experience and theological reflection, is the experience of objectivity. Consequently, theology can be considered a science. But what of atheists and agnostics, who fail to understand and appreciate this? Their failure to come to this same conclusion is due to "a distorting one-sidedness in their mode of apprehending that whole whose parts are the data of theology."[32] For Baynes, the editor of the encyclopaedia, philosophy was the organizing discipline of the whole. For Gifford and for Flint, this integrating function is performed, not by philosophy, but by theology, and specifically, by natural theology. Because this understanding of natural theology as the greatest and, in some senses, the only science, parallels the view lying behind the encyclopaedia, it is not surprising that many of the early Gifford lecturers were contributors to the *Britannica*.[33]

The elements of the worldview on which the *Britannica* is based are evident. That view assumed that there is a common rationality, to which all educated people would agree. Following the standards and methods of such a rationality would lead to a comprehensive scientific understanding of the whole, in which everything fit within a logical place. This whole mode of

---

[30]Ibid.
[31]Ibid., p. 21.
[32]Ibid., p. 22.
[33]Ibid., p. 23.

life, including the understandings of rationality and science, is part of a history of inevitable progress.[34]

MacIntyre had taken as his topic for the Gifford Lectures the last in the list that Adam Gifford had included in his will: "the Knowledge of the Nature and Foundation of Ethics or Morals, and of all Obligations and Duties thence arising." Consequently, his comparison of different approaches is in terms of this grounding of ethics. For Gifford, this question was not a different one from natural theology, but was part of it, for he held that there was an eternal, unchangeable scheme of morality, founded on God's unchanging nature. It is therefore instructive to see what morality was for Adam Gifford. First, he regarded it as a distinct and autonomous domain, as distinguished from the aesthetic, religious, economic, legal, and scientific. Second, it was primarily a matter of rules. Third, these rules were negative prohibitions, rather than positive injunctions. Fourth, in the culture of Gifford's time and place, a strong sense of impropriety was attached to violations of the customs, and this impropriety was thought of as a variety of immorality. Fifth, agreement on the content of morality coexisted with significant disagreements about how it is to be intellectually justified. There was, however, an agreement that morality, thus understood, must be rationally justifiable somehow.[35]

The genealogist approach. MacIntyre points out that the form of presentation of the encyclopaedist view also fit its content well. The article was the ideal medium of expression, because it assumed the common rationality of the writer and the reader, and drew its justification from the authority of the author's expertise. This was not the only genre, however. The lecture similarly assumed this same rationality, being in effect a spoken encyclopaedia article. In light of this, MacIntyre does not think it surprising that one of the leading nineteenth-century critics of the encyclopaedist approach, Friedrich Nietzsche, abandoned the genre of the lecture by leaving the university.[36]

Nietzsche raised several types of objections to this objectivistic and universally rationalistic approach of the encyclopaedists. The first objection is psychological. The idea that there is one common rationality that all men possess is a case of failing to recognize an unconscious motive. Those who function in the encyclopedist mode are part of a fraternity, as it were, which has systematically institutionalized lack of self-knowledge. Persons who are part of that professorial fraternity are deformed. They are involved in complicity with a system of suppressions and repressions of any opposition to

---

[34]Ibid., p. 24.
[35]Ibid., p. 26.
[36]Ibid., pp. 32-33.

such an approach. This is part of what Nietzsche was later to call the *will to power*.[37]

Epistemologically, what is involved in this lack of self-knowledge is a blindness to "the multiplicity of perspectives from which the world can be viewed and to the multiplicity of idioms by means of which it can be characterized; or rather, a blindness to the fact that there is a multiplicity of perspectives and idioms, but no single world which they are of or about." It is a case of supposing that there is a world that would remain even if one subtracted the perspective from which one views it.[38]

Nietzsche's critique is also historical in nature. He writes the history of the process in which social and psychological factors distorted the will to power into the will to truth, which then also concealed it. Ostensibly, this was a concern for purity of truth, but it was actually a case of malice and hate. He sees this as a new kind of asceticism, in which scholarship prided itself on its freedom from the illusions, theological and otherwise, that had preceded the Enlightenment. In pointing out these limitations of the philosophers, Nietzsche does not claim to have refuted them by the use of a more effective or more accurate dialectic. Rather, he was simply mocking the claims of dialectic.[39]

This approach is radically different from that of the encyclopaedists. The encyclopedists thought there was a single framework for knowledge, a rationality common to all humans, a truth that could be arrived at by applying the ideal methodology, whose rules were the rules of rationality as such. This methodology was basically the same in all disciplines, the difference being only in the specifics of the subject matter. For Nietzsche, on the other hand, there is a multiplicity of perspectives. From each of these one may develop a truth from a point of view, but not a truth as such. The latter is an empty notion, as is the idea of *the* world. Instead of universal and objective rules or rationality, there are simply strategies of insight. There are also strategies of subversion, including the type of endeavor he has engaged in with respect to the encyclopaedist's approach.[40]

A similar contrast can be seen in ethics. In the encyclopaedist's view there is a set of conceptions of right and good that are superior to those of pre-Enlightenment views, both in terms of the quality of moral conduct and the justification of the moral judgments. To the genealogist such as Nietzsche, however, following the view just described is itself a case of bad-

---

[37]Ibid., p. 35.
[38]Ibid., p. 36.
[39]Ibid., pp. 41-42.
[40]Ibid., p. 42.

ness. It is a sign of inadequately managed resentment, as a will to power. What must be done is subversion, the breaking down of such conceptions and the breaking up of fixed patterns or systems of rules.[41] It is not a matter of showing the superior rationality of one's own view, but of undermining the whole idea of rational, universal rules that guide our behavior.

If we now have two opposed views, what can be done by way of engaging them with one another, or fostering genuine dialogue and understanding? MacIntyre points out that each of these approaches has its own characterization of the other, and indeed must. To the encyclopaedist, the genealogist is just spelling out familiar irrationalist themes. So genealogy is just one more case of relativism, and is therefore susceptible to the arguments Socrates made against Protagoras. On the other hand, to the genealogist the encyclopaedist is imprisoned within metaphors that he fails to recognize as such. And both of them regard any attempt to describe this conflict between the two from some third, noncommittal point as impossible, because there is no neutral ground.[42]

One can, of course, attempt to learn the two idioms as new first languages, the way an anthropologist attempts to learn the language and culture of a group of which he is not antecedently a part. When one does that, however, it becomes apparent that any attempt by either of the two parties to translate the other's view into their own inevitably leads to distortion of sorts. It is possible to see the other as in some sense a variant of one's own view, so that the genealogist sees the encyclopaedist as a reified extension of his own much more limited concept, and the encyclopaedist sees genealogy as a diminished and self-destructive reworking of his own truth as such. The two even differ in their characterization of the nature of the difference, since the encyclopaedist approach necessarily requires that there be only one point of view, into which all others must be incorporated, while the genealogist's approach must insist on the possibility of genuinely alternative schemes.[43]

MacIntyre at this point engages in an extended discussion of the problems of self-referentiality and related issues faced by the genealogist, and brings Michel Foucault into the picture. That discussion need not concern us at this point. He describes as an alternative a third approach, which he terms the approach of tradition, as exemplified by such figures as Augustine and Thomas Aquinas. Seeing the fragmented nature of the contemporary university, he advocates that lecturers become explicit about the partisan

---

[41]Ibid., pp. 42-43.
[42]Ibid., p. 43.
[43]Ibid., pp. 43-44.

character of their work. They should acknowledge frankly their own traditions, seek to advance inquiry from within them, and engage representatives of other traditions in dialogue.[44]

Nancey Murphy and James W. McClendon Jr.

The late James W. McClendon Jr. and Nancey Murphy, husband and wife, have developed a scheme for distinguishing modern and postmodern theologies. As such, this scheme also sheds light on the nature of modernism and postmodernism in general. They begin by asserting that there is an increasing awareness that the modern period, ushered in by Descartes and the Enlightenment, is passing or has passed in science, philosophy, and theology, but that it is less clear what its successor is and will be. They suggest that the term *postmodern* has thus far been used in three contexts: art and architecture, deconstructionist literary criticism, and American theology. They proceed by delineating modernism in terms of the three axes, and then defining postmodernism negatively by showing how it departs from these axes.[45]

Modern thought. Murphy and McClendon identify modernism in terms of three philosophical motifs: epistemological foundationalism, the representational-expressivist theory of language, and atomism or reductionism. Each of these areas constitutes an axis on which modern views can be represented.

Epistemological foundationalism is the view, most fully exemplified in the thought of René Descartes, that knowledge can only be justified by finding some indubitable or incorrigible beliefs on which the reasoning process can begin. In so doing, it sees philosophy as making possible all other disciplines, by establishing their starting points. The reasoning is that if any tenet is to be certain, its support cannot be circular or involve an infinite regress.[46]

Modern epistemology has had a strong concern with skepticism. The reason for this is that, if the foundation is not secure, knowledge has lost its justification and skepticism follows. It should be noted that modern skeptics and modern foundationalists share the same view of knowledge, the former seeing problems with the foundationalist program. So they may be thought of as opposite ends of a line between foundationalist certainty and skepticism. Descartes was at the extreme foundationalist end of the line, starting

---

[44]Ibid., pp. 216-36.
[45]Nancey Murphy and James W. McClendon Jr., "Distinguishing Modern and Postmodern Theologies," *Modern Theology* 5, no. 3 (1989): 191.
[46]Ibid., p. 192.

with intuitions (clear and distinct ideas) and reasoning from them deductively. David Hume made the foundation of his beliefs sense experience, but concluded that deductive reasoning was not adequate as a means of constructing a view from the sensory impressions. There are varying interpretations of Hume, some of which would place him at the skeptical end of the continuum, but others that see him as somewhere in the middle.[47]

Murphy and McClendon assert that modern philosophy of language has for the most part thought of the meaning of language inhering in the fact that it refers to objects in the world, naming and representing facts about them. The problem is, however, that some sentences having the grammatical form of statements do not appear to refer to objects, ethics being one such type of sentence. Since this representational theory of language was not deemed adequate to cover such areas, a supplementary view of meaning was appended to the representational theory, namely, the expressivist or emotivist theory. According to such a view, emotional discourse expresses the speaker's attitudes or emotions. Thus, various types of discourse could in theory be distributed along the continuum, but in practice they tend to be found at either one end or the other. Logical positivists and philosophers such as Bertrand Russell and the early Ludwig Wittgenstein sought to develop artificial languages that would mirror the structures of reality.[48]

The final area defining the modern view is reductionism, individualism, and the generic view of community. In the premodern period the church's traditional authorities, the philosopher and the Bible, had prevailed, but in the modern period, the flight from these external authorities led to a focus on the individual as the basis of authority. Descartes, the solitary individual seeking to ascertain truth for himself, was an example, but political authority similarly was based on the consent of individuals.[49]

In modern political theory there were at least two forms of individualism, according to Murphy and McClendon. One was the idea that the individual has priority over the collective. The group is simply a collection of individuals, who alone are real. There has also more recently been a methodological thesis which maintains that to comprehend the functioning of groups it is necessary to understand the laws governing the behavior of individuals. Some thinkers taking exception to this thesis, such as Hegel and Marx, emphasized the group as the key to the reality of the individual.[50]

Murphy and McClendon consider methodological individualism an

---

[47]Ibid., p. 193.
[48]Ibid., pp. 194-95.
[49]Ibid., p. 196.
[50]Ibid., pp. 196-97.

instance of a more general tendency in modern science: reduction. This was especially inspired by the success of mechanism in physics, where the macro properties of gases can be explained on the basis of the properties of their molecules. This was also seen in the philosophy of language, where the meaning of sentences was understood as a function of the meaning of words, and in epistemology, where atomic facts were the building blocks from which other knowledge is constructed.[51]

These three axes then form, in the judgment of Murphy and McClendon, the three-dimensional "space" within which modern thought can be located. They acknowledge that additional dimensions could also be developed, such as a rhetorical dimension, with poles of detachment or objectivity and of subjectivity or self-involvement.[52]

These three axes constitute the basis for Murphy and McClendon's definition of postmodernism. They state, "We propose to define as postmodern any mode of thought that departs from the three modern axes described above without reverting to premodern categories."[53] There is not, at this point, complete correlation between postmodernism and relationship to each of these categories. Some postmodern philosophers and theologians have moved outside one or two of the axes, but not all of them. There are, however, connections among these axes, and several philosophical motifs cluster together: holism in epistemology, the relating of meaning to use in philosophy of language, and an organic but not premodern view of community in ethics and political philosophy, which Murphy and McClendon refer to as a "corporate metaphysics." The break between modern and postmodern is not sharp, just as was the case between the premodern and the modern, and there have been precursors of postmodernism. Nonetheless, it is possible to identify some philosophers who have enabled the significant shifts of perspective.[54]

Willard Quine judged that even the logical positivists' emphasis on sentences referred to units that were too small to be reducible to experience. Rather, he asserts that there is a whole fabric to our knowledge. This impinges on experience only along the edges. It is also possible to think of science as being like a great force field, the boundaries of which are experience. Conflict with experience at the edges produces changes in the interior, but not in a direct fashion. It does so indirectly, through affecting the equilibrium of the whole. For Quine, changes made are governed by such prag-

---

[51] Ibid., p. 198.
[52] Ibid.
[53] Ibid., p. 199.
[54] Ibid.

matic considerations as conservatism and simplicity. In justifying belief, there are two kinds of questions: whether individual beliefs fit properly within the network, and why this network rather than another. Thomas Kuhn's work in philosophy of science is also holistic, because he asserts that paradigms are accepted or rejected as a whole.[55]

In the philosophy of language, the later Wittgenstein and J. L. Austin represent postmodernism. Wittgenstein insisted that meaning is to be understood in terms of the use of language, and that there are different language games. Austin developed the idea of speech acts. Rather than being reducible to two functions, the representational and the expressive-emotive, all language is to be understood in terms of the social world. The issue is what the language is intended to effect, such as promises, commands, questions, and so on. Rather than being termed true or false, which would apply only to representational sentences, he uses the broader categories of "happy" and "unhappy" utterances.[56]

Alasdair MacIntyre represents postmodernism in ethics by the way he tries to avoid emotionalism, which he believes will always lead to manipulation. The only way to support the common good, MacIntyre insists, is through a corporate or organic view of society. In such a view, the individual members of society are complementary to one another. He begins with the idea of a practice, which is a complex form of human activity that systematically extends human powers to achieve excellence and human good. Human qualities needed for successful participation in such practices are candidates for virtues, but this does not include skills as safecracking and seduction. The definition of virtue requires broad considerations, such as how well it contributes to an individual's life story from birth to death, and how it contributes to that person's life, not in isolation, but in relationship to a group, such as family, state, and so on. So MacIntyre rejects the idea that the individual is logically prior to the group, and the opposition between individual good and good of the group.[57]

There is, Murphy and McClendon insist, a growing unity in postmodern thought. These several issues or areas are related to one another, so that changes in one are increasingly affecting the others.[58]

In this chapter, we have examined three different characterizations of the broad phenomenon commonly known as postmodernism. Neither this nor

---

[55]Ibid., pp. 200-201.

[56]Ibid., pp. 201-2.

[57]Ibid., pp. 203-4.

[58]Ibid., pp. 204-5. For a more complete and later description of one type of postmodernism by one of the authors, see Nancey Murphy, *Anglo-American Postmodernity: Philosophical Perspectives on Science, Religion and Ethics* (Boulder, Colo.: Westview, 1997).

any other survey could begin to do justice to the variety and complexity of
the movement. It is a variety of architecture, representing a reaction against
modernism. It is a school of art, of literary criticism, of history (the "new
historicism"), of philosophy (deconstruction on one hand, and neopragmatism on the other); within each of these fields, it has many and varied representatives. In addition, it is characteristic of much popular culture,
including popular music. In particular, the popular cultural form or "po-mo,"
as it is sometimes called, shows virtually infinite permutations. The treatment of popular postmodernism will be the subject of another book.

Three ways of elaborating postmodernism could be followed. One would
be to attempt to describe all of these nuances in detail, but that would produce, not a book, but a whole library. Another would be to give several summary statements, seeking to encompass all of postmodernism, but that
would be either hopelessly general and vague or skewed toward one variety
of postmodernism. A third would be to take several major spokespersons for
postmodernism, examine their thought in some detail, and let them speak
for the whole movement. While this again fails to do full justice to the variety within the movement, it at least has the virtue of introducing readers to
significant spokespersons. It is this third option that I have chosen to follow.
But before we can begin the examination of these postmodern thinkers, considerable background must be examined, and to that we now turn.

2

premodernism

Not only is postmodernism a relatively recent arrival on the intellectual scene of humanity, so also is modernism when compared with premodernism. For that way of thinking has, in various forms, been held by the majority of humans for a much longer time than either modernism or postmodernism. It even lingers on in some segments of the human race to the present day. If one cannot understand postmodernism without understanding the modern mentality out of which it grew, then similarly one cannot understand modernism without seeing the premodern mentality that preceded it.

Some readers may think that including such an extensive discussion of the premodern period is unnecessary. I would contend, however, that it is important, first because of the realization of the historically conditioned character of beliefs. A comparison of postmodernism, not only with modernism but also with that which preceded it, will help us see this more clearly. Further, while some characterize postmodernism as basically a reaction against modernism, especially in its Enlightenment form, this examination of premodernism will enable us to see that what postmodernism is turning from is of a broader nature than simply that period. Moreover, just as modernism is by no means extinct, there are also significant segments of the world population who still are basically living in a premodern orientation. In addition, seeing the contrast of postmodernism with premodernism should help us to understand the senses in which postmodernism is genuinely postmodern, and not merely antimodern. Finally, viewing the transition first from premodernism to modernism and then from modernism to postmodernism helps us to see that in all likelihood there is no chronological ultimacy to postmodernism either.

Premodernism could be expounded in several ways. One would be to give a general summary of the whole ethos. That, however, would suffer the liability of potential abstractness. A second approach would be to examine a large number of different representatives of this view. Such an approach, however, might easily fall into superficiality. The approach we have chosen to follow here is to look in some depth at three specific representatives of premodernism, one nonreligious or philosophical, one religious or theological, and one who is both a philosopher and a Christian theologian. We will then attempt in summary to draw together common features of the thought of these three men, supplemented by observations from other instances of premodern thought. The three spokespersons whose thoughts we will examine—Plato, Augustine, and Thomas Aquinas—were truly giants in their own right. While the premodern period covers a long span of time and involves a variety of conceptions, these three men, one from the pre-Christian era, one from the early centuries of the Christian church, and one from medieval times, provide us with a good sampling of the spirit of the period.

Plato

There is no question that Plato has had a tremendous impact on Western thought. Alfred North Whitehead said of political theory, "Every problem which Plato discusses is still alive today,"[1] and developed his book around the seven Platonic generalities.[2] Raphael Demos says that "Plato has exerted a greater influence over human thought than any other individual with the possible exception of Aristotle; this is due both to the intrinsic vitality of his ideas and the fact that he appears at a comparatively early stage in Western culture."[3]

Plato was born in Athens of aristocratic parents in 427 B.C. and died in 346 B.C. He was a student of Socrates from about age twenty to twenty-eight, and his early interest in poetry was replaced but not extinguished by his love for philosophy. Upon Socrates' death in 399 B.C., Plato left Athens and traveled, although the exact details of his travels are difficult to ascertain. The Platonic Academy, founded in 387, was the means of preservation of his writings. It

---

[1] Alfred North Whitehead, *Adventures of Ideas* (New York: Macmillan, 1961), p. 15.
[2] Ibid., p. 366.
[3] Raphael Demos, "Introduction," in *Plato: Selections*, ed. Raphael Demos (New York: Scribner's, 1927), p. v.

persisted for more than nine centuries, going out of existence in A.D. 529, when Justinian embezzled its funds. Although Plato's dialogues feature Socrates as enunciating and defending such concepts as the theory of ideas, it is apparent that in many cases these were thoughts propounded by Plato, rather than Socrates.

Theory of ideas. To a modern-day commonsense person, Plato's most central affirmation about reality seems mistaken or confused. For to such a person, concrete, specific objects and instances seem to be the most real things in the universe. For Plato, however, just the opposite is true. Concrete or empirical objects are shadowy, less real than the concepts they represent. Thus, a courageous man or a courageous act is not as real as is courage itself. This metaphysic is present in many of Plato's writings, but is especially clearly expounded in the *Republic*. While an extensive literature has grown up regarding the development of Plato's views during the course of his writing, that will not be our concern here, since we are primarily interested in his overall conception as an example of the premodern view of things. We will consequently merely examine four passages in the *Republic* as indicative of his general view.

In the first of these Plato discusses two kinds of persons and two corresponding states of mind. There are those who may properly be termed philosophers. They are distinguished by their recognition of the existence both of the Ideas and of sensible objects, and their ability to distinguish between these. The other type of person is capable of recognizing beautiful objects and enjoying them. They are lovers of sounds and sights. They, however, are incapable of "apprehending and taking delight in the nature of the beautiful in itself." Such people have to be thought of as dreaming, whether asleep or awake. They mistake resemblance for identity. The philosopher, however, does not simply experience various beautiful objects, but recognizes beauty in itself. He "is able to distinguish that self-beautiful, and the things that participate in it, and neither supposes the participants to be it, nor it the participants." This person is understood to be awake, very much awake, and his state is understood as knowledge, while the other's is opinion.[4] Plato then engages in a discussion of the difference between these two states, and of the objects involved in each. Knowledge is of what is, the completely real. Ignorance has as its objects the unreal. Opinion then is concerned with what lies between these two, the realm of semi-reality.

After defining justice, sobriety, bravery, and wisdom, Plato asks about what it is "by reference to which just things and all the rest become useful and beneficial." This, he says, is the most important to know and is the idea

---

[4]Plato *Republic* 5.476.

of good. Knowledge of it is crucial: "And if we do not know it, then, even if without the knowledge of this we should know all other things never so well, you are aware that it would avail us nothing, just as no possession either is of any avail without the possession of the good."[5] No one will really know, nor be a fit guardian of, such matters as justice, unless he knows in what respect it is good. To know this, to know the idea of good, is truly to have knowledge. Those who hold true opinion but without intelligence are really no different from blind men who happen to go the right way.[6]

In the dialogue Socrates wants to know the good, but he thinks it helpful to begin by studying the offspring of the good. He notes that we speak of many beautiful things and many good things. Beyond that, however, we speak of the self-beautiful and the good that is only and merely good. He speaks of the former, the particulars, as the objects of sight, by which he means sense in general, and the latter as objects of thought. He then points out a distinctive characteristic of seeing versus hearing. In hearing, no additional factor is needed beyond the one who hears and that which is heard. In the case of seeing, however, an additional factor is needed. Without light nothing will be seen and colors will remain invisible. The sun is that which makes all objects of sight visible.[7] Just as the sun is with respect to sight and the objects of sight, so is the idea of good with respect to knowledge and its objects, the ideas: "This reality, then, that gives their truth to the objects of knowledge and the power of knowing to the knower, you must say is the idea of the good, and you must conceive as being the cause of knowledge and truth, in so far as known."[8] And just as neither light nor sight is the sun, so also neither truth nor knowledge is the good. They are what they are because of something greater, namely, the idea of the good. There is another dimension to the simile between the sun and the idea of the good. The sun not only furnishes illumination, but the power of generation and growth and nurture. So also "the objects of knowledge not only receive from the presence of the good their being known, but their very existence and essence is derived to them from it, though the good itself is not essence but still transcends essence in dignity and surpassing power."[9]

The dialogue then moves to one of the most famous images or similes in Plato's thought, the divided line. In many ways, this is the very heart of his theory of ideas, and one place where the relationship between the intelligible and the visible is etched in sharpest fashion. He likens two types of

---

[5]Ibid., 6.505.
[6]Ibid., 6.506.
[7]Ibid., 6.507-8.
[8]Ibid., 6.508E.
[9]Ibid., 6.509B.

objects, or two realms, to a line, which is divided into two parts, and then each of these parts again divided into two subparts. In the lower part, that of the visible, the lower subpart is made up of shadows and reflections, the upper subpart of this lower half is "that of which this is a likeness or an image, that is, the animals about us and all plants and the whole class of objects made by man."[10]

In the upper part of the line, the realm of the intelligible, there are again two subparts. The first appears to consist of mathematical objects. Here, those who know them utilize the images from the lower half, but not as ends in themselves. They are used as means to rise to an understanding of that of which they are likenesses. So the mathematician studies the characteristics of an actual existent square object, but in order to understand the idea of the square as such and the diagonal as such. One is reminded here of Socrates' famous dialogue with the slave boy in the *Meno*, in which by making squares and diagonals, he is able to lead him to "remember" a principle of geometry.[11] The upper subsection is not so easily described or understood. Plato says of it that here the soul "advances from its assumptions to a beginning or principle which transcends assumption, and in which it makes no use of the images employed by the other section, relying on ideas only and progressing systematically through ideas."[12] He seems to be saying that, unlike the first subpart, where visible objects are utilized, the mind or soul here does not rely on any such objects. Further, whereas in the case of the first subsection the soul moves to conclusions from the hypotheses by means of assumptions, here it moves from hypotheses to a single unhypothetical first principle.

This second subsection clearly appears to be dealing with the ideas, but what of the first subsection of the upper half of the line? Are the objects involved there some sort of intermediary between the visible and the intelligible? Are they the mathematical, as contrasted with the ideas? As appealing as this interpretation may be, it seems unjustified. Plato, who is known for his explicitness, did not suggest any basic difference between them, and he speaks of the *mathematica* in the singular, not the plural. Further, he uses of them the expression "itself" (αὐτό), which is the very hallmark of an idea. Further, the whole idea of the divided line seems to hinge on the dichotomy between the upper and lower halves, the intelligible and the visible, and in the passage in which he likens the idea of the good to the sun, he identifies the intelligible with the ideas.

---

[10]Ibid., 6.510A.
[11]Plato *Meno* 82-86.
[12]Plato *Republic* 6.510B.

The third connected passage shedding light on Plato's conception of the two classes of objects, the two states of soul, and the two types of persons is that of the cave. Here he describes men who are in a subterranean cavern, with their backs to the entrance. They are so restrained that they are unable to turn and look toward the opening. They can only look at the wall before them. Behind them a fire is burning, which casts its illumination on them and on the wall. Then between the fire and the men there is a road along which a low wall has been built, of the type that puppeteers use, to conceal themselves beneath and behind, and to display their puppets above. Along this road travel various persons, carrying a variety of implements that rise above the wall, as well as human images and shapes of animals. The men in the cave cannot see these directly, however. They see only the shadows, which are cast on the wall before them by the objects between them and the fire. In such a situation it is natural that they would mistake the shadows on the wall, confusing them with reality. Even sounds would fit this picture, for the voices of those behind them would echo off the wall, and would be thought to be the voices of the shadow men on the wall.

What if one of the men is freed and compelled to look directly at the objects behind the group, and the light? This would be a painful experience. The effect would be to blind the man. He would now not be able to see the objects clearly, until a period of adjustment to the light had transpired. When, however, he did, he would not want to return to the cave, and would consider of no real value the prizes these men confer on their number who excel in judging the shadows.

Supposing that he then returned to the cave, and reassumed his own position, an interesting result would follow. It has been the practice of the chained men to engage in various kinds of contests regarding the images before them. They have commented on them, attempted to discern the shadows as quickly as possible, to remember the sequences of the events, and to predict what would come next. When this man takes his earlier place, he would have to go through a process of readjustment to the darkness like that which he had formerly experienced in relation to the bright light. Now he would have difficulty for a time in seeing clearly the shadows and correctly interpreting them. He would be laughed at by his fellow prisoners for the disability that he now seemed to have. They would consider him to have been ruined by his ascent, and they would resist and even kill anyone who attempted to lead them up out of the cave, as their colleague had been.[13]

Plato is clear in his application of this metaphor. Socrates says to Glaucon, "This image then, dear Glaucon, we must apply as a whole to all that

---

[13]Ibid., 7.514A-517A.

has been said, likening the region revealed through sight to the habitation of the prison, and the light of the fire in it to the power of the sun. And if you assume that the ascent and the contemplation of the things above is the soul's ascension to the intelligible region, you will not miss my surmise, since that is what you desire to hear. But God knows whether it is true."[14] Some confusion is introduced into the metaphor by the presence of both the fire and the sun, and of the objects in the cave between the men and the fire, and the objects outside the cave, illuminated by the sun. We should probably consider the fire in this metaphor to correspond to the sun in the earlier metaphor, rather than attempting to identify the sun in each of the metaphors. On this basis, there is an elaboration of what Socrates has said earlier: "the idea of good, and that when seen it must needs point us to the conclusion that this is indeed the cause for all things of all that is right and beautiful, giving birth in the visible world to light, and the author of light and itself in the intelligible world being the authentic source of truth and reason, and that anyone who is to act wisely in private or public must have caught sight of this."[15]

Knowledge, true knowledge, then is not received primarily by exposure to the visible, the physical objects. It is rather obtained by attention to the higher realm. Plato says, "Even so this organ of knowledge must be turned around from the world of becoming together with the entire soul, like the scene-shifting periactus of the theater, until the soul is able to endure the contemplation of essence and the brightest region of being. And this, we say, is the good, do we not?"[16]

The relationship of the particulars or individual instances to the forms is of further importance to us. In *Parmenides*, Parmenides suggests that the individual things are what they are because they "partake in" the corresponding form and Socrates agrees.[17] This does not mean, however, says Socrates, that the particular thing receives a part of the form.[18] Here is something of an ambiguity regarding what partaking or participating means. On the one hand, it seems that the form is "in" the particular. He also speaks of the relationship in terms of "communing."[19] On the other hand, he uses terminology of the likeness of the particulars to the form, thus suggesting something of an imitation of archetypes by particulars. Socrates says that "this participation they come to have in the forms is nothing but their being made in their

---

[14]Ibid., 517B.
[15]Ibid., 517B-C.
[16]Ibid., 518C.
[17]Plato *Parmenides* 130B-E.
[18]Ibid., 131B.
[19]Plato *Phaedo* 100D; *Republic* 476A.

image."[20] Whether there is an ambiguity in Plato's thought here, or whether one of these modes of participation should be understood in light of the other or both in light of some third concept, the point is that each instance of a particular quality is what it is because of the respective form. In part, the issue is the nature of the forms themselves. Some have argued on the basis of the "third man argument" in *Parmenides* that the forms must themselves exemplify the qualities that they represent.[21] Probably the best interpretation of the passage is one that treats the forms, not as instances of the quality possessed by the particulars, but rather as more nearly a formula for that quality, just as the formula for a circle is not itself circular.[22]

One additional metaphysical problem is the relationship of God to the form of the good. Although present in the earlier dialogues, reference to God increases in the later dialogues. A number of theories of the relationship of the two have been offered, and Demos is correct when he says that "no answer can be made which is not tinged with doubt."[23] There appear to be four possible explanations of the relationship:

1. God is the cause or the ground of the idea of the good.

2. God's existence derives from the idea of the good.

3. The two are coordinate principles.

4. They are identical.

Serious arguments have been offered in support of each of these, and serious difficulties in turn attach to each.[24]

Each of these and many other interpretive issues have provoked great amounts of discussion and debate, which go beyond the scope of the treatment here. We may summarize briefly the thought of Plato as it bears on our understanding of premodernism.

1. What is most real is not the physical or perceptible, but the ideal, or the conceptual.

2. Each particular instance of a particular quality exists because of its relationship to a universal or an abstract quality.

3. Knowledge consists in knowing the intelligible and ideal, not the concrete and sensory. It is dialectics or reasoning that leads us to truth, not primarily sense perception.

---

[20]*Parmenides* 132D.

[21]William David Ross, *Plato's Theory of Ideas* (Oxford: Clarendon, 1951), pp. 87-88.

[22]Cf. A. E. Taylor, "I—On the First Part of Plato's *Parmenides*," *Mind*, n.s. 12 (January 1903): 1-20.

[23]Raphael Demos, *The Philosophy of Plato* (New York: Octagon, 1966), p. 123.

[24]For discussions of these several theories and the respective arguments offered for them, see Ross, *Plato's Theory of Ideas*, pp. 43-45; and W. T. Stace, *A Critical History of Greek Philosophy* (London: Macmillan, 1920), pp. 202-4.

4. There is a correspondence theory of truth here. Something is true because it corresponds to or expresses that which really is, independently of our thought.[25]

Augustine

If Plato was the supreme philosopher of early Western civilization, then Augustine certainly occupied a similar position among theologians. The events of his life are well known. Born in 354 at Tagaste in North Africa as the son of a devout woman and a pagan father, he early displayed strong passions, so that baptism, which was believed to remove sin, was delayed until quite late. He left Africa on a ship in the middle of the night, since he anticipated that otherwise his mother's tears would have restrained him from going. Earlier he had become deeply involved in Manichaeism, a philosophy that emphasized the primacy of two principles, good and evil. This accounted for the struggle he found within his own will, but it ultimately proved unsatisfying. He was attracted to Neo-Platonism, and then underwent a conversion to Christianity. He became a priest and then bishop of Hippo in North Africa. His writings covered many topics, and set the direction of Christian theology for many centuries to come. For our purposes, the most significant of all his works is his massive *City of God,* written over a period of thirteen years. It had arisen out of a crucial event of history. In the year 410 the city of Rome was conquered and sacked by the Goths under the leadership of Alaric. This provoked not only a political crisis, but also a crisis of faith for many Roman citizens. In 412 the pagan Volusianus addressed a series of objections to the Christian faith to Marcellinus, who in turn passed them on to Augustine.

There were two main criticisms of Christianity in relationship to the disaster that had befallen Rome. First, Christianity taught a renunciation of the world, which turned citizens away from service of the state. In fact, certain of the virtues it proclaimed were antithetical to the empire's success. Christ's injunction to turn the other cheek when slapped, for example, would hardly result in defense of the empire. Second, when Rome had converted to Christianity under Constantine, the pagans proclaimed that their own gods would bring terrible consequences on Rome. This had now occurred in the fall of Rome.

Marcellinus put the objection this way: "It is manifest that very great

---

[25]Stace contends that the doctrine of ideas is founded upon the correspondence theory of truth. If I have a true idea of a concept, such as justice or largeness, then there must exist something such as justice in itself or largeness in itself, to which my idea corresponds (Stace, *Critical History of Greek Philosophy*, pp. 183-85).

calamities have befallen the country under the government of emperors practising, for the most part, the Christian religion."[26] Marcellinus begged Augustine to make some reply to these charges, and out of this came the *City of God.* Its influence has been great. The emperor Charlemagne, who used to have serious works read to him as he ate his dinner, enjoyed hearing the works of Augustine, and especially, the *City of God.*[27] Augustine himself indicates the motivation for this writing in his *Retractions:*

> Meanwhile, Rome was overthrown by a raid of Goths, led by King Alaric, a most destructive invasion. The polytheistic worshippers of false gods, whom we commonly call "pagans," endeavoured to bring this overthrow home to the Christian religion, and began to blaspheme the true God with unusual sharpness and bitterness. This set me on fire with zeal for the house of God, and I commenced to write the books *Of the City of God* against their blasphemies or errors. This work occupied me for a number of years, owing to numerous interruptions of businesses that would not brook delay and had a prior claim on me. . . . These first ten books, then, are a refutation of these two vain opinions adverse to the Christian religion. But not to expose ourselves to the reproach of merely having refuted the other side without establishing our own position, we have made that assertion of our own position the object of the second part of this work.[28]

Although this work was originally conceived as a response to the problem just described, it became much more than that. The first ten books are in large part a negative or defensive response to those charges, but the last twelve books are a positive demonstration of the value of Christianity, as contrasted with paganism. The *City of God* constitutes a thorough philosophy of history, for the whole understanding of what is transpiring on the stage of history must be seen as the contrast between the stories of two cities.

This constructive portion of the treatise begins with a frank declaration of Augustine's epistemology. He is, with respect to ultimate truths, clearly not an empiricist. He is going to speak of God, but acknowledges that only seldom does anyone move from the observation of material objects to the knowledge of God as creator. This is because God does not speak with humanity through the medium of matter, "but He speaks by means of the truth itself, and to all who can hear with the mind rather than with the body."[29] Because the human was made in the image of God and therefore

---

[26]Augustine *Letter* 136.2.
[27]Edward R. Hardy Jr., "The City of God," in *A Companion to the Study of St. Augustine,* ed. Roy W. Battenhouse (New York: Oxford University Press, 1955), p. 257.
[28]Augustine *Retractions* 2.
[29]Augustine *City of God* 11.2.

comes closer to him than does any other part of the creation, one would think that humans would be able to know God, at least through their highest part. Unfortunately, however, "the mind, which was meant to be reasonable and intelligent, has, by dark and inveterate vices, become too weak to adhere joyously to His unchangeable light (or even to bear it) until, by gradual renewal and healing, it is made fit for such happiness, its first need was to be instructed by faith and purified."[30] It was in order to bring humans into truth that the Son of God became incarnate, thus becoming the mediator of truth. Consequently, through the prophets, by Jesus' own words, then through the apostles, God made this necessary knowledge known to humans, and inspired the Scripture. We customarily know by our own witness those things presented to our senses, but when they are not, we seek out and believe other witnesses. "If, however, our perceptions are of invisible things remote from our own interior sense, we ought to believe either those who have learned these truths as revealed in the Incorporeal Light or those who contemplate these truths in an abiding Vision of God."[31]

Augustine then offers us a great epic, depicting the origin, progression, and ultimate end of the history we observe. It all began with God's creation of everything that is. This is something taken by faith, in this case, reliance upon the witness of Moses, one of those prophets of whom Augustine has spoken. Yet although revealed, this truth should be apparent to all who observe the universe: "For, quite apart from the voice of the Prophets, the very order, changes, and movements in the universe, the very beauty of form in all that is visible, proclaim, however silently, both that the world was created and also that its Creator could be none other than God whose greatness and beauty are both ineffable and invisible."[32]

It should be apparent that Augustine is working with a strong theism. This God of whom he speaks is the originator of all things, not Plato's demiurge, who works with the material that he finds at hand. This God has created, and his creation is complete. It is good because he is good. This includes even those things within creation that we might tend to consider "unsuitable and even harmful" to us, such as fire, cold, and wild beasts. Yet those who raise this objection have not really considered the nature of these things, how valuable to us if we use them "well and wisely." Augustine takes as an example poison, which is deadly if improperly used, but if properly employed can be a health-giving medicine, while food, drink, and sunlight,

---

[30]Ibid.
[31]Ibid., 11.3.
[32]Ibid., 11.4.

if taken immoderately and unwisely, can be harmful.[33]

In Augustine's understanding of the creation, there is a great hierarchy of created objects. Some, the angels, are heavenly, and many are earthly. Some are better than others, and the reason for this inequality is to make possible the existence of each and all. In this hierarchy, God is the highest, then in descending order, the angels, humans, animals, plants, and inanimate objects. This is objective, being the very way reality has been structured. There is also a subjective order of valuations, which results from free created intelligences' ability to value things differently from the way God had created them. Our place is to see this objective order, and to see ourselves in the proper place within it.[34]

Interestingly, these created objects all bear the image of God, each in its own way. Since God is triune, the image must also be triune in nature. In the human, for example, this is seen in the fact that we are, we know that we are, and we love to be and know that we are.[35] Here is an echo of what Augustine developed much more extensively in *The Trinity*. Everything else in creation, even the inanimate, reflects this same triune pattern.[36]

The city of God is to be seen as including not only God himself and all those humans who love and obey him, but also a great heavenly host of angels. Indeed, much of what God accomplishes in the world he carries out by means of the angels. Like humans, they are free intelligences, and it was the use of their freedom that initiated the grand story after creation. Augustine clearly wrestles with the problem of evil. He is not willing to take the approach of Manicheism, which had appealed to him so strongly during his earlier years, according to which there were two ultimate principles, good and evil. Rather, God created everything, and it was all good. The presence of evil occurred through a disruption of the order of things. As noted above, there is a great order of things, and the preservation of this order is good: "All natures, then, are good simply because they exist and, therefore, have each its own measure of being, its own beauty, even, in a way, its own peace. And when each is in the place assigned by the order of nature, it best preserves the full measure of being that was given to it."[37] The good angels are those that persisted in the place assigned to them; the evil angels are those that rebelled against God and turned to themselves. They were able to do this because, being made in the image of God, they possessed the freedom of choice to do so. If, however, we seek for some additional explana-

---

[33]Ibid., 11.22.
[34]Ibid., 11.16.
[35]Ibid., 11.26.
[36]Ibid., 11.27, 28.
[37]Ibid., 12.5.

tion, some efficient cause of evil, none is forthcoming. There is nothing in the creation that itself is evil, that could have caused this choice.[38]

This same history also marked the beginning of the human race. Although Augustine does not know the time of the creation, he is careful to reject two erroneous views: the position that humans were not created, but are eternal, as is God; and the Greek cyclical view that history simply repeats itself. He is committed to a linear view of time, in which history is moving toward a definite goal, which God has established.[39] The question is not so much the date at which humanity came into being, but rather the fact that there is an end, which is ultimately meaningful.

Just as the angels, the humans misused their freedom and fell. This had significant effects, especially death. Whereas angels were created immortal and even sin could not deprive them of that immortality, humans can die physically, which involves the separation of body and soul. There is also the death of the soul, when God leaves it. These two together constitute the first death. Beyond that there is the second death, which is the eternal punishment suffered by the reunited body and soul.[40]

If creation brought the City of God upon earth, the fall of humanity introduced the earthly city. These two cities and the relationship between them constitute Augustine's explanation of history. All the human race is descended from the one person Adam, and all would have experienced the endless misery of the second death, had not God in his mercy intervened. Despite all the differences of culture and appearance among the peoples of the world, all belong to one or the other of these two cities: "One city is that of men who live according to the flesh. The other is of men who live according to the spirit. Each of them chooses its own kind of peace and, when they attain what they desire, each lives in the peace of its own choosing."[41] While these two groups are found intermingled within this world, they are quite different, in both their orientation and their destiny: "In regard to mankind I have made a division. On the one side are those who live according to man; on the other, those who live according to God. And I have said that, in a deeper sense, we may speak of two cities or two human societies, the destiny of the one being an eternal kingdom under God while the doom of the other is eternal punishment along with the Devil."[42] While it might be tempting to identify the City of God with the church, Augustine appears not to be doing so. He uses the term *church* in several different senses, and in

---

[38]Ibid., 12.6, 7.
[39]Ibid., 12.10-18.
[40]Ibid., 13.2, 12.
[41]Ibid., 14.1.
[42]Ibid., 15.1.

the *Enchiridion* appears to be making such an identification, but in reality he distinguishes the City of God from the visible or empirical church. In his discussion of the final judgment, he makes clear that there will be a separation, even from within the church:

> And from the Church those reapers shall gather out the tares which He suffered to grow with the wheat till the harvest, as He explains in the words "The harvest is the end of the world; and the reapers are the angels. As therefore the tares are gathered together and burned with fire, so shall it be in the end of the world. The Son of man shall send His angels, and they shall gather out of His kingdom all offenses." Can He mean out of that kingdom in which are no offenses? Then it must be out of His present kingdom, the Church, that they are gathered.[43]

This great drama that is unfolding will come to a final end, which Augustine describes in the last four books of the *City of God*. Christ will return personally in the last times, and will then judge the living and the dead.[44] The basis of this judgment, however, is not the works of humans as such. If God had simply administered justice, none would have been saved. Rather, Christ came as the mediator, to reconcile God and humans, who by their sin had introduced a great gulf between themselves and God. This mediator could only accomplish this if he himself were God.[45] Those who are judged worthy of eternal life are those who have freely chosen to accept this reconciling work of the mediator.

Thus, this final judgment will not bring to an end either of the two kingdoms that have coexisted during this earthly lifetime: "After the resurrection, however, when the final, universal judgment has been completed, there shall be two kingdoms, each with its own distinct boundaries, the one Christ's, the other the devil's; the one consisting of the good, the other of the bad, both, however, consisting of angels and men."[46] Neither of these groups will be able to sin—the former because they have no will to do so, the latter because they have no power to do so. The former will continue endlessly in bliss, but the latter will suffer forever. There will, however, be degrees, both of reward and of punishment, for the respective groups.[47]

Because there is a divine sovereignty, the events of history are driven not by human action, but by the willing of God. What he decides will come to pass, and nothing can frustrate that will. Even the ultimate fate of individual

---

[43]Ibid., 20.9.
[44]Ibid., 20.1.
[45]Augustine *Enchiridion* 108.
[46]Ibid., 111.
[47]Ibid.

humans is the result of God's will, in the well-known doctrine of predestination. Throughout Augustine's writings there is an apparent tension between human freedom and divine sovereignty. The relationship of these two in his thought is a problem exceeding the scope of this book. Augustine considers the question of in what sense it can be said that God wills all to be saved, but yet not everyone is actually saved. This would seem to indicate that humans by their will are able to frustrate the will of God, and that they actually do so. Nonetheless, he saves even those who are unwilling, if he so chooses, because he is able to change the wills of sinful men, whenever and wherever he chooses, and to direct those wills to good ends.[48] And the fact that he decides to do this in the case of one and not in the case of another, is not injustice, it is grace and mercy. There is nothing of merit in the one that causes God to choose him or her. When he does it for one, that is mercy, but when he does not do it for another, that is justice.[49]

In part, Augustine's doctrine of divine sovereignty developed more fully into the doctrine of predestination as he interacted with the Pelagians, who believed in human goodness and ability. Augustine eventually saw the implications of the position he took on human sinfulness and inability as involving the necessity of total predestination.

Augustine's view as premodern. A number of dimensions of Augustine's thought influenced the nature of the view of reality that came to characterize the medieval church's understanding, and thus the belief of large parts of the Western world for many centuries.

1. We are given here an explanation of reality that is intended to be rational. This is not to say that all of reality can be comprehended by unaided human reason, but that it is believed to follow a rational pattern and the laws of logic. Nor does this mean that everything will be comprehensible to the unaided human mind, but that truth is interrelated. Because the same God who made the external world created the human mind, it follows the same patterns of order that are found in that created world.

2. This is a comprehensive account. All of history is encompassed within this explanatory scheme; indeed, it goes beyond what is usually termed history, to cover the eternal future. It is also universal in the sense of being the story, not merely of one group of people or one geographical area, but of the entire human race. It is not presented as merely one idiosyncratic account of things, but as universal truth.

3. This is clearly a theology, not a philosophy. Repeatedly, Augustine declares that he is going to base his view primarily on the specially revealed

---

[48]Ibid., 97-98.
[49]Ibid., 98; Augustine *On the Predestination of the Saints* 19.

Scripture, rather than on human reasoning power. Thus, what he gives us is generically a philosophy of history, but more specifically, a theology of history. The categories he uses to explain the story of history are drawn not from experience of history, but from supernatural concepts. To use the categories developed much later, in the twentieth century, this is history "from above," rather than "from below."

4. The ultimate explanation of reality and history is that the moving, causing force is not any force or set of forces within nature, but is supernatural. What occurs is a product of a transcendent being's planning, initiating, and directing activity.

5. Humanity's final end is defined, not in terms of physical satisfaction or comfort within the confines of this earthly life, but in relationship to a life to follow this one and in a locale removed from earth. The object of life is to relate oneself correctly to a supernatural, eternal, infinite, and unseen being.

Thomas Aquinas

Theological reflection continued to refine Christian doctrine during the centuries following Augustine. Much of this was based on variations of the philosophy of Plato. In the thought of St. Thomas Aquinas, we find both the culmination of that process and a turn to a new direction. What is clear is that his thought has had far-reaching effects, in the fields of both theology and philosophy. For centuries to follow, he was the major theologian of Roman Catholicism, to such an extent that his theology could almost be said to be the official theology of the Catholic Church. In 1567 the Council of Trent in enunciating the Catholic response to Protestantism gave Thomas the title "Universal Doctor of the Church."

As we noted, many theologians followed the lead of Augustine by utilizing Platonism and Neo-Platonism as their philosophical resource. In the thirteenth century, the philosophical works of Aristotle began to become known in Christian circles. It was the genius of Thomas to develop a synthesis between Aristotle and Christian theology. This is not to say that Thomas followed Aristotle blindly. He sometimes followed Plato more closely, especially where it seemed to him that Aristotle's views on an issue were not fully compatible with revealed Christianity.

Thomas was born at Roccasecca, Italy, probably in 1225. He was a large man, who spoke little, leading his fellow students to label him the dumb ox. After taking his early education at the monastery of Monte Cassino, he enrolled at the University of Naples, where he came in contact with the philosophy of Aristotle and with the order of Dominicans. This was a reform movement with special appeal to intellectuals but regarded by the upper classes of society as extreme and fanatical. When Thomas entered the order, his father had him kidnapped by his brothers and held prisoner in the family castle for two years, during which time they sought to dissuade him from membership in the order. Upon being released, Thomas returned to the order. He went on to study at the University of Paris, a center of the rising Aristotelianism, and began his teaching career there in 1256.

Thomas's two major works are the *Summa Theologica* (or more correctly, *Theologiae*) and the *Summa Contra Gentiles.* The former was his statement of Christian belief, for the instruction of Christians. It was his systematic theology, as it were. The *Summa Contra Gentiles* was his apologetic, designed to assist Christians in their refutation of other religions, at a time when Christianity was encountering Muslims in Spain and North Africa. These works were written using the scholastic method, a style that seems strange to us today, but was familiar to theologians and other scholars of the time. Thomas states a particular doctrine, then observes the objections commonly raised to it. Following that, he replies to the objections, stating his own view, often with citations from earlier Christian theologians or from "the philosopher," his designation of Aristotle.

To understand Thomas's theology and philosophy, it is important to see his distinctions between nature and grace, between reason and faith, which underlie all of his specific positions. The whole set of distinctions could be summarized in terms of natural and supernatural. The natural can be known by reason, but the supernatural can only be grasped by faith. Yet there is no real conflict between the two. Since both derive ultimately from God, they are in harmony, if properly understood. The lower realm was the domain of philosophy, by which Thomas of course has in mind especially the philosophy of Aristotle, whereas the supernatural can be known only by revelation. Whereas Augustine saw faith as seeking understanding, in Thomas's thought it was more a matter of understanding leading one to faith.

All of this means that the existence of God can be known by human reason, without appeal to the authority of the Scriptures or of special revelation. His essence, however, can only be known by consulting his special revelation. So, for example, it is possible to prove by rational argument that God exists, but not that he is triune. The method of philosophy is to start with the particulars of sense perception, to build from those to the abstract forms and relations of science, and ultimately to the abstract principles of metaphysics. Theology's method is the reverse of this. It begins with the data of revelation, from which as its principles it deduces the conclusions that it elaborates and systematizes.

As I observed, Thomas does not believe it is necessary to appeal to special revelation to know the existence of God. Neither, however, does he hold that this divine existence is known immediately or intuitively. It is true that the knowledge that God exists is implanted within us in a general and confused way, insofar as God is the human's source of happiness and all persons desire happiness. This is not to know absolutely that God exists.[50] Rather, God's existence must and can be established by the use of rational proofs. Thomas does this in his famous fivefold proof for the existence of God. Whereas Anselm in his ontological proof had argued for God's existence from an analysis of God's nature, showing that it necessarily included his existence, Thomas will begin with what all persons can observe.

The first proof is from motion. In Thomas's thought, causing motion is bringing something from a state of potentiality to one of actuality. Nothing can be changed from potentiality to actuality except by something actual, and nothing can be at the same time potential and actual. Consequently, nothing can be the cause of its own motion. What is in motion must therefore be put in motion by something else, which is actuality, and that in turn by yet something else. It is impossible, however, for this sequence of causes and effects to be infinite, for if that were the case, there would be no first mover and, consequently, no subsequent movers. "Therefore, it is necessary to arrive at a first mover, put in motion by no other; and this everyone understands to be God."[51]

The second proof is from efficient causation. In the sensible world, we find an order of efficient causes. Nothing can be its own efficient cause, because then it would be prior to itself. Again it is not possible to go on to infinity, because that would take away intermediate cause, which in turn is the cause of the ultimate cause. Therefore, it is necessary to posit a first cause, which everyone names God.[52]

The third proof is taken from an analysis of the possible (or contingent) and the necessary. Contingent things have the possibility of being or not being, and that which can not be, at some time is not. If, however, all things were contingent, there would have been a time when there was nothing. Then, however, nothing could now exist, because the nonexistent cannot come into existence except through something that is. If that were the case, there would be nothing now, which is obviously absurd. Therefore there must be some necessary being, who has his being, whose being does not depend on anything else, and this necessary being we call God.[53]

The fourth proof is based on the degrees of perfection that we find in

---

[50]Thomas Aquinas *Summa Theologiae* Part 1, Question 2, Article 1, Reply to Objections 1.
[51]Ibid., P1, Q2, A3.
[52]Ibid.
[53]Ibid.

experience. The greater more closely approximates to the greatest in that genus. That maximum is the cause of the other members of the series, as fire, being the maximum of heat, is the cause of all hot things. "Therefore," Thomas concludes, "there must be something that is to all things the cause of their being, goodness, and every perfection, and this we call God."[54]

Thomas's final argument is the design argument. He observes that there are things lacking intelligence, such as natural bodies, that act for an end, producing the best result. This could not be by chance, however, and since something that lacks intelligence cannot move toward an end in itself, there must be some intelligent being that directs all things to their ends, and this being we call God.[55]

This type of reasoning can succeed with respect to the natural world, establishing thereby the existence of the supernatural. Specific knowledge of that supernatural world cannot be attained simply by the use of reason, however. While some had contended that it was possible to establish by reason that God is triune, Thomas does not think so. This is part of God's essence, which is undiscoverable by human reason.

One important question relates to how we are able to predicate anything about God. We attribute to God qualities that we also predicate of human beings, such as intelligence and love, using the same language. Do these terms mean the same thing when applied to God as they do when applied to us? Here Thomas points out that the same word is used differently in many cases. Thus, for example, the word *healthy* is used differently of medicine and animal, since medicine is the cause of health in the animal. Similarly with respect to terms predicated of God and of humans:

> And in this way some things are said of God and creatures analogically, and not in a purely equivocal nor in a purely univocal sense. For we can name God only from creatures. Thus whatever is said of God and creatures, is said according to the relation of a creature to God as its principle and cause, wherein all perfections of things pre-exist excellently. Now this mode of community of idea is a mean between pure equivocation and simple univocation. For in analogies the idea is not, as it is in univocals, one and the same, yet it is not totally diverse as in equivocals; but a term which is thus used in a multiple sense signifies various proportions to some one thing; thus "healthy" applied to urine signifies the sign of animal health, and applied to medicine signifies the cause of the same health.[56]

Thus, we can use the natural realm to understand the supernatural realm

---

[54]Ibid.
[55]Ibid.
[56]Ibid., P1, Q13, A5.

because there is an analogy or proportion between the two. It would not be proper to say that God and his love and intelligence resemble us, but rather that we resemble him. He is the perfection and completion of what we are only in part.

Thomas is working with a hierarchical conception of reality. At the top of this scheme is God, who is pure actuality, without any mixture of potentiality. His essence and existence are identical. He knows all things in himself and by his knowledge he is the cause of all being. Next are the separate intellectual substances, the various levels of angels. They are pure spirits. Then there are humans, who are human souls united with material bodies.[57]

The human thus participates, as it were, in the reality of that which is above it in the hierarchy of being and that which is below. The human soul is immortal. The souls of animals are not self-subsistent, but those of humans are. The souls of animals can be corrupted when their bodies are corrupted, but humans' souls can only be corrupted in themselves. But Thomas says, "This, indeed, is impossible, not only as regards the human soul, but also as regards anything subsistent that is a form alone. For it is clear that what belongs to a thing by virtue of itself is inseparable from it; but existence belongs to a form, which is an act, by virtue of itself. Wherefore matter acquires actual existence as it acquires the form; while it is corrupted so far as the form is separated from it. But it is impossible for a form to be separated from itself; and therefore it is impossible for a subsistent form to cease to exist."[58]

The human is made in the image of God. In what does this image consist? Thomas says, "Man is said to be after the image of God, not as regards his body, but as regards that whereby he excels other animals. Hence, when it is said, 'Let us make man to our image and likeness,' it is added, 'And let him have dominion over the fishes of the sea' (Genesis 1:26). Now man excels all animals by his reason and intelligence; hence it is according to his intelligence and reason, which are incorporeal, that man is said to be according to the image of God."[59] This is what enables him to understand the revealed truth about God, and also to discover from the natural world the existence of God.

Thomas as premodern. In a number of respects, Thomas exemplifies premodernism.

1. There are two realms of reality, that of the natural and the supernatural.

---

[57]Ibid., P1, Q50, A1.
[58]Ibid., P1, Q75, A6.
[59]Ibid., P1, Q3, A1, R2.

2. The supernatural is the cause of the existence of the natural, and of what happens within it.

3. Humans may by reason discover the natural, but they can only know the supernatural by God's gracious special revelation.

4. There is no contradiction between the realm of nature and of grace, and thus no contradiction between reason and faith.

Summary of Premodernism

I have chosen to approach the understanding of premodernism by examining three representatives. Plato and Augustine are fundamentally rationalistic in their epistemology, favoring the idea that knowledge comes through the reasoning process, rather than through sense experience. Thomas Aquinas, on the other hand, emphasizes sense experience, and is therefore more consonant with the modern scientific method. Yet even his thought displays notable differences from the modern, and particularly the postmodern, view.

While the thoughts of each of these men show unique variations, it is possible to observe some general themes, which summarize the premodern orientation:

1. There is an overall explanation of things, in terms of inclusiveness with respect to all of reality and of the whole of history.

2. Reality has a rational character. History is going somewhere, fulfilling some discernible pattern, whether linear or circular in nature. It is therefore possible to make sense of reality. Humans are capable of understanding reality, at least to some degree, whether that knowledge results from personal discovery or from acceptance of special revelation from a divine being.

3. Observable nature does not exhaust all of reality. There are real and important entities lying beyond nature. Indeed, these entities, whether personal or impersonal, are considered to have a strong and perhaps even decisive influence on what transpires within the observable world.

4. The happiness and fulfillment of humans is believed to require correct adjustment to these unseen realities. Because they are the source of meaning or of life, they must be understood and followed. Thus, full human existence requires an element of faith, as it were.

5. Time, as we know it, is not the whole of reality. An additional dimension of life, and in many ways its most important aspect, lies beyond time.

6. The unchanging and permanent are most important. Without these, the flux of experience would have no real meaning.

3

modernism

Gradually, the way of thinking identified as premodernism gave way to a view that in some respects agreed with it, but in other significant ways, contradicted it. This new thinking characterized science as well as philosophy. It can be understood by examining four major representatives of the modern mind: René Descartes, Isaac Newton, John Locke, and Immanuel Kant.

René Descartes

Often referred to as the father of modern philosophy, Descartes in many ways deserves that title. He embodies many of the characteristics of the modern period intellectually, and in some ways does that so fully that he is the basis for some of the caricatures that have been offered regarding modern thinkers in general. He was a mathematician, who invented analytic geometry, and that specialization colors all of his thinking. It was the precision, objectivity, and finality of mathematics that he sought for in all areas of knowledge.

Born in Touraine, France, in 1596, he studied at the Jesuit College of La Flèche. Here he found himself considerably disillusioned with much that he was learning. He came to consider as false anything that he found to be only probable. He was looking for that whose truth could be clearly and definitely seen. Because he was supported by his parents he did not need to occupy himself with any definite employment, although he did engage in military service for a time. Consequently, he traveled extensively, studying and observing life. During this period he formulated his philosophy and began committing it to writing.

Many of Descartes's general conceptions and goals are to be found in his *Rules for the Direction of the Understanding.* He is clear that what he is seeking is a universal type of knowledge, both in the sense of what is true for everyone and of what is true of all areas of knowledge. He observes that in the arts, it is not possible to learn all of them at once. One makes far more progress by concentrating on one at a time. Some think this is also true of the sciences, but such is not the case. "For all the sciences are nothing else but human wisdom, which always remains one and the same, however different the subjects to which it is applied, and which receives no more alteration from those subjects than does the light of the sun from the variety of things it illumines. Hence there is no need to impose any boundaries upon the mind: the knowledge of one truth does not, like the practise of one art, keep us from the discovery of another, but rather helps us."[1] The reason for this is that there is an interconnectedness of the sciences. In fact, Descartes says, "they are all interconnected and reciprocally dependent." Instead of studying merely one of these sciences, therefore, one who wishes to gain knowledge should aim at "increasing the natural light of reason," rather than solving particular scholastic problems. This will enable the intellect to show the will what choice to make.[2]

In this process, the objects that we should study are those about which we can gain "certain and indubitable knowledge." The only disciplines of which this is true are arithmetic and geometry, which should lead us to inquire why this is. Such inquiry reveals that knowledge can be obtained by two means: experience and deduction. The reason for the superior certainty found in these two disciplines is that "they alone are concerned with an object so pure and simple that they suppose absolutely nothing which experience has rendered uncertain, but consist entirely in consequences rationally deduced." The conclusion is not that persons should restrict their study to these two fields, but that they "ought not to occupy themselves with any object, concerning which they cannot possess a certainty equal to that of the demonstration of arithmetic and geometry."[3] Descartes is skeptical of the knowledge commended to one by others, since scholars have frequently taken obscure matters on which they have only probable knowledge, given them complete faith, and mixed them with matters that are true and cer-

---

[1]René Descartes, *Rules for the Direction of the Understanding,* rule 1.
[2]Ibid.
[3]Ibid., rule 2.

tain.[4] Here is the picture of the individual knower, who must personally verify all knowledge that he would accept. Indeed, Descartes indicates that he was born with a mind such that he found greater pleasure in discovering things by his own devices than in hearing others explain them.[5]

There are only two acts of the intellect by which we can arrive at truth without any fear of error. These two are intuition and deduction. By intuition Descartes means not merely a fleeting sensory experience, but "a conception of a pure and attentive mind so easy and so distinct, that no doubt at all remains about that which we are understanding. Or, what comes to the same thing, intuition is the undoubting conception of a pure and attentive mind, which arises from the light of reason alone, and is more certain even than deduction, because simple."[6] Examples of such intuitions are that one exists, that he thinks, that a triangle has only three sides. These are actually more numerous than most persons think, because "they scorn to turn their minds toward matters so easy."[7] By deduction Descartes means the process by which certain truths are "necessarily concluded from other facts certainly known." It is no less certain than is intuition, but is distinguished from it by involving some movement or succession, which intuition does not. An example is the knowledge that the last link in a chain is connected with the first, even though we do not take in all the links in a single glance, as we would in intuition, but by a process in which successively we see each of the different links. These are two most certain paths to scientific knowledge, and no others should be admitted. This conclusion, however, does not preclude our believing those things that are divinely revealed to be more certain than all knowledge, because faith in these is a matter of will rather than of intellect. However, "if they have a basis in the intellect, they can and ought to be, more than all other things, discovered by one or other of the two ways already mentioned."[8] This will emerge in our later examination of Descartes' thought.

It is extremely important that one proceed in the quest for knowledge by following some definite method of inquiry. Descartes shows a certain condescension toward average humans, who, he says, "often lead their minds through unknown paths," hoping to find truth by chance, whom he likens to persons who seek treasure by roaming about on roads, hoping to find something lost by a stranger. While it is possible by good fortune to find something this way on occasion, "it is much better never to think of investigating

---

[4]Ibid., rule 3.
[5]Ibid., rule 10.
[6]Ibid., rule 3.
[7]Ibid.
[8]Ibid.

the truth of anything at all, than to do it without method." What does he mean by method? "By method, then, I understand certain and simple rules, such that if a man follows them exactly, he will never suppose anything false to be true, and, spending no useless mental effort, but gradually and steadily increasing his knowledge, will arrive at the true knowledge of all those things to which his powers are adequate."[9]

In the *Meditations* we see an application of this methodology Descartes has been discussing. He begins by confessing that several years earlier he had come to realize that many of the things that he had believed since his youth were false opinions. At that time he resolved to rid himself of all those opinions, and to commence anew "the work of building from the foundation, if I desired to establish a firm and abiding superstructure in the sciences."[10] Here is foundationalism: the attempt to establish some absolutely certain starting point on which all knowledge could rest, and which would then have its truth guaranteed as well. To do this, Descartes will seek to doubt everything until he comes to something truly indubitable.

There are, Descartes notes, many things the truth of which it seems to be impossible to doubt. Among these are some firsthand sense experiences: "that I am in this place, seated by the fire, clothed in a winter dressing-gown, that I hold in my hands this piece of paper, with other intimations of the same nature." If he denies such obvious truths, certainly he would have to be classed as insane. Yet there are other possibilities. He is a human, in the habit not only of sleeping, but of dreaming similar things to these. Since there are no certain marks for distinguishing the state of waking from that of sleeping, he cannot be sure that he is not now dreaming. We must acknowledge that their existence is doubtful. Although this is the case, there seem to be some indubitable objects: "but that Arithmetic, Geometry, and the other sciences of the same class, which regard merely the simplest and most general objects, and scarcely inquire whether or not these are really existent, contain somewhat that is certain and indubitable: for whether I am awake or dreaming, it remains true that two and three make five, and that a square has but four sides; nor does it seem possible that truths so apparent can ever fall under a suspicion of falsity [or incertitude]."[11]

Yet even here there is the possibility of error. Suppose that the all-powerful God has so arranged things that I am deceived about these matters. Descartes notes that he sometimes thinks that others are in error. How does he know that he himself is not similarly in error? It might seem that the good-

---

[9]Ibid., rule 4.
[10]Descartes, *Meditations on First Philosophy*, meditation 1.
[11]Ibid.

ness of God is the guarantee in this matter, for how could a good God have created him in such a way as to be liable to constant deception? But if this is the case, it would seem that this divine goodness would also be contrary to his being occasionally deceived. Yet he realizes that he is sometimes in error. Thus this epistemological deus ex machina does not solve the problem. Perhaps it is not God but some malignant demon who does the deceiving. In light of all these considerations, Descartes must diligently guard against credulity on his part.[12]

In the second meditation Descartes moves from the negative doubt to the positive of that which cannot be doubted successfully. Just as Archimedes had wished for a firm and immovable spot from which to move the world, so Descartes acknowledges that he is looking for such a metaphysical spot, one thing that is indubitable. Here again is Descartes's foundationalism, his desire to find a foundation on which to build his philosophy with certainty.

Suppose, he says, that he was convinced that there was absolutely nothing in the world. Would that also mean that he was convinced that he did not exist? By no means:

> I assuredly existed, since I was persuaded.
>
> But there is I know not what being, who is possessed at once of the highest power and the deepest cunning, who is constantly employing all his ingenuity in deceiving me. Doubtless, then, I exist, since I am deceived; and let him deceive me as long as he may, he can never bring it about that I am nothing, so long as I shall be conscious that I am something. So that it must, in fine, be maintained, all things being maturely and carefully considered, that this proposition (*pronunciatum*) I am, I exist, is necessarily true each time it is expressed by me, or conceived by me in my mind.[13]

This is the argument that has come to be known popularly as "I think, therefore I am." If anything, the argument here should be summarized as "I doubt, therefore I am."[14] The point is that from the activity of doubting, Descartes infers the existence of himself as the subject.

It is important that we analyze carefully the nature of this argument. It has come under a number of criticisms. One of these is that the starting point itself is the conclusion of a deductive argument. On this basis, what Descartes has actually done is to argue as follows: "all thinking beings exist; I am a thinking being; therefore I exist." This, however, runs

---

[12]Ibid.

[13]Ibid., meditation 2.

[14]L. J. Beck, *The Metaphysics of Descartes: A Study of the Meditations* (Oxford: Clarendon, 1965), p. 80.

counter to what Descartes had said about the two means of gaining knowledge: "Let us enumerate all the acts of our intellect through which we can
arrive at the cognition of things without any fear of error. There are only
two: namely intuition and induction."[15] He goes on to explain what he
means by induction: "By *intuition* I understand, not the fleeting testimony
of the senses, nor the deceptive judgment of the imagination with its false
constructions; but a conception of a pure and attentive mind so easy and
so distinct, that no doubt at all remains about that which we are understanding. Or, what comes to the same thing, intuition is the undoubting
conception of a pure and attentive mind, which arises from the light of
reason alone, and is more certain than deduction, because simpler."[16]aa
That this type of intuition is involved in the first principle of the argument
is seen from this statement: "When we become aware that we are thinking
things, this is a primitive act of knowledge derived from no syllogistic reasoning. He who says '*I think, hence I am or exist*' does not infer existence
from thought by a syllogism, but, by a simple act of mental vision, recognizes it as if it were a thing that is known *per se.*"[17]

It is still necessary, however, to inquire further about the nature of the
objects of intuition. How can we be certain that they indeed are true, or that
our intuition is genuine? It is because the objects of intuition are clear and
distinct, a pair of adjectives that play a very important part in Descartes's
epistemology. He acknowledges, in connection with the *cogito* ("I think,
therefore I am") that there is some difficulty in establishing this certainty.
"And having remarked that there was nothing at all in the statement '*I think,
therefore I am,*' which assures me of having thereby made a true assertion,
excepting that I see very clearly that to think it is necessary to be, I came to
the conclusion that I might assume, as a general rule, that the things which
we conceive very clearly and distinctly are all true—remembering, however,
that there is some difficulty in ascertaining which are those that we distinctly conceive."[18] He explains that he terms "that clear which is present
and apparent to an attentive mind." By distinct he means "so precise and different from all other objects that it contains within itself absolutely nothing
but what is clear."[19]

It is not our purpose here to examine his discussion of the role of deity in

---

[15]Some editors emend this to read "deduction."

[16]Descartes, *Rules for the Direction of the Understanding*, rule 3.

[17]René Descartes, *Reply to Second Objections,* in *The Philosophical Works of Descartes,* trans.
Elizabeth S. Haldane and G. T. Ross (New York: Dover, 1955), 2:38.

[18]René Descartes, *Discourse on the Method of Rightly Conducting the Reason and Seeking for
Truth in the Sciences,* in *Philosophical Works,* 1:101-2.

[19]Descartes, *Principles,* 1.45.

guaranteeing the veridical character of these clear and distinct ideas, nor of asking about the validity of his contention. The point we have sought to illustrate is that knowledge can be certain because it rests on the firm bed-rock of some indubitable first principles, from which it proceeds by valid deduction.

Isaac Newton

What Descartes has done for the discipline of philosophy, Isaac Newton did for science. Although he did not publish his magnum opus until 1687, Newton had made his major discoveries at the age of twenty-three. The discoveries that immediately preceded him made possible his insights. Newton was born in the year that Kepler died, and just eight years before the death of Descartes. It was an outstanding example of the coincidence of a gifted human and an opportune time.

Much of the work that had been done was in the field of mathematics, and it is significant that the title of Newton's major work is *Mathematical Principles of Natural Philosophy.* Descartes had invented analytical geometry, and Newton invented calculus (Leibnitz also invented it independently). Yet it was not merely abstract mathematics that was the basis of Newton's scientific theory or "natural philosophy," as he termed it. Mathematics combined with experimentation was the source of his knowledge of nature. Numerous significant discoveries in a period of twenty years formed the material on which Newton drew. Torricelli, a student of Galileo, had invented the barometer and measured the atmosphere in 1643. Pascal confirmed his measurements and formulated the laws of pressure in fluids. Boyle discovered the laws of pressure in gases. So the method of science was to discover the laws of nature, confirming thereby the computations derived from mathematics. Newton's great contribution to science was to draw on the recent experimental data, and apply the mathematical method universally to mechanical motion. It was the fulfillment of Descartes's dream of giving a complete mechanical interpretation of the world in exact, mathematical, deductive terms. Newton formulated a famous rule and corollaries:

> Rule I. We are to admit no more causes of natural things than such as are both true and sufficient to explain their appearances. . . .
>
> Rule II. Therefore, to the same natural effects we must, as far as possible, assign the same causes. . . .
>
> Rule III. The qualities of bodies, which admit neither intensification nor remission of degree and are found to belong to all bodies within the reach of our experiments, are to be esteemed the universal qualities of all bodies whatsoever. For since the qualities of bodies are only known to us by experiments, we are to hold for universal all such as universally agree with experiments. . . . We are certainly

not to relinquish the evidence of experiments for the sake of dreams and vain fictions of our own; nor are we to recede from the analogy of Nature, which sues to be simple, and always consonant to itself.[20]

It is clear that his aim is "to subject the phenomena of nature to the laws of mathematics."[21] There is a universal order within nature, and this order can be described mathematically. Kepler had discovered the laws of planetary motion from induction of the facts he had observed, and Galileo had formulated the laws of falling bodies on the earth. Newton included both of these in one all-inclusive set of principles. The same laws governing occurrences on the surface of the earth apply throughout the entire solar system. This premise enabled later scientists to calculate and predict light, heat, magnetism, and electricity.

The makeup of reality. In Newton's understanding, the world is made up of hard and indestructible particles called atoms. These particles are predominantly mathematical, but they are simply smaller elements of objects that we experience with our senses. So, for example, he says, "That all bodies are impenetrable, we gather not from reason, but from sensation. The bodies which we handle we find impenetrable, and thence conclude impenetrability to be a universal property of all bodies whatsoever."[22] Changes in nature are to be understood to be the results of the separations, union, and motion of these particles.

Space and time. Newton's own position can be most clearly discerned with respect to his conceptions of space and time, and here also the contrast with a later type of physics is sharply etched. Newton was attempting to distinguish his view of space and time, the true views thereof, from relativist views. On those views, space and time were thought of entirely in terms of distances between objects or events. They did not have any separate or independent status of their own. Newton, however, spoke of both absolute and relative time and space: "Absolute, true, and mathematical time, of itself, and from its own nature, flows equably without relation to anything external, and by another name is called duration: relative, apparent, and common time, is some sensible and external (whether accurate or unequable) measure of duration by the means of motion, which is commonly used instead of true time; such as an hour, a day, a month, a year."[23] Absolute time can be seen here to have an intrinsic reality, for which it does not depend on anything, and is not affected or altered by anything. A similar

---

[20]Isaac Newton, *Mathematical Principles of Natural Philosophy*, 3.1-3.
[21]Ibid., author's preface.
[22]Ibid., 3.3.
[23]Isaac Newton, *Principles, Definitions,* scholium 1.

distinction is made with respect to space: "Absolute space, in its own nature, without relation to anything external, remains always similar and immovable. Relative space is some movable dimension or measure of the absolute spaces; which our senses determine by its position to bodies, and which is vulgarly taken for immovable space."[24] It may be popular to define space in relationship to certain objects. In reality, according to Newton, we should think in the reverse fashion. These objects are located within absolute space, which exists independently of these objects, and is not affected or altered by them.

Corresponding to absolute and relative space is the idea of absolute and relative motion, which is correlated with the idea of force. Absolute motion is that which takes place as a result of application of force. There cannot be absolute motion without the application of force, and conversely, where force is applied, there must inevitably be absolute motion as a result. Relative motion involves no application of force, as when the object in question remains motionless, but another moves, thus altering the relationship between the two.

Human beings. Newton's view of the human person and its relationship to the rest of the world follows what was by this time becoming a rather widely accepted view, namely, dualism. The human's soul, which for Newton is identical with the mind, is locked up as it were in the human body. It has no direct contact with the outside world. It is located in a particular part of the brain, called the *sensorium*, to which motions are conveyed from external objects by means of nerves, and it in turn transmits motions to muscles by animal spirits. In vision, the motions that come to the brain do not come directly from the external object, but from the image the object forms on the retina.[25] Newton's doctrine of secondary qualities enters into play at this point. These have no existence outside of human brains, except as a potential of certain objects to reflect or propagate certain motions.[26] On this understanding, the human is essentially a spectator. The world of qualities perceived by the human is simply the effects of the mechanistic external world on the brain of the person.

God. Although this is a mathematical world, known empirically, Newton, as a Christian believer, did not dispense with God. As alluded to earlier, God is the one who has created this great machine of creation. Although Newton apparently had a theism based on his personal religious experience, it was as the Lord of the creation that God played a significant part in his system of

---

[24] Ibid., scholium 2.
[25] Isaac Newton, *Optics*, 1.1.7.
[26] Ibid., 2.1.

thought. Newton had a developed natural theology, according to which the orderliness of the heavenly bodies required a God: "This most beautiful system of the sun, planets and comets could only proceed from the counsel and dominion of an intelligent and powerful Being. And if the fixed stars are the centres of other like systems, these, being formed by the like wise counsel, must be all subject to the dominion of One."[27] It is not merely astronomical considerations that require belief in God, however: "Blind metaphysical necessity, which is certainly the same always and every where, could produce no variety of things. All that diversity of natural things which we find suited to different times and places could arise from nothing but the ideas and will of a Being necessarily existing."[28]

Newton is concerned to define and describe this God in such a way as to distinguish his view from both deism and pantheism. God is infinite in every respect: he is supreme or most perfect, in eternity, knowledge, and power. The world is not to be thought of as his body, nor even as a machine that he has once created and in the affairs of which he never again involves himself.

> This Being governs all things, not as the soul of the world, but as Lord over all; and on account of his dominion he is wont to be called *Lord God* παντοκρά-τωρ, or *Universal Ruler*; for *God* is a relative word, and has a respect to servants: and *Deity* is not the dominion of God over his own body, as those imagine who fancy God to be the soul of the world, but over servants.[29]

John Locke

Quite different in many ways is John Locke's epistemology. He was strongly attracted to Descartes' philosophy, and one commentator suggests that Descartes had more influence on Locke than did any other metaphysical philosopher, in terms of both his analytical approach and his introspective method. Locke's interests were more in facts than in abstractions, however, and he became critical of Descartes' rationalism, and soon developed his own thought in considerable contrast to this view.[30]

Locke was born August 29, 1632, in Wrington, Somersetshire, England, but spent his boyhood near Bristol. He was the oldest of two sons in a family of Roundhead and Puritan sympathies. In 1652 he received a scholarship to Christ Church, Oxford, which was to be his home for the next fifteen years.

---

[27]Newton, *Principles*, 2nd ed., book 3, general scholium.
[28]Ibid.
[29]Ibid.
[30]Alexander Campbell Fraser, "Prolegomena, Biographical, Critical, and Historical," in John Locke, *An Essay Concerning Human Understanding* (New York: Dover, 1959), 1:xix-xx.

This was a time when experimental research was becoming popular, and Locke became occupied with chemical experiments and meteorological observations; he also studied medicine. Although he did not take a degree in medicine, he engaged in something of an amateur practice in Oxford.

Two events occurred which were to shape his thought and interests for some time to come. First, a physician, Dr. Thomas, in his absence entrusted oversight of his practice to Locke. One patient who came during that time was the Earl of Shaftesbury. He was so favorably impressed with Locke that he invited him to regard his home as Locke's own. This friendship introduced Locke into the society of scientists such as Sydenham and Boyle. The second event was a meeting of five or six friends in the winter of 1670. These friends were discussing some issues of morality and revealed religion, and found themselves unable to reach agreement. It occurred to Locke that they were taking a wrong approach, and that they should inquire into the objects and method of understanding. This became, by his own testimony, the inquiry that led to the production of his *Essay*. It proved to be one of the major works on the problems of epistemology within the history of philosophy.

No innate ideas. The first major point in Locke's epistemology is a rejection of the conception of innate ideas. While some have claimed that the view he attacks is a straw man, John Yolton has documented the widespread acceptance of the innate idea conception in seventeenth-century England.[31] The theory Locke is reacting against insists that humans have unlearned ideas that are part of their very makeup, something which the soul receives in its very first being and brings into the world with it. The most common argument offered in support of this contention is that of general assent, the fact that there are certain ideas that everyone agrees on. This, however, Locke asserts, would only be effective if it could not be shown that there is no other way that people come to such a view, which he believes can be done. Worse than that, however, the argument is self-defeating, for the simple reason that there is no single conception such as this on which everyone agrees.[32]

Having thus disposed of the conception that there are ideas that are innate within us, Locke presents his alternative view. All our ideas, he contends, come from either sensation or reflection, which together he terms *experience*. By the former he means the senses conveying into the mind perceptions of things. This is the great source of most of our ideas, depending wholly on our senses. The other is the perception of the operations of our

---

[31]John W. Yolton, *Locke and the Way of Ideas* (Oxford: Clarendon, 1956), chap. 2.
[32]John Locke, *Essay Concerning Human Understanding*, 1.1.2-4.

own mind within us, working on ideas it has received. It is very like sense, and Locke indeed refers to it as *internal sense*. He calls this reflection, which he defines as "that notice which the mind takes of its own operations, and the manner of them, by reason whereof there come to be ideas of these operations in the understanding." These two, he says, "are to me the only originals from whence all our ideas take their beginnings."[33]

Here then is foundationalism of a different sort from that of Descartes. Rather than beginning with indubitable first principles obtained introspectively and drawing inferences from them, the basic starting point is sense experience. Although reflection also produces ideas, nothing can be produced without sensation first supplying the raw material. Qualities are the powers that objects have to cause ideas. Locke divides qualities into primary and secondary qualities. Primary qualities are those that all bodies have, including solidity, extension, figure, and mobility. Secondary qualities are those powers that cause the sensations of sound, color, odor, and taste in the perceiver. Locke does not hold that the secondary qualities, such as redness, are in the object, but certain primary qualities cause phenomena, such as the appearance of red, to the observer. There is no resemblance between this phenomenon, the idea in the mind, and the quality that causes it. That which causes it is objectively present in the object, however. Locke says, "Simple ideas are not fictions of our fancies, but the natural and regular productions of things without us, really operating upon us; and so carry with them all the conformity which is intended; or which our state requires."[34] In addition to simple ideas there are complex ideas, which the mind forms from simple ideas by combining two or more of them. What it cannot do, however, is to form a new simple idea.

Political philosophy. Locke's other major contribution to the modern period was his political philosophy, which had considerable influence on the American Constitution. He holds that all humans are originally in "a state of perfect freedom to order their actions, and dispose of their possessions, and persons as they see fit, within the bounds of the Laws of Nature, without asking leave, or depending upon the Will of any other man."[35] These laws have been established by God, and as rational creatures, humans must be governed by the law of nature. The assumption is that by the use of reason, a human could discover these laws of nature, which constitute the fundamental principles of morality.[36] In the state of nature, humans are bound

---

[33]Ibid., 2.1.122-23.
[34]Ibid., 4.4.4.
[35]John Locke, *Two Treatises on Government*, 2.2.4.
[36]See John Locke, *Essays on the Law of Nature*.

to maintain peace, preserve humankind, and refrain from harming one another. Because of human partiality, however, it is necessary to have civil government, by which humans form a social contract with one another. When someone attempts to gain absolute power over others, he has created a state of warfare. The people then have the right to revolt, which is actually an extension of the right to punish an aggressor in the state of nature. Interestingly, Locke, who was essentially a social conservative, justified slavery on the grounds that the slaves are persons who originally were in a state of wrongful war against those who conquered them. He believed that property rights also were based on the law of nature, but it was the duty of government to preserve them.

Religion. Locke was a strong believer in the voluntary nature of religion. Since persons of various religions are equally sure of the truth of their position, it is likely that no one has all of truth, and thus toleration is to be extended to all. He did not, however, believe this tolerance should be extended to atheists, because, being atheists, they would not be bound by promises, oaths, and covenants. Although Socinians, deists and Unitarians took inspiration from Locke's writing, his own views were rather orthodox. He believed in the divine inspiration of the Bible, but held that even such revelation must be tested by reason.

Immanuel Kant

In Immanuel Kant we find a full expression of the modern mentality in philosophy, although there are already elements in his thought that contained some of the seeds of postmodernism. He was born, educated, taught, and lived his entire life in a single town, Königsberg, in East Prussia (now Kaliningrad, Russia), never married, and did not travel widely. Yet his influence has been profound in the Western world. Although there is no pure Kantian philosopher now alive and writing, either in Germany or elsewhere, the issues that he raised continue to influence a number of discussions in philosophy and other disciplines. Kant was born in 1724 and died in 1804, thus doing his entire productive literary work in the last half of the eighteenth century. In many ways, he was the prime philosopher of the Enlightenment.

Kant's thought must be seen against the background of the major philosophical debate of the time, between the rationalists and the empiricists, on how knowledge is gained. The rationalists, Descartes, Spinoza, and Leibnitz, contended that by the use of deduction and drawing on certain innate ideas, it is possible to have knowledge of the supersensible. The empiricists, Locke, Berkeley, and Hume, on the other hand, argued that there are no innate ideas, and that all knowledge comes from sense experience. There had been an extensive debate between Leibnitz and Locke on this subject, and Kant, who had felt considerable affinity for the rationalist view, testifies that Hume "awakened me from my dogmatic slumbers." In the concluding words of his *Enquiry*, Hume had dismissed metaphysics by saying, "If we take in our hand any volume; of divinity or school metaphysics, for instance; let us ask, *Does it contain any abstract reasoning concerning quantity or number:* No. *Does it contain any experimental reasoning concerning matter of fact and existence?* No. Commit it then to the flames: for it can contain nothing but sophistry and illusion."[37] In his precritical phase, Kant had basically agreed, but came to see that there must be a basis for such metaphysical inquiry. His aim, then, was to find an approach to the theory of knowledge that would combine what he considered to be the valid insights of both these views.

The discussion may be set within the context of the different kinds of sentences. A priori sentences are those that do not claim to be dependent on or logically posterior to, sensory experience. The propositions of mathematics are of this type. These are not arrived at by actual measurement of the physical world, but by deduction from fixed premises. A posteriori sentences, on the other hand, such as scientific propositions, are derived from sense experience, or are logically posterior to it. Analytical sentences are those in which the predicate adds nothing that is not contained, at least implicitly, within the subject, and simply explicates that meaning. "All bachelors are unmarried" would be an example of this type. Synthetic sentences are those in which the predicate adds some information not contained within the subject, such as "That tree is tall." There had been considerable debate about these several types of sentences. Kant's particular contribution was in his claim that there are a priori synthetic sentences, in which, without the benefit of sensory data, one may, by pure inference, arrive at truths not implicit in the subject of the sentence: "We must discover on the largest scale the ground of the possibility of synthetical judgments *a priori*; we must understand the conditions which render every class of them possible, and endeavour not only to indicate in a sketchy outline, but to define in its fulness and practical completeness, the whole of that knowledge, which forms a class by itself, systematically arranged according to its original sources, its divisions, its extent and its limits."[38]

Kant wrote three great critiques, together with several smaller treatises.

---

[37]David Hume, *An Enquiry Concerning Human Understanding* (La Salle, Ill.: Open Court, 1949), p. 184.

[38]Immanuel Kant, *Critique of Pure Reason*, 2nd ed., trans. F. Max Müller (Garden City, N.Y.: Doubleday, 1961), p. 31.

Roughly, the first of these critiques, *The Critique of Pure Reason,* is concerned with epistemology, the second, *The Critique of Practical Reason,* addresses the basis of ethical judgments, and the third, *The Critique of Judgment,* is oriented to issues of aesthetics. It is primarily the *Critique of Pure Reason,* together with the *Prolegomena to Any Future Metaphysics,* that is of relevance to our concerns here.

Kant tells us that he is engaged in a transcendental philosophy, and identifies this by defining transcendental knowledge as that "which is occupied not so much with objects, as with our *a priori* concepts of objects."[39] In his use of *transcendent* here Kant means that the argument transcends experience, and attempts to discern the a priori conditions of experience. While a system of such concepts might be called Transcendental Philosophy, he declares such an undertaking to be too much for him at present. He is concerned with a transcendental critique, but not a doctrine. The difference is that the contribution of a critique, unlike that of a doctrine, is only negative, not positive. Its aim is to purge rather than expand reason, preserving it against errors.[40] He likens his endeavor, not to a building, but to "an architectonic plan, guaranteeing the completeness and certainty of all parts of which the building consist."[41]

Kant divides his treatment of transcendentalism into the elements of transcendentalism and the method of transcendentalism. The former consists of the transcendental aesthetic, dealing with time and space, and the transcendental logic. The transcendental logic is in turn divided into the transcendental analytic and the transcendental dialectic.

Kant explains the basis of our knowledge by his statement that "there are two stems of human knowledge, which perhaps may spring from a common root, unknown to us, viz. *sensibility* and the *understanding,* objects being given by the former and thought by the latter."[42] In the transcendental aesthetic, he investigates the former, and in the transcendental logic, the latter. There is one means by which knowledge reaches its objects directly and forms the ultimate material of all thought, namely, intuition *(Anschauung).* "Sensibility alone," he says, "supplies us with intuitions *(Anschauungen).* These intuitions become thought through the understanding *(Verstand),* and hence arise conceptions *(Begriffe).* All thought therefore must, directly or indirectly, go back to intuitions *(Anschauungen),* i.e. to our sensibility *[Sinnlichkeit],* because in no other way can objects be given to us."[43] If, however,

---

[39] Ibid., p. 32.
[40] Ibid.
[41] Ibid., p. 33.
[42] Ibid., p. 34.
[43] Ibid., p. 37.

sensibility gives us the matter of the phenomenon, what gives that unde-
fined object of empirical intuition its form, what causes it to be arranged in a
certain order? To put it another way, what enables sensation to become intuition, or what are the a priori conditions of a posteriori knowledge? These,
contributed by the mind, are space and time.[44]

Kant first sets himself the task of demonstrating the a priori character of
space. He offers two arguments in support of his contention. The first is that
the concept is necessary in order to distinguish between any two objects: "in
order that I may be able to represent them [two objects] *(vorstellen)* as side by
side, that is, not only as different, but as in different places, the representation *(Vorstellung)* of space must already be there."[45] The second is more basic
and more convincing: "It is impossible to imagine that there should be no
space, though one might very well imagine that there should be space without objects to fill it."[46]

Kant's treatment of time is similar to that of space. Again his contention
is that time is not an empirical concept obtained from experience. If it were,
"neither coexistence nor succession would enter into our perception, if the
representation of time were not given *a priori.*"[47] As with space, its independence is a major evidence of its a priori character: "We cannot take away
time from phenomena in general, though we can well take away phenomena out of time. Time therefore is given *a priori*. In time alone is reality of
phenomena possible. All phenomena may vanish, but time itself (as the
general condition of their possibility) cannot be done away with."[48]

It is important to see what Kant is saying here. He had considered three
possibilities regarding the status of space and time: that they are "real
beings" in themselves; that they are determinations or relations of things,
which they would possess even if they were not perceived; that they are
determinations inherent in the form of intuition, and therefore within our
mind, without which space and time would never be ascribed to anything.[49]
His choice clearly is with the last of these. He makes no claim as to whether
the objects of intuition are really or in themselves the way we perceive
them to be. There is no way of knowing them but through our intuition, and
that must necessarily be through the forms of space and time. Kant believes
he has uncovered the nature of human perception, a quality or structure
common to all humans: "We know nothing but our manner of conceiving

---

[44]Ibid., pp. 38-39.
[45]Ibid., p. 39.
[46]Ibid., p. 40.
[47]Ibid., p. 43.
[48]Ibid., pp. 43-44.
[49]Ibid., p. 39.

them [the objects], that manner being peculiar to us, and not necessarily shared in by every being, though, no doubt, by every human being."[50]

This then is, in brief, Kant's discussion of sensibility. He also regards understanding as a source of knowledge. In the transcendental logic he intends to identify and demonstrate the a priori elements within understanding, and to show how these are to be properly applied, as well as to identify illegitimate applications of them. The former endeavor, showing the correct application of the categories of understanding, he refers to as the transcendental analytic, and the latter, the improper application of the categories, he identifies as the transcendental dialectic.

The categories are not abstracted from perception. To identify them, therefore, we must examine thinking or judging, which for Kant is the application of the categories. This process involves the unifying of the presentations of sensation into concepts. His method in some ways anticipates that of phenomenology. It is one of examination of the functioning of any faculty: "When we watch any faculty of knowledge, different concepts, characteristic of that faculty, manifest themselves according to different circumstances, which, as the observation has been carried on for a longer or shorter time, or with more or less accuracy, may be gathered up into a more or less complete collection."[51] What we must do is to ignore the specific content of judgments and focus solely on their form. This will give us a listing of the various types of judgment that are being made. Kant believes that this gives us four headings of the function of thought in a judgment, each heading of which includes three subdivisions:

  I. *Quantity of Judgments*
    Universal
    Particular
    Singular
  II. *Quality*
    Affirmative
    Negative
    Infinite
  III. *Relation*
    Categorical
    Hypothetical
    Disjunctive
  IV. *Modality*
    Problematical

[50]Ibid., p. 50.
[51]Ibid., p. 63.

Assertory

Apodictic

Kant's next step is to contend that corresponding to each of these judgments is a category of the mind or understanding, since all knowledge presupposes the content or matter being given by experience, which is manifold in the pure intuition. But that manifold must in some sense be synthesized or brought into unity. If this were not the case, then we would have simply disorganized sensation. For the sensation of color in space, and the sensation of cubeness, there must be a synthesis or combination of these, to form, for example, the concept of a colored cube. With respect to cause, Hume had argued that there is no such thing in experience as the experience of the cause. Rather, there is simply the constant conjunction of events. If the striking of one ball by another is always followed by the rolling away of the first ball, we say that the contact and the force resulted in or caused the motion of the first ball. However, since Hume could not find this judgment in the actual sensory experience, he attributed it to psychological sources, a tendency to attribute some sort of causative influence. In effect, what Kant does is to concede the validity of Hume's argument, at least up to a certain point. Instead of simply attributing the judgment of causation to psychological factors, he contended that this is evidence of an a priori factor, contributed by the knowing subject. A specific illustration of his is the activity of counting: "Thus our counting (as we best perceive when dealing with higher numbers) is a synthesis according to concepts, because resting on a common ground of unity, as for instance, the decade. The unity of the synthesis of the manifold becomes necessary under this concept."[52]

The exact nature and content of Kant's argument justifying the transition from judgments to categories is not as clear as we might wish. A number of commentators have pointed this out. Roger Scruton, for example, says, "An argument to that effect is hard to find, and it is significant that Kant was so dissatisfied with 'The Transcendental Deduction' that he rewrote it entirely for the second edition of the *Critique*, changing its emphasis from the subjective conclusion given above towards the objective deduction presently under discussion. Even so, the result is very obscure. . . . The flavour of the argument is more apparent than its substance."[53] Stephan Körner offers a reconstruction of the argument, but prefaces it by saying, "The following is but a crude outline, indeed almost a caricature, of Kant's procedure; and yet it fits his derivation of *some* of his Categories fairly well." He concludes his interpretation by saying, "I must desist from this crude exegetical game, and not

---

[52]Ibid., p. 71.

[53]Roger Scruton, *Kant* (Oxford: Oxford University Press, 1982), p. 33.

even try to refine it to the high degree of subtlety which would do justice to a Kantian argument."[54]

It may be helpful to recapitulate what Kant is saying, as compared to his predecessors and contemporaries. In the knowing process, what typically happens is that sensory data from the object known enters the consciousness of the knower through the pure forms of intuition, space and time. They thus are experienced as in space, having location and separation from other objects, and in time, being located prior to, simultaneous with, or subsequent to, other occurrences. They then enter the understanding, where they are further organized by the categories of the mind. Thus, they are known with respect to quantity as either universal ("all"), particular ("these"), or singular ("this one"). As to the other types of categories, similar judgments are made. Instead of a confused mass of sensory data, the object is experienced with this sort of coherence and intelligibility.

It is not entirely clear whether in Kant's view, the mind finds these qualities because they are present in the object and the mind fits its object, or whether it imparts these qualities to what is known, thus making it knowable. Two things can be said definitely about Kant's view, however. The mind does not simply create the objects. Unlike Berkeley's idealism, the objects exist independently of the knowing mind. Kant even added an explanation, "Against Idealism," to make this clear. Further, the mind does not simply passively find the qualities in the object, as Hume would contend. Whether combining the judgments to make the object of knowledge coherent, or actually introducing these qualities, the object simply could not be known as it is, without the mind's activity in applying the categories.

An illustration may help. When looking at a painting, one is exposed to a manifold of colors and shapes. When seeing it as a painting, however, rather than a collection of such stimuli, the person finds certain patterns within the painting. Depending on the nature of the painting, there may be recognizable objects within it. Similarly, in hearing speech, one hears a variety of sounds. If one knows the language being spoken, those are not merely interesting sounds, but a pattern of meaning emerges. In the same way, the role of the conscious subject in knowing is, according to Kant, like this. Rather than a mass of sense data, the person knows an object. The active power of the mind transforms sensation into knowledge.

Kant also contends that there are principles, which he says "are nothing but rules for the objective use of the former [the categories]."[55] The highest principle of all analytical judgments is the principle of contradiction, "that

---

[54]Stephan Körner, *Kant* (Harmondsworth, U.K.: Penguin, 1955), p. 55.
[55]Kant, *Critique of Pure Reason*, p. 117.

no subject can have a predicate which contradicts it."[56] The synthetic principles are listed as

I. Axioms of Intuition

II. Anticipations of Perception

III. Analogies of Experience

IV. Postulates of Empirical Thought in General[57]

While space will not permit thorough examination of each of these
principles, one may prove instructive as an example. The principle of axioms of intuition is that "all phenomena are, with reference to their intuition, extensive qualities." By an extensive quality Kant means "that in
which the representation of the whole is rendered possible by the representation of its parts, and therefore preceded by it." This means that one
cannot represent to oneself a line "without drawing it in thought, that is,
without producing all its parts one after the other, starting from a given
point, and thus, first of all, drawing its intuition."[58] It may be said roughly
that if the categories represent judgments that the knowing subject
makes, the principles are descriptions and prescriptions of how it makes
those judgments.

Improper use of the categories. It will be recalled that knowledge involves
both the logical structure supplied by the understanding as form and sensation to provide content. Without one or the other, there is no knowledge.
Kant's famous dictum, stated in several different ways, was, *"Thoughts without contents are empty, intuitions without concepts are blind."*[59] It is not uncommon, however, to attempt to apply the categories without having sensory
content for them. This is the case in some major issues of metaphysics.
What happens, however, when this is done, is that two equally possible
opposing statements can be made. So Kant examines each of several such
antinomies in his Transcendental Dialectic. An example is the first anti-
nomy of cosmology, which pairs the thesis: "The world has a beginning in
time, and is limited also with regard to space," with the antithesis, "The
world has no beginning and no limits in space, but is infinite, in respect both
to time and space." He then offers proofs for both thesis and antithesis.[60]
Both positions, derived from a common assumption, appear to be true. It is
not possible to resolve this contradictory situation, unless one recognizes
that the assumption on which both rest is mistaken. Just as "a square circle
is round" and "a square circle is not round" rest upon the contradictory idea

[56]Ibid., p. 111.
[57]Ibid., p. 117.
[58]Ibid., p. 118.
[59]Ibid., p. 55.
[60]Ibid., pp. 262-67.

of a square circle,[61] so each of these antinomies rests on a false assumption. This is an indication of the illusory character of apparent metaphysical statements about supersensible objects.

The modernist character of Kant's critical philosophy. Kant's *Critique of Pure Reason* embodies certain characteristics of modernism. Perhaps the most significant is the belief in objectivism, and in a particular way. One way to argue for the objectivity of knowledge would be to contend that the order of things is present in the world that is known empirically. Thus, the quality is in the object, regardless of knowledge of it. Kant's approach is somewhat different. There is an objective quality to judgments because the structure of the reason is the same for all persons. He would say that the form of intuition is the same for all humans, and in the case of the categories of the understanding, apparently these are the same for all rational beings. In other words, there is a common quality of reason in all persons. This means that one individual knower can have knowledge that is the same as another individual.

We have noted that for Kant both the sensory and the logical elements are necessary for there to be knowledge. This means, however, that we cannot get outside of our categories to know the object of intuition in itself, apart from the way our mind structures that knowledge. This is the famous Kantian distinction between the noumenal world, the world as it is in itself, and the phenomenal world, the world as it appears to us. Because of this distinction, contrasting interpretations of Kant have arisen, some (such as Fichte, Schelling, and Schopenhauer) emphasizing that our thought determines the nature of the world, the more idealistic form, and others emphasizing that the world determines how we think of it. It appears, rather, that both must be held together. There is a harmony or a correspondence between the mind of the knower and the object known. The laws governing the one correspond to the laws governing the other, so that knowledge is possible.

To be sure, the world that Kant discussed in his critiques was the world of Newtonian physics and Euclidean geometry. He did not anticipate the coming of alternative physics and geometry, according to which these understandings would be understood not as perfect renditions of the world, but as one way of dealing with it.

Summary of Modernism

The major content of modernism can be summarized in several affirmations.

1. Knowledge is considered to be a good that is to be sought without

---

[61]Körner, *Kant*, p. 114.

restriction. Knowledge will provide the solution to humanity's problems. This confidence in knowledge therefore contributes to a belief in progress.

2. Objectivity is both desirable and possible. It is believed that any personal or subjective factors can be eliminated from the knowing process, thus rendering the conclusions certain.

3. Foundationalism is the model for knowledge. All beliefs are justified by their derivation from certain bedrock starting points or foundational beliefs.

4. The individual knower is the model of the knowing process. Each person must assess the truth for himself or herself, even though the truth is the same truth for everyone.

5. The structure of reality is rational. It follows an orderly pattern. The same logical structure of the external world is also found in the human mind, thus enabling the human to know and organize that world. In most cases, this order or pattern is believed to be immanent within the world, rather than deriving from some transcendent source.

4

nineteenth-century precursors to postmodernism

While postmodernism represents a sharp contrast with the preceding modern period, it did not simply burst upon the scene suddenly and completely. There had always been contrary voices, protesting the modern view of reality. In the nineteenth century, however, two solitary philosophical voices were raised that were to develop into existentialism in the twentieth century, and then to provide inspiration for a full-blown postmodernism. These two early warning signals of a coming postmodernism were in many ways quite different from one another, and yet their thoughts and writings contained significant common elements.

Søren Kierkegaard

Søren Kierkegaard was born in 1813 and died in 1855, but was in many ways more a man of the twentieth than of the nineteenth century. Although he exerted little real influence on his contemporaries, he had a profound effect on the twentieth century. Anyone who reads him before reading the theologies of Karl Barth, Emil Brunner, Rudolf Bultmann, Paul Tillich, and Reinhold Niebuhr, will be impressed by the echoes of his thought in the works of these men.

It is not only in theology, however, that his influence has been felt. For Kierkegaard became the father of twentieth-century existentialism, and aspects of his thought therefore also appear in the work of persons like Martin Heidegger. In many ways, his thought also anticipates many of the emphases of postmodernism. Derrida wrote an interpretation of Kierke-gaard's *Fear and Trembling*.[1] John Caputo says, "The genealogical lines and links of deconstruction run back, not only to Nietzsche, but also, as I am constantly insisting, to Kierkegaard and Levinas, who are arguably the most important religious philosophers, or philosophical men of religion, or think-ers engaged in a philosophical repetition of religion (DM 52-53/GD 49), in the last two centuries."[2] While Nietzsche's influence has been widely recog-nized, Kierkegaard's is frequently overlooked.[3]

Deconstruction of the Hegelian system. Although certainly not using the term, Kierkegaard was engaged in the vigorous deconstruction of two domi-nant entities of his day, one a philosophical movement and the other an institution. These were, respectively, the inclusive philosophy of Georg Hegel and the Danish Lutheran state church.

Hegel had attempted to reduce all of reality to one great logical system, which would explain everything that is. He thought that his system accounted for everything within history. A personal filing system that for-merly was quite widely promoted utilized the slogan "a place for everything, and everything in its place." This in many ways aptly characterizes the Hegelian system. History was the thinking of the great mind, the Absolute, and he (or it) thinks in a definite dialectical pattern. The famous thesis-antithesis-synthesis schema allowed even the seemingly contradictory items to be included within this great system. Everything was to be ratio-nally explained. Within this system, in a sense the individual had no signifi-cance, other than as a part of the whole. It is this to which Kierkegaard is reacting when he speaks of the "system."

In the *Postscript*, Kierkegaard deals at length with this system. He contends that a logical system is possible, but that an existential system is not, except for God. In fact, in the *Philosophical Fragments,* he had explored the possibility of making Christianity a problem of thought. The difficulty, however, is that a system, to be a system, must be final, that is, it must include everything. To do this, it must exclude anything that is subject to an existential dialectic. Hegel assumed that he could introduce movement into logic, but that is an

---

[1] Jacques Derrida, *The Gift of Death*, trans. David Wills (Chicago: University of Chicago Press, 1995).

[2] John D. Caputo, "A Commentary," in Jacques Derrida, *Deconstruction in a Nutshell: A Con-versation with Jacques Derrida*, ed. John D. Caputo (New York: Fordham University Press, 1997), p. 159.

[3] Stanley Grenz, for example, makes no mention of Kierkegaard (*A Primer on Postmodern-ism* [Grand Rapids, Mich.: Eerdmans, 1996]) and D. A. Carson makes only one reference, basically positive, to Kierkegaard (*The Gagging of God: Christianity Confronts Pluralism* [Grand Rapids, Mich: Baker, 1996], p. 105).

illusion. While he everywhere assumes it, he never tries to prove it.[4]

According to Hegel, the system begins with the immediate. This means that, to use terminology and categories introduced later, Hegel's philosophy was foundationalist. To say, however, that one begins with the immediate is not to give the answer, but to pose a question, namely, *"How does the System begin with the immediate? That is to say, does it begin with it immediately?"*[5] Kierkegaard's answer to this is in the negative. There are a large number of possible beginning points, and either the thinker would have to wade through an infinite process of reflection, and would not be able to begin the system before he died, or he must make a choice, or he would have to choose the beginning point by an act of will.[6] Thus, the idea that the system is without presuppositions vanishes.

More serious is the fact that a system by its very nature excludes the individual. Hegel's system claimed to take in everything. Unfortunately, however, it had to omit one crucial matter: the individual who constructed the system. It was a philosophy that could account for everything except the philosopher himself. Kierkegaard asks about the identity of the one who has authored such a system.

> Is he a human being, an existing human being? Is he himself *sub specie aeterni*, even when he sleeps, eats, blows his nose, or whatever else a human being does? Is he himself the pure "I am I"? This is an idea that has surely never occurred to any philosopher; but if not, how does he stand existentially related to this entity, and through what intermediate determinations is the ethical responsibility resting upon him as an existing individual. Does he in fact exist? And if he does, is he then not in the process of becoming? . . . In that case I readily understand that it is not a human being I have the honor to address.[7]

Only God can form an existential system. The reason for this is that when a particular existence has become part of the past, it is now final or complete, and therefore can be grasped systematically. But, the question is, for whom can this be a system? It is only from outside of existence, and yet the one who himself is in existence, "who is in his eternity forever complete, and yet includes all existence within himself—it is God."[8]

The system turns reality and life into thought. When there is the claim of an absolute logical system, there is nothing left for an existing individual.

---

[4]Søren Kierkegaard, *Concluding Unscientific Postscript* (Princeton, N.J.: Princeton University Press, 1941), p. 99.
[5]Ibid., p. 101.
[6]Ibid., pp. 102-3.
[7]Ibid., p. 302.
[8]Ibid., p. 108.

Kierkegaard's recommendation is a strange one: "For suicide is the only tolerable existential consequence of pure thought, when this type of abstraction is not conceived as something merely partial in relation to being human, willing to strike an agreement with an ethical and religious form of personal existence, but assumes to be all and highest."[9] Kierkegaard is not necessarily recommending suicide as a course of action. What he is saying is that when an absolute system is in place, it deprives the individual of passionate decision. That makes life less passionate than suicide would be.

The life of a monk in a cloister seems unreal to us. Actually, however, the philosopher is more out of touch with reality. Kierkegaard finds "the passionate forgetfulness of the hermit, which takes from him the entire world, is much to be preferred to the comical distraction of the philosopher engrossed in the contemplation of universal history, which leads him to forget himself."[10] He likens the philosophers to men who build huge castles, but themselves live in shacks nearby.[11]

Attack on Christendom. If Kierkegaard's criticism of the Hegelian system was the great passion of his early writing, then surely his attack on the existent Christendom, as represented especially by the Danish Lutheran state church, was the consuming concern of his later writings. He had, of course, been born into the state church, as was every person born in Denmark. Before he had any opportunity to make a choice for himself, he had been inducted into this form of Christendom, or institutional Christianity. He had studied for the state examinations in theology, and had argued frequently with his father as to whether he should take those exams. He concluded, however, after his father died, that he must now take them, for as he said, "one cannot argue with a dead man." He did this, but had no immediate intention of becoming a priest.

Off and on throughout his life he wrestled with the issue of whether to seek appointment as a parish priest, but was unable to resolve the matter. Particularly when the estate he had inherited from his father began to expire, he again considered seeking a parish position. Over the years, his objections to the church had been building up. He hesitated to express these, however, out of respect for Bishop Mynster, a friend of Søren's father and for whom he personally had strong affection. When, however, Mynster died, and Professor Martensen, who was to succeed him as bishop, eulogized him in a sermon as a genuine witness to the truth,

---

[9]Ibid., p. 273.
[10]Ibid., pp. 283-84.
[11]*The Journals of Søren Kierkegaard: A Selection*, ed. and trans. Alexander Dru (Oxford: Oxford University Press, 1938), p. 156 (#583).

Kierkegaard could restrain himself no longer.[12] He began an attack on Christendom, both in his more formal writings and even more in his writings in popular publications, which was to last to the end of his life.

It is instructive to note the attacks Kierkegaard made on Mynster, the bishop, and Martensen, the professor, for they epitomize the criticisms he leveled against the church and the clergy in general. As Walter Lowrie put it, "S. K. was inclined to aim his shafts only at shining marks . . . he was not interested in denouncing the baser deviations from Christian faith and practice which were obvious enough to all, but rather the glittering corruptions which were held in high repute."[13]

In the sermon mentioned above, preached on the Sunday between Mynster's death and his funeral, Martensen had eulogized Mynster as a witness to the truth, one of a great series of such witnesses. He had urged his hearers to imitate the faith of the deceased bishop, which, he said, was a witness "not merely by word and profession, but in deed and in truth."[14] Against this contention, Kierkegaard protested violently:

> Bishop Mynster's preaching soft-pedals, slurs over, suppresses, omits something decisively Christian, something which appears to us men inopportune, which would make our life strenuous, hinder us from enjoying life, that part of Christianity which has to do with dying from the world, by voluntary renunciation, by hating oneself, by suffering for the doctrine, etc.—to see this one does not have to be particularly sharp-sighted, if one puts the New Testament alongside of Mynster's sermons.[15]

It was not just the bishop's preaching that must be challenged as a true witness, however. It was also his life, since Kierkegaard believed that one's life should express what one was preaching about. A witness to the truth, he said, is "a man whose life from first to last is unacquainted with everything which is called enjoyment . . . a man who in poverty witnesses to the truth— in poverty, in lowliness, in abasement, and is so unappreciated, hated, abhorred, and then derided, insulted, mocked . . . scourged, maltreated, dragged from one prison to the other, and then at last— . . . crucified, or beheaded, or burnt, or roasted on a gridiron."[16]

The Christianity-is-suffering theme echoes throughout Kierkegaard's religious writings. Instead of suffering, Martensen has in his sermon substi-

---

[12]George E. Arbaugh and George B. Arbaugh, *Kierkegaard's Authorship: A Guide to the Writings of Kierkegaard* (Rock Island, Ill.: Augustana College Library, 1967), p. 358.

[13]Walter Lowrie, *Kierkegaard* (New York: Harper & Brothers, 1962), p. 504.

[14]Kierkegaard, *Attack upon Christendom* (Princeton, N.J.: Princeton University Press, 1946), p. 5.

[15]Ibid.

[16]Ibid., p. 7.

tuted power, worldly goods, advantages, enjoyment of luxuries. To do this is "more contrary to Christianity, and to the very nature of Christianity, than any heresy, any schism, more contrary than all heresies and schisms combined." This is to *play* Christianity, the way a child plays soldier. What Martensen has done is to play the game that Mynster was a great witness to the truth, standing in the line of apostles and martyrs.[17] The contrast between the suffering and poor Jesus and the prestigious and comfortable life of the bishop is a major theme of Kierkegaard's attack on the church.

The established church came in for extended criticism by Kierkegaard, especially its clergy. He had much to say about baptism of infants. This was an involuntary matter on the part of the subject of baptism, and Kierkegaard felt that the priests desired to keep it that way. If, instead, persons were permitted at the age of discretion to decide upon their religion, the priests would no doubt have much less business. He satirizes: "A person has no religion; but by reason of family circumstances, first because the mother got into the family way, the paterfamilias in turn got into embarrassment owing to that, and then with the ceremonies connected with the sweet little baby— by reason of all this a person has . . . the Evangelical Lutheran religion."[18]

It is essential to be a baptized Christian, a member of the Lutheran church, to succeed within Danish society. Kierkegaard articulates a harsh assessment of this: "To be or to call oneself a Christian is a condition so essential for getting on in life that I suppose no one could get permission to earn his living by keeping a brothel unless he could produce proof that the was baptized and is (*i.e.* calls himself) a Christian. That is to say: to earn a living in this way is admissible, says the State, but only on the assumption and understanding and condition that you are a Christian. God in heaven!"[19]

The clergy are depicted as those who, under the guise of being servants and followers of Christ, have managed to make a rather comfortable living from the exercise of their ministry. The following appears in his journals under the heading "The Preaching of the Gospel."

Parson: Thou shalt die unto the world.—The fee is one guinea.

Neophyte: Well, if I must die unto the world I quite understand that I must fork out more than one guinea; but just one question: Who gets the guinea?

Parson: Naturally I get it, it is my living, for I and my family have to live by preaching that one must die unto the world. It is really very cheap, and soon we will have to ask for considerably more. If you are reasonable you will

---

[17]Ibid., p. 8.
[18]Ibid., p. 206.
[19]*Journals of Søren Kierkegaard*, p. 499 (#1306).

understand that to preach that one must die unto the world, if it is done seriously and with zeal, takes a lot out of a man. And so I really have to spend the summer in the country with my family to get some recreation.[20]

The several attacks on the church boil down to a few. The established church is Christendom, an institution in which everyone is automatically a Christian, but which therefore means nothing. It has departed from the truth of Christianity, which Jesus preached and exemplified, by substituting for the suffering that is at the heart of Christianity the comfort, ease, and advantage of being a Christian. Even those who are called on to preach the gospel do so in such a way as to benefit from it, thus contradicting by their actions the words they are proclaiming.

Subjective truth. One of Kierkegaard's major contributions to subsequent thought was his concept of subjective truth. To understand this concept, it is important to see his distinction between two types of truth, each appropriate in its own realm and for its own purpose.

Objective truth is the type of truth found in the study of science, history, mathematics, and any number of other realms where it is of primary importance to come to know and understand some object as precisely as possible. Here, as the name would seem to indicate, emphasis is placed on the object to be known, and the involvement of the subject who is doing the knowing must be minimized:

> When the question of truth is raised in an objective manner, reflection is directed objectively to the truth, as an object to which the knower is related. Reflection is not focussed upon the relationship, however, but upon the question of whether it is the truth to which the knower is related. If only the object to which he is related is the truth, the subject is accounted to be in the truth.[21]

Kierkegaard makes clear that he does not wish to reject the appropriateness of this view to the realm of science. He insists that he holds to the "sacred security of the precincts of science."[22] In this approach the subject becomes quite indifferent in the matter of truth, and conversely, the truth becomes indifferent. Objectivity claims to offer a kind of security. There is a danger that attaches to subjectivity, namely, madness, which in the last analysis is indistinguishable from truth, for they both have inwardness. The absence of inwardness also is madness, however. Kierkegaard tells of a patient who escapes from an asylum. He knows that when he returns to his village, he will be recognized and sent back to the asylum, and so resolves

---

[20]Ibid., p. 471 (#1267).
[21]Kierkegaard, *Postscript*, p. 178.
[22]Ibid., p. 135.

that he will demonstrate that he has objective truth. He picks up a ball, which he puts in the back pocket of his coat. Each time the ball strikes his posterior, the man says, "Bang, the earth is round!" Certainly, it is true that the earth is round, but by stating something so generally accepted, does not the man demonstrate that he is indeed insane?[23]

The real problem, however, comes when this view is extended to existential matters. As we noted earlier, Kierkegaard holds that an existential system is impossible. The objective approach involves what he calls an "approximation process," whereby one continually gathers more data and comes closer to a correct description of the object. So with respect, for example, to historical matters, one can only have relative certainty.[24] Similarly, the objective approach with respect to Christianity holds that since the New Testament is a historical document, one may simply approach it as a matter of historical inquiry, determining thereby what is Christian truth.[25] Here, however, as also in the realm of ethics, the approach works precisely contrary to the intention and goal. For the objective approach makes one into an observer, so objective that he becomes almost a ghost.[26] Matters such as Christianity and ethics, however, require a decision, and a decision is a matter of subjectivity.

Because the objective approach can never reach complete certainty, it can never make a decision. Indeed, the objective approach assumes that there is a direct transition from the objective inquiry to the subjective acceptance. One simply gathers enough knowledge to make the decision and then does so. This approach, however, is either a disillusionment because of ignorance of the subjective mode, or it is a means of shirking one's duty.[27] Similarly, the approach that attempts to bring God to light objectively is impossible, because God is a subject, and thus only exists for subjectivity in inwardness.[28] Rather than the direct or mediated approach, "the subjective acceptance is precisely the decisive factor; and an objective acceptance of Christianity *(sit venia verbo)* is paganism or thoughtlessness."[29]

Very different is the subjective approach: "*When the question of truth is raised subjectively, reflection is directed subjectively to the nature of the individual's relationship; if only the mode of this relationship is in the truth, the individual is in the truth even if he should happen to be thus related to what is not*

---

[23]Ibid., p. 174.
[24]Ibid., p. 25.
[25]Ibid., p. 38.
[26]Ibid., p. 118.
[27]Ibid., pp. 115-16.
[28]Ibid., p. 178.
[29]Ibid., p. 116.

true."[30] This is not merely what goes beyond the objective certainty; it is what flies in the face of objective certainty. But where lies the greater truth, in the objective approach or in the subjective? Kierkegaard poses the issue in several different areas. He first notes this with respect to religion, by introducing a hypothetical situation.

> If one who lives in the midst of Christendom goes up to the house of God, the house of the true God, with the true conception of God in his knowledge, and prays, but prays in a false spirit; and one who lives in an idolatrous community prays with the entire passion of the infinite, although his eyes rest upon the image of an idol: where is there most truth? The one prays in truth to God though he worships an idol; the other prays falsely to the true God, and hence worships in fact an idol.[31]

The same applies to an issue like immortality. Take Socrates, who did not have any proof of immortality, who said, *if* there is an immortality, and thus could be considered a doubter, compared with some modern thinkers, who can offer three proofs for the truth of immorality. Socrates, who lived with passion with respect to this issue, risked his entire life. The modern thinkers, however, with their three proofs, do not live their lives in conformity with this idea. Kierkegaard's comment is unflinching: "if there is an immortality it must feel disgust over their manner of life: can any better refutation be given of the three proofs? The bit of uncertainty that Socrates had, helped him because he himself contributed the passion of the infinite; the three proofs that the others have do not profit them at all, because they are dead to spirit and enthusiasm, and their three proofs, in lieu of proving anything else, prove just this."[32]

One way to characterize this difference between the two forms of truth is that "*The objective accent falls on WHAT is said; the subjective accent on HOW it is said.*"[33] It is not simply that the subjective enters in because of the objective, and goes beyond it. It is actually in opposition to any objective certainty. The paradoxical nature of the truth is what evokes the necessary inward passion: "For the objective situation is repellent; and the expression of the objective repulsion constitutes the tension and the measure of the corresponding inwardness."[34] Whereas in objective truth there is an approximation process, of getting closer and closer to the truth, in subjective truth the lack of objective certainty requires what in other contexts Kierkegaard

---

[30]Ibid., p. 178.
[31]Ibid., pp. 179-80.
[32]Ibid., p. 180.
[33]Ibid., p. 181.
[34]Ibid., p. 183.

calls a leap but here refers to as an appropriation-process: *"An objective uncertainty held fast in an appropriation-process of the most passionate inwardness is the truth,* the highest truth attainable for an *existing* individual."[35]

This shift, from the object known as the locus of truth to the subject as the center, was a revolutionary development, which in the coming century was to have a marked manifestation in a number of areas, particularly with respect to literary texts.

Friedrich Nietzsche

Friedrich Nietzsche is the other major nineteenth-century philosophical precursor of postmodernism. Like Kierkegaard, his influence was greater in the twentieth century than during his own lifetime, and the two are often cited as founders of existentialism. Nietzsche was born October 15, 1844, the birthday of Friedrich Wilhelm, the king of Prussia, for whom he was named. His father was the Lutheran pastor of the church in Röcken and both his grandfathers had also been pastors. His father died of a mental disorder when Friedrich was five years of age, and he consequently grew up as the sole male member of a household that included his mother, sister, grandmother, and two unmarried aunts.[36] As a student he so distinguished himself that Friedrich Ritschl declared that he was the best student he had taught, and recommended Nietzsche for an appointment as professor of classical philology at the University of Basel. He received this appointment, although he had not submitted his doctoral dissertation or his *Habilitationschrift,* the additional treatise necessary to become a professor. Nonetheless, in light of this appointment, the University of Leipzig conferred the doctorate on him.[37]

Nietzsche's work has been the object of widely differing interpretations. There does not appear to be a systematic design behind the writings, so that they can be fit into some kind of overall project. It also is difficult to know how literally to take his writing, and how great a weight to rest on certain passages. Some of this results from the varying values placed on different parts of his corpus, and specifically, the relative place to be assigned in interpretation to his published and his posthumous works, the *Nachlass,* which consist of notes from various periods of his life. Much of the work of collecting and publishing Nietzsche's work was done by his sister, Elisabeth Förster-Nietzsche. It was her interpretation of his works that came to be accepted, even though Kaufmann contends that "few writers today would

---

[35]Ibid., p. 182.
[36]Walter A. Kaufmann, *Nietzsche: Philosopher, Psychologist, Antichrist* (Princeton, N.J.: Princeton University Press, 1950), p. 19.
[37]Walter Kaufmann, "Nietzsche," in *The Encyclopedia of Philosophy*, ed. Paul Edwards (New York: Macmillan, 1967), 5:506.

cite her as a reliable interpreter but her influence is still tremendous, if unrecognized."[38] For instance, she made the judgment to include unpublished notes in his posthumous work, *The Will to Power*. It is therefore more difficult than would otherwise be the case, to determine the exact content of his views. He died in 1900, suffering from mental illness, and apparently also from syphilis.

One issue that affects the interpretation of Nietzsche is the lineage claimed for his ideas by some later movements. The Nazis, for example, made much of his concept of the *Übermensch*, which caused considerable aversion for his thought, but that appropriation should not be taken as determinative for understanding the meaning of his thought. One widely influential interpretation of the place of Nietzsche has been that of Jürgen Habermas, who referred to Nietzsche's thought as the "entry into postmodernity,"[39] and says that Nietzsche "renounces a renewed revision of the concept of reason and *bids farewell* to the dialectic of enlightenment."[40] According to this interpretation, Hegel and Nietzsche represent two forms of the European response of dissatisfaction with the Enlightenment ideal. Hegel attempted to reinstate the Enlightenment hopes by replacing the logistic method with a dialectical approach, in which contradictions were overcome in a new synthesis. Instead of replacing the Enlightenment rationalism with a new rationalism, Nietzsche introduced a type of irrationalism, and thus completely rejected the hope for an inclusive rational explanation of reality.

Nietzsche as deconstructionist. To what extent is Nietzsche advocating a rejection of the entire age and culture within which he was working? There are several indications of the similarity of his task to that of postmodernism and even deconstructionism.

It is apparent, even from the titles of his work, that Nietzsche sees a change of era or paradigm. Something is dying or fading, something else is arising or coming into being. Note some of these: *Beyond Good and Evil; The Birth of Tragedy; Daybreak: Thoughts on the Prejudices of Morality; Twilight of the Idols*. This is seen, however, more fully in his actual discussions of ideas, institutions, and even the modern period. These must be interpreted in light of the fact that Nietzsche is not self-consciously concerned with the Enlightenment or modernity per se. He is rather addressing or criticizing certain features or institutions of it.

---

[38] Kaufmann, *Nietzsche*, p. 4.

[39] Jürgen Habermas, *The Philosophical Discourse of Modernity*, trans. Frederick Lawrence (Cambridge, Mass.: MIT Press, 1987), p. 85.

[40] Ibid., p. 86.

Conventional morality. One of these characteristics of modernity is most evident in his criticism of conventional morality. It should be pointed out that Nietzsche is not simply attempting to destroy morality as such. He is not merely tearing down, out of opposition to morality. He critiques morality in order that a new and better alternative may be substituted for it. Indeed, the subtitle of *The Will to Power* is *An Attempted Transvaluation of All Values.* He claims in *Ecce Homo* that although *The Dawn of Day* was the work in which he began his campaign against morality, it was a positive, not a negative book. He then, however, gives his reason for writing what he did:

> My life-task is to prepare for humanity a moment of supreme self-consciousness, a Great Noontide when it will give both backwards and forwards, when it will emerge from the tyranny of accident and priesthood, and for the first time pose the question of the Why and Wherefore of humanity as a whole. This life-task is a necessary result of the view that mankind does *not* follow the right road of its own accord, that it is by no means divinely ruled, but rather, that it is precisely under the cover of its most sacred values that the tendency to negation, corruption, and decadence has exerted such seductive power. The question as to the origin of moral values is therefore a question of primary importance to me because it determines the future of mankind.[41]

This leads him to point out the origin of the problem: "We are asked to believe that at bottom everything is in the best hands, that the book, the Bible, gives us definite assurance of a divine guidance and wisdom overlooking man's destiny."[42] Nietzsche maintains that the exact opposite is the truth, namely, that the control by priests, not only of the church, but throughout society, has led to what he terms "the morality of decadence." By this he means the establishment of altruism as the supreme virtue, with the concomitant suppression of egoism. He regards anyone who disagrees with him on this point as "infected."

In *An Attempt at Self-Criticism*, he refers to Christianity as "the most extravagant burlesque of the moral theme to which mankind has hitherto been obliged to listen." In this particular context, he is discussing Christianity in relationship to esthetics, but here it illustrates more general themes. The Christian dogma, which is only moral, considers itself true and therefore sets up absolute standards, in relationship to which all art is relegated to the realm of falsehood. Under the disguise of a better life, Christianity has become a rejection of life.[43] In a long sentence he says:

---

[41]Friedrich Nietzsche, *Ecce Homo*, in *The Philosophy of Nietzsche* (New York: Random House, n.d.), pp. 887-88.
[42]Ibid., p. 888.
[43]Ibid., p. 941.

The hatred of the 'world,' the condemnation of emotion, the fear of beauty and sensuality, a beyond, invented to slander this world all the more, at bottom a longing for Nothingness, for the end, for rest, for the 'Sabbath of Sabbaths'—all this, together with the unconditional insistence of Christianity on the recognition *only* of moral values, has always appeared to me as the most dangerous and ominous of all possible forms of a 'will to perish'; at the very least, as the symptom of a most fatal disease, of the profoundest weariness, faint-heartedness, exhaustion, anemia—for judged by morality (especially Christian, that is, absolute morality) life *must* constantly and inevitably be the loser, because life is something essentially unmoral,—indeed, bowed down under the weight of contempt and the everlasting No, life *must* finally be felt as unworthy of desire, as in itself unworthy.[44]

Nietzsche's disaffection for morality was of wider grounding than simply his displeasure with Christianity, however. It is the conflict of conventional morality with the principle of the will to power that renders it suspect. This was a basic principle, developed as a modification of Schopenhauer's concept of the will to life, which he virtually identified with life. Morality is an expression of the will to power, but the question is, whose will to power. Nietzsche contends that three powers lie concealed behind morality: "(1) The instinct of the herd against the strong and independent; (2) the instinct of the suffering and underprivileged against the fortunate; (3) the instinct of the mediocre against the exceptional."[45] The difficulty is that this morality is developed at the cost of the ruling classes, and so retrains Nature's efforts to produce a higher type. Values are established and certified in relationship to the mass, the herd. He says:

How much or how little dangerousness to the community or to equality is contained in an opinion, a condition, an emotion, a disposition or an endowment—that is now the moral perspective; here again fear is the mother of morals. . . . The lofty independent spirituality, the will to stand alone, and even the cogent reason, are felt to be dangers; everything that elevates the individual above the herd, and is a source of fear to the neighbour, is henceforth called *evil;* the tolerant, unassuming, self-adapting, self-equalising disposition, the *mediocrity* of desires, attains to moral distinction and honour.[46]

The primary difficulty of conventional morality is that it impedes the development of the extraordinary individual, or as Nietzsche termed it, the *Übermensch,* or Superman. He believes that up to this point the aim of education has been utility, with respect to the society currently existing, rather than what could and will be. The herd is desirable, as it serves as a founda-

---

[44]Ibid., pp. 941-42.
[45]Friedrich Nietzsche, *The Will to Power,* ed. Walter Kaufmann (New York: Random House, 1967), p. 274.
[46]Nietzsche, *Beyond Good and Evil* §201, in *Philosophy of Nietzsche,* p. 492.

tion for the development of the higher race of men.[47] The human race can only be elevated by the rise of this higher form of humanity. Nietzsche is quite clear that his goal is this Superman, not humanity, and that such a single individual may justify whole millenniums of existence.[48] It is not simply Christianity that by its morality has resisted the higher values, however. Even philosophy, with its advocacy of moral "truths," has said no to Life.

Christianity. One of Nietzsche's most sustained attacks was on religion, and specifically, on the Christian religion. Although he had been born into a pastor's home and was at some points quite appreciative of his heritage, he came increasingly to reject it as antithetical to what is most important. At one point, his objection to Christianity was largely on the basis of historical criticism. In his more mature phase, however, with the full development of his idea of the Superman, the opposition to Christianity took a predictable form.

In his work *The Antichrist,* Nietzsche again asserted the value of the will to power: "What is good? Everything that heightens the feeling of power in man, the will to power, power itself. What is bad? Everything that is born of weakness."[49] Christianity is then evaluated in relationship to this value structure: "Christianity should not be beautified and embellished: it has waged dead war against this higher type of man; it has placed all the basic instincts of this type under the ban; and out of these instincts it has distilled evil and the Evil One: the strong man as the typically reprehensible man, the 'reprobate.'"[50] In particular, this effect can be seen in the value it places on pity as a virtue. Pity, however, makes suffering contagious and impedes the production of the higher values: "Quite in general, pity crosses the line of development, which is the law of *selection*. It preserves what is ripe for destruction; it defends those who have been disinherited and condemned by life; and by the abundance of the failures of all kinds which it keeps alive, it gives life itself a gloomy and questionable aspect. . . . Pity is the *practice* of nihilism. To repeat: this depressive and contagious instinct crosses those instincts which aim at the preservation of life and at the enhancement of its values."[51]

We should, however, note the distinction between Nietzsche's attitudes toward empirical Christianity and Christ himself. The former should not be confused with the one root to which its name refers. The other roots from

---

[47]Nietzsche, *Will to Power* §897, p. 477.

[48]Ibid. §§997, 1001, pp. 518, 519.

[49]Friedrich Nietzsche, *The Antichrist*, book 1, aphorism 2, in *The Portable Nietzsche*, ed. Walter Kaufmann (New York: Viking, 1954), p. 570.

[50]Ibid., aphorism 5, p. 571.

[51]Ibid., aphorism 7, p. 573.

which it has sprung are actually far more important. Nietzsche says: "What did Christ *deny*? Everything that today is called Christian."[52] This includes the Christian creed: "The entire Christian teaching as to what shall be believed, the entire Christian 'truth,' is idle falsehood and deception and precisely the opposite of what inspired the Christian movement in the beginning."[53] Neither, however, was it a matter of practices or of the social entity of the church: "Precisely that which is Christian in the ecclesiastical sense is anti-Christian, in essence: things and people instead of symbols; history instead of eternal facts; forms, rites, dogmas instead of a way of life. Utter indifference to dogmas, cults, priests, church, theology is Christian."[54] What Christ preached was a life, a real life. The kingdom of heaven is a state of the heart, and is manifested in deeds.[55]

Nietzsche's conception of philosophy. Some philosophers have questioned whether Nietzsche can be correctly termed a philosopher, in view of his rejection of much traditional philosophy and philosophers. It is true that in several respects he does not engage in the type of endeavor often associated with philosophy. He is not attempting to develop a system, an all-inclusive synoptic scheme that ties together all of the phenomena of our experience. Nor does he work out a thoroughgoing epistemology, or offer rigorous rational proofs for his contents or extensive theoretical refutations of the views he rejects. In so doing, however, despite his extensive criticisms of philosophers, he seems to be helping establish a new type of philosophy and philosopher. This is particularly true of his later writings, beginning with *Thus Spoke Zarathustra.*

Nietzsche is engaged in doing topical or problem philosophy. Even in the writings of his middle period, where this does not necessarily appear to be the case, he indicates in his reflection on them in *Ecce Homo*, that they were indeed formulated on such a basis. Some may question whether this is philosophy, because of the nature of the topics he addresses. His writing is distinguished by the neglect of such traditional problems of philosophy as the existence of God, the basis of moral judgments, and the nature and basis of knowledge. He is not interested in the usual disputes that arise in connection with these problems and then produce conflicting propositions, the truth or falsity of which must be debated. Rather, he deals with topics such

---

[52]Nietzsche, *Will to Power* §158, p. 98.
[53]Ibid., §159, p. 98.
[54]Ibid.
[55]Ibid., §§161-63, pp. 98-99. Nietzsche had read carefully the works of the Hegelian left, and one can detect in his thoughts the influence of David Strauss's *The Life of Jesus* and of Ludwig Feuerbach's *The Essence of Christianity.*

as ascetic ideals, the will to truth, and the bad conscience. These matters pose problems requiring new interpretation and evaluation, and this is what Nietzsche thinks to be the primary task of philosophy.

Further, Nietzsche approaches the problems not in an inclusive or fundamental fashion, but through a case treatment. Socrates, David Strauss, Schopenhauer, Wagner, and many others are introduced and examined. He then uses these cases to address a particular problem. He ranges cases for and against various interpretations. The unique nature of his philosophical method emerges at this point. Schacht summarizes well:

> Nietzsche does not for the most part present arguments of the customary sort. But he recognizes the need to do more than merely say what he thinks, in order to make his criticisms stick and his own ideas convincing. On the attack, he typically seeks to *make cases against* certain ways of thinking. He proceeds by presenting an array of considerations to make us suspicious and aware of just how problematical these methods are, ultimately to deprive them of their credibility. He generally does not claim that the considerations he marshals actually *refute* his targets. Rather, he aims and purports to *dispose* of them. He attempts to undermine them sufficiently to lay them to rest, exposed as unworthy of being taken seriously—at least by those possessed of intellectual integrity.[56]

Finally, Nietzsche's philosophizing can be seen to consist to a large extent of what is actually ad hominem argumentation. He is not concerned about theoretical truth but rather life, and ideas and systems are evaluated by the way they contribute to life. In discussions of matters such as morality and religion he is not so much refuting a given view as undermining it, creating suspicion, showing the motives that lie behind it. The discussion of pride and pity, the herd mentality, the slavish values often espoused, proceeds along these lines. It is indeed appropriate that one movement that claims Nietzsche as a forerunner is termed "existentialism," for these existential concerns are of the greatest importance in his thought.

The rejection of customary metaphysics. One of Nietzsche's more significant contributions was his perspectivity. This was in effect an attack on the Enlightenment view of knowledge as fixed, objective, and absolute. His comments appear in several different contexts. One of these is his opposition to positivism. Positivism restricted knowledge to phenomena, and insisted that facts are all that there are. Nietzsche, however, takes the exact opposite view: "I would say: No facts is precisely what there is not, only

---

[56]Richard Schacht, "Nietzsche's Kind of Philosophy," in *The Cambridge Companion to Nietzsche*, ed. Bernd Magnus and Kathleen Higgins (Cambridge: Cambridge University Press, 1996), pp. 157-58.

interpretations. We cannot establish any fact 'in itself': perhaps it is folly to want to do such a thing." He then goes on to soften somewhat this rather extreme statement: "Insofar as the word 'knowledge' has any meaning, the world is knowable: but it is *interpretable* otherwise, it has no meaning behind it, but countless meanings—'Perspectivism.'"[57]

He also brings this criticism to bear on the Kantian "thing in itself." Whereas language is supposed to be the expression of all realities, it "designates only the relations of things to men, and to express these relations he uses the boldest of metaphors."[58] This is seen especially in the matter of the formation of concepts. Here Nietzsche clearly identifies himself as a nominalist, as against any form of realism. The formation of a concept is achieved by grouping together similar particulars. This, however, is an artificial matter:

> Every concept originates by the equation of the dissimilar. Just as no leaf is ever exactly the same as any other, certainly the concept "leaf" is formed by arbitrarily dropping those individual differences, by forgetting the distinguishing factors, and this gives rise to the idea that besides leaves there is in nature such a theory as the "leaf," i.e., an original form according to which all leaves are supposedly woven, sketched, circled off, colored, curled, painted, but by awkward hands, so that not a single specimen turns out correctly and reliably as a true copy of the original form.[59]

So, with honesty, there is no essence referred to as that. There are merely many unequal cases, which we equate by omitting what is different or unequal.

What, then, is truth? Nietzsche contends that truths are illusions.

> Truth is a mobile army of metaphors, metonyms, anthropomorphisms, in short, a sum of human relations, which were poetically and rhetorically heightened, transferred, and adorned, and after long use seem solid, canonical, and binding to a nation. Truths are illusions about which it has been forgotten that they are illusions, worn-out metaphors without sensuous impact, coins which have lost their image and now can be used only as metal, and no longer as coins.[60]

What we call truth is actually in large part a product of the creative work of the human knower.

---

[57]Nietzsche, *Will to Power* §481, p.267.

[58]Nietzsche, "On Truth and Lying," in *Friedrich Nietzsche on Rhetoric and Language*, ed. Sander L. Gilman, Carole Blair, and David J. Parent (New York: Oxford University Press, 1969), p. 248.

[59]Ibid., p. 249.

[60]Ibid., p. 250.

The laws of logic, such as the law of identity and the law of contradiction, seem self-evident. In reality, says Nietzsche, these are not undeniable principles. Supposedly one cannot think and function without assuming them: "We are unable to affirm and to deny one and the same thing: this is a subjective empirical law, not the expression of any 'necessity' but only of an inability."[61] From the fact that we cannot do this, we assume that it is a necessary truth, but that does not follow. It reveals more about us than about the nature of reality. The problem with these supposedly necessary principles is that to assert that they are necessary assumes a prior and independent knowledge of the nature of the object, of Being. Rather than being adequate to reality, these are the means by which we create realities or the concept of reality. Nietzsche says, "Logic is the attempt to comprehend the actual world by means of a scheme of being posited by ourselves; more correctly, to make it formulatable and calculable for us."[62]

It is not only the outer world, the objects of knowledge, which is at least in part constructed by us. The same is true of the subject of knowledge itself, the ego.

This same perspectivity is seen in Nietzsche's discussion of moral issues. He is particularly critical of a natural law ethic—the view that values and even laws are embedded within nature, and ethics is a matter of discovering these and conforming our actions to them. There is, however, no such law. Rather, "it exists only owing to your interpretation and bad 'philology.' It is no matter of fact, no 'text,' but rather just a naively humanitarian adjustment and perversion of meaning, with which you make abundant concessions to the democratic instincts of the modern soul!"[63] This can be seen in the different conclusions drawn on the basis of some such imagined natural law. One person finds basis there for equality. Another, however, justifies quite a different position, such as the tyrannical claims to power, on the basis of the same data. Thus people assert about the world "that it has a 'necessary' and 'calculable' course, *not*, however, because laws obtain in it, but because they are absolutely *lacking*, and every power effects its ultimate consequences every moment."[64] Thus, Nietzsche makes a statement about ethics very similar to that which he made in the case of epistemology: "There is no such thing as moral phenomena, but only a moral interpretation of phenomena."[65]

---

[61]Nietzsche, *Will to Power* §516, p. 279.
[62]Ibid.
[63]Nietzsche, *Beyond Good and Evil* §22, p. 405.
[64]Ibid.
[65]Ibid., §108, p. 459.

5

twentieth-century transitions to postmodernism

If the persons in the previous chapter can be said to anticipate postmodernism, then the persons and movements we are considering here should be thought of as actually participating in it, at least partially. They combined elements of modernism with postmodernism, and in the biography of at least one of them, Ludwig Wittgenstein, we see the transition from the former to the latter from his earlier to his later thought.

Martin Heidegger

A great deal of dispute has focused on the person and thought of the philosopher Martin Heidegger. Although often thought of as the father of modern German existentialism, Heidegger disavows the title of existentialist. There is considerable debate about the extent of difference between the thought of the early and the late Heidegger, of whether there are in effect two Heideggers or only one. There has been controversy over his relationship to Nazism, since in his installation address as rector of the University of Freiburg he offered a certain amount of endorsement for that philosophy, although he gradually withdrew from that movement and in the 1940s was even forbidden to publish. What is not questioned, however, is the extent of his influence on twentieth-century thought. Numerous philosophers, including Derrida and other deconstructionists, have acknowledged his contribution to their thinking. Especially because of his association with Rudolf Bultmann during their time together at the University of Marburg, he exerted considerable impact on theology.

Heidegger was born in 1889 in Messkirch, Baden, in the Black Forest of Germany. Both his parents were Catholics, and Martin initially planned his education with the goal of becoming a priest. This interest soon turned to philosophy, however, and he was especially influenced by the work of Franz Brentano, Heinrich Rickert, Edmund Husserl, and Nicolai Hartmann. Although he departed from Husserl's teaching at a number of points, the latter requested that Heidegger be named his successor at the University of Freiburg, and Heidegger's major work, *Being and Time*, was dedicated to Husserl. Heidegger was a largely private man. Although invited in 1930 and 1933 to become a professor at Berlin, he declined, preferring to remain in the solitude of the Black Forest, where he felt there were fewer distractions.

Heidegger's thought is complex, and any attempt to convey it in brief fashion must necessarily produce distortion. For our purposes, however, it is sufficient to sketch a few motifs that indicate the transition in orientation that was taking place in the twentieth century.

Dasein. In his major early work, *Being and Time*, Heidegger developed at some length the concept of *Dasein.* Various translators and commentators have translated this as "being-there" (the literal meaning), "being-here," or various other English terms. Perhaps the wisest approach is simply to leave the term untranslated and to derive its meaning inductively from observing Heidegger's use of it.

In one sense, we could almost render *Dasein* as "human being," since it is a way of understanding our human existence, and thus derivatively, of understanding being in general. Here Heidegger reverses the common tendency to understand Being, or even the being of humans, from an understanding of the being of specific objects. For Heidegger, humans cannot be approached as things or objects. In fact, *Dasein* rejects the distinction of object and subject, even in the Kierkegaardian form that stresses subjectivity. He says, "Dasein is not only close to us . . . we *are* it, each of us, we ourselves."[1]

Dasein must be understood in light of Heidegger's conception of the world, for it is very much wrapped up with human relationship to the world. In fact, we cannot conceive of *Dasein* apart from the world. He says that modes of *Dasein*'s Being "must be seen and understood *a priori* as grounded upon that state of Being which we have called '*Being-in-the-world.*'"[2] By being "in" the world, however, Heidegger does not mean "in" as location spatially, the way a car is in the garage. Rather, it means something like "being associ-

---

[1]Martin Heidegger, *Being and Time* (New York: Harper & Row, 1962), p. 36.
[2]Ibid., p. 78.

ated with," or "being familiar with." *Dasein* and the world are not two entities that could be conceived of as existing side by side: "Being-in is not a
'property' which Dasein sometimes has and sometimes does not have. . . .
Taking up relationship towards the world is possible only *because* Dasein, as
Being-in-the-world, is as it is."[3] In other words, *Dasein* is a relationship, a
quality of the way we are related to the world.

The world here is being understood as our environment, that in which we
are found. The German *Umwelt* carries the idea of "the world around."
Dasein then is a way of being so related to the world that its contents are not
merely regarded as objects, to be known or studied, but in a more practical
way. Objects may be regarded either as *vorhanden* or as *zuhanden,* perhaps
best rendered as "present at hand" and "ready to hand." In seeing objects as
present at hand, we are thinking of them in terms of their discernible qualities or attributes, which may be examined, analyzed, classified, and the like.
This, however, says Heidegger, is not the primordial way of relating to them.
It is a derived or secondary way of reflecting on them.

The more primary or the primordial way of relating to the objects is in
terms of how we may use them. Thus, regarding a hammer in terms of its
size, shape, composition, color, and so on, is not the way we ordinarily initially conceived of it. The primordial way, treating it as "ready to hand," is in
terms of using it to drive nails or pound on other objects. Heidegger is quite
clear about this priority: "The kind of dealing which is closest to us is . . . not
a bare perceptual cognition, but rather that kind of concern which manipu-
lates things and puts them to use."[4] Because this pragmatic orientation is so
immediate, we may tend to overlook it. If, however, the hammer were to
break, we would become very conscious of the importance of the ready to
hand dimension. Although Greek philosophy had this pragmatic dimension,
it became neglected in the fuller development of Greek philosophy, he contends.

Heidegger contrasts his view of the world with that of Descartes. This can
be seen, for example, in his discussion of space. Space can be thought of
objectively or mathematically, as the actual distance of remoteness, as a category. It can also be thought of in terms of what he terms *Entfernung,* or "de-
severance," the practical distance. What is near spatially may actually be far
practically, and vice versa. To use a contemporary illustration, a computer
program may be close at hand, but if I am unfamiliar with it, it may be quite
inaccessible. Conversely, although it may be some distance away, a program
that I know well will actually be closer or "ready to hand," although it is not

---

[3]Ibid., p. 84.
[4]Ibid., p. 95.

"present at hand." Heidegger says, "A pathway which is long 'Objectively' can be much shorter than one which is 'Objectively' shorter still but which is perhaps 'hard going' and comes before us as interminably long. *Yet only in thus 'coming before us' is the current world authentically ready-to-hand.* The Objective distances of Things present-at-hand do not coincide with the remoteness and closeness of what is ready-to-hand within-the-world."[5]

We should note that Heidegger is not rejecting the legitimacy of the scientific approach, but rather its exclusiveness, or even its primacy. The scientific approach to a hammer would be to measure it or test it. While that has a definite bearing on the hammer's utility, it is not the exclusive truth about the hammer, or even the most important way of understanding it. What is thought of as scientific objectivity must be seen as emerging only at a secondary level, the level of abstraction. According to Heidegger, Descartes, who was a mathematician, thought that not only the best but virtually the only way of truly knowing the world "lies in knowing *[Erkennen] intellectio,* in the sense of knowledge *[Erkenntnis]* we get in mathematics and physics. Mathematical knowledge is regarded by Descartes as the one manner of apprehending entities which can always give assurance that their Being has been securely grasped."[6]

There are, to be sure, differences of emphasis between Heidegger's earlier and later thought. Yet, for our purposes, we may note the continuation and even elaboration of this distinction of different ways of relating to or knowing the world. In his *Gelassenheit* Heidegger distinguishes between what he terms calculative thinking and meditative thinking. While each has its own proper place. Heidegger is fearful that the former will increasingly overwhelm the latter: "The approaching tide of technological revolution in the atomic age could so captivate, bewitch, dazzle, and beguile men that calculative thinking may someday come to be accepted and practised as *the only* way of thinking."[7] One effect of this reduction of creative thinking to calculative thinking is the division of knowledge into compartments of specialization. Another, more basic, is the split of subject-object thinking. Here the world is viewed through one's own categories. This split began with Plato's division of the world of appearance below and the realm of real being above, which led then to the dualism of things and ideas. Heidegger agrees with Nietzsche's contention that Christianity is simply Platonism for the people.[8]

---

[5]Ibid., pp. 140-41.
[6]Ibid., p. 128.
[7]Martin Heidegger, *Discourse on Thinking: A Translation of Gelassenheit* (New York: Harper & Row, 1966), p. 56. See also his "Question Concerning Technology," in *The Question Concerning Technology and Other Essays* (New York: Garland, 1977), pp. 3-35.
[8]Martin Heidegger, *Introduction to Metaphysics* (New Haven, Conn.: Yale University Press, 1959), p. 106.

Hans-Georg Gadamer

Hans-Georg Gadamer exerted a powerful influence on later-twentieth-century thought through his work in the field of hermeneutics, broadly conceived, and especially his concept of the two horizons. The magnitude of his influence is indicated by the statement of even his critic, E. D. Hirsch: "Hans-Georg Gadamer has published the most substantial treatise on hermeneutic theory that has come from Germany this century."[9]

To understand Gadamer's hermeneutic it is necessary to grasp his conception of philosophy. To Gadamer, philosophy is a purely descriptive, rather than a prescriptive, activity. Despite the title of his major work, he writes, "I am *not proposing a method*, but I am describing *what is the case.*"[10]

Gadamer's magnum opus is divided into three parts. In the first, he examines "the question of truth as it emerges in the experience of art"; in the second, the subject is "the extension of the question of truth to understanding in the human sciences"; in the third, he looks at "the ontological shift of hermeneutics guided by language." An examination of the first of these gives us an understanding of his paradigm for all hermeneutics. It should be understood that in this context, hermeneutics means something much broader than simply the interpretation of texts. In the introduction, Gadamer equates hermeneutics with "the phenomenon of understanding and of the correct interpretation of what has been understood."[11] The investigation he is engaged in "is concerned to seek that experience of truth that transcends the sphere of the control of scientific method wherever it is to be found, and to inquire into its legitimacy."[12] He sees himself going beyond the hermeneutics of Schleiermacher or Dilthey. While Dilthey had separated the *Geisteswissenschaften*, or human sciences from the *Naturwissenschaften*, or natural sciences, hermeneutics applied only to the former. The latter were still science, which could be unfolded by using the correct method.

For Gadamer, however, his approach was both broader and further-reaching: "I did not wish to elaborate a system of rules to describe, let alone direct, the methodical procedure of the human sciences. . . . My real concern was and is philosophic: not what we do or what we ought to do, but what happens to us over and above our wanting and doing."[13] He sees himself as continuing, in some sense, Kant's endeavor: "He [Kant] asked a philosophic

---

[9]E. D. Hirsch Jr., *Validity in Interpretation* (New Haven, Conn.: Yale University Press, 1967), p. 245.
[10]Hans-Georg Gadamer, *Truth and Method* (New York: Seabury, 1975), p. 465.
[11]Ibid., p. xi.
[12]Ibid., p. xii.
[13]Ibid., p. xvi.

question: What are the conditions of our knowledge, by virtue of which modern science is possible, and how far does it extend? Thus the following investigation also asks a philosophic question. But it does not ask it only of the so-called human sciences. . . . It does not ask it only of science and its modes of experience, but of all human experience of the world and human living. It asks (to put it in Kantian terms): how is understanding possible?"[14] Thus art is a logical starting place for such an inquiry.

Gadamer is aware of a powerful philosophic tradition of belief in the inclusive power of theoretical reason. This, however is not a permanent or inherent characteristic of philosophy. Rather, it is related to specific historical factors, particularly the Enlightenment. It was exposed by Hume's skepticism and by Kant's first *Critique*. While it is often thought of as characteristic of Greek philosophy, in that tradition reason was not merely a theoretical capacity, but rather a human attitude, presupposing practical knowledge.[15]

The specific form Gadamer's inquiry takes relates to the human sciences. It was common in the twentieth century to seek to assimilate them to the methodology of the natural sciences, which means that a strong emphasis is placed on the use of statistical method. Gadamer believes this has been a fundamentally mistaken direction: "The real problem that the human sciences present to thought is that one has not properly grasped the nature of the human sciences if one measures them by the yardstick of an increasing knowledge of regularity. . . . Historical research does not endeavour to grasp the concrete phenomenon as an instance of a general rule."[16] It is apparent that history is here being made the representative human discipline: "Its ideal is rather to understand the phenomenon itself in its unique and historical concreteness. . . . The aim is not to confirm and expand these general experiences in order to attain knowledge of a law, e.g. how men, peoples and states evolve, but to understand how this man, this people or this state is what it has become—more generally, how has it happened that it is so."[17] Instead of science, he believes that the clue to doing human sciences is to be found in rhetorical and humanist culture.[18]

This is what leads Gadamer to his discussion of esthetics. Interacting with Kant, he asks, "Is it right to reserve the concept of truth for conceptual knowledge? Must we not also admit that the work of art possesses truth? We shall see that to acknowledge this places not only the phenome-

---

[14]Ibid., pp. xvii-xviii.
[15]Hans-Georg Gadamer, "The Power of Reason," *Man and World* 3 (1970): 5-15.
[16]Gadamer, *Truth and Method*, p. 6.
[17]Ibid.
[18]Ibid., p. 23.

non of art but also that of history in a new light."[19]

Gadamer contends that rather than being just one kind of experience, aesthetic experience represents the essence of experience itself.[20] It can therefore give us a clue to the very nature of knowledge in general. What happens in the aesthetic experience is that "it suddenly takes the person experiencing it out of the context of his life, by the power of the work of art, and yet relates him back to the whole of his existence."[21] Yet this is not merely an experience of something foreign to the one having the aesthetic experience. It is a matter of self-understanding.

Aesthetic experience also is a mode of self-understanding. But all self-understanding takes place in relation to something else that is understood and includes the unity and sameness of this other. Inasmuch as we encounter the work of art in the world and a world in the individual work of art, this does not remain a strange universe into which we are magically transported for a time. Rather, we learn to understand ourselves in it, and that means that we preserve the discontinuity of the experience in the continuity of our existence. Therefore it is necessary to adopt an attitude to the beautiful and to art that does not lay claim to immediacy, but corresponds to the historical reality of man.[22]

If, however, aesthetic experience is not a unique type of experience but reveals the nature of experience in general, then, as Gadamer says, "this involves a far-reaching hermeneutical consequence, inasmuch as all encounter with the language of art is an encounter with a still unfinished process and is itself part of this process."[23] This is because "in the experience of art we see a genuine experience induced by the work, which does not leave him who has it unchanged."[24]

This analysis of art is extended into a treatment of play, since art is a kind of play. Three notable characteristics of play are pertinent to our understanding. Just as "the work of art has its true being in the fact that it becomes an experience changing the person experiencing it," so "the players are not the subjects of play; instead play merely reaches presentation through the players."[25] This can be seen in drama and music as well: "Rather, in the performance, and only in it—as we see most clearly in the case of music—do we encounter the work itself, as the divine is encountered in the

---

[19]Ibid., p. 39.
[20]Ibid., p. 63.
[21]Ibid.
[22]Ibid., p. 86.
[23]Ibid., p. 88.
[24]Ibid., p. 89.
[25]Ibid., p. 92.

religious rite . . . . It itself belongs to the world to which it represents itself. A drama exists really only when it is played, and certainly music must resound."[26] It appears that Gadamer has arrived at his answer to the age-old conundrum of whether when a tree falls in the forest and no one is there to hear it, there is any sound. "This is seen most clearly in the interpretative arts, especially in drama and music, which wait for the occasion in order to exist and find their form only through that occasion. . . . The work itself is what 'takes place' in the performative event. It is its nature to be occasional in such a way that the occasion of the performance makes it speak and brings out what is in it."[27]

From these considerations, then, Gadamer draws his conclusion: "If my argument is correct, however, then the real problem of hermeneutics is quite different from its common acceptance. . . . Understanding must be conceived as a part of the process of coming into being of meaning, in which the significance of all statements—those of art and those of everything else that has been transmitted—is formed and made complete."[28]

The final concept in Gadamer that I will be discussing is probably his most famous concept: that of the fusing of horizons. In the model of human sciences developed in the modern or Enlightenment period, the goal is an objectivity similar to that believed to be present in the natural sciences. The aim is to understand past events in terms of the historical horizon of those events. By horizon he means "the range of vision that includes everything that can be seen from a particular vantage point."[29] This sort of objectivity, however, is both impossible and unrealistic. In order to understand another's horizon we must have our own horizon,[30] and can only understand the concepts of the historical past by comprehending them through our own concepts.[31] This fusion of the two horizons of the past and the present or the interpreter and the text is true understanding.[32]

Ludwig Wittgenstein

One of the pivotal figures in the rise of postmodernism is the Austrian philosopher, Ludwig Wittgenstein. Indeed, in many ways, he personally embodies the change from the modern to the postmodern period. For in the transition from his earlier to his later thought we see the contrast

---

[26]Ibid., p. 104.
[27]Ibid., p. 130.
[28]Ibid., p. 146.
[29]Ibid., p. 269.
[30]Ibid., p. 271.
[31]Ibid., p. 104.
[32]Ibid., pp. 273-74.

between the mentalities of these two periods.

Wittgenstein was born in Vienna in 1889 into a well-to-do Jewish family. His father was an engineer, but various family members displayed strong artistic qualities. Both his parents and some of his seven brothers and sisters were musical, his brother Paul being the one-armed pianist for whom Ravel wrote the piano concerto for left hand. Johannes Brahms was a frequent visitor in their home. Ludwig himself made a number of sculptures.[33]

Wittgenstein studied engineering in Berlin and then in Manchester. He was very interested in technical aeronautical problems, especially the construction of propellers. This study involved him in numerous mathematical calculations, and revived his interest in the foundations of mathematics. He had already become interested in philosophy, especially Schopenhauer's *Die Welt als Wille und Vorstellung* ("The World as Will and Imagination"). These two worlds, the metaphysical and logical or positivist, continued to have an influence on him throughout his academic life. In his early work he distinguished between them, but in his later writings they are brought together.

During the period of his study in England he made a number of trips to the Continent, and visited several times with Gottlob Frege, mathematics professor at Jena, who was primarily concerned with the logical problems of mathematics. Frege encouraged Wittgenstein to study with Bertrand Russell, who with Alfred Whitehead had written *Principia Mathematica*. Wittgenstein began jotting down his philosophical observations, which he continued while serving in the Austrian army during World War I, and even as an Italian prisoner of war. These notes were eventually published as *Tractatus Logico-Philosophicus*.

In this early work Wittgenstein attempts, like the logical positivists, to construct a logical language that would include all of the sciences. At this point he held to the mirror view of language, which maintains that the logical and positive language most fully embodied in the exact sciences mirrors or pictures reality. A fact is what is the case, and propositions which when compared with reality are seen to correctly mirror it are to be considered true and those which do not are false.[34] There was strong similarity between Wittgenstein's views at this point and those of the logical positivists, and even some influence of the former on the latter. Nonetheless, they differed at two points. First, Wittgenstein's logical atomism is not found in quite this form in logical positivism, and, second, whereas logical positivists rejected

---

[33]For the most part, these biographical details are taken from C. A. van Peursen, *Ludwig Wittgenstein: An Introduction to His Philosophy* (London: Faber & Faber, 1969), chap. 1; and Anthony Kenny, *Wittgenstein* (Cambridge, Mass.: Harvard University Press, 1973), chap. 1.

[34]Ludwig Wittgenstein, *Tractatus Logico-Philosophicus* (London: Routledge & Kegan Paul, 1922), 4:5-6.

metaphysics, Wittgenstein recognizes it, but says that one can say nothing about it. Thus, at the end of the *Tractatus*, discussing the question of his own propositions' meaningfulness, Wittgenstein says that after one has climbed through or over them, he will finally recognize them as senseless. He says, "Whereof one cannot speak, thereof one must be silent."[35] While this might seem mystical and inconsistent with the remainder of the *Tractatus*, it will seem so only to one unfamiliar with Wittgenstein's background and temperament.

In 1929 Wittgenstein returned to Cambridge, becoming a fellow of Trinity College in 1930; in 1939 he was named G. E. Moore's successor. It soon became apparent that his views had shifted considerably since his earlier work, although these changes were not really documented in print until after his death in 1951. About 1933 he began circulating his new ideas in two sets of lecture notes, in a brown and a blue folder. These were published posthumously in 1958. In 1953 the *Philosophical Investigations* appeared.

In the *Tractatus* Wittgenstein, like the logical positivists, had sought to construct an ideal language that would reveal the hidden structure of all true discourse. In his later thought, however, he expressed a broader view of language. Language is used in many different ways, and these cannot simply be inferred from the surface of language on the basis of ordinary grammar. A transitional statement of his views is found in the *Philosophical Remarks*: "But the essence of language is a picture of the essence of the world; and philosophy as custodian of grammar can in fact grasp the essence of the world, only not in the propositions of language, but in rules for this language, which exclude nonsensical combinations of signs."[36]

This distinction between surface grammar and depth grammar becomes important in Wittgenstein's later thought. While the former is the grammar of language as it appears to us, the latter is an examination of actual language as found in usage, and is often incomplete. It is to this ordinary language that he turns. He had written in the *Tractatus* that language is as complicated as a living organism, and in the later writings he is seeking to examine this life of language. He is not, however, simply proposing a commonsense approach to language, as some British philosophers such as Moore had advocated. Wittgenstein says, "There is no commonsense answer to a philosophical problem. One can defend common sense against the attacks of philosophers only by solving their puzzles, i.e., by curing them of the temptation to attack common sense; not by restating the views of com-

---

[35]Ibid., §7.
[36]Ludwig Wittgenstein, *Philosophical Remarks* (New York: Barnes & Noble, 1975), §54.

mon sense. A philosopher is not a man out of his senses, a man who doesn't see what everybody sees." The aim of philosophy is to elucidate the ordinary functioning of language. The problem is that ordinary language, which pervades all of our life, tends to keep the mind in one position, thus effecting a mental cramp. Philosophy aims to remove this mental cramp.[37]

Wittgenstein uses a number of analogies to convey his understanding of philosophy's role. In *The Blue and Brown Books* he speaks of a jigsaw puzzle. We are unable to solve it and think that we either have the wrong pieces, or that some pieces are missing. What is actually the case, however, is that all the pieces are present, but are mixed up. Instead of forcing or distorting the pieces, we should examine them carefully and sort them out correctly. Then the puzzle will be solved.[38] In his last writings he appeals to the image of different language games and suggests that this is the task of philosophy, to look carefully at the pieces of the puzzle and only then attempt to fit them together.[39] Problems occur when language is running idle.[40]

In *The Blue and Brown Books* Wittgenstein gives a rather helpful illustration. He begins with a simple language, composed of a few words, like *cube, brick, slab,* and *column,* which in turn refer to objects such as cubes, bricks and slabs, and columns. A builder calls out a word, *slab,* to his assistant, who then brings him the object corresponding to that word. What is happening here, however, is that through training the assistant has learned that when the builder speaks that word, the assistant is to perform a certain action. *Brick* is not a description, but an order, within the language game in which these two are engaged.[41]

Language, then, does not simply name objects. It may be put to several different uses, such as giving orders, framing conjectures, making up a story, play-acting, telling a joke, translating, praying, cursing, greeting. While on the surface the same forms or words appear, in terms of depth grammar they are functioning differently: "Here the term 'language-*game*' is meant to bring into prominence the fact that the *speaking* of language is part of an activity, or of a form of life. . . . It is interesting to compare the multiplicity of the tools in language and of the ways they are used, the multiplicity of kinds of word and sentence, with what logicians have said about the structure of language. (Including the author of the *Tractatus Logico-Philosophicus.*)"[42]

---

[37]Ludwig Wittgenstein, *Preliminary Studies for the "Philosophical Investigations," Generally Known as the Blue and Brown Books* (New York: Harper & Row, 1958), pp. 58, 59.

[38]Ibid., p. 46.

[39]Ludwig Wittgenstein, *Philosophical Investigations,* 3rd ed. (New York: Macmillan, 1958), §109.

[40]Ibid., §132.

[41]Wittgenstein, *Preliminary Studies,* pp. 77-83.

[42]Wittgenstein, *Philosophical Investigations,* §23.

Philosophy's task, then, is to observe the way language is functioning in a given instance, rather than prescribing the way it must function. To fail to do this, and to confuse one language game for another, is to fall into the mental cramp Wittgenstein has described. Such a mental cramp may also occur in connection with the question, "What is the meaning of a word?" He criticizes Frege's understanding of meaning, in which words have a sort of meaning, independent of anyone's understanding of them. On that scheme, there is a dead meaning, and then an organic part, the understanding of the signs. Rather, says Wittgenstein, the meaning, which gives life to the sign, is not something existing separately from the sign, in something called the mind, but is actually the use made of the sign, which may vary in different activities, or language-games.[43] So the word *bishop* has different meanings in ecclesiastical settings and in the game of chess. One cannot determine the meaning of *bishop* in chess by an analysis of the material of which it is composed. Rather, its meaning is involved in the moves that can be made with it in a game of chess.[44]

Thomas Kuhn

If the developments we have been discussing were related to particular issues in specific fields, the one we now turn to is much more general, involving the understanding of the whole scientific enterprise and the nature of scientific methodology. To a certain extent, the developments we have previously examined contributed to Kuhn's discussion, for it was concerned with the question of why one paradigm comes to replace another in scientific endeavors.

Thomas Kuhn is a historian of science, who gravitated to that field from theoretical physics, where he was nearing the end of his dissertation work. At the time, he was involved in teaching an experimental college course on physical science for nonscience majors. Here he was exposed for the first time to the history of science, and to his surprise found he had to revise his views of the nature of science and the reasons for its success. Consequently, he shifted his specialization to the history of science, and particularly of the philosophical issues that had led him to study the history of science.[45]

Kuhn begins by in effect offering an apologetic for the discipline he will use to solve the problem he wants to undertake. He contends that the usual source for the understanding of the nature of science has been the study of

---

[43]Wittgenstein, *Preliminary Studies*, pp. 1-25.

[44]Wittgenstein, *Philosophical Investigations*, §108.

[45]Thomas S. Kuhn, *The Structure of Scientific Revolutions* (Chicago: University of Chicago Press, 1970), p. v.

finished scientific accomplishments. The problem with this approach, however, is that it is intended to be pedagogic and persuasive, that is, to perpetu-
ate the views in which current practitioners have been schooled. Kuhn
makes his goal clear: "This essay attempts to show that we have been misled
by them in fundamental ways. Its aim is a sketch of the quite different concept of science that can emerge from the historical record of the research
activity itself."[46] In other words, rather than drawing the understanding of
science from the results of its endeavor, he is going to examine the actual
process by which those conclusions were reached. It is not merely the
employment of historical data that constitutes his contribution, however.
Sometimes the data of history are utilized in an unhistorical manner. They
have simply been scrutinized from the standpoint of the questions drawn
from science texts. On that approach, science is seen as a constellation of
facts, methods, and theories, and scientists are seen as those who contribute
to the stockpile of scientific technique and knowledge, in a piecemeal fashion.[47]

On the model usually propounded regarding science, the difference
between paradigms or views is objective in origin. One group comes to
adopt a new view because they more rigorously or carefully follow the scientific method, or because they take note of data that the other group has
not discerned or factored into their thinking. In contrast, Kuhn argues that
historically this is not how paradigm changes have taken place. Rather, he
contends, the methodological directives are insufficient to dictate particular
scientific conclusions in the case of many scientific questions. Certain other
less "objective" factors enter in. What experiment does a researcher choose
to perform first, and what data resulting seem to him to be especially relevant to the problem under consideration? The differences between different
schools of thought arise because of incommensurable ways of seeing the
world and practicing science within it. These differences are the result of
arbitrary factors: "Observation and experience can and must drastically
restrict the range of admissible scientific belief, else there would be no science. But they cannot alone determine a particular body of such belief. An
apparently arbitrary element, compounded of personal and historical accident, is always a formative ingredient of the beliefs espoused by a given scientific community at a given time."[48]

By its very nature, what Kuhn calls "normal science," working within the
received framework, proceeds on the assumption that the scientific commu-

---

[46]Ibid., p. 1.
[47]Ibid., pp. 1-2.
[48]Ibid., p. 4.

nity knows what the world is like. Consequently, it endeavors to suppress any novelties. Yet, Kuhn contends, progress in science requires taking those novelties or anomalies seriously. When they become so numerous or so serious that they can no longer be ignored, what he terms a scientific revolution, a change in the very way of understanding and doing science, takes place. Such changes are never merely incremental changes in the established view or approach, but rather involve a reconstruction of theory and a re-evaluation of prior fact. And, since normal science specifies not only what sorts of entities there are in the universe but also what are not, these revolutions may come from the discovery of some hitherto unknown entity, such as oxygen or x-rays.[49]

In the early stages of a science's development, different persons encountering the same data or range of phenomena interpret them in different ways. Kuhn offers an explanation for this. The interpretation of such phenomena requires some antecedent factors: "No natural history can be interpreted in the absence of at least some implicit body of intertwined theoretical and methodological belief that permits selection, evaluation, and criticism. If that body of belief is not already implicit in the collection of facts—in which case more than 'mere facts' are at hand—it must be externally supplied, perhaps by a current metaphysic, by another science, or by personal and historical accident."[50] The acceptance of a theory requires that it seem better than its competitors, but this cannot account for all the facts. When a new theory attracts more of the next generation's practitioners in the field, the older schools of thought gradually disappear, in part through the conversion of their members to the new view, but there are always some who cling to the old view. These individuals are simply read out of the profession, which ignores their work.[51]

Kuhn illustrates his thesis through the examination of a number of such revolutions, one of the most prominent being the Copernican revolution. His fundamental thesis is what is most important to us. Science has been considered and has claimed to be the most nearly objective of endeavors. It involves the study of facts, and it improves its conclusions by more complete and accurate understanding of these facts. Subjective personal matters, or influences arising from the historical setting, are to be ignored or neutralized. Kuhn's contention is that the actual nature of scientific discovery and work is quite different. The "facts" can be understood in more than one way, and what leads a scientist to select particular facts to include, and to inter-

---

[49]Ibid., p. 7.
[50]Ibid., pp. 16-17.
[51]Ibid., pp. 17-19.

pret them in a particular way, is a function of personal and local factors. New theories arise because one scientist views the phenomena differently than does another. There is an arbitrary element even in scientific method.

The Sociology of Knowledge

The sociology of knowledge has in a general way had a rather long history, yet in the form that the term currently designates, it is a mid- to late-twentieth-century phenomenon. In its simplest and most general form, it is the idea that beliefs and ideas grow out of the social setting in which they are held, and in more extreme forms, they are thought of as having been determined by that social setting. As such the sociology of knowledge is a reaction against positivist views in the discipline, which held that although different cultures may have differing insights into issues, there is one generally valid or objective truth. In the influence of the Enlightenment, social sciences attempted to rid their methodology of any local or particular influences, thus arriving at some ahistorical or timeless form of understanding or a common human nature. Further, impressed by the vast achievements in the natural sciences, the social sciences had sought to emulate that methodology.[52]

Karl Marx was in some ways the initial contributor to this theory, with his contention that human consciousness is determined by social forces, and specifically, by material life processes. This reversed the usual way of thinking of things: "Life is not determined by consciousness, but consciousness by life."[53] This is part of a general rule, but what is distinctive about ideas is that persons who hold them claim that their ideas are *true.* Those who control the means of material production also control the production of ideas: "The ruling ideas are nothing more than the ideal expression of the dominant material relationships, the dominant material relationships grasped as ideas: hence of the relationship which makes the one class the ruling one, therefore the ideas of its dominance."[54]

The early real pioneers of sociology of knowledge, however, were Max Scheler and Karl Mannheim. Scheler, a philosopher, advocated a rather limited theory, based on a distinction between ideal factors and real factors. The latter affect the conditions under which the former can appear, but not their content. Because most of Mannheim's works have been translated into English while Scheler's have not, Mannheim's influence in the English-speaking world has been much more significant. Mannheim was reacting quite

---

[52]Susan J. Hekman, *Hermeneutics and the Sociology of Knowledge* (Notre Dame, Ind.: University of Notre Dame Press, 1986), p. 5.
[53]Karl Marx and Friedrich Engels, *The German Ideology, Parts I and III* (New York: International Publishers, 1947), p. 15.
[54]Ibid., p. 39.

strongly to Marxism. He distinguished three senses of ideology: the particular, the total, and the general. These refer respectively to ideology as only a portion of an opponent's thought; as the whole of his thought; and as characteristic of one's own thought, as well as of one's opponent's thought.[55]

In the mid-twentieth century, the movement of sociology of knowledge became somewhat diffused into varying schools of thought. Two general clusters can be observed, however. One group, following the lead of Alfred Schutz, has concentrated on the social origins of commonsense reality, or everyday knowledge. The other concentrated more on the empirical relationship between knowledge, in the more formal or technical sense, and social factors. This latter group can, in a sense, be considered adherents to the classical form of sociology of knowledge.

Despite these differences, certain common traits and conclusions can be noted. Robert Bierstadt observes that the questions that are important to answer in one age and society may not even be considered in another: "No one in modern industrial societies wonders whether, if God is all-powerful, he can restore virginity to a prostitute; no one debates whether the mouse that steals into the cathedral and eats the consecrated wafer has partaken of the body of Christ; and no one asks himself why God, who is presumed to be eternal, did not create the universe, say, some 600,000 years earlier than he did."[56]

One's situation affects not only the choice of topics. The content of the knowledge is also socially determined. Mannheim distinguished two forms of the sociology of knowledge. The first is "a purely empirical investigation through description and structural analysis of the ways in which social relationships, in fact, influence thought." These, he says, may then pass into the second form, "an epistemological inquiry concerned with the bearing of this interrelationship upon the problem of validity." He contends that these two types are not necessarily connected and that "one can accept the empirical results without drawing the epistemological conclusions."[57] He maintains that the emergence and crystallization of thought is influenced in many cases and at important places by what he terms "extra-theoretical factors of the most diverse sort." This is what he calls the existential determination of thought.[58] The world is known through many different orientations. The difference, he says, cannot be in the object, which is basically the same for all.

---

[55]Peter L. Berger and Thomas Luckmann, *The Social Construction of Reality: A Treatise in the Sociology of Knowledge* (Garden City, N.Y.: Doubleday, 1966), pp. 8-9.

[56]Robert Bierstadt, "Introduction," in Judith Willer, *The Social Determination of Meaning* (Englewood Cliffs, N.J.: Prentice-Hall, 1971), p. 2.

[57]Karl Mannheim, "The Sociology of Knowledge," in *Ideology and Utopia: An Introduction to the Sociology of Knowledge* (New York: Harcourt, Brace & World, 1936), p. 239.

[58]Ibid.

It must rather be found in "the very different expectations, purposes, and impulses arising out of experience."[59]

Mannheim does not wish to draw the implication of the relativity of knowledge from his argument. He distinguishes between relativism and relationism. The former concludes that establishing that all knowledge is socially determined means that it is relativized, that it has no validity beyond the situation of its origin. Relationism, on the other hand, recognizes this social origin of all knowledge, but refuses to use this principle reductively, to conclude to relativism.

There are three possible answers to the question of whether we can make any statements about a statement's truth or falsity, once we have shown that it derives from a particular social setting. The first is the relativist view, which holds that the absolute validity of an assertion is denied by showing its derivation from a given social situation. The second regards such argumentation as irrelevant, believing that drawing conclusions of truth or falsity from a social explanation would be a case of the genetic fallacy. The third, which Mannheim espouses, differs from both of these. Sociology of knowledge cannot make absolute judgments of truth or falsity, but it "also becomes a critique by redefining the scope and the limits of the perspective implicit in given assertions."[60]

Whether or not Mannheim drew the implication of relativism from the method of the sociology of knowledge, others are inclined to do so. To take the reflection a step further, however, one should also apply the method of sociology of knowledge to itself. In other words, its knowledge is socially determined, and thus is also relative. Interestingly, sociologists of knowledge have declined to do this, offering various reasons. Berger and Luckmann suggest that raising such questions is like trying to push a bus in which one is riding. While not brushing such questions aside, they propose that these questions are not part of the empirical discipline of sociology, but rather belong to the methodology of the social sciences, and they therefore decline to discuss them.[61] Bierstadt sees very clearly the implications of the position when he says that "we unhappily confront a situation in which knowledge has lost its truth and so also have all propositions in the sociology of knowledge. The ultimate and unresolvable paradox . . . is that the sociology of knowledge destroys the possibility of a sociology of knowledge." He says that this is an unresolvable paradox, and he can only throw up his hands and quote Kant's statement that reason has the ability to raise questions to which it cannot give answers.[62]

---

[59]Ibid., p. 241.
[60]Ibid., pp. 253-56.
[61]Berger and Luckmann, *Social Construction of Reality*, pp. 12-13.
[62]Bierstadt, "Introduction," p. 3.

part 2

major intellectual voices
of postmodernism

6

jacques derrida

In many ways, the father of modern deconstruction is Jacques Derrida. Primarily a philosopher, he has also exerted a strong influence in the field of literary criticism. It is customary to say that Derrida's thought and writing are difficult to understand. In fact, this difficulty is legendary. Any attempt to unfold what he is actually doing and saying will therefore require unusual patience and attention.

Elements of Derrida's Thought
Background. Derrida is a French Algerian of Jewish extraction. Born in Algeria in 1931, he moved to France as a young student. There he studied phenomenology with Emmanuel Levinas and Paul Ricoeur. His earliest writings were comments on and reactions to the thought of Edmund Husserl, and among the strongest early influences on his thought was Martin Heidegger. He acknowledges the influence of phenomenology:

> My philosophical formation owes much to the thought of Hegel, Husserl, and Heidegger. Heidegger is probably the most constant influence, and particularly his project of "overcoming" Greek metaphysics. Husserl, whom I studied in more detailed and painstaking fashion, taught me a certain methodical prudence and reserve, a rigorous technique of unraveling and formulating questions. But I never shared Husserl's pathos for, and commitment to, a phenomenology of presence. In fact, it was Husserl's method that helped me to suspect the very notion of presence and the fundamental role it has played

in all philosophies. My relationship with Heidegger is much more enigmatic and extensive; here my interest was not just *methodological* but *existential*. The themes of Heidegger's questioning always struck me as necessary—especially the "ontological difference," the critique of Platonism and the relationship between language and Being.[1]

Husserl had sought by the method of "bracketing" to use his phenomenological methodology to establish a type of foundationalism. He sought a pure intuition of essences, without any presuppositions. Ultimately, Husserl concluded that this attempt was a failure: "Philosophy as science, as serious, rigorous, indeed apodictically rigorous, science—*the dream is* over."[2] This acknowledgment by Husserl led Derrida to pursue further the idea of deconstruction, including deconstructing even the phenomenology of Husserl himself.

The idea of deconstruction. What is it that Derrida is attempting to do in deconstruction? He is quite clear about what he is not trying to do, which he feels his critics have unjustly and inaccurately accused him of doing. He insists that he is not contending for any suspension of reference, or proposing that there is nothing beyond language. He says:

> Deconstruction is always deeply concerned with the 'other' of language. I never cease to be surprised by critics who see my work as a declaration that there is nothing beyond language, that we are imprisoned in language; it is, in fact, saying the exact opposite. Every week I receive critical commentaries and studies on deconstruction which operate on the assumption that what they call "post-structuralism" amounts to saying that there is nothing beyond language, that we are submerged in words—and other stupidities of that sort. Certainly, deconstruction tries to show that the question of reference is much more complex and problematic than traditional theories supposed. It even asks whether our term "reference" is entirely adequate for designating the "other." The other, which is beyond language and which summons language, is perhaps not a "referent" in the normal sense which linguists have attached to this term. But to distance oneself from the habitual structure of reference, to challenge or complicate our common assumptions about it, does not amount to saying that there is *nothing* beyond language.[3]

Similarly, Derrida's response to a question about his treatment of the subject indicates his real intention, as contrasted with the incorrect statements

---

[1] Jacques Derrida, in Richard Kearney, *Dialogues with Contemporary Continental Thinkers* (Manchester: Manchester University Press, 1984), p. 109.
[2] Edmund Husserl, *The Crisis of European Sciences and Transcendental Phenomenology: An Introduction to Phenomenological Philosophy*, trans. David Carr (Evanston, Ill.: Northwestern University Press, 1970), p. 389.
[3] Derrida, in Kearney, *Dialogues*, pp. 123-24.

that have been made about his view: "I have never said that the subject should be dispensed with. Only that it should be deconstructed. . . . The subject is not some meta-linguistic substance or identity, some pure *cogito* of self-presence; it is always inscribed in language. My work does not, therefore, destroy the subject; it simply tries to resituate it."[4]

In light of these denials, why has there been such apparent widespread misunderstanding of Derrida's thought? In responding to the charge of nihilism, he contends that such misinterpretation of his thought is "symptomatic of certain political and institutional interests—interests which must also be deconstructed in their turn."[5] The question which will have to be asked is whether there are elements of his thought that state or imply this kind of interpretation.

Rejection of logocentrism. Derrida's deconstruction should be seen in light of a long and hallowed tradition to which he is reacting. While it bears several names, he terms it logocentrism. This is the idea that understanding, meaning, can be given a fixed reference point by grounding it in logos, some fixed principle or characteristic of reality; in other words, in a presence. Among the principles that have been recited as the basis of this logos in the history of philosophy are the familiar ones of Greek thought. "It could be shown that the names related to fundamentals, to principles, or to the center have always designated an invariable presence—*eidōs, archē, telos, energeia, ousia*, (essence, existence, substance, subject), *alētheia*, transcendentality, consciousness, God, man, and so forth."[6] Spivak, who translated Of Grammatology, says that logocentrism is "the belief that the first and last things are the Logos, the Word, the Divine Mind, the infinite understanding of God, an infinitely creative subjectivity, and, closer to our time, the self-presence of full self-consciousness."[7]

Derrida himself says "That the logos is first imprinted and that that imprint is the writing-resource of language, signifies, to be sure, that the logos is not a creative activity, the continuous full element of the divine word, etc."[8] He states that the fabric of signs is "preceded by a truth, or a meaning already constituted by and within the element of the logos. Even when the thing, the 'referent,' is not immediately related to the logos of a creator God where it began by being the spoken/thought sense, the signified has at any rate an immediate relationship with the logos in general (finite or

[4]Ibid., p. 125.
[5]Ibid., p. 124.
[6]Jacques Derrida, *Writing and Difference* (Chicago: University of Chicago Press, 1978), pp. 279-80.
[7]G. V. Spivak, "Translator's Preface," in Jacques Derrida, *Of Grammatology* (Baltimore: Johns Hopkins University Press, 1976), p. lxviii.
[8]Derrida, *Of Grammatology*, p. 68.

infinite), and a mediated one with the signifier, that is to say, with the exteriority of writing."[9]

Although logocentrism has had a long history, it is no longer a viable approach. A rupture has taken place, making impossible such a centering: "Henceforth, it was necessary to begin thinking that there was no center, that the center could not be thought in the form of a present-being, that the center had no natural site, that it was not a fixed locus but a function, a sort of nonlocus in which an infinite number of sign-significations came into play."[10]

What is this logos on which logocentrism centers? It is not logos in the meaning of word, or language. Rather, it is logos in the sense of reason, or organizing pattern. It is the idea that there is a meaning outside of language, thus a kind of foundationalism. John Ellis says logocentrism "is not a fixation on words, as one might expect, but instead a belief that there is an order of meaning existing *independently* of the structure of any given language that is a foundation for all else. . . . Logocentrism here turns out to be much the same as the more familiar *essentialism*, the belief that words simply label real categories of meaning existing independently of a language."[11]

The primacy of writing. Closely allied with logocentrism is the idea of phonocentrism. This is the idea that speech is more basic than writing, that in speech the meaning of the words is present. This goes back to Plato, who referred first to silent or inward speech. Plato described this in the *Phaedrus* as "a silent dialogue of the soul with itself." This is the case because of the immediate presence of the speaker to himself, so that truth is pure self-immediacy, uncontaminated by any outside influence. Meaning is identical with itself. Speaking is the next nearest approximation to this pure identity of meaning and sign. Here the speaker and the hearer are present with one another, both spatially and temporally. Writing, however, according to Plato's interpretation and the classic understanding is secondary to speaking. Here the writer and the reader are not physically present with one another. In fact, they may not even be present in the same time. The writer may already be dead, yet the words live on. This means that they are subject to interpretations different from what the original writer intended. Plato spoke, consequently, of the abuses that may occur when speeches "have been once written down, they are tumbled about anywhere among those who may or may not understand them, and

---

[9]Ibid., pp. 14-15.

[10]Derrida, *Writing and Difference*, p. 280.

[11]John M. Ellis, *Against Deconstruction* (Princeton, N.J.: Princeton University Press, 1989), p. 35.

know not to whom they should reply, to whom not: and, if they are mal-treated or abused, they have no parent to protect them; and they cannot protect or defend themselves."[12]

Derrida believes that this favoring of speech, or phonocentrism, has been characteristic of the entire history of thought. It is not just Plato and Aristotle who have done this, but it is the *"ethnocentrism* which, every-where and always, had controlled the concept of writing . . . from the pre-Socratics to Heidegger, always assigned the origin of truth in general to the logos: the history of truth, of the truth of truth, has always been—except for a metaphysical diversion that we shall have to explain—the debase-ment of writing, and its repression outside 'full' speech."[13] Derrida con-tends that Saussure, who protested this contamination by writing, gave this protest a very prominent place in his writing, and in a tone that indi-cated how strongly he felt about the matter: "The contamination by writ-ing, the fact or the threat of it, are denounced in the accents of the moralist or preacher by the linguist from Geneva. The tone counts; it is as if, at the moment when the modern science of the logos would come into its autonomy and its scientificity, it became necessary again to attack a heresy."[14]

Logocentrism is related to a metaphysics of presence, in which the sym-bol is present to the person using it, the person hearing it, and that which it represents. In writing, on the other hand, the author and the reader are sep-arated from one another in time and in space. Western metaphysics, there-fore, considers this a disadvantage, and consequently has favored speaking over writing. It is this preference for speaking over writing that Derrida crit-icizes so vehemently in his attack on logocentrism. In its place, he proposes the primacy of writing over speaking. By this he does not mean that writing is chronologically prior to speaking, but that it is preferable to speaking. He will make a virtue of what seems to some to be the problem with writing, that instead of affirming the identity of sign and referent, it creates a differ-ence—or to use his word, a *différance*. John Caputo claims that what Derrida is trying to do is not to destroy objective meaning, but to show that meaning does not rest on some ultimate principle, such as logos, the mind of God, or something of that type: "Rather than on a firm foundation or perfectly enclosed system he is trying to pull the plug on any leak-proof system of acknowledging a still lower un-principle, an unsettling, dis-placing 'neces-sity' we are under to labor always under a play of traces, having to cope with

---

[12]Plato *Phaedrus* §275.
[13]Derrida, *Of Grammatology*, p. 3.
[14]Ibid., p. 34.

an irrepressible iterability that can never be contained or decisively regu-
lated."[15]

It should be noted that Derrida does not always simply mean writing in
the customary sense of literal writing. While the term often is used in that
sense, it is also frequently equated with language in general.

> If "writing" signifies inscription and especially the durable institution of a sign
> (and that is the only irreducible kernel of the concept of writing), writing in
> general covers the entire field of linguistic signs. In that field a certain sort of
> instituted signifiers may then appear, "graphic" in the narrow and derivative
> sense of the word, ordered by a certain relationship with other instituted—
> hence "written," even if they are "phonic's"—signifiers. The very idea of insti-
> tution—hence of the arbitrariness of the sign—is unthinkable before the possi-
> bility of writing and outside its horizon.[16]

Différance and meaning. If meaning does not inhere in or derive from
some great fixed, eternal principles, or some metaphysical principle such
as being, from where does it come? This is where, in the concept of writing, there is the idea of *différance.* The history of metaphysics had in effect
been a series of arguments over the center, in which one philosopher contended that what he thought to be the center should replace the previous
idea of the center. The shift for Derrida came in seeing that there is no
center: "Henceforth, it was necessary to begin thinking that there was no
center, that the center could not be thought in the form of a present-being,
that the center had no natural site, that it was not a fixed locus but a function, a sort of nonlocus in which an infinite number of sign-substitutions
came into play."[17]

The word *différance,* which Derrida created, contains two ideas within it:
differing and deferring. The differing is a matter of showing a series of
"traces," of showing the difference between things. This is how reference
works, such as dictionaries, function. They define something by showing
how it differs, or is distinct from, other things. We understand the sign by
seeing, not so much what it is, but what it is not. This trace (the French
word carries strong implications of track, footprint, imprint) is a word for
which we could also substitute other terms of Derrida's, such as *arche-writ-
ing* or *différance,* according to Spivak, in the translator's preface to *Of Grammatology.*[18] The meaning of the sign, rather than deriving from some

---

[15]John D. Caputo, in *Deconstruction in a Nutshell: A Conversation with Jacques Derrida* (New
York: Fordham University Press, 1997), p. 102.
[16]Derrida, *Of Grammatology,* p. 44.
[17]Derrida, *Writing and Difference,* p. 280.
[18]Spivak, "Translator's Preface," pp. xv-xvii.

absolute principle such as being, is built up by the free play of traces, by the successive substituting of one trace for another, thus distinguishing it from other signs.

This is where the latter part of the meaning of the word *différance* comes in. It is the endless play of signifiers, in which one gives way or defers to the next, that builds up the meaning of the sign. Caputo says, "Derrida . . . thinks of users of language invoking coded, that is, repeatable, marks or traces that build up or constitute from within certain unities of meaning as 'effects' of the code. These traces are not inherently meaningful in themselves but 'arbitrary' and 'conventional.' . . . The meaning—and reference—is a function of the difference, of the *distance* or the 'spacing' between the traces, what is called, in a perfectly serious way, the 'play' of differences or traces."[19] Here is a strong rejection of the idea of essentialism, the idea that there are some ideal meanings, or what Derrida calls "presence," which antedate the play of traces and to which that play must conform. Rather, "meaning and reference are always built up slowly and tentatively from below, from within the networks of codes and assumptions within which we all always and already operate."[20] If there were a centering in a point of fixed reference outside the play of signifiers, or what he terms *logocentrism*, there would obviously be a limit to this play of signifiers. Without that, however, the play is endless.

This concept of *différance* in Derrida is not restricted to language, although that is where it is most obvious. Caputo contends that it applies to "everything—institutions, sexuality, the worldwide web, the body, whatever you need or want. . . . He is arguing that, *like* language, all these structures are marked by the play of differences, by the 'spacing' of which *différance* is one of the names."[21] An example of this can be seen in the area of sexual relationships. As Derrida sees it, the debate over homosexuality is actually "a debate about an over-organized, over-regulated, narrowly oppositional space in which there are only two hierarchically ordered places, a 'binarity' of male and female, of male over female. For Derrida, the way to break this up is to open all the *other* places that this binary scheme closes off."[22]

Play. What Derrida has done is to take the Saussurian concept of contrast and substitute for it the term *play*. This exchanges the idea of specific differences for less controlled and specific differentiation than what was previously envisioned. The lack of a center leads to this: "This field is in effect

---

[19]Caputo, *Deconstruction in a Nutshell*, p. 100.
[20]Ibid., p. 101.
[21]Ibid., p. 104.
[22]Ibid.

that of *play*, that is to say, a field of infinite substitutions only because it is finite, that is to say, because instead of . . . being too large, there is something missing from it: a center which arrests and grounds the play of substitutions. One could say— . . . that this movement of play, permitted by the lack or absence of a center or origin, is the movement of *supplementarity*."[23] He also says, "The meaning of meaning (in the general sense of meaning and not in the sense of signalization) is infinite implication, the indefinite referral of signifier to signified."[24]

It is not just that there is no "transcendental signified," no independent concept. That would signal the end of the chain of signifiers, referring to no other signified. Rather, there is no end to the chain of signifiers. Every signified is itself a signifier: "On the contrary, though, from the moment that one questions the possibility of such a transcendental signified, and that one recognizes that every signified is also in the position of a signifier, the distinction between signified and signifier becomes problematical at its root."[25]

This endless play of signs in which there is no final or transcendental signified, no signified that is not also a signifier, leads us to the conclusion that there is no final meaning. Derrida says, "From the moment that there is meaning there are nothing but signs. *We think only in signs.* Which amounts to ruining the notion of the sign at the very moment when, as in Nietzsche, its exigency is recognized in the absoluteness of its right. One could call *play* the absence of the transcendental signified as limitlessness of play, that is to say as the destruction of onto-theology and the metaphysics of presence."[26]

Writing under erasure. Related to this matter of free play and trace is the practice of writing *sous rature*, or "under erasure." Derrida takes this idea from Heidegger and adapts it. Derrida writes a word, crosses it out, then prints both the word and its deletion. This is because the word is inaccurate, so it must be crossed out, yet it is necessary, so it remains legible. An example is his discussion of the word *sign*, which relates to the idea of trace. Here is where his use of erasure differs from that of Heidegger. For Heidegger, Being means that there is a presence, but it cannot be articulated. For Derrida, "trace is the mark of the absence of a presence, an always already absent presence, of the lack at the origin that is the condition of thought and experience."[27]

Autodeconstruction. The execution of this methodology of Derrida can be

---

[23]Derrida, *Writing and Difference*, p. 289.

[24]Ibid., p. 25.

[25]Jacques Derrida, *Positions,* trans. Alan Bass (Chicago: University of Chicago Press, 1972), pp. 19-20.

[26]Derrida, *Of Grammatology,* p. 50.

[27]Spivak, "Translator's Preface," p. xvii.

seen in his treatment of the traditional logocentrisms, or ontotheologies. The usual understanding of them has been in terms of their identity, that is, the ability to gather everything into one all-inclusive system, to which there are no unresolved factors, or internal contradictions. Derrida claims that in a sense, what he is doing is not so much deconstructing these philosophies, as showing their auto-deconstruction. His aim is to demonstrate that even within a philosophy such Plato's there are elements that do not fit, that it contains its own otherness or difference. He insists on a thorough reading of Plato; in fact, "I think we have to read them [Plato and Aristotle] again and again and I feel that, however old I am, I am on the threshold of reading Plato and Aristotle. I love them and I feel I have to start again and again and again. It is a task which is in front of me, before me."[28] We must understand, however, the correct way of reading these classics:

> Now, nevertheless, the way I tried to read Plato, Aristotle, and others is not a way of commanding, repeating, or conserving this heritage. It is an analysis which tries to find out how their thinking works or does not work, to find the tensions, the contradictions, the heterogeneity within their own corpus. What is the law of this self-deconstruction, this "auto-deconstruction"? Deconstruction is not a method or some tool that you apply to something from the outside. Deconstruction is something which happens and which happens inside; there is a deconstruction at work within Plato's work, for instance. As my colleagues know, each time I study Plato I try to find some heterogeneity in his own corpus, and to see how, for instance, within the *Timaeus* the theme of the *khōra* is incompatible with this supposed system of Plato.[29]

It may therefore be helpful to us, in seeking to understand this deconstructive methodology, to examine Derrida's use of it in the specific case of Plato. He has done this in a work titled *Khōra*, the English translation of which bears the title *On the Name*. Derrida distinguishes between Platonism and the text of Plato. While the philosophy known as Platonism is certainly based on the text, it does this by abstracting and simplifying, whereas the text is complex and heterogeneous. The elimination of these heterogeneous elements, however, has created Platonism: "This will be called Platonism or the philosophy of Plato, which is neither arbitrary nor illegitimate, since a certain force of thetic abstraction at work in the heterogeneous text of Plato can recommend one to so do. . . . 'Platonism' is thus certainly one of the effects of the text signed by Plato, for a long time, and for necessary reasons, the dominant effect, but this effect is

---

[28]Derrida, in Caputo, *Deconstruction in a Nutshell*, p. 9.
[29]Ibid.

always turned back against the text."[30] The philosophy of Plato is a collection of theses or dominant themes in Plato, which can be turned against the text of Plato. This philosophy then controls the text, "dominating, according to a mode which is precisely all of philosophy, other motifs of thought which are also at work in the text."[31] What must be done, according to Derrida, is to retain and draw out these heterogeneous elements that have been neutralized or numbed: "Hence the necessity to continue to try to think what takes place in Plato, with Plato, what is shown there, what is hidden, so as to win there or to lose there."[32]

The standard understanding of Plato is usually drawn from such images as the allegory of the cave or the divided line in the *Republic.* This divides all of reality rather neatly into two spheres, the intelligible, the realm of the ideas; and the sensible, the realm of the shadows cast by these ideas. What Derrida does is to look for some overlooked or omitted element in the text of Plato, something that the philosophy of Platonism does not take into account. He finds this in the concept of *khōra.*

In the *Timaeus,* Plato himself supplies this missing third element. *Khōra* is the indeterminate receptacle in which the sensible instances of the forms or ideas are inscribed. This is neither the intelligible nor the sensible, although it has something in common with each of these. It has not come into being, although it really does not have the eternality of the forms. It is not an object of the senses, yet is not an intelligible object of the mind. This unclassifiable third thing is what attracts Derrida's attention. It is beyond philosophy's grasp, but nonetheless must be an object of our attention and inquiry.[33] This *khōra* is not simply something marginal, inserted in some out-of-the-way part of the text, but is in the middle of the text of the *Timaeus.* This being the case, it is as if Plato is inviting us to do this deconstruction of his thought.

Bricolage. If, then, we cannot reduce the thought of Plato, or for that matter, any other thinker, to a homogeneous systematized body of ideas, how can we proceed? It is helpful here to look at Derrida's discussion of the *bricoleur,* an idea he borrows from Lévi-Strauss. The *bricoleur,* according to Spivak, is to be thought of roughly as a professional do-it-yourself man, although of a different standing than the English handyman, jack of all trades, odd job man. He uses things for purposes other than those for which they were originally intended.[34] Derrida says that according to Levi-Strauss he "is

---

[30]Jacques Derrida, *On the Name,* ed. Thomas Dutoit (Stanford, Calif.: Stanford University Press, 1995), p. 120.
[31]Ibid.
[32]Ibid., p. 121.
[33]Ibid., pp. 90, 125.
[34]Derrida, *Of Grammatology,* p. xix.

someone who uses 'the means at hand,' that is, the instruments he finds at his disposition around him, those which are already there, which had not been especially conceived with an eye to the operation for which they are to be used and to which one tries by trial and error to adapt them, not hesitating to change them whenever it appears necessary, or to try several of them at once, even if their form and their origin are heterogeneous—and so forth."[35] This is in seeming contrast to the engineer, who works with instruments specifically designed for the task at hand. Yet one will not find in Derrida any envy of the seemingly greater objectivity and efficiency of the so-called hard sciences. The engineer is actually a myth. "A subject who supposedly would be the absolute origin of his own discourse and supposedly would construct it 'out of nothing,' 'out of whole cloth,' would be the creator of the verb, the verb itself. The notion of the engineer who supposedly breaks with all forms of *bricolage* is mythopoetic, the odds are that the engineer is a myth produced by the *bricoleur.*"[36] Thus it appears that all knowledge, even supposedly scientific, objective knowledge, is characterized by this sort of incompleteness. Spivak comments, "Sign will always lead to sign, one substituting the other (playfully, since 'sign' is 'under erasure') as signifier and signified in turn. Indeed, the notion of play is important here. Knowledge is not a systematic tracking down of a truth that is hidden but may be found. It is rather 'the field of *freeplay*, that is to say, a field of infinite substitutions in the closure of a finite ensemble.'"[37]

Justice and the limits of deconstruction. But, we may ask, is there no limit to deconstruction? Is there nothing that is undeconstructible? To answer this question may help us understand more fully what deconstruction really intends, and what it does not. This is probably best seen in Derrida's discussion of justice. In the Villanova roundtable, Derrida was asked about his understanding of justice, and how the impossibility of the ethical life and the impossibility of justice formed the condition of the appearance of justice. He indicated that although justice had been on his mind for some time, it was a conference at the Cardozo Law School that forced him to address the issue thematically. He draws a distinction between right and law, or the law and justice. By the law, he means "the history of right, of legal systems."[38] He concludes that the law can be deconstructed:

> There is a history of legal systems, of rights, of laws, of positive laws, and this history is a history of the transformation of laws. That why they are there [*sic*].

[35]Derrida, *Writing and Difference*, p. 285.
[36]Ibid.
[37]Derrida, *Of Grammatology*, p. xix.
[38]Derrida, in Caputo, *Deconstruction in a Nutshell*, p. 16.

You can improve law, you can replace one law by another one. There are constitutions and institutions. This is a history, and a history, as such, can be deconstructed. Each time you replace one legal system with another one, one law by another one, or you improve the law, that is a kind of deconstruction, a critique and deconstruction. So, the law as such can be deconstructed and has to be deconstructed. That is the condition of historicity, revolution, morals, ethics, and progress.[39]

By way of contrast to the law as specific rules, codes, regulations, there is justice, and this, in Derrida's judgment, is undeconstructible. In fact, it is the basis or the driving force behind deconstruction, or that for the sake of which deconstruction is engaged in: "But justice is not the law. Justice is what gives us the impulse, the drive, or the movement to improve the law, that is to deconstruct the law. Without a call for justice we would not have any interest in deconstructing the law. That is why I said that the condition of possibility of deconstruction is a call for justice. Justice is not reducible to the law, to a given system of legal structures. That means that justice is always unequal to itself. It is non-coincident with itself."[40]

There is a sense in which justice is never complete or perfect. Derrida speaks of how justice implies "non-gathering, dissociation, heterogeneity, non-identity with itself, endless inadequation, infinite transcendence."[41] There is no such thing as being just, and if anyone says, "I am just," you can be sure that he or she is wrong, "because being just is not a matter of theoretical determination."[42] Derrida distinguishes between being right and being just. One can know that he is right, because that means acting in agreement with norms, such as stopping at a red light. The fact that justice is not merely a matter of calculation has interesting implications for the administration of justice.

> To speak of justice is not a matter of knowledge, of theoretical judgment. That's why it's not a matter of calculation. You can calculate what is right. You can judge; you can say that, according to the code, such and such a misdeed deserves ten years of imprisonment. That may be a matter of calculation. But the fact that it is rightly calculated does not mean that it is just. A judge, if he wants to be just, cannot content himself with applying the law. He has to reinvent the law each time. If he wants to be responsible, to make a decision, he has not simply to apply the law, as a coded program, to a given case, but to reinvent in a singular situation a new just relationship; that means that justice cannot be reduced to a calculation of sanctions, punishments, or rewards. That

---

[39]Ibid.
[40]Ibid., pp. 16-17.
[41]Ibid., p. 17.
[42]Ibid.

may be right or in agreement with the law, but that is not justice. Justice, if it has to do with the other, with the infinite distance of the other, is always unequal to the other, is always incalculable.[43]

If law, thought of as specific statutes, can and must be deconstructed, that does not mean that justice is deconstructible as well. Indeed, justice is undeconstructible and is the reason for the deconstructibility of law. Derrida says, "Justice in itself, if such a thing exists, outside or beyond law, is not deconstructible. No more than deconstruction itself, if such a thing exists. Deconstruction is justice."[44]

On the face of it, this sounds as if justice is some transcendental signified, a bit of ontology or the logocentrism or the metaphysics of presence. If so, it would indicate that Derrida's project is not as complete or as consistent as one would hope. Caputo, seeing this problem, is quick to defend Derrida against such a charge.

> Justice is not deconstructible. After all, not everything is deconstructible, or there would be no point to deconstruction. While it is true that there is no end to deconstruction, no *telos* and no *eschaton*, it is not true that there is no point to deconstruction, no spur or stylus tip, no thrust, no cutting edge. Everything cannot be deconstructible or, better, every *thing* is deconstructible, but justice, if such a thing "exists," is not a *thing*. Justice is not a present entity or order, not an existing reality or regime; nor is it even an ideal *eidos* toward which we earthlings down below heave and sigh while contemplating its heavenly form. Justice is the absolutely unforeseeable prospect (a paralyzing paradox) in virtue in which the things that get deconstructed are deconstructed.[45]

There are what Derrida calls "aporias of justice," paradoxes as it were, which block our way, which prevent us simply proceeding in some automatic fashion. There are at least three of these, or perhaps a single one that appears in three different domains.

1. Suspension of the law. There is justice only when the law is not simply applied, but suspended or lifted. The judge must make a fresh judgment, stretching the law if need be, to deal with a new, unique situation. Derrida makes much of Kierkegaard's treatment of Abraham, in which there was a "teleological suspension of the ethical." Since every case is different, it is not a case, but a singularity.[46]

---

[43]Ibid.

[44]Derrida, "Force of Law: The Mystical Foundation of Authority," in *Deconstruction and the Possibility of Justice*, ed. Drucilla Cornell, Michel Rosenfeld, and David Gray Carlson (New York: Routledge, 1992), pp. 14-15.

[45]Caputo, *Deconstruction in a Nutshell*, pp. 131-32.

[46]Derrida, "Force of Law," pp. 22-24.

2. *Undecidability.* The just decision is one that "gives itself up to the impossible decision."[47] Caputo explains this by telling us that "the opposite of 'undecidability' is not 'decisiveness' but programmability, calculability, computerizability, or formalizability. Decision-making, judgment, on the other hand, positively *depends upon* undecidability, which gives us something to decide. . . . That does not mean that it is 'decisionistic,' for that would break the tension in the opposite direction, by dropping or ignoring the law altogether and substituting subjectivistic autonomy for responsibility to the other."[48] Only a decision is just, not a law, a rule, or even the person deciding.[49]

3. *Urgency.* Even if justice could be derived from a system of calculation of right and wrong, it cannot wait for the completion of such a system. It must deal with the situation that is at hand now. Here again, Derrida's view appears to be strongly influenced by Kierkegaard. A major difference, however, is that in Kierkegaard it is the lonely individual seeking his eternal happiness, whereas for Derrida, deconstruction is always concerned for the justice due the other, "the other's coming as the singularity that is always coming."[50]

An alternative logic. Standard discussion proceeds on the basis of a two-valued or bimodal logic, in which the laws of logic apply: the law of identity (A is A); the law of contradiction (something cannot be both A and not-A at the same time and in the same respect); and the law of excluded middle (something must be either A or not-A). In the use of such logic, proof often consists of disproving the contradictory of a proposition, or disproof in showing the truth of its contradictory.

Derrida, however, claims to be presenting and working with a different kind of logic. For example, he discusses at some length the work of Mallarmé, and specifically the question of whether it should be considered either Platonic or Hegelian, and concludes: "It is thus not simply false to say that Mallarmé is a Platonist or a Hegelian. But it is above all not true. And vice versa."[51] Barbara Johnson comments on this passage:

> Instead of a simple "either/or" structure, deconstruction attempts to elaborate a discourse that says *neither* "either/or," *nor* "both/and" nor even "neither/nor," while at the same time not totally abandoning these logics either. The very word *deconstruction* is meant to undermine the either/or logic of the opposition

---

[47]Ibid., p. 24.

[48]Caputo, *Deconstruction in a Nutshell*, p. 137.

[49]Jacques Derrida, *Deconstruction and the Possibility of Justice*, pp. 24-26.

[50]Ibid., p. 139.

[51]Jacques Derrida, *Dissemination*, trans. Barbara Johnson (Chicago: University of Chicago Press, 1981), p. 207.

"construction/destruction". Deconstruction is both, it is neither, and it reveals the way in which both construction and destruction are themselves not what they appear to be. Deconstruction both opposes and redefines; it both reverses an opposition and reworks the terms of that opposition so that what was formerly understood by them is no longer tenable.[52]

This alternative logic might be mistakenly taken to be simply Hegelianism, in which contradictories, thesis and antithesis, are brought into a synthesis, in which neither persists unmodified, but are gathered up (*Aufgehoben*), in a modified form. We can note both the similarities and differences between Derrida's logic and that of Hegel:

It has been necessary to analyze, to set to work, *within* the text of the history of philosophy, as well as *within* the so-called literary text . . . certain marks . . . that *by analogy* . . . I have called undecidables, that is, unities of simulacrum, "false" verbal properties (nominal or semantic) that can no longer be included within philosophical (binary) opposition, resisting and disorganizing it, *without ever* constituting a third term, without ever leaving room for a solution in the form of speculative dialectics (the *pharmakon* is neither remedy nor poison, neither good nor evil, neither the inside nor the outside, neither speech nor writing; the *supplement* is neither a plus nor a minus, neither an outside nor the complement of an inside, neither accident nor essence, etc.; the *hymen* is neither confusion nor distinction, neither identity nor difference, neither consummation nor virginity, neither the veil nor the unveiling, neither the inside nor the outside, etc. . . . Neither/nor, that is *simultaneously* either or.[53]

Derrida acknowledges that he is using a dialectic of the Hegelian type, and even says of *différance* that it is "at a point of almost absolute proximity to Hegel," yet finally breaks with Hegel, for he says that this *différance* "can never be totally resolved."[54]

Although none of the commentators suggest this, it appears to me that Derrida's practice of erasure is another indication of this alternative logic. For in that practice, a word is written and then crossed out, indicating that it cannot be simply taken literally or at face value. Yet it is not obliterated. It is allowed to continue to stand, even in this negated form, so that both the concept and its negation are simultaneously presented to the reader.

Derrida and religion. There has been a considerable interest of late in Derrida's views of religion, and even his own personal religious faith, attitudes, and practice. While much of this attention has focused on his later

---

[52]Barbara Johnson, "Nothing Fails Like Success," in *A World of Difference* (Baltimore: Johns Hopkins University Press, 1987), pp. 12-13.
[53]Derrida, *Positions*, pp. 42-43.
[54]Ibid., p. 44.

writings, there has also been an effort to identify elements of religious reference even in his earlier writings, or at least to reconcile his earlier positions with the later religious references.[55]

As to his own religious orientation, Derrida was born into a Jewish family, and his mother, Georgette Safar Derrida, not unlike Augustine's mother Monica, apparently worried greatly about his lack of faith. In 1976 Derrida attempted to describe his broken covenant with Judaism.[56] Caputo, who knows Derrida's biography well, says, "For Derrida is Jewish without being Jewish, Jewish *sans* Judaism, married outside Judaism, his sons uncircumcised, he an atheist."[57] Yet Derrida says that "the constancy of God in my life is called by other names," admits that he does "quite rightly pass for an atheist," yet asserts that he has an "absolved, absolutely private language" in which he speaks of God all the time.[58] Since this statement comes from 1976, it indicates that Derrida's interest in religion is not simply a late development. Caputo, perhaps Derrida's most sympathetic and perceptive commentator, says of the "religion" of Derrida that "no one understands, not even his mother," and suggests that attempting to understand Derrida's (cir)cumfessions is a "daunting—impossible—task."[59]

What, then, is Derrida's "religion," if he describes himself as an atheist? It appears that this is a pursuit of something transcendent. He speaks of messianic and prophetic eschatology, which differs from philosophy by dispensing with objective or absolute criteria. He says that he does not presume that his deconstruction has a prophetic function, but then goes on to say:

> But I concede that the style of my questioning as an exodus and dissemination in the desert might produce certain prophetic resonances. It is possible to see deconstruction as being produced in a space where the prophets are not far away. But the prophetic resonances of my questioning reside at the level of a certain rhetorical discourse which is also shared by several other contemporary thinkers. The fact that I declare it "unfortunate" that I do not personally

---

[55]Bruce Ellis Benson ("Traces of God: The Faith of Jacques Derrida," *Books and Culture* 6, no. 5 [2000]: 42-45), interprets Derrida in a basically positive fashion, finding considerable areas of value in Derrida for orthodox Christianity. He does not, however, discuss some of Derrida's key concepts, such as an alternative logic and his criticism of ontotheology, and fails to mention Derrida's important essay, "Faith and Knowledge" (see documentation below).

[56]Jacques Derrida, *Circumfession: Fifty-Nine Periods and Periphrases,* in Geoffrey Bennington and Jacques Derrida, *Jacques Derrida* (Chicago: University of Chicago Press, 1993), p. 154.

[57]John D. Caputo, *The Prayers and Tears of Jacques Derrida* (Bloomington: Indiana University Press, 1997), p. xvii. Caputo agrees with Mark C. Taylor in understanding tears both as cries and as cuts (p. 340, n. 1). Thus *tears* may rhyme with *ears* or *bears*.

[58]Derrida, *Circumfession*, pp. 155-56.

[59]Derrida, *Prayers and Tears*, p. xviii.

feel inspired may be a signal that deep down I still hope. It means that I am in fact still looking for something. So perhaps it is no mere accident of rhetoric that the search itself, the search without hope for hope, assumes a certain prophetic *allure.* Perhaps my search is a twentieth century brand of prophecy? But it is difficult for me to believe it.[60]

Caputo contends that this is what should be called Derrida's "religion," this search for the unrepresentable, unimaginable, unforeseeable, impossible. He says, "It [deconstruction] is moved—it has always been moving, it gives words to a movement that has always been at work—by the provocation of something calling from afar that calls it beyond itself, outside itself. . . . Deconstruction is a passion and a prayer for the impossible, a defense of the impossible against its critics, a plea for/to the experience of the impossible which is the only real experience, stirring with religious passion."[61] This is the quest for the wholly other, the *tout autre,* which gives the prophetic or messianic bent to deconstruction, its air of expectancy.

Derrida has professed to be an atheist. Yet there is a sense in which he has a god that is the object of his attention, a god who is not external but internal. In *The Gift of Death* he says: "God is the name of the possibility I have of keeping a secret that is visible from the interior but invisible from the exterior." This structure of consciousness, this being within oneself, then takes on special significance: "once I can have a secret relationship with myself and not tell everything, once there is secrecy and secret witnessing within me, (it happens that) I call myself God—a phrase that is difficult to distinguish from 'God calls me,' for it is on that condition that I can call myself or that I am called in secret. God is in me, he is the absolute 'me' or 'self,' he is that structure of invisible interiority that is called, in Kierkegaard's sense, subjectivity."[62]

Derrida speaks of messianicity without messianism. By this he means *"the opening to the future or to the coming of the other as the advent of justice, but without horizon of expectation and without prophetic prefiguration."*[63] Just what is this messianicity? *"An invincible desire for justice is linked to this expectation. By definition, the latter is not and ought not to be certain of anything, either through knowledge, consciousness, conscience, foreseeability or any kind of programme as such. This abstract messianicity belongs from the very beginning to the experience of faith, of believing, of a credit that is irreducible to knowledge and of a*

---

[60]Derrida, *Dialogues,* p. 119.

[61]Derrida, *Prayers and Tears,* pp. xix-xx..

[62]Jacques Derrida, *The Gift of Death* (Chicago: University of Chicago Press, 1995), pp. 108-9.

[63]Jacques Derrida, "Faith and Knowledge: The Two Sources of 'Religion' at the Limits of Reason Alone," in *Religion,* ed. Jacques Derrida and Gianni Vattimo (Stanford, Calif.: Stanford University Press, 1996), p. 17.

trust that 'founds' all relation to the other in testimony."[64] That justice, of course, as we have seen, is not simply to be equated with right, or with any particular laws.

This understanding of messianicity fits well with Derrida's discussion of the Kantian distinction between two types of religion. The religion of cult alone seeks favors of God. Moral religion, by contrast, "*is interested in the good conduct of life* (die Religion des guten Lebenswandels); *it enjoins him to action, it subordinates* knowledge *to it and* dissociates *it from itself, prescribing that man become better by* acting *to this end, in accordance with the following principle: 'It is not essential and hence not necessary for everyone to know what God does or has done for his salvation,' but it is essential to know what* man himself must do *in order to become worthy of this assistance.*"[65]

Derrida speaks of the importance of gauging two temptations. One of these is the Hegelian: "*ontotheology which determines absolute knowledge as the truth of religion.*" Derrida contends that "*dogmatic philosophies and natural religions should disappear and, out of the greatest 'asperity', the harshest impiety, out of kenosis and the void of the most serious privation of God* (Gottlosigkeit), *ought to resuscitate the most serene liberty in its highest totality. Distinct from faith, from prayer or from sacrifice, ontology destroys religion, but, yet another paradox, it is also perhaps what informs, on the contrary, the theological and ecclesiastical, even religious, development of faith.*"[66]

This ontotheology is not restricted to the Hegelian form of religion. It is found in the various forms of fusion of Greek thought with Hebrew and even Christian thought, in what Derrida calls the "Graeco-Abrahamic hybridization, which remains anthropo-theological." This synthesis, however, is resisted by *khōra*, which we have examined above, and which represents that which cannot be assimilated by such a system.

There are, of course, many other themes in Derrida's thought that relate either directly or indirectly to religion. These can never be reduced to a system. This is particularly true of his "Faith and Knowledge," which is an anthology of his comments at a seminar on religion, held on the isle of Capri in 1994. It reads much like Pascal's *Pensées*—a collection of ideas, but without systematic interrelationship. Nonetheless, it is possible to summarize briefly some of the major themes of his view of religion.

1. The religious is not to be identified with specific religions, or with belief in God per se. Rather, in the case of deconstruction, it is found in a

---

[64]Ibid., p. 18.
[65]Ibid., p. 10.
[66]Ibid., p. 15.

quest for transcendence, for something beyond.

2. In terms of the distinction between religion as belief or doctrine, and religion as ethics, Derrida's emphasis is far more on the latter, especially in terms of justice.

3. Ontotheology, or the blending of theology with metaphysics, especially of a Greek type, not only contributes to religion, but actually militates against it. Derrida personally is more oriented to "prayer" than to doctrinal formulation.

4. In keeping with this, Derrida is "Augustinian," that is, he is much more inclined to see religion in the areas of uncertainty, than in rational and logical formulations and proofs of doctrines.[67]

Analysis of Derrida's Thought

With this data before us, it is possible to draw some conclusions regarding the nature and intention of Derrida's deconstruction.

1. The proclaimed intention is not to eliminate any sort of objective truth or any nonlinguistic references. This is seen both in Derrida's complaints about those who have misunderstood him in this fashion, and in similar complaints by his defenders. He emphasizes that this is deconstruction, rather than either construction or destruction. By this he seems mean something rather similar to analysis, or perhaps, dissection. This is the attempt to take apart a particular position, its assertions and arguments, in order to discover within it conflicting elements. The assumption here is that a text has conflicting elements of signification within it, because it signifies in more than one way.[68] He especially objects to the truth of any text being grounded in some absolute truth or unqualified being. So it is not truth, but unqualified or nonrelative or unopposed truth that is the object of his critique.

2. There is an assumption of, and emphasis on, the presence of paradoxes, of internal conflict, of disharmonies of thought and expression, rather than an expectation of harmony and an attempt to bring disparate elements into a harmonious whole. This is of the nature of a presupposition and reflects the existentialist background of Derrida's thought. The search for and expectation of finding internal disparity and the aversion to any kind of inclusion system is strongly reminiscent of the thought of Kierkegaard.

3. Derrida's own statements are seldom unequivocal. He either makes a statement and conjoins it with its contradictory, or makes a statement and then in another place says something very different on the subject. This

---

[67]For more complete treatment of Derrida and religion, see his *Circumfession* and Caputo's *Prayers and Tears.*

[68]Barbara Johnson, "Translator's Introduction," in Derrida, *Dissemination*, p. xvi.

enables his sympathizers to give a rather conservative interpretation of his thought, its scope and import, while providing justification for a much more radical interpretation by negative critics. Yet it is clear that Derrida and his advocates believe that there is a definite meaning to what he has written, as evidenced by their strong and frequently emotive complaints about the misunderstanding of his thought by those critics.

4. One of these equivocations can be seen with respect to the term *writing*. It is used in the usual and specific sense, and also in a generic sense, in which it is roughly synonymous with language. Spivak says, "the name 'writing' is given here to an entire structure of investigation, not merely to 'writing in the narrow sense,' a graphic notation on tangible material."[69]

5. There are limits to deconstruction. Although all other views are proper targets of deconstruction, deconstruction itself is not. Nor is justice, which is the basis of and driving force behind Derrida's deconstructive endeavor.

---

[69]Spivak, in Derrida, *Of Grammatology*, p. lxix.

7

michel foucault

F or many thinkers, it must be said that their thoughts really cannot be understood apart from the events of their lives. This is especially the case with Michel Foucault.[1]

Foucault was born October 15, 1926, in Poitiers, a provincial French city, as the second child of Paul and Anne Malapert Foucault. His father and both his grandfathers were physicians, and it was expected that he would follow that profession as well. He was named Paul, as were his father and paternal grandfather. His mother, however, added to "Paul" a hyphen and the additional name Michel. At a fairly early age he changed his name, however, to simply Michel, because he did not want to bear the same name as the father whom he hated.

Although the family attended Mass regularly, there apparently was something of an anticlericalism in this family. Paul-Michel became an acolyte and choirboy for a time. He did well in school, excelling in every subject except math. Suddenly, in eighth grade, he began to do poorly, so his mother decided to send him to a local Catholic school. During this time he developed an intense dislike for religion and monks. After a period of study at preparatory schools, he was granted entrance to the École Normale Supérieure in Paris, the most prestigious college-level school in France.

---

[1]The contents of this brief biographical summary are drawn especially from Didier Eribon, *Michel Foucault* (Cambridge, Mass.: Harvard University Press, 1991), and from James Miller, *The Passion of Michel Foucault* (New York: Doubleday, 1993).

Here, however, he was unsociable, unpopular, and unhappy, and even attempted suicide. His father took him to a psychiatrist, his first encounter with a member of that profession. In the process of therapy he admitted to the psychiatrist that he was homosexual, and again attempted suicide on numerous occasions.

He developed a strong interest in psychology and psychoanalysis. He became a member of the Communist Party in 1950, but left it in 1953, shortly after Stalin's death. In 1952, he became an assistant lecturer at the University of Lille. Then for about six years of apparently self-imposed exile, he worked at a variety of jobs, in Uppsala, Warsaw, and Frankfurt, following which he received an appointment at the University of Clermont-Ferrand, where from 1960 to 1966 he commuted one day a week from Paris. He then departed for Tunisia, where he taught philosophy until 1968. He returned to France to a new university being established at Vincennes, where he recruited the most radical philosophers he could find, and became involved in demonstrations and controversy. After two years there, however, he was successful in being appointed to the faculty of the Collège de France.

Beginning in the late 1970s, he frequently taught at the University of California at Berkeley as a visiting professor. During this time he became an active participant in the homosexual community in San Francisco, including the subculture of sado-masochism, and also became involved in the use of various types of drugs. He was urged by his friends to practice caution, but this was contrary to his very approach to life, and at some point he acquired the HIV virus. AIDS was still relatively unfamiliar in the early 1980s, and it is possible that Foucault did not actually realize that he had AIDS. While it has been rumored that he knowingly infected members of the gay community with this virus, there is no confirmation. Some gay persons have criticized Foucault for not using the situation of his own disease to speak out on behalf of AIDS sufferers. In early 1984 he became ill and in June was hospitalized, dying on June 25.

The difficulty of understanding and interpreting Foucault's thought is well known. There are a number of reasons for this. One is that his thought was developing over the years of his active career. It is commonplace to think of Foucault's work in terms of three periods of his life or three phases of his thinking. On this model, the first period of his writing involved a concentration on discourses or disciplines of knowledge. This was the period in which he wrestled with the most epistemological questions. Then, in the second period, he especially discussed power and the way it is used to control populations, whether in mental institutions, hospitals, or prisons. The final period then is understood as being concerned with the attempt to reconstruct some sort of theory of the self or the subject.[2] It was, however, not merely the subject matter Foucault dealt with that changed with the passage of time. He also altered his viewpoint on some matters, but did not necessarily inform the reader of that change. In some cases, he changed the terminology employed in expressing his thoughts. For example, what he referred to as "thought" in *Madness and Civilization* is roughly equivalent to what he meant by "discourse" in *The Order of Things.*[3]

Even within a given work, however, Foucault is not a model of logical consistency. He makes statements that seem to contradict one another. Part of the reason for this is that he is not attempting to present a theory of anything, a complete explanation of the structure of things. To attempt to do so, he says on one occasion, would be to concede the very position he is rejecting, since "theory still relates to the dynamic of bourgeois knowledge."[4] He seems to have a virtual antipathy to the idea of system. Thus, the charge of inconsistency would not be applicable to him, he would contend. This does mean, however, that it is possible to construct at least two different Foucaults from his writing. When charged with holding one of the views that he seems to espouse, he (or another interpreter of him) can charge the original interpreter with misunderstanding him. An example of this is his vigorous disavowal of the charge that he is a structuralist,[5] even though he earlier identified himself by using that term.[6]

Finally, some of the confusion that Foucault generates is a matter of his very style of expressing himself. When asked a question in the interviews and dialogues which we have, he often appears not to answer the question. Part of the problem is that he really does not define his terms, but simply makes predications about them, or proceeds to use them, leaving the listener or reader to draw his or her own conclusions in the matter. His sentences are frequently lengthy and convoluted and their syntax difficult to follow

In the exposition that follows, I will not attempt complete coverage of Foucault's thought, but I will emphasize those aspects that bear most directly

---

[2]Alec McHoul and Wendy Grace, *A Foucault Primer: Discourse, Power and the Subject* (New York: New York University Press, 1993), p. viii.

[3]Allen McGill, *Prophets of Extremity: Nietzsche, Heidegger, Foucault, Derrida* (Berkeley: University of California Press, 1985), p. 252.

[4]Michel Foucault, "Revolutionary Action: 'Until Now,'" in *Language, Counter-Memory, Practice: Selected Essays and Interviews,* ed. Donald F. Bouchard (Ithaca, N.Y.: Cornell University Press, 1977), p. 231.

[5]Michel Foucault, *The Order of Things: An Archaeology of the Human Sciences* (New York: Vintage, 1973), p. xiv.

[6]Michel Foucault, "Je suis tout au plus . . . ," interview, *La Presse de Tunis*, April 2, 1967. See Eribon, *Michel Foucault*, p. 231.

upon my purposes in examining him. Thus, for example, the issue of whether he was really still a structuralist late in his life and career will not be given much attention. Similarly, the extent to which a structured outline of his thought should be placed on it is questionable. Since he did not write in a fashion intended to be a system, some of his cardinal conceptions are inferences, rather than direct assertions, and thus cannot be arranged as neatly as we might ordinarily wish.

The Function of Power

One of the most pervasive themes in Foucault's thought is his view of power and the role it plays in society. This is seen in his analysis of social institutions, such as hospitals, particularly mental hospitals, and even the very dynamics of the body of accepted knowledge.

When I was taking my first introductory course in psychology as a college sophomore, the instructor made an interesting comment one day: "The only difference between the people in mental institutions and those of us on the outside is that there are more of us. If there were more of them, they would put us inside." Apart from the obvious additional qualification that we are also better organized than they are, I thought that quite a humorous thought. Yet, in a sense, Foucault has built an entire system on that thought, in his *Madness and Civilization.* Beginning with a historical treatment of society's handling of the "mentally ill," he seeks to demonstrate how society has wielded power in this area.

Foucault's work as a whole cannot be classified neatly into either the discipline of history or that of philosophy. Indeed, an entire book has been devoted to the question of whether he is a historian or a philosopher.[7] Actually, he does not appear to see these as separate disciplines. He is what can be termed an historicist.[8] He is not looking for grand inclusive explanations, or for transcendental principles lying behind the observable phenomena. He will draw his conclusions from what can be observed, including the historical.

Foucault begins his discussion of madness with the observation that leprosy was a major problem in Europe in the middle ages, so that large numbers of leprosariums were created to deal with those who had to be kept separated from the rest of society, lest they infect them. By the early seventeenth century, however, leprosy had virtually disappeared. This left a different kind of problem: what to do with these physical plants and their

---

[7]Clare O'Farrell, *Foucault: Historian or Philosopher?* (New York: St. Martin's, 1989).
[8]See William Dean, *History Making History: The New Historicism in American Religious Thought* (Albany: State University of New York Press, 1988), pp. 1-22.

endowments. At the same time that the actual disease vanished, what remained were "the values and images attached to the figure of the leper as well as the meaning of his exclusion, the social importance of that insistent and tearful figure which was not driven off without first being inscribed within a sacred circle."[9] The aim of the exclusion of the leper had been his salvation. These values and concerns were now transferred to a new group within society: "Poor vagabonds, criminals and 'deranged minds' would take the part played by the leper, and we shall see what salvation was expected from this exclusion, for them and for those who excluded them as well. With an altogether new meaning and in a very different culture, the forms would remain—essentially that major form of a rigorous division which is social exclusion but spiritual reintegration."[10]

Another institution must also be observed in this historical survey: the "ship of fools." Originally a literary composition, the ship of fools eventually became a real, physical ship. Madmen were driven from cities, and frequently they were handed over to boatmen, to be transported away from their native place. Yet madmen were not universally expelled. Some were put in hospitals and places of detention. So Foucault speculates that it was only the outsider, the foreigner, who was driven away or placed on the ship of fools. Not only did the ship accomplish the purpose of ridding a given place of its madmen; it was thought of as purifying. Although confined to the ship, the madman was thrust out upon the water, with its great uncertainty.[11]

In the seventeenth century, large houses of confinement were built. Varied groups of people were imprisoned within them: the poor, the unemployed, prisoners, and the insane. Foucault sees the date of 1656 as a landmark, the time of the decree establishing the Hôpital Général in Paris. Although the name of the place would suggest that this was a medical establishment, Foucault insists that this was not the case: "It is rather a sort of semijudicial structure, an administrative entity which, along with the already constituted powers, and outside of the courts, decides, judges, and executes. . . . a strange power that the King establishes between the police and the courts, the limits of the law: a third order of repression. The insane whom Pinel would find at Bicêtre and at La Salpêtrière belonged to this world."[12] Foucault contends that these institutions had nothing to do with medicine and everything to do with imposing order and power on people.

---

[9]Foucault, *Madness and Civilization*, p. 6.
[10]Ibid., p. 7.
[11]Ibid., p. 11.
[12]Ibid., p. 40.

The economic significance of these places of confinement should not be overlooked or minimized. Whereas the fifteenth century had been largely a time of economic expansion, which had continued into the seventeenth century, by 1640 recession had set in, at least in France. A number of coinciding factors—"reduction of wages, unemployment, scarcity of coin"—were, in Foucault's judgment probably due to a crisis in the Spanish economy.[13] An edict was established that was intended to solve some of the problems: the unemployed were to be confined. On Monday, May 14, 1657, the militia began rounding up beggars and confining them in the Hôpital Général.[14]

More was involved in these actions than merely confinement, however: "It was no longer merely a question of confining those out of work, but of giving work to those confined and thus making them contribute to the prosperity of all. The alternation is clear: cheap manpower in the periods of full employment and high salaries; and in periods of unemployment, reabsorption of the idle and social protection against agitation and uprisings."[15] Conditions in these places were not good. They were places of filth and punishment. There was little difference between the hospitals and the prisons, and the insane could be found somewhat indifferently in either of them. They both served the same purpose: negating threats to the social order.[16]

The same type of historical analysis of power is carried over into Foucault's treatment of imprisonment, in *Discipline and Punish*. The book begins with a gory description of the torture death of a murderer, Damiens. This is followed by a description of the daily regimen in a model prison. Each activity is exactly specified, and is announced by drumrolls. These are two rather contrasting approaches to punishment. The first is directed toward the flesh, and is administered under the authority of the king. The second, however, is the rule of law, and is more methodical and restrained. Foucault's comment on the latter is: "The age of sobriety in punishment had begun."[17]

The study that follows is not merely of prisons in the sense of physical places of incarceration, however. It is also, says Foucault, about the "prison" within, those internal forces that control the person's thoughts and actions. The book is, according to Foucault, an allegory about the soul: "The soul is the effect and instrument of political anatomy; the soul is the prison of the body."[18]

---

[13]Ibid., p. 49.
[14]Ibid.
[15]Ibid., p. 51.
[16]Ibid., pp. 65-84.
[17]Michel Foucault, *Discipline and Punish: The Birth of the Prison* (New York: Vintage, 1979), p. 14.
[18]Ibid., p. 30.

What type of endeavor is this study? Foucault claims it is an attempt to get at the truth. The problem, he acknowledges, as with all his studies, is that the categories involved in truth are themselves the products of historical situations: "What historical knowledge is possible of a history that itself produces the true/false distinction on which such knowledge depends?"[19] Yet, here an interesting dual orientation appears. On the one hand, Foucault speaks of his use of the standard methods of historiography: "I use methods drawn from the classical repertoire: demonstration, proof of historical documentation, reference to texts, recourse to authorized commentaries, [interpretation of] relations between ideas and facts, proposition of explanatory schemes, etc."[20] Yet on the other hand, he introduces the element of fiction into his supposedly factual writing. He said in an interview, "It seems to me that the possibility exists for fiction to function in truth, for a fictional discourse to induce effects of truth, and for bringing it about that a true discourse engenders, or 'fabricates' something that does not yet exist, that is, 'fictions' it."[21] So, he indicates in *Discipline and Punish*, he "makes use of 'true' documents, but in such a way that through them it is possible to effect not only a certification of the truth, but also an *experience* that authorizes an alteration, a transformation in the relationship that we have with ourselves and with our cultural universe: in a word, with our 'knowledge.'"[22] Miller's explanation of the role of fiction in Foucault's writing is this: "The 'fictive' part of his book is, in effect, designed to evoke a kind of 'limit-experience' in the reader, triggering a change in our selves, in our 'souls,' and in our understanding of 'truth,' all together."[23]

Foucault is admittedly indebted to and influenced by Nietzsche, who in the *Genealogy of Morals* had theoretized about how societies endeavor to mold their citizens, to "tame," as it were, the unruly and disruptive. Nietzsche had seen Christianity as part of this process, with its insistence on subjugating the body. Foucault picks up Nietzsche's theme and extends it, so that the modern human sciences, as he terms them, have taken over this function of Christianity.

Somewhere around the French Revolution, Foucault contends, the nature of

[19]"Question of Method: An Interview with Michel Foucault," in *After Philosophy: End or Transformation?* ed. Kenneth Baynes, James Bohman, and Thomas McCarthy (Cambridge, Mass.: MIT Press, 1987), p. 111.

[20]Michel Foucault, *Remarks on Marx: Conversations with Duccio Trombadori,* trans. R. James Goldstein and James Cascaito (New York: Semiotext[e], 1991), pp. 32-33.

[21]Michel Foucault, *The History of Sexuality,* in *Power/Knowledge,* ed. Colin Gordon (New York: Pantheon, 1980), p. 193.

[22]Foucault, *Remarks on Marx,* p. 37.

[23]Miller, *Passion of Michel Foucault,* p. 212.

punishment changed. The grisly form that he describes in the case of Damiens was replaced by more discreet forms of punishment. According to him, the aim was "not to punish less, but to punish better; to punish with an attenuated severity perhaps, but in order to punish with more universality and necessity; to insert the power to punish more deeply into the social body."[24] This change took place primarily through the arising of society's ability to exercise surveillance and thus supervision of its members. This is what Foucault calls "panopticism," a term drawn from the eighteenth-century philosopher Jeremy Bentham.

Bentham had devised a form of architecture for prisons to make their task more efficient. The prison was designed in a sort of semicircle, with the cells on the outside of the circle and the guard station at the center. With windows on both the outside and the inside of the cell, the guard could observe every prisoner without moving from his station. The term *panopticon* came from the Greek word *panoptos*, and meant "all-seeing." This is the fashion in which discipline is now exercised, humanly and invisibly. And, it should be noticed, this observation, this inspecting gaze, is not to be found merely in the prison situation. Its practice is extended to all sorts of areas.

This can be seen in very efficient fashion in the military, in which even the body is brought under control. New recruits are transformed into soldiers. It might even be said that soldiers are constructed from these recruits. The body is made physically fit. A certain posture is learned.[25] In a perfect military camp, all is laid out with geometrical exactness.[26] An orphanage was observed to have the same degree of detailed control of the behavior of the inmates.[27] Foucault comments upon the inclusiveness of this control:

> The workshop, the school, the army were subject to a whole micro-penality of time (lateness, absences, interruptions of tasks), of activity (inattention, negligence, lack of zeal), of behaviour (impoliteness, disobedience), of speech (idle chatter, insolence), of the body ("incorrect" attitudes, irregular gestures, lack of cleanliness), of sexuality (impurity, indecency). At the same time, by way of punishment, a whole series of subtle procedures was used, from light physical punishment to minor deprivations and petty humiliations. It was a question both of making the slightest departures from correct behaviour subject to punishment, and of giving a punitive function to the apparently indifferent elements of the disciplinary apparatus: so

---

[24]Foucault, *Discipline and Punish*, p. 82.

[25]Michel Foucault, "Docile Bodies," in *Discipline and Punish: The Birth of the Prison* (New York: Vintage, 1979), pp. 135-36.

[26]Michel Foucault, "Means of Correct Training," in *Discipline and Punish: The Birth of the Prison* (New York: Vintage, 1979), p. 171.

[27]Ibid., p. 177

that, if necessary, everything might serve to punish the slightest thing; each subject find himself caught in a punishable, punishing universality.[28]

The examination is a particularly effective form of observation, whether the academic examination in school or the military review. Here are combined both "hierarchical surveillance" and "normalizing judgment," with the result that the individual is made the effect and object of power and of knowledge.[29]

One area that has come in for especially intense attention is sex and sexuality. Foucault projected a six-volume treatment of the history of sexuality, three volumes of which were completed before his death. The reason he gives for the extensiveness of this treatment is that historians had criticized his *Madness and Civilization* for incomplete treatment of the historical data.[30] The first volume opens with a familiar type of theme. He observes the repression of sex that took place in the Victorian period. Not only was sex restricted, or confined to marriage; it was not even to be discussed.[31] Thus, even the discussion of sex was a way of breaking the prohibitions. His aim in the projected series was not to inquire why society is so repressed with respect to sex. Rather, it is to ask by what process society has come to say that it is repressed. We must not only ask why sin was made to be a sin, but to ask "why we burden ourselves today with so much guilt for having once made sex a sin."[32]

In the interview "The Confession of the Flesh," Foucault explains further what he was attempting to do. He indicates that in an earlier draft, he started with sex as sort of a pre-given datum, and "sexuality figured as a sort of simultaneously discursive and institutional formation which came to graft itself on to sex, to overlay it and perhaps finally to obscure it." When he showed the manuscript to some others, however, he came to the conclusion that this understanding was flawed: "couldn't it be that sex—which seems to be an instance having its own laws and constraints, on the basis of which the masculine and feminine sexes are defined—be something which on the contrary is *produced* by the apparatus of sexuality? What the discourse of sexuality was initially applied to wasn't sex but the body, the sexual organs, pleasures, kinship relations, interpersonal relations, and so forth."[33]

The special object of Foucault's polemic is the idea that there is a nature of sexuality, to which it must conform. He says:

---

[28]Ibid., p. 178.
[29]Ibid., p. 184.
[30]Michel Foucault, "The Confession of the Flesh," trans. Alain Gosrichard, in *Power/Knowledge*, ed. Colin Gordon (New York: Pantheon, 1980), p. 209.
[31]Foucault, *History of Sexuality*, pp. 3-4.
[32]Ibid., p. 9.
[33]Foucault, "Confession of the Flesh," p. 210.

Sexuality must not be thought of as a kind of natural given which power tries to hold in check, or as an obscure domain which knowledge tries gradually to uncover. It is the name that can be given to a historical construct: not a furtive reality that is difficult to grasp, but a great surface network in which the stimulation of bodies, the intensification of pleasures, the incitement to discourse, the formation of special knowledges, the strengthening of controls and resistances, are linked to one another, in accordance with a few major strategies of knowledge and power.[34]

This is simply the specific application of a general principle Foucault had enunciated in *The Order of Things*: "What is essential is that thought, both for itself and in the density of its workings, should be both knowledge and a modification of what it knows, reflection and a transformation of the mode of being of that on which it reflects."[35] The older Western ethic, whether in its Epicurean or Stoic form, was a "natural law ethic." It "was articulated upon the order of the world, and by discovering the law of that order it could deduce from it the principle of a code of wisdom or a conception of the city; even the political thought of the eighteenth century still belongs to this general form."[36] Modern thought, however, is quite different: "[It] formulates no morality, since any imperative is lodged within thought and its movement towards the apprehension of the unthought."[37]

Power and knowledge. This function of power carries over to the matter of knowledge as well. It has been customary to say that knowledge is power, that the possession of knowledge enables one to exercise influence and control. In Foucault's judgment, the relationship is reciprocal, rather than unilateral. He says that "'Truth' is linked in a circular relation with systems of power which produce and sustain it, and to effects of power which it induces and which extend it. A 'regime' of truth."[38] Elsewhere he elaborates upon this concept:

Power produces knowledge. . . . Power and knowledge directly imply one another; . . . there is no power relation without the correlative constitution of a field of knowledge, nor any knowledge that does not presuppose and constitute at the same time power relations. These 'power-knowledge relations' are not to be analysed, therefore, not on the basis of a subject of knowledge who is or is not free in relation to the power system, but, on the contrary, the subject who knows, the objects to be known and the modalities of knowledge must be regarded as so many effects of these fundamental implications of power-knowledge and their historical transformations. In short, it is not the activity of the subject of knowledge that produces a corpus of knowledge, useful or

---

[34]Foucault, *History of Sexuality*, pp. 105-6.
[35]Foucault, *The Order of Things*, p. 327.
[36]Ibid., pp. 327-28.
[37]Ibid., p. 328.
[38]"Michel Foucault, "Truth and Power," in *Power/Knowledge*, ed. Colin Gordon (New York: Pantheon, 1980), p. 133.

resistant to power, but power-knowledge, the processes and struggles that traverse it and of which it is made up, that determines the forms and possible domains of knowledge.[39]

For those who have thought of truth as independent of power or at least of producing, rather than following from it, this may come as a surprising statement. The ideal of the intellectual dispassionately seeking and discovering truth and following its leading is replaced here by the concept of power producing truth, and those who possess the former dictating or creating the latter. Foucault says, "The important thing here, I believe, is that truth isn't outside power, or lacking in power: contrary to a myth whose history and functions would repay further study, truth isn't the reward of free spirits, the child of protracted solitude, nor the privilege of those who have succeeded in liberating themselves. Truth is a thing of this world: it is produced only by virtue of multiple forms of constraint."[40]

The attempt to demonstrate the connection between power and knowledge was what had motivated Foucault's study of asylums and madness. It is not that this connection does not function in such supposedly objective disciplines as physics or chemistry, but if one attempts to raise the question of the connection of such fields with political and economic structures of society, one is dealing with an unnecessarily complicated question. This lifts the threshold of possible explanations impossibly high. However, if one raises the question with respect to psychiatry, asks Foucault, "won't the question be much easier to resolve, since the epistemological profile of psychiatry is a low one and psychiatric practice is linked with a whole range of institutions, economic requirements and political issues of social regulation?" Here the "interweaving of effects of power and knowledge" could be "grasped with greater certainty."[41]

It is helpful to see concretely how this power is exercised. We are familiar with more overt forms of such exercise of power, as in censorship. It is frequently more subtle, however. The intellectual is no longer really necessary to gain knowledge and share it with the masses. They already know and understand, but a whole system exists that represses this knowledge. It is part of the whole societal network.[42]

In a discussion about repression and revolution, Foucault observes that repression is exercised in the educational system in two ways: in terms of whom it excludes from the process, and in terms of "the model and the stan-

---

[39]Foucault, *Discipline and Punish*, pp. 27-28.
[40]Foucault, "Truth and Power," p. 131.
[41]Ibid., p. 109.
[42]Foucault, "Intellectuals and Power," in *Language, Counter-Memory, Practice*, p. 207.

dard (the bars) it imposes on those receiving this knowledge."[43] Even the content of this education is determined, as the students are asked to learn certain matters and ignore others. Certain kinds of knowledge, such as that generated by the workers at the beginning of the nineteenth century into their material conditions, have not been considered, except as it entered into the work of Marx.[44] Even the way knowledge is approached is predetermined. In France, up to the age of sixteen, students are taught issues from a historical perspective, rather than being exposed to contemporary problems. They are taught that the present is to be understood using categories drawn from the past, and historical continuity, rather than discontinuity, is emphasized.[45]

> In the broadest sense, both the nature of events and the fact of power are invariably excluded from knowledge as presently constituted in our culture. This is to be expected since the power of a certain class (which determines this knowledge) must appear inaccesible [sic] to events; and the event, in its dangerous aspect, must be dominated and dissolved in the continuity of power maintained by this class, by a class power which is never defined. On the other hand, the proletariat develops a form of knowledge which concerns the struggle for power, the manner in which they can give rise to an event, respond to its urgency, avoid it, etc.; this is a knowledge absolutely alien to the first kind because of its preoccupation with power and events. For this reason, we should not be fooled by the modernized educational program, its openness to the real world: it continues to maintain its traditional grounding in 'humanism' while emphasizing the quick and efficient mastery of a certain number of techniques, which were neglected in the past. Humanism reinforces social organization and these techniques allow society to progress, but along its own lines.[46]

By humanism, Foucault means everything in our Western civilization that restricts the desire for power. It does this by encouraging subjugation of oneself to God, society, or other types of sovereignties. At the heart of this effort is the theory of the subject, so that our culture vigorously opposes anything that would weaken its hold on us. This hold can be attacked in two ways. One is a "desubjectification" of the will to power. By this Foucault means the use of "political struggle in the context of class warfare." The other is destruction of the subject as pseudosovereign. Here he has in mind an attack on culture, the rejection of the prohibitions society imposes on persons: "the suppression of taboos and the limitations and divisions

---

[43]Foucault, "Revolutionary Action," p. 219.
. [44]Ibid., pp. 219-20.
[45]Ibid., p. 220.
[46]Ibid., pp. 220-21.

imposed upon the sexes; the setting up of communes; the loosening of inhibitions with regard to drugs; the breaking of all the prohibitions that form and guide the development of a normal individual."[47]

This destruction of the subject is also what is meant by genealogy. Foucault is opposed not only to the systems that inculcate, but even to the idea of the constituent subject. While some may be content simply to relativize the phenomenological subject by placing it in its historical setting, evolving through the course of history, Foucault has something more radical in mind. He says:

> One has to dispense with the constituent subject, to get rid of the subject itself, that's to say, to arrive at an analysis which can account for the constitution of the subject within a historical framework. And this is what I would call genealogy, that is, a form of history which can account for the constitution of knowledges, discourses, domains of objects etc., without having to make reference to a subject which is either transcendental in relation to the field of events or runs in its empty sameness throughout the course of history.[48]

Of great importance is Foucault's understanding of subjugated knowledges. He calls for an insurrection of these knowledges. The primary meaning of this expression is not just that certain historical contents are buried within a formal systematization. More than that, he is referring to "a whole set of knowledges that have been disqualified as inadequate to their task or insufficiently elaborated: naive knowledges, located low down on the hierarchy, beneath the required level of cognition or scientificity."[49] This is the knowledge possessed by the unqualified, that of the psychiatric patient and the ill person. This is what Foucault calls popular knowledge, although it is not simply general commonsense knowledge. In fact, it is a particular, local, differential knowledge, which cannot achieve unanimity. Yet, he says, "it is through the re-appearance of this knowledge, of these local popular knowledges, these disqualified knowledges, that criticism performs its work."[50] What were these buried, subjugated knowledges concerned with? It was the historical knowledge of struggles. The process of unfolding these subjugated knowledges gives us a genealogy, a rediscovery of these struggles. There is one essential condition, however, without which such genealogy would not be possible: "[they] were not possible and could not even have been attempted except on one condition, namely, that the tyranny of globalising discourses with their hierarchy and all their privileges of a theoretical *avant-*

---

[47]Ibid., p. 222.
[48]Foucault, "Truth and Power," p. 117.
[49]Michel Foucault, "Two Lectures," in *Power/Knowledge*, ed. Colin Gordon (New York: Pantheon, 1980), p. 82.
[50]Ibid.

garde was eliminated."[51] Here again Foucault's opposition to universal theories is evident. He is not talking about an opposition between abstract unitary theory and concrete multiplicity of facts, nor is he speaking of an empiricism or positivism that underwrites the genealogical project:

> Genealogies are therefore not positivistic returns to a more careful or exact form of science. They are precisely anti-sciences. Not that they vindicate a lyrical right to ignorance or non-knowledge: it is not that they are concerned to deny knowledge or that they esteem the virtues of direct cognition and base their practice upon an immediate experience that escapes encapsulation in knowledge. It is not that with which we are concerned. We are concerned, rather, with the insurrection of knowledges that are opposed primarily not to the contents, methods or concepts of a science, but to the effects of the centralising powers which are linked to the institution and the functioning of an organised scientific discourse within the society such as ours.[52]

A clear indication of this effort to subjugate certain kinds of knowledge can be seen in the question which for a long time was asked about Marxism: "Is it a science?" The same question could be asked and was asked about other views, such as psychoanalysis and semiology of literary texts. How would genealogy reply to this? "'If you really want to know, the fault lies in your very determination to make a science out of Marxism or psychoanalysis or this or that study.' If we have any objection against Marxism, it lies in the fact that it could effectively be a science."[53] Before we can pose such a question, we must rather "question ourselves about our aspirations to the kind of power that is presumed to accompany such a science."[54] The real issues concern what types of knowledge and what subjects one is trying to disqualify by such a question, and conversely, what one is trying to enthrone by so doing. Foucault affirms what he considers to be the real motivation behind asking whether Marxism is a science: "For me you are doing something altogether different, you are investing Marxist discourses and those who uphold them with the effects of a power which the West since Medieval times has attributed to science and has reserved for those engaged in scientific discourse."[55]

The understanding of truth is crucial at this point. Foucault does not offer one of the classical definitions of truth, such as correspondence or coherence. Rather, he defines it as "a system of ordered procedures for the produc-

---

[51]Ibid., p. 83.
[52]Ibid., pp. 83-84.
[53]Ibid., p. 84.
[54]Ibid.
[55]Ibid., p. 85.

tion, regulation, distribution, circulation and operation of statements."[56] He is averse to the idea of there being any such thing as "objective" knowledge. The foundationalism epitomized in Descartes is part of what he is attacking. In that sort of view, theory and knowledge are objective, and then that objective material is applied as practice. For Foucault, there is no such distinction:

> In this sense theory does not express, translate, or serve to apply practice: it is practice. But it is local and regional, as you said, and not totalizing. This is a struggle against power, a struggle aimed at revealing and undermining power where it is most invisible and insidious. It is not to "awaken consciousness" that we struggle (the masses have been aware for some time that consciousness is a form of knowledge; and consciousness as the basis of subjectivity is a prerogative of the bourgeoisie), but to sap power, to take power; it is an activity conducted alongside those who struggle for power, and not their illumination from a safe distance. A "theory" is the regional system of this struggle.[57]

This understanding has a bearing on the role of the intellectual in society. Traditionally, the intellectual was thought of as the master of truth and justice, who acted as the spokesman of the universal: "To be an intellectual meant something like being the consciousness/conscience of us all. . . . The intellectual is thus taken as the clear, individual figure of a universality whose obscure, collective form is embodied in the proletariat."[58] This universal role of the "left" intellectual, frequently derived from Marxism, has not been played for some time now. Instead, the connection between theory and practice is now specific, exercised at those points where the intellectuals' own life situation place them, such as housing, the hospital, the laboratory, and so on. Although not now covering the universal issues, the intellectual is now part of a network of lateral connections between specific fields of knowledge. The specific intellectual, in Foucault's judgment, has emerged since the Second World War, with the atomic scientist, and specifically, Oppenheimer, serving as the transition point between the universal and the specific intellectual. Such a person, however, runs a number of risks, not the least of which is the danger of being manipulated by such groups as political parties and trade unions.[59]

How is this repressive exercise of power through knowledge to be dealt with? Some might suggest that what is needed is an alternative theory. Indeed, in a discussion on revolution, two of Foucault's dialogue partners pro-

---

[56]Foucault, "Truth and Power," p. 133.
[57]Foucault, "Intellectuals and Power," p. 208.
[58]Foucault, "Truth and Power," p. 126.
[59]Ibid., pp. 127-30.

pose that what is needed is a utopian model and a "theoretical elaboration that goes beyond the sphere of partial and repressed experiences,"[60] and another suggests that the movement that culminated in the student uprisings of May 1968 "could have gone much further if it had been supported by an adequate theory, a thought capable of providing it with new perspectives."[61] Foucault disagrees with both ideas, however. His proposal is not for an alternative of the same type. Rather, he says, "Reject all theory and all forms of general discourse. This need for theory is still part of the system we reject." What he proposes instead is opposition on the basis of actual experiences: "It is possible that the rough outline of a future society is supplied by the recent experiences with drugs, sex, communes, other forms of consciousness, and other forms of individuality."[62] Nor does he accept the contention that the revolutionary actions of May lacked staying power because there was no sustaining theory behind it. He believes it was important that "thousands of people exercised a power which did not assume the form of a hierarchical organization." The decline of the effect was for a different reason: "Unfortunately, since power is by definition that which the ruling class abandons least readily and recaptures on the first occasion, it was impossible to maintain the experience for longer than a few weeks."[63] Nor does he wish to replace the institutions with better, counterinstitutions, such as the free universities in the United States: "If you wish to replace an official institution by another institution that fulfills the same function—better and differently—then you are already being reabsorbed by the dominant structure."[64]

It should be apparent by now that if for Foucault power is not exclusively the result of knowledge but its cause, the means of its production, then the solution to the problem is not to argue against it, to seek to refute it. Rather, the effort must be to alter the conditions that produce it. There must be a "political" solution, in which a new politics of truth is established: "The essential political problem for the intellectual is not to criticise the ideological contents supposedly linked to science, or to ensure that his own scientific practice is accompanied by a correct ideology, but that of ascertaining the possibility of constituting a new politics of truth. The problem is not changing people's consciousnesses—or what's in their heads—but the political, economic, institutional regime of the production of truth."[65]

---

[60]Foucault, "Revolutionary Action," p. 231.
[61]Ibid., p. 232.
[62]Ibid., p. 231.
[63]Ibid., p. 232.
[64]Ibid.
[65]Foucault, "Truth and Power," p. 133.

Analytical Summary

What are the major tenets and implications of these thoughts? While Foucault's thought cannot be reduced to a system, a cluster of motifs can be observed.

1. A salient feature of all of life is power, in terms of what we generally term *political power*. This is the ability to control the thoughts and behavior of individuals within society.

2. Those possessing power exercise it in such a way as to determine what is right and allowable, true and believable. This gives the resultant actions and declarations an appearance of absoluteness, but these could have been different if other centers of power had been in control.

3. Right and wrong are actually expressions of normal and abnormal, or that which conforms to and that which does not conform to the dominant forms within a given culture.

4. Power does not flow from knowledge in a unilateral way. It also creates knowledge, by decreeing what is true.

5. Truth is not to be understood as correspondence to reality, or as "the way things really are." It is historically and politically produced, it is what the possessors of power say is true.

6. To establish truth in this fashion, certain knowledges are subjugated. For example, the psychiatrist declares what is truth, but the opinion of the patient is ignored.

7. One primary criterion employed in such subjugation is "science," which is regarded as the purest, most complete, and most accurate form of knowledge. The degree to which a discipline or discourse is scientific is the measure of its admissibility as knowledge.

8. Theory and practice are not to be separated, so that the latter is the application of the former. The very concept of "theory" and employment of "theory" is a mark of the established order.

9. System is a sign of the exercise of power, organizing all truth into an integrated whole, in the process discarding information that does not fit.

10. Reality is not simply reported by discourse, but is constructed by it. This is true of sex, for example, and even of the self.

11. The basis for many of Foucault's analyses and conclusions is ostensibly history. Yet it is not literal history, which could be confirmed or refuted by historical data, but "fictive history," or history fictionalized.

12. Pleasure, as exemplified in sex, is of a very high value, and is to be pursued without limitation.

13. The way to alter truth is not by intellectual argumentation or refutation, but by changing the political conditions that produce truth.

8

richard rorty

T he persons we have examined thus far have been continental European thinkers. They approach the issues out of that context, and with a European orientation. Richard Rorty, on the other hand, is an American, and has traveled a different journey to the conclusions that he holds. While some of his intellectual heritage, in terms of Hegel, Husserl, and Heidegger, has been the same as that of Derrida and Foucault, his route to their thought has been rather indirect, and has included the unique influence of American pragmatism.

Rorty's own intellectual biography is seldom discussed and perhaps not widely known. It does, however, help us to understand something of his thought and how he came to it. A hint is given in the dedication of his *Contingency, Irony, and Solidarity:* "In memory of six liberals: my parents and grandparents."[1] His parents were Trotskyites who had broken with the American Communist Party in 1932. When he was twelve, the most significant books on his parents' shelves were *The Case of Leon Trotsky* and *Not Guilty,* which together made up the report of the Dewey Commission of Inquiry into the Moscow Trials.[2] His parents worked at the Workers Defense League office, and at twelve years of age he worked as an office boy, deliver-

---

[1] Richard Rorty, *Contingency, Irony, and Solidarity* (Cambridge: Cambridge University Press, 1989), p. v.
[2] Richard Rorty, "Trotsky and the Wild Orchids," in *Wild Orchids and Trotsky: Messages from American Universities,* ed. Mark Edmundson (New York: Penguin, 1993), pp. 33-34.

ing press releases, which he read as he traveled. He says that, as a result, at that age he "knew that the point of being human was to spend one's life fighting social injustice."[3]

Rorty had wide and unusual interests. One of these was Tibet, and he sent a present and congratulations to the Dalai Lama, a fellow eight-year-old who had made good. He became very interested in the wild orchids that grew in the mountains of northwest New Jersey, where his family spent part of their time. At age fifteen he enrolled in the so-called Hutchins College of the University of Chicago. There he was searching for some all-encompassing view, which would enable him to hold together in one vision, reality and justice.[4] The intellectual leaders of the university, such as Robert Hutchins and Mortimer Adler, regarded pragmatism as relativistic and self-refuting. Rorty found himself searching for stable absolutes, and tried Christianity and the philosophy of Plato. By the age of twenty, however, he gave up this quest, having become convinced that there was no "noncircular justification of any debatable stand on any important issue." That led him to the conclusion that there was no neutral standpoint from which first principles could be evaluated, and that the best test for philosophical truth was the test of coherence.[5] Nonetheless, coherence could be manipulated, and the winner of the philosophical debate was generally the person most skilled at drawing distinctions to avoid contradiction.

The next forty years of Rorty's life he described as an attempt to determine what, if anything, philosophy is good for. For a time, that pursuit involved the study of Hegel, from whom he concluded that rather than producing some eternal understanding outside of time, if philosophy could simply understand its time, it could change the world. This concern with his time led him back to Dewey, who seemed to have learned what Hegel had to say about avoiding certainty and eternity, but by taking Darwin seriously, had protected his thought against pantheism. This insight coincided with his discovery of Derrida, through whom he was led to Heidegger. Rorty was struck by the resemblance among Dewey's, Wittgenstein's, and Heidegger's criticisms of Descartes' thought. He found himself no closer to the sort of single vision, tying together one's Trotskyism and wild orchids, that he had gone to college to get thirty years earlier. He says:

> As I tried to figure out what had gone wrong, I gradually decided that the whole idea of holding reality and justice in a single vision had been a mistake—that a pursuit of such a vision had been precisely what led Plato astray.

---

[3]Ibid., p. 35.
[4]Ibid., p. 36.
[5]Ibid., p. 39.

More specifically, I decided that only religion—only a nonargumentative faith in a surrogate parent who, unlike any real parent, embodied love, power, and justice in equal measure—could do the trick Plato wanted done. Since I couldn't imagine becoming religious, and indeed had gotten more and more raucously secularist, I decided that the hope of achieving a single vision by becoming a philosopher had been a self-deceptive atheist's way out. So I decided to write a book about what intellectual life would be like if one could manage to give up the Platonic attempt to hold reality and justice in a single vision.[6]

That book—*Contingency, Irony, and Solidarity*—should be understood in light of this self-declaration.

The Nature of Philosophy

Rorty's disillusionment with a certain type of philosophy comes through repeatedly in his writings. It can be seen clearly in his distinction between two types of philosophy.

Formal or traditional philosophy. While there have been many variations of this philosophy, some of them to be found in surprising places, Plato's thought was the epitomization of this approach. This type of philosophy is concerned with isolating the True or the Good, of defining the words *true* and *good*. Whether of a Platonic or a Kantian variety, the transcendental philosophy attempted to identify these norms, so as to obey them: "The idea is to believe more truths or do more good or be more rational by knowing more about Truth of Goodness or Rationality."[7] This type of philosopher believes in real essences, and is attempting to identify them. There have been both transcendental and empirical varieties of this view, or in a different set of categories, premodern and modern varieties. Philosophers like Plato thought there was a reality beyond space and time, whereas empirical philosophers believed the only reality is made up of space and time. Both varieties, however, believed in the existence of truth and goodness as objectively present in reality, independent of our consciousness, and the aim of the philosopher was to discover, correctly describe, and then act upon this independent goodness and truth. All such philosophies can be represented as Philosophy, with a capital P.[8]

Pragmatism. Pragmatism, as Rorty sees it, is not a set of alternative answers to the questions that Philosophy has asked. Rather, it holds that the attempt to answer those questions has not proven fruitful, and therefore

---

[6]Ibid., pp. 41-42.
[7]Richard Rorty, "Introduction: Pragmatism and Philosophy," in *Consequences of Pragmatism* (Minneapolis: University of Minnesota Press, 1982), p. xv.
[8]Ibid.

should be abandoned. When pragmatists suggest that we cease asking questions about Truth and Goodness, however, they do so not from some theory about the nature of reality. They are not saying that there is no such thing as Truth or Goodness, nor do they have a relativistic view of Truth and Goodness. "They would simply like to change the subject," says Rorty.[9]

Pragmatism is philosophy with a small p. Both the empirical and the transcendental philosophers were attempting to isolate the reality to which ideas and language supposedly correspond. "Pragmatism cuts across this transcendental/empirical distinction by questioning the common presupposition that there is an invidious distinction to be drawn between kinds of truth. For the pragmatist, true sentences are not true because they correspond to reality, and so there is no need to worry what sort of reality, if any, a given sentence corresponds to—no need to worry about what 'makes' it true."[10]

Rorty sees even analytic philosophy as having gone through a process of "de-transcendentalization." Although analytic philosophy is often thought of as empirical and scientific, and thus opposed to transcendentalism, that is misleading. Rorty believes there has been a development in analytic philosophy, paralleling that in pragmatism from Peirce to Dewey, in Wittgenstein's thought from the early *Tractatus* to the later *Investigations*, and in Heidegger's project of *Fundamentalontologie* to that of his *Andenken*.[11] This process, which is away from any sort of foundationalism, is one by which philosophy, "which starts off by announcing that it will construct a permanent neutral framework for the criticism of culture, consisting of apodictic truths (usually identified as 'logical' or 'structural') differing in kind from those found outside of philosophy, 'de-transcendentalizes' itself by gradually blurring the distinctions between logic and fact, structure and content, atemporal essence and historical accident, theory and practise, philosophy and non-philosophy."[12]

Rorty sees the major element in this process of detranscendentalization as being the abandonment of the idea of epistemology as first philosophy. This in turn results from the criticism of the idea that certain representations, whether of sense-data or meanings, are privileged and foundational. Russell's concern with "logical form" and Husserl's "purely formal" aspects of the world which remained when the contingent or nonformal aspects

---

[9]Ibid., p. xiv.
[10]Ibid., p. xvi.
[11]Richard Rorty, "Epistemological Behaviorism and the De-Transcendentalization of Analytic Philosophy," in *Hermeneutics and Praxis*, ed. Robert Hollinger (Notre Dame, Ind.: University of Notre Dame Press, 1985), p. 89.
[12]Ibid.

had been "bracketed" represented attempts to find some sort of apodictic truths. Both Quine and Sellars, however, raised what Rorty calls "behaviorist questions" about these supposedly apodictic truths. By this he means that instead of asking for some ontological foundation for epistemology, we should treat epistemology simply as a study of certain ways that human beings interact. This difference can be seen in the area of morals:

> The two schools of moral philosophy do not differ on the point that human beings have rights worth dying for. What they differ about is whether, once one has understood when and why these rights have been granted or denied, in the way in which social and intellectual historians understand this, there is more to understand. They differ, in short, about whether there are "ontological foundations for human rights," just as the Sellars-Quine approach differs from the empiricist and rationalist traditions about whether, once one understands when and why various beliefs were adopted or discarded (as historians and sociologists of knowledge do), there is something called "the relation of knowledge to reality" left over to be understood.[13]

Rorty recognizes, of course, that to say that the True and the Right are matters of social practice will incur the charge of relativism. Such a charge, however, presupposes the sort of transcendentalism in which there is a permanent neutral matrix for all inquiry and all history.[14]

The differences between these two types of philosophy are also revealed in Rorty's discussion of the concepts of objectivity and solidarity. These are two ways in which human beings try to give their lives sense by placing them in a larger context. Objectivity is the way that has been attempted by Philosophy. It is the effort to think of oneself in relation to some nonhuman reality. Solidarity, on the other hand, involves "telling the story of their contribution to a community." In the case of a person seeking solidarity, "she does not ask about the relation between the practices of the chosen community and something outside that community."[15] The approach of solidarity does not require either a metaphysics or an epistemology. Adherents of this position view truth as "what is good for *us* to believe. . . . From a pragmatist point of view, to say that what is rational for us now to believe may not be *true*, is simply to say that somebody may come up with a better idea. It is to say that there is always room for improved belief, since new evidence, or new hypotheses, or a whole new vocabulary, may come along." What is involved in the desire for objectivity on the part of a pragmatist? It is "sim-

---

[13]Ibid., p. 101.

[14]Ibid., pp. 101-2.

[15]Richard Rorty, "Solidarity or Objectivity?" in *Objectivity, Relativism, and Truth* (Cambridge: Cambridge University Press, 1991), p. 21.

ply the desire for as much intersubjective agreement as possible, the desire to extend the reference of 'us' as far as we can. Insofar as pragmatists make a distinction between knowledge and opinion, it is simply the distinction between topics on which such agreement is relatively easy to get and topics on which agreement is relatively hard to get."[16]

Basic Tenets of Rorty's Pragmatism

At a number of points Rorty has taken the earlier pragmatism and extended it further than the original pragmatists had. This includes his view of epistemology of the self, and of language.

Antirepresentationalism. Much of Rorty's early work, especially *The Mirror of Nature*, was concerned with rejecting and refuting the realist view that we know external reality as it is. At the time, although the background of his thought was Wittgenstein, Heidegger, and Dewey, his primary inspiration came from Sellars and Quine. In *Objectivity, Relativism, and Truth*, he brings that discussion up to date, indicating that his more recent mentor has been Donald Davidson. He also notes that although philosophical thought at the end of the twentieth century was grappling with the same problem of realism that it did at the beginning of the century, there was now a significant difference.

In 1900, the opposite of realism was idealism. Now, however, it is not the mind that is thought of as standing over against reality, but language. The question now is what statements, if any, stand in representational relationship to something nonlinguistic. Consequently, the opposite of realism is today termed merely "antirealism."[17]

Rorty's view goes beyond merely antirealism, however, for that term has two different senses. In the first sense, it means the claim with respect to some specific true statements, that there is no state of affairs that they represent. As such, this is a dispute among representationalists, those philosophers who hold that mind or language contains representations of reality. In the second and more radical sense, however, antirealism means the claim that "*no* linguistic items represent *any* nonlinguistic items." Here it is properly termed antirepresentationalism, the "attempt to eschew discussion of realism by denying that the notion of 'representation,' or that of 'fact of the matter,' has any useful role in philosophy."[18]

It is important, however, to see that Rorty is not proposing antirealism as some sort of new epistemology. The claim by Williams that "the determi-

[16]Ibid., pp. 22-23.
[17]Richard Rorty, "Introduction," in *Objectivity, Relativism, and Truth*, p. 2.
[18]Ibid.

nacy of reality comes from what we have decided or are prepared to count as determinate" must be rejected, because it suggests some sort of causal dependence. Rather, says Rorty:

> "determinacy" is not what is in question—that neither does thought determine reality nor, in the sense intended by the realist, does reality determine thought. More precisely, it is no truer that "atoms are what they are because we use 'atom' as we do" than that "we use 'atom' as we do because atoms are as they are." *Both* of these claims, the antirepresentationalist says, are entirely empty. Both are pseudo-explanations.[19]

The reason the former view must be considered a pseudo-explanation is because there simply is no independent way of verifying that our language does indeed somehow correctly represent some nonlinguistic reality. There is no God's-eye view from which we can break out of our language and beliefs and test things as they really are. The reason the latter view must also be considered a pseudo-explanation is because we cannot posit any such thing as mind. The alternative views seem to be something like this:

1. Our beliefs are caused by the objects they represent.

2. Our beliefs are caused by our minds, not by some external object.

3. Our beliefs are caused by our language, which in turn is shaped by the community of which we are a part.

Rorty appears to be advancing the last of these three views. His further argument therefore consists of demonstrating the contingency of each of these components, often presented as factors in the knowing process.

The contingency of language. As noted earlier in the discussion of Rorty's view of philosophy, he sees himself as standing over against the traditional types of philosophy, which are trying to give true accounts of the nature of things. He sees the idea that truth is something made rather than discovered as going back about two hundred years to the French Revolution, which demonstrated that "the whole vocabulary of social relations, and the whole spectrum of social institutions could be replaced almost overnight."[20] At about same time, the rise of the Romantic poets had a similar effect by showing that art is no longer to be thought of as imitation, but as "the artist's self-creation."[21] The joining of these two forces has now achieved a cultural hegemony. For most intellectuals, the question of how to make sense of one's life and community is no longer the domain of religion, philosophy, or science, but rather of art, politics, or both. This has, consequently, led to a split within philosophy, with some allying their effort with the paradigm of

---

[19]Ibid., p. 5.
[20]Rorty, *Contingency, Irony, and Solidarity*, p. 3.
[21]Ibid.

science, whose goal is to discover, rather than to create, truth, and with others conceiving their discipline and their efforts along the line of art.[22]

Rorty sees his own work as having much more in common with the second view, of philosophy as art, than with the first, of philosophy as science. He is not an idealist, in the sense of denying the reality of the existence of the world external to us. We must distinguish between the idea that the world is out there and the claim that truth is out there. To say, however, that truth is not out there is to affirm that truth is a quality of sentences, not of objects. Where there are no sentences there is no truth. But since sentences are elements of human languages, which in turn are human creations, to say that truth is a function of sentences is to say that truth is a human creation.[23]

What Rorty is especially objecting to here is the idea of essences, or intrinsic natures. On that model, the objects in the external world have intrinsic natures, and the truth-process is one of discovering and accurately expressing those essences. Rorty believes that the idea that truth, as well as the world, is out there derives from "an age in which the world was seen as the creation of a being who had a language of his own."[24] Although that idea has been largely abandoned now, there still is a strong belief in the concept of self-subsistent facts, as a result of which it is easy to begin capitalizing "truth," so that it either takes the place of God or of the world as God's project. Further, confusion between single sentences and entire vocabularies takes place. While the world often enables us to decide between alternative specific sentences, such as "Red wins" and "Black wins," that is not true of whole broad vocabularies, or language games, as they are called. The shift from one of these to another, from one way of describing the world to an alternative description, does not take place because of any influence of the objects discussed. Nor is it a decision, based on the knowers applying certain criteria to their discussion of the universe of discourse.

Rorty agrees with Thomas Kuhn that the change involved in the Copernican revolution was not a decision made on the basis of telescopic observations. He says, "Cultural change of this magnitude does not result from applying criteria (or from 'arbitrary decision') any more than individuals become theists or atheists, or shift from one spouse or circle of friends to another, as a result either of applying criteria or of *actes gratuits*. We should not look within ourselves for criteria of decision in such matters any more than we should look to the world."[25] In Rorty's judgment, the belief in the

---

[22]Ibid., pp. 3-4.
[23]Ibid., p. 5.
[24]Ibid.
[25]Ibid., p. 6.

human subject making such decisions on the basis of such criteria represents a belief in the idea of the human self possessing an intrinsic nature or essence, paralleling the belief that the external world has such an essence. His statement is a strong one:

> As long as we think that there is some relation called "fitting the world" or "expressing the real nature of the self" which can be possessed or lacked by vocabularies-as-wholes, we shall continue the traditional philosophical search for a criterion to tell us which vocabularies have this desirable feature. But if we could ever become reconciled to the idea that most of reality is indifferent to our descriptions of it, and that the human self is created by the use of a vocabulary rather than being adequately or inadequately expressed in a vocabulary, then we should at last have assimilated what was true in the Romantic idea that truth is made rather than found. What is true about this claim is just that *languages* are made rather than found, and that truth is a property of linguistic entities, of sentences.[26]

Rorty contends that the insight of these revolutionaries and poets who introduced such significant changes two centuries earlier was that "anything could be made to look good or bad, important or unimportant, useful or useless, by being re-described."[27]

Rorty recognizes the natural charge that can be brought against his view: that he is claiming that his suggestion "gets something right," that it is the correct way of doing philosophy. To make such a suggestion, however, would be to fall back into the old intrinsicalist way of viewing reality, to think that there are real essences of things, which his view more accurately describes than do the alternative views. In his judgment, however, to say that a view "fits the world" is like saying that opium makes one sleepy because of its dormative power. He is not proposing an alternative explanation that is superior because it more adequately fits the facts.

> To say that there is no such thing as intrinsic nature is not to say that the intrinsic nature of reality has turned out, surprisingly enough, to be extrinsic. It is to say that the term "intrinsic nature" is one which it would pay us not to use, an expression which has caused more trouble than it has been worth. To say that we should drop the idea of truth as out there waiting to be discovered is not to say that we have discovered that, out there, there is no truth. It is to say that our purposes would be served best by ceasing to see truth as a deep matter, as a topic of philosophical interest, or "true" as a term which repays "analysis." "The nature of truth" is an unprofitable topic resembling in this respect "the nature of man" and "the nature of God," and differing from "the

---

[26]Ibid., pp. 6-7.
[27]Ibid., p. 7.

nature of the positron," and "the nature of Oedipal fixation." But this claim about relative profitability, in turn, is just the recommendation that we in fact *say* little about these topics, and see how we get on.[28]

Although Rorty is sometimes characterized as an anti-realist, and as offering a different epistemology or a different theory of truth than the familiar correspondence view, he claims not to be doing so. It is not a particular theory of knowledge that he is attempting to refute, but rather the whole view of philosophy that seeks to find more and more adequate epistemologies. Whether his view may require or may imply some such theory is another question, but he is offering a different approach than conventional theoretical philosophy. In other words, rather than the philosopher as scientist, Rorty is proposing the idea of the philosopher as poet. He contends that philosophers should not be asked for arguments against such views as the correspondence theory of truth or the idea of the intrinsic nature of reality. He is not, strictly speaking, saying that such views are untrue and should be rejected. Rather, he is saying, such discussions are not helpful and should be ignored or avoided.

An attempt at refutation would consist, typically, of such criticisms as that they are internally inconsistent. Such criticisms can never be established, however, for they are inconclusive, and worse yet, they are expected to be phrased in the very vocabulary that they attempt to reject. They "are always parasitic upon, and abbreviations for, claims that a better vocabulary is available. Interesting philosophy is rarely an examination of the pros and cons of a thesis. Usually it is, implicitly or explicitly, a contest between an entrenched vocabulary which has become a nuisance and a half-formed new vocabulary which vaguely promises great things."[29]

What is the nature of this new type of philosophy? How does it operate? This philosophy does not offer arguments against the philosophy Rorty is trying to replace. Nor does this philosophy proceed by a piecemeal analysis of one concept after another, or by testing thesis after thesis. Rather, such a method proceeds to "redescribe lots and lots of things in new ways, until you have created a pattern of linguistic behavior which will tempt the rising generation to adopt it, thereby causing them to look for appropriate new forms of nonlinguistic behavior, for example, the adoption of new scientific equipment or new social instruments." It works holistically. It says such things as "try thinking of it this way," or "try to ignore the apparently futile traditional questions by substituting the following new and possibly interesting questions." Specifically, it does not claim to be a better way of dealing

---

[28]Ibid., p. 8.
[29]Ibid., p. 9.

with or answering the old questions. Rather, it suggests that those old questions be ignored, that one stop doing what one has been doing. The reason for this is important to understand: "It does not argue for this suggestion on the basis of antecedent criteria common to the old and the new language games. For just insofar as the new language really is new, there will be no such criteria."[30]

With this background, Rorty proceeds to show the contingency of three important factors in our culture: language, self, and community. He particularly follows the work of Donald Davidson in his treatment of the consequences of the contingency of language, which he believes to be basic to the other two considerations. Davidson is critical of the traditional view, according to which there is a core self that holds a set of beliefs, the adequacy of which is to be evaluated by the extent to which they accurately correspond to a reality exterior to the network of beliefs itself. On that model, language is a medium, standing between the human self and the nonhuman reality that it purports to contact. Two varieties of this model have contended for pre-eminence. The representationist view holds that the function of language is to correctly represent to the self external reality, while the expressionist view sees language as articulating what lies within the self.

Davidson, following the later Wittgenstein, avoids both of these conceptions. He does not see alternative vocabularies as pieces of a jigsaw puzzle, according to which all vocabularies are either dispensable, reducible to other vocabularies, or capable of being united with all other vocabularies into one super vocabulary. Rather, vocabularies are like alternative tools, which may be exchanged for one another. In the traditional approach, vocabularies were evaluated by their adequacy, the extent to which they effectively either represented or expressed, according to the particular variety of theory involved. Davidson, however, rejects the traditional uses of terms like "fact" and "meaning," and, indeed, the "scheme-content model" of thought. Even further, he rejects the idea that there is an entity called "language," and that it has a fixed task to perform. He uses the concept of "a passing theory" to make his point.

Suppose that we think of meeting a new person, perhaps from a quite different culture. We would try to anticipate what that person would do under certain circumstances. Such a theory would have to be constantly corrected to take into account "mumbles, stumbles, malapropisms, metaphors, tics, seizures, psychotic symptoms, egregious stupidity, strokes of genius, and the like." All that is needed for two persons to understand one another through speech, is "the ability to converge on passing theories from utter-

---

[30]Ibid.

ance to utterance." So the idea of language as a third entity, between the self and the object, is dispensed with:

> To say that one's previous language was inappropriate for dealing with some segment of the world (for example, the starry heavens above, or the raging passions within) is just to say that one is now, having learned a new language, able to handle that segment more easily. To say that two communities have trouble getting along because the words they use are so hard to translate into each other is just to say that the linguistic behavior of inhabitants of one community may, like the rest of their behavior, be hard for inhabitants of the other community to predict.[31]

It is helpful, in grasping this understanding of language, to see Davidson's treatment of metaphor. He follows Mary Hesse's thought of scientific revolutions as metaphoric redescriptions of nature, rather than different insights into its intrinsic nature. In this respect, even new paradigms in the natural sciences are more like the redescriptions in history or social sciences than vice versa. Talk of DNA or of the Big Bang are products of causal forces, just as is talk of "secularization" or of "late capitalism." Rather than being thought of in terms of a telos, such as the discovery of truth or the freeing of humanity, they should be thought of causally, or in terms of what Aristotle called efficient causation. So, Rorty says, "These various constellations are the random factors which have made some things subjects of conversation for us and others not, have made some projects and not others possible and important." He says of Aristotle's use of *ousia*, Paul's use of *agape*, and Newton's use of *gravitas:* "for all we know, or should care [they] were the results of cosmic rays scrambling the fine structure of some crucial neurons in their respective brains. Or, more plausibly, they were the result of some odd episodes in infancy—some obsessional kinks left in these brains by idiosyncratic traumata. It hardly matters how the trick was done. The results were marvelous. There had never been such things before."[32]

Metaphor, on Davidson's understanding and that of Rorty as well, must be understood differently than it has been in the past. Usually, metaphorical and literal meaning had been thought of as two different types of meaning or two different sorts of interpretation. Rather, proposes Davidson, these should be thought of as the distinction between familiar and unfamiliar uses: "The literal uses of noises and marks are the uses we can handle by our old theories about what people will say under various conditions. Their metaphorical use is the sort which makes us get busy developing a new the-

---

[31]Ibid., p. 14.
[32]Ibid., p. 17.

ory."[33] Conventional theories of language had seen metaphors as having meanings distinct from their literal ones. Rather, says Rorty, "Tossing a metaphor into a text is like using italics, or illustrations, or odd punctuation or formats."[34]

Rorty's inclusive view comes in the conclusion to the chapter where he summarizes Blumenberg, Nietzsche, Freud, and Davidson as suggesting that "we try to get to the point where we no longer worship *anything*, where we treat *nothing* as a quasi divinity, where we treat *everything*—our language, our conscience, our community, as a product of time and chance. To reach this point would be, in Freud's words, to 'treat chance as worthy of determining our fate.'"[35]

The contingency of self. This contingency is also to be understood to apply to the self. Here Rorty feels that Freud especially led the way, in de-divinizing the self. He did this by "tracking conscience home to its origin in the contingencies of our upbringing."[36] Kant had given up on the idea that in scientific knowledge of hard facts we have a contact with a power outside of ourselves. He reintroduced it, however, with the idea of a righteousness deep within us. Freud, however, offers causal explanations of such experiences as guilt, pity, and love. Whereas the conventional understanding of the self was that there was a real power called Reason, which judged among the claims to adequacy of different courses of moral action, Freud, by showing the sophistication of our unconscious strategies of self-justification, calls in question the idea that there is any such central faculty as reason. In both the Platonic and the Kantian views of morality, the central concept was that morality involves bringing specific actions under general principles. Freud, on the other hand, does not give reasons why we should act in a particular way, or choose a particular course of action, but rather presents a causal explanation of why it is that we do actually so act.[37]

This powerful explanation of the unconscious processes is extended to every area of life. The intellectual is to be understood on this model as well, as simply someone who deals with particular marks and noises. These fantasies can be understood in a fashion parallel to the understanding Davidson offered of metaphor. We can refer to these as "fantasy" when they do not catch on, rather than as poetry or philosophy, and as "genius," rather than eccentricity or perversity, when they do: "The difference between genius and fantasy is not the difference between impresses which lock on to some-

---

[33]Ibid.
[34]Ibid., p. 18.
[35]Ibid., p. 22.
[36]Ibid., p. 30.
[37]Ibid., p. 33.

thing universal, some antecedent reality out there in the world or deep within the self, and those which do not. Rather, it is the difference between idiosyncrasies which just happen to catch on with other people—happen because of the contingencies of some historical situation, some particular need which a given community happens to have at a given time."[38]

So, it appears, Freud has done for the understanding of human nature or of the self what Wittgenstein and Davidson did for the understanding of human language: removed any idea of an essence of it. Rorty summarizes:

> To sum up, poetic, artistic, philosophical, scientific, or political progress results from the accidental coincidence of a private obsession with a public need. Strong poetry, commonsense morality, revolutionary morality, normal science, revolutionary science, and the sort of fantasy which is intelligible to only one person, are all, from a Freudian point of view, different ways of dealing with blind impresses—or, more precisely, ways of dealing with different blind impresses: impresses which are unique to an individual or common to the members of some historically conditioned community. None of these strategies is privileged over others in the sense of expressing human nature better. No such strategy is more or less human than any other, any more than the pen is more truly a tool than the butcher's knife, or the hybridized orchid less a flower than the wild rose.[39]

The contingency of community. The final area of application of the principle of contingency, that of community, stems from Rorty's awareness of a criticism leveled against a view such as his. That is the contention that to say that truth is not "out there" is relativism and irrationalism. His response is that such distinctions are obsolete, clumsy tools, which belong to a vocabulary that we should try to replace. This will not, however, be a matter of argument, strictly speaking. That would be to grant the critic his choice of weapons. Rather, the method Rorty will follow is that which he has already explained, of redescribing certain things, of outflanking the objections by enlarging the scope of the metaphors he uses. His strategy is, in other words, to try to make the vocabulary in which the objections are phrased look bad.[40]

Rorty notes Michael Sandel's criticism, that if one's convictions are only relatively valid, why should one stand for them unflinchingly, and contends that Sandel is herein taking the vocabulary of Enlightenment rationalism for granted. Once again Davidson observes that there is no point outside the historically conditioned particular situation from which we could make such

---

[38]Ibid., p. 37.
[39]Ibid., pp. 37-38.
[40]Ibid., p. 44.

judgments as would be required by an "absolutely valid" viewpoint. What must be done is to accept that which is "relatively valid." In a liberal society there is a belief in the value of a free and open encounter, and *"A liberal society is one which is content to call 'true' whatever the upshot of such encounters turns out to be."*[41] The charge of relativism should not be answered, but rather evaded. A question like "How do you *know* that freedom is the chief goal of social organizations?" should be brushed aside like the question, "How do you *know* that Jones is worthy of your friendship?" Rorty says, "We should see allegiance to social institutions as no more matters for justification by reference to familiar, commonly accepted premises—but also no more arbitrary—than choices of friends or heroes. Such choices are not made by reference to criteria. They cannot be preceded by presupposition-less critical reflection, conducted in no particular language and outside of any particular historical context."[42]

Virtue and a liberal society. From the standpoint of traditional philosophy, with its belief in intrinsic qualities of Truth and Goodness within Reality, it would appear that it would not be possible for Rorty to maintain an ethic. In what would virtues and vice inhere, if such are created by the community? How can one maintain that something ought to be done, on this seemingly arbitrary basis?

Rorty, however, is quick to insist on the combination of individual irony (that is, the belief that the true and the good do not inhere in reality) with liberal community. He is quite unequivocal about the negative value of cruelty. He is aware of the criticisms that it is not possible to combine this private irony with a public liberal hope. The first criticism is that the public-private split he is talking about simply will not work. Without some metaphysical undergirding, a liberal society will dissolve. While granting that it may turn out to be the case that this fear is true, he thinks there is good basis for thinking it false, and that is the analogy to the decline of religious faith. There were those who argued that without some sort of postmortem reward or punishment, liberal societies would be weakened, but Rorty contends that just the opposite has actually been the case: "As it turned out," Rorty says, "however, willingness to endure suffering for the sake of future reward was transferable from individual rewards to social ones, from one's hopes for paradise to one's hopes for one's grandchildren."[43]

The second objection is the more serious: that it is psychologically impossible to be a private ironist and a public liberal, in other words, "to be some-

---

[41]Ibid., p. 52.
[42]Ibid., p. 54.
[43]Rorty, "Private Irony and Liberal Hope," in *Contingency, Irony, and Solidarity*, p. 85.

one for whom 'cruelty is the worse thing we do,' and to have no meta-physical beliefs about what all human beings have in common."[44] Does not the idea that we all have an obligation to overcome cruelty presuppose some common quality within human beings that deserves respect, regardless of the vocabulary they use?

The ironist differs from the metaphysician in two important respects. On the one hand, the ironist believes that the "redescriptions" which serve a liberal society are those which ask, "What humiliates?" whereas the metaphysician also wants to ask, "Why should I avoid humiliating?" The metaphysician wants to bolster the wish to be kind with arguments, whereas the ironist simply wants to improve the chances of being kind.[45]

What, then, does the ironist see as uniting him or her to the rest of the human race? It is not a common language but a common susceptibility to a sort of pain that humans do not share with animals: humiliation. Rorty says, "On her [the ironist's] conception, human solidarity is not a matter of sharing a common truth or a common goal but of sharing a common selfish hope, the hope that one's world—the little things around which one has woven into one's final vocabulary—will not be destroyed."[46] Unlike the liberal metaphysician, who sees liberal culture as centering around theory, the liberal ironist thinks it centers around literature.[47]

In the end, Rorty makes a sort of admission, which is also something of a disclaimer:

> The suspicion that ironism in philosophy has not helped liberalism is quite right, but that is not because ironist philosophy is inherently cruel. It is because liberals have come to expect philosophy to do a certain job—namely, answering questions like "Why not be cruel?" and "Why be kind?"—and they feel that any philosophy which refuses this assignment must be heartless. But that expectation is a result of a metaphysical upbringing. If we could get rid of the expectation, liberals would not ask ironist philosophy to do a job which it cannot do, and which it defines itself as unable to do.[48]

Analytical Summary
The several strands of Rorty's thought, sometimes rather repetitious in nature, now need to be drawn together.

1. Rorty's thought is a nonessentialism. While not denying the existence of an external world, Rorty rejects the idea that truth is out there, waiting to

---

[44]Ibid.
[45]Ibid., p. 91.
[46]Ibid., p. 92.
[47]Ibid., p. 93.
[48]Ibid., p. 94.

be discovered. He has no confidence in real essences, either in the world external to our consciousness or in the self. This is not a dogma of positive belief, but simply a type of agnosticism.

2. There is, accordingly, an antirealism, and an antirepresentationalism with respect to language. Language is not seen as representing any nonlinguistic reality.

3. There is a contingency and a historical conditionedness to the understanding of the world, the self, language, and community. These are products of our community.

4. Truth is not to be understood as agreement with or correspondence of our ideas or language to the "real world." It is rather that which works, which enables us to cope with, or to deal with, reality.

5. For the most part, the traditional questions of philosophy should not be answered, but simply ignored, or the subject should be changed. This pragmatism should not be understood as offering alternative answers to the traditional questions, but simply as ignoring the questions as unfruitful. Solutions are not found in appealing to a better set of facts, but in redescribing the situation, enabling us to see things in a better way.

6. Ethical values are not grounded on some metaphysical basis, but simply are the consensus of one's community. The concern is for finding ways to minimize cruelty, for example, but not to give final answers as to why cruelty is wrong.

7. This is a pragmatism, but genuinely a *neo*-pragmatism. While sharing many of the features of the later pragmatists, such as James and Dewey, it also goes beyond that. James, for example, said of the definition of truth: "Truth, as any dictionary will tell you, is a property of certain of our ideas. It means their 'agreement,' as falsity means their disagreement, with 'reality.' Pragmatists and intellectualists both accept this definition as a matter of course. They begin to quarrel only after the question is raised as to what may precisely be meant by the term 'agreement,' and what by the term 'reality,' when reality is taken as something for our ideas to agree with."[49] It is difficult to imagine Rorty making the first part of that statement, even with the qualifications in the latter part.

---

[49]William James, "Pragmatism's Conception of Truth," in *"Pragmatism," and Four Essays from "The Meaning of Truth"* (New York: Meridian, 1955), p. 132.

9

---

stanley fish

Ιn the United States, a major form of postmodernism has been as a school of literary criticism, especially associated with the "Yale school" of criticism, including Harold Bloom, J. Hillis Miller, and Paul de Man. Another whose thought has been especially influential is Stanley Fish.

Communities and Interpretation

The essay that gives its title to what is probably Fish's most influential book is drawn from an incident that occurred following the opening day of the class of one of Fish's colleagues when he was at Johns Hopkins. A student came to the professor and asked him, "Is there a text in this class?" Without hesitating, the teacher replied, "Yes; it's the *Norton Anthology of Literature*." The student then said, "No, No. I mean in this class do we believe in poems and things, or is it just us?" While realizing that there are those who would regard this anecdote as an illustration of the dangers of listening to people like Fish, who "preach the instability of the text and the unavailability of determinate meanings," his intention is to use it to show "how baseless the fear of these dangers finally is."[1]

Criticism of postmodern critics. If the incident just recounted was one facet of the immediate occasion for the writing of this and several other

---

[1]Stanley Fish, *Is There a Text in This Class? The Authority of Interpretive Communities* (Cambridge, Mass.: Harvard University Press, 1980), p. 305.

essays reprinted in the book, there was also another origin of it, namely, Meyer Abrams's paper "How to Do Things with Texts." That was an attack on the thought of Jacques Derrida, Harold Bloom, and Fish, whom Abrams terms "Newreaders." The specific charge brought by Abrams is that each of the Newreaders engages in a double game, of "introducing his own inter- pretive strategy when reading someone else's text, but tacitly relying on communal norms when undertaking to communicate the methods and results of his interpretations to his own readers." By using the standard language in deconstructing the standard language, the presumption that they are understood argues against their own position.[2]

Fish says that Abrams's most persistent charge against these Newreaders is that they ignore the literal normative meanings of texts, and move those texts into a realm of indeterminacy, in which "no text can mean anything in particular" and "we can never say just what anyone means by anything he writes."[3] Thus, the literal meaning, which somehow resides objectively within the text, is overridden by the actions of willful interpreters.

Status of normative meaning. In light of this debate Fish raises the ques- tion of the normative or literal or linguistic meaning of the question the stu- dent presented initially to the professor. He contends that within the framework of the current critical debate there seemingly could only be two answers to that question: "either there *is* a literal meaning of the utterance and we should be able to say what it is, or there are as many meanings as there are readers and no one of them is literal."[4] On the contrary, he sug- gests that the answer is that the utterance, "Is there a text in this class?" actually has *two* literal meanings. In the circumstances that the professor assumed, the utterance is an inquiry about the nature of the course require- ments, whether there is a required textbook. On the other hand, in the cir- cumstances which the student had in mind and to which she then alerted the instructor, the question is "about the instructor's position on the status of the text."[5]

In Fish's interpretation of the situation, the instructor did not choose between two possible meanings; he simply responded in terms of what seemed the obvious meaning of the statement, and when the student altered his understanding of the situation he responded in terms of an equally inescapable meaning. In neither case was meaning imposed on the text. Rather, says Fish, "both interpretations were a function of precisely the

---

[2]Ibid., p. 303. The quotation from Abrams is from *Partisan Review* 4 (1979): 587.
[3]Ibid., p. 305.
[4]Ibid., pp. 305-6.
[5]Ibid., p. 306.

public and constituting norms (of language and understanding) invoked by Abrams." The difference between Fish and Abrams comes in the interpretation of the status of those norms. Rather than being "embedded in the language," whence they could be read out by any unbiased reader, they "inhere in an institutional structure within which one hears utterances as already organized with reference to certain assumed purposes and goals." Since both the professor and the student are situated within the same structure, "their interpretive activities are not free, but what constrains them are the understood practices and assumptions of the institution and not the rules and fixed meanings of a language system."[6]

Fish contends that neither meaning of the utterance would be immediately available to all native speakers of the language. The meaning that the instructor assumed would only be available to someone familiar with what transpires on the first day of class. Such a person does not apply the knowledge of that particular phenomenon to the utterance after the fact, but rather, the person hears it under the influence of that knowledge. It is actually present and operative in the very hearing of what is said. Similarly, for someone to hear and understand the meaning as explained by the student would require a familiarity with the issues of contemporary literary theory. Further, Fish says he is not saying that there are some hearers for whom the words would be completely unintelligible, but that for some, they would be understood in a sense different from either of these. For example, it could be understood as an inquiry regarding the location of an object, as for example, "I think I left my text in this class; have you seen it?" This possibility raises for some the fear that there is an infinite number of possible meanings. Such is not the case, however, according to Fish. In any of the possible settings of the utterance, there are severe constraints on the possible meaning, so that there could not be an infinite plurality of meanings. But such a fear is justified only if sentences existed not already embedded in some situation or other. Such a state, "if it could be located, would be the normative one, and it would be disturbing indeed if the norm were free-floating and indeterminate. But there is no such state; sentences emerge only in situations, and within those situations, the normative meaning of an utterance will always be obvious or at least accessible, although within another situation that same utterance, no longer the same, will have another normative meaning that will be no less obvious and accessible."[7]

To be sure, in most such alternative options of meaning, there is one that will be accessible to more people, simply because more people are familiar

---

[6]Ibid.
[7]Ibid., pp. 307-8.

with the situation in which it is embedded. In this case, the understanding the professor initially had of the utterance would be the one that more people would think of, simply because the meaning the student had in mind presupposes a situation with which fewer persons would be familiar. When the group of those familiar with such a situation includes a great many people, that particular meaning will appear so customary and even obvious that it seems "natural."[8] Indeed, that will seem to many to be *the* meaning of the text.

Fish considers this an important point, because it counters a contention made by Abrams and E. D. Hirsch. Hirsch argues from a shared understanding of ordinary language that there is a core of determinate meanings. He offers as an example, ""The air is crisp," and expects his readers to agree on the shared and normative verbal meaning of that statement. Hirsch does not even feel it necessary to argue for it, and Fish considers his optimism regarding the meaning of this particular phrase to be well founded. The obviousness of the meaning is not, says Fish, because the meaning is in a linguistic system independent of any context. Rather, it is because such a phrase is heard as already embedded in a context. That this is the case can be seen by thinking of these words, "The air is crisp," as being in the context of a discussion of music, so that the meaning would be, "When the piece is played correctly, the air is crisp." Actually, the meaning of the sentence was in a context, and Fish claims that the evidence for that is that no specification of the context was given. He says, "That is, it is impossible even to think of a sentence independently of a context, and when we are asked to consider a sentence for which no context has been specified, we will automatically hear it in the context in which it has been most often encountered."[9]

Certain conclusions can be drawn from these two examples. The first is that the hearer or reader of these utterances is not constrained by some meaning that words have in a normative linguistic system. Yet, one is not free to confer on them any meaning one wishes. Indeed, says Fish, the word *confer* is misleading, because it suggests a two-stage process of scrutinizing a sentence and then giving it a meaning. He summarizes: "The argument of the preceding pages can be reduced to the assertion that there is no such first stage, that one hears an utterance within, and not as preliminary to determining, a knowledge of its purposes and concerns, and that to so hear it is already to have assigned it a shape and given it a meaning."[10]

The role of expectations in interpretation. Fish makes his point further in

---

[8]Ibid., pp. 308-9.
[9]Ibid., p. 310.
[10]Ibid.

the chapter "How to Recognize a Poem When You See One." Here he tells of listing a group of names, one to a line, and then telling the students that this was a poem. That next class was a group of students who were engaged in the study of English religious poetry of the seventeenth century. When they saw the list of names, they immediately attempted to interpret the "poem," finding religious significance in it. Fish contends that the students were not simply responding to meanings that inhered in the symbol itself. They recognized that they were dealing with a poem, and then the distinguishing features followed. He puts it clearly: "In other words, acts of recognition, rather than being triggered by formal characteristics, are their source. It is not that the presence of poetic qualities compels a certain kind of attention but that the paying of a certain kind of attention results in the emergence of poetic qualities."[11] Interpretation is therefore understood quite differently than it has been previously. Whereas skilled reading has been thought to be a matter of discernment, of being able to detect what was there, it can now be seen to be a matter of knowing how to *produce* what is then said to be there. Thus interpreters, rather than decoding poems, make them.[12] This is not, according to Fish, an isolated incident. He has been able to reproduce it, and others can do the same as well. The students would be able to do what they did, regardless of the name we choose to describe their action.[13]

This constituting argument is not restricted to poems, or even to assignments, however. Some would argue that there is a bedrock level on which the names constitute neither an assignment nor a poem, but rather a list. Fish insists, however, that this argument also fails, because for this to be seen as a list requires the concepts of seriality, hierarchy, subordination and so on. While these seem to be available to almost everyone, they are not somehow inherent, either in the names known or in the knower, but are learned concepts. Even if one attempts to take the more basic entities, such as letters, paper, and graphite as objective, these also are constituted as they are only because of some system or other. He concludes "that all objects are made and not found, and that they are made by the interpretive strategies we set in motion."[14]

Rebuttal of the charge of subjectivism. At this point, the usual charge is that Fish's view falls into subjectivism. Fish is unwilling to accept the validity of such a contention, however. What prevents his view from becoming subjectivism is that the means by which these interpretive strategies are carried

---

[11]Ibid., p. 326.
[12]Ibid., p. 327.
[13]Ibid., p. 328.
[14]Ibid., p. 331.

out are not individual and hence subjective, but rather social and conventional. That is to say, the "you" who does the interpreting is not an isolated individual, but a collective or communal you. In the language of Southern American English, it is always "y'all," rather than simply "you."[15] While we indeed create objects, we create "through interpretive strategies that are finally not our own but have their source in a publicly available system of intelligibility."[16]

It is not merely the objects, such as poems and lists, which are created, however. It is also ourselves. The system, which in this case is a literary system, also fashions us who are creating these objects. It does so by furnishing us with the categories of understanding that we use in constructing these objects. Fish has thus removed the self as well as the externally known realities from the realm of free-standing, intrinsic entities.[17]

Returning to the external world, Fish generalizes his contention that poems and lists are created to include "every object or event that becomes available within an institutional setting."[18] He illustrates this with another classroom incident. While he was lecturing, one student began vigorously waving his hand. Fish asked the class what it was that the student was doing, and they all answered that the student was seeking permission to speak. When asked how they knew that this was the case, they replied that it was obvious. Actually, Fish asserts, the meaning that they found in the student's action would not have been available to someone who did not know what was involved in being a student. Such a person might have thought that the student was pointing to the lights or to something that was about to fall. Or, if the student had actually been an elementary or middle-school student, he might have been seeking permission to go to the bathroom. Here again Fish makes the point that there is neither objectivism nor subjectivism involved. The meaning of the student's gesture is not simply present in an obvious fashion on the surface of the event, nor is the interpretation put on it merely individual and idiosyncratic.[19]

Communal origin of categories of perception. Fish extends his theory further. He contends that these categories, supplied by the community, constitute the very shape of seeing itself. There is not a perceptual ground more basic than this. By that, he means that perceiving and interpreting are not separate acts. There is not a moment in which the students simply see the action of their fellow student, and then give it a significance: "To be in the

---

[15]Ibid.
[16]Ibid., p. 332.
[17]Ibid.
[18]Ibid.
[19]Ibid., pp. 332-33.

situation (this or any other) is to 'see' with the eyes of its interests, its goals, its understood practices, values, and norms, and so to be conferring significance *by* seeing, not after it."[20] When the students perceive their fellow student waving his hand, they do so with the categories in which they understand themselves to be functioning as students. The objects appear to them in forms related to that functioning, rather than in some objective or pre-interpretive form. Even if the object is seen as not related, that itself is specifying what something is not, and thus this is a type of relation. Perception is always situation-specific. Even if someone who was not a student were to enter the room, while he might not see the raised hand as the students do, he would certainly see it in some way. He might consider it evidence of a disease, as a political salute, as a muscular exercise, or as an attempt to kill flies. He would never see it as purely physical data, uninterpreted. His way of seeing would, further, not be individual or idiosyncratic, but a product of an institutional structure.[21]

Fish says that the account he has offered removes the urgency of the arguments of Hirsch, Abrams, and others. They fear that without some normative system of meanings, the reader will simply substitute a purely idiosyncratic meaning for the meaning that the text brings with it, which is usually identified as the intention of the author. Such a fear is unfounded, however, according to Fish, for the meanings the reader finds are not merely his or hers as an individual, but have their source in the interpretive community.[22]

The distinction of subjective and objective is not a helpful one. It could either be said that these meanings are neither subjective nor objective or that they are both subjective and objective. They are not simply read off from the object; they are, however, not merely individual, but are public and conventional. Fish believes that even the use of the terms *subjective* and *objective* has the effect, not of facilitating inquiry, but of shutting it down. The reason for this is that such use assumes the distinction between the interpreter and the object interpreted. That distinction in turn assumes that interpreters and their objects are two different kinds of acontextual entities. Given these two assumptions, the issue can only be one of control: "will texts be allowed to constrain their own interpretation or will irresponsible interpreters by allowed to obscure and overwhelm texts."[23]

Resolution of problems. When viewed in this way, Fish claims, a number of

---

[20]Ibid., p. 334.
[21]Ibid., pp. 334-35.
[22]Ibid., p. 335.
[23]Ibid., p. 336.

problems disappear, not because they have been solved, but rather because we can see they were never problems in the first place. For example, Abrams wonders how, if there is no normative system of stable meanings, two persons could ever agree on the interpretation of a work or even a sentence. This is only really a concern, however, says Fish, if the persons are thought of as isolated individuals, whose agreement must be compelled by something external to them. His characterization of Abrams's view at this point is interesting and instructive.

"There is something of the police state in Abrams's vision, complete with posted rules and boundaries, watchdogs to enforce them, procedures for identifying their violation as criminals."[24] If, however, says Fish, their understandings are informed by the same interpretive principles, "then agreement between them will be assured, and its source will not be a text that enforces its own perception but a way of perceiving that results in the emergence to those who share it (or those whom it shares) of the same text."[25]

This optimism expressed at the end of the chapter on how to recognize a poem may seem to exceed the discussion that has preceded it. Actually, it should be noted that in the examples Fish gives, there is unanimity. All of the students found religious symbolism within the poem, although the understanding of the exact nature of that symbolism differed among them. All of the students understood similarly the waving of the student's hand as a request for permission to speak. This confidence in the potential agreement of different interpreters forms another topic for his discussion.

Accounting for agreement and disagreement. Fish contends further that the ability of his theory to account, not just for agreement, but for disagreement, supports the cogency of his account. On the objectivist account, determinate meaning lies on the surface of things, there to be readily discovered. Some, however, according to Fish, choose not to see it. They perversely substitute their own meanings for the obvious meanings of the texts. There is, however, he claims, no explanation for such waywardness, and he suggests that original sin would seem to be the only relevant model. On this objectivist view, disputes are to be settled simply by referring persons to the relevant facts.[26]

Fish maintains, on the contrary, that it is not possible to resolve disagreements by appeal to the facts, for facts emerge only in the context of some point of view or other. Persons do not disagree because some pay attention to the facts and others do not, but because they hold different points of view,

---

[24]Ibid., p. 337.
[25]Ibid.
[26]Ibid., p. 338.

so that the facts are constituted differently for them: "what is at stake in a disagreement is the right to specify what the facts can hereafter be said to be. Disagreements are not settled by the facts, but are the means by which the facts are settled."[27] In literary criticism this can be seen quite clearly, for everyone claims that his or her interpretation fits the facts best, but everyone's purpose is to persuade others of his or her interpretive principles, in the light of which those facts will appear most indisputable. So, for example, Kathleen Raine and E. D. Hirsch each advance an interpretation that each claims to be definite and obvious, and each claims the same word as internal and confirming evidence for the interpretation.[28]

Finite number of possible interpretations. This is not to say, however, that there can be an infinite number of interpretations of a given piece of writing, that no interpretation can be ruled out. Fish agrees with Wayne Booth that it is right to rule out at least some interpretations, but disagrees on the reason. As a pluralist, Booth holds that there is something in the text that rules out some readings while admitting others. Since the text is always a function of interpretation, however, then for Fish it cannot be the basis of rejection of some interpretations. That leaves him with an apparent impasse: that while there seems to be no basis for labeling an interpretation unacceptable, we actually do it all the time.[29]

This problem only exists, says Fish, if we assume that the activity of interpretation is unconstrained. Actually, the shape of that activity is under the limitation that the literary institution will at any time allow only a limited number of interpretive strategies. There are unwritten rules as to what it means to operate within the literary institution. While there is always a category of things that are not done, the makeup of that category is continually changing. The change happens in two ways. One is laterally, as one moves from one subcommunity to another. The other is the change of what was once considered an unacceptable interpretive strategy becoming acceptable.[30]

There are currently unacceptable readings of each piece of literature. Fish considers the possibility of an "Eskimo reading" of Faulkner's "A Rose for Emily": it describes an Eskimo. Anyone who proposes such a reading would find that it would not be accepted in the literary community. The reason for this is that there are currently no recognized interpretive strategies for producing the text in this fashion. Yet, such an interpretive strategy

---

[27]Ibid.
[28]Ibid., p. 339.
[29]Ibid., p. 342.
[30]Ibid., pp. 342-44.

could arise, in which case there would be an Eskimo "A Rose for Emily," in addition to a Freudian, a mythological, a christological, a regional, a socio-logical, and a linguistic "A Rose for Emily."[31] It is not some inherent content or feature of texts that rules out certain interpretations, but rather the absence of recognized interpretative strategies.

Two Models of Critical Activity

Fish's final contribution in this book is a chapter contrasting two models of critical activity: demonstration and persuasion. He acknowledges again the objectivist's fear that if interpretation determines what will count as fact, or text, there will be no limitation on the conclusions that can be reached. On that way of thinking, interpretation is in need of constraints, to limit what it can do. Actually, says Fish, interpretation is a structure of constraints. It has its own internal set of rules and regulations, its own list of prescribed and proscribed activities.[32]

The problem critics see with the approach Fish is advocating is that there cannot be any end to the succession of interpretations. For if changes in interpretation are not based on more accurately presenting an independent text, but rather on conventions of criticism that may be exchanged for oth-ers, then there is no assurance that one such criticism will not and should not be exchanged for another. If this is the case, then criticism becomes a cynical activity, in which one advocates a particular point of view simply because it is likely to win points or because no one has as yet propounded it.[33]

In fact, the charge is that on Fish's view, the whole institution of liter-ary education is actually something of a hoax. The question posed by E. D. Hirsch, "On what grounds does [the teacher of literature] claim that his 'read-ing' is more valid than that of any pupil?" is a pertinent one.[34] Fish asserts that what we believe at a given time we consider true, even though we know that we have previously held with an equal degree of certainty views that we now do not hold, and know that this present view will at some point in the future be replaced in our thinking. The mind is constituted by the categories of understanding and is not capable of achieving the sort of distance from them that would make skepticism possible. Consequently one believes what one believes and does so without reservation. Knowing that one's perspective is limited does not make one's convictions seem any less real.[35]

---

[31] Ibid., pp. 346-47.
[32] Ibid., p. 356.
[33] Ibid., p. 358.
[34] Ibid., p. 359.
[35] Ibid., pp. 360-61.

Demonstration versus persuasion. Fish draws a distinction between two approaches in teaching. The approach of demonstration is based on the assumption that there are objective facts, independent of any awareness of them, and proceeds by attempting to demonstrate how these support a given interpretation. The approach of persuasion, on the other hand, frankly acknowledges that it comes from a particular orientation, and that the facts that one appeals to are available only from a perspective already assumed. Here one tells students and readers what one already sees and attempts to persuade them to adopt this same perspective, so that they also may see what the teacher sees.[36]

The status of arguments. Two questions remain for Fish. One is the status of the argument he has been presenting. He has been saying that all arguments are made from some particular perspective, based on certain assumptions or presuppositions. Does not this argument also apply to itself, however? Does it not make the argument no more secure than that which it is trying to oppose? His answer is, yes, but "so what?" Since there is no privileged point of view, everyone will have to engage in persuasion, of the type that he has engaged in. In the case of his view, much of this has been showing the groundlessness of the fears some have of what will happen if his view is adopted.[37]

Practical consequences. The other question that must be raised concerns the practical consequences of Fish's argument. If his view is adopted, how will that affect the practice of literary criticism, or the way one reads and teaches poetry? His answer is that it has no implications whatsoever. The assumption that for something to be interesting it must affect our everyday experiences of poetry is tied to the ideology of the New Criticism, and therefore is not an assumption he makes. Moreover, discussion of such matters as the status of the text simply does go on, and anyone who is able to advance the discussion of them will be accorded a hearing. The fact that people were willing to come and hear his lectures is evidence of that.[38]

Ethical Judgments

In the book *There's No Such Thing as Free Speech, and It's a Good Thing, Too,* Fish addresses somewhat broader issues, although the basic thesis and position is largely the same as that which we have examined in his earlier writing. Here he approaches what might be called broadly, ethical issues, or at least the basis of ethical judgments, whereas the material we have already

---

[36]Ibid., p. 365.
[37]Ibid., pp. 368-69.
[38]Ibid., pp. 370-71.

looked at was more concerned with the basis of literary critical judgments. He is particularly concerned to discuss the objectivist position in these matters. On that conventional approach, there are certain concepts and phrases that serve to settle matters, because they are considered to be absolute in some sense. These are terms like *justice, reason, neutrality, free speech*, and the like. By Fish's own declaration he is going to approach these with considerable skepticism; indeed, the title, *There's No Such Thing as Free Speech*, indicates that he holds these concepts to be rather mythical. He states his thesis clearly: "My argument is that when such words and phrases are invoked, it is almost always as part of an effort to deprive moral and legal problems of their histories so that merely formal calculations can then be performed on phenomena that have been flattened out and no longer have their real-world shape."[39]

Historical conditioning. Fish's point is that our understanding of such concepts as justice, and our judgment of what fulfills them, is historically conditioned. There is no absolute or transcendental standard to which these could be compared, or by which they might be measured. He illustrates this point in his opening chapter. In the movie version of *How to Succeed in Business Without Really Trying*, two men, one of them the boss's nephew, are assigned to the mailroom. One of them is to be made head of the mailroom, and the executive who is to choose which it will be announces, "I've been told to choose the new head of the mailroom on merit alone." The boss's nephew responds, "That's not fair."[40]

Is or is not such a policy fair? Most of us would tend to respond, "Of course it is fair that a person should be selected on the basis of merit, not on the basis of family relationship." That, however, does not seem to be the case in the mind of the boss's nephew. He has come to his position expecting that his family connection will gain him the promotion. Now, in his judgment, the rules are being changed in the middle of the game. That seems clearly unfair. Fish's point is that although ideas like merit and fairness seem to be perspicuous, or obvious to anyone, they actually "have different meanings in relation to different assumptions and background conditions," in other words, that they are conditioned by our setting, background, experience, and various aspects of our identity.[41] To the nephew, his family relationship is part of merit.

The contest over setting the terms. The usual understanding of much of the

---

[39]Stanley Fish, *There's No Such Thing as Free Speech, and It's a Good Thing, Too* (New York: Oxford University Press, 1994), p. viii.
[40]Ibid., p. 3.
[41]Ibid., p. 4.

debate that goes on in relationship to the law assumes that there is some sort of absolute justice, fairness, or merit. Winning the debate over who should be treated in a particular way is a matter of showing how that side's cause more fully conforms to this pure concept of justice. Fish advances a quite different interpretation and argument, however. What happens in these situations is that one side manages to define merit in such a way that it accords with its own assumptions and practice. He says that "getting hold of the concept of merit and stamping it with your own brand is a good strategy."[42] He claims that those who have opposed multiculturalism, feminism, ethnic studies, and the like in recent years have been particularly adept at this strategy. The usual method of doing this is to claim that the movement or position opposed is insufficiently general to be the basis of a judgment or a program. It is, in other words, a *special interest.* Those who advance such a program as feminism have an axe to grind, whereas, presumably, those who oppose it are much more objective and more broadly concerned. The "isms" are narrow and political, rather than genuinely aesthetic or rational. They cannot be compared to the claims made in the name of "truths that pass beyond time and circumstance; truths that, transcending accidents of class, race and gender, speak to us all."[43]

Reason and faith. In his discussion of a pamphlet by Lynne Cheney advocating certain general truths, Fish says that two important questions must be raised: "What are these truths and how and *by whom* are they to be identified?" The reason these questions must be raised, and in this form, is that no one thinks himself or herself to be consciously choosing untruth. All think themselves to be representing the truth. In light of these conflicting claims, it is necessary to ask which of these are timeless and which are temporally and locally conditioned. The usual way of making such a determination is through the use of reason, but the problem is what seems a reason for one person may not seem to be that at all to another. Fish makes a significant assertion: "Reasons do not confirm or shore up your faith; they are extensions of your faith and are reasons *for you* because of what you already believe at a level so fundamental that it is not (at least while you are in the grip of belief) available for self-conscious scrutiny."[44] This leads to a rather universal inference: "It would seem, then, that no one is or could be capable of making the necessary determination (the determination of which proffered truths are the genuinely transcendent ones) because everyone is so enmeshed in time and circumstance that only circumstantial and timely

---

[42]Ibid., p. 6.
[43]Ibid., p. 7.
[44]Ibid.

(i.e., historically bounded) truths will be experienced as perspicuous."[45]

Those who have most vigorously opposed political correctness and similar movements have done so by contending that these are indeed political movements, and as such, have inappropriately intruded into the academic or scholarly realm. Fish's response is not to defend political correctness by denying that it is political. Rather, he claims that all participants in the debate are political. While many bill themselves as nonpolitical or apolitical, many conservatives actually want a campus that comports with their standard of political correctness.[46]

The charge of relativism. This statement of course evokes the charge of relativism, but such a charge assumes that judgments of such issues as fairness are made by identification with some transcendent or general standards. If, then, there is no source of authority capable of commanding everyone's acceptance, there will be no way to distinguish right from wrong, to choose one argument over another. Such concerns, however, says Fish, reflect a conception of humans as standing apart from all contexts of judgment. This is not the case. In fact, he argues, "none of us is ever in that 'originary' position, unattached to any normative assumptions and waiting for external guidance; rather, we are always and already embedded in one or more practices whose norms, rules, and aspirations we have internalized, and therefore we are not only capable of making distinctions and passing judgments but cannot refrain from doing so."[47]

The main part of the *Free Speech* book is a report of Fish's side of a series of debates between himself and Dinesh D'Souza. He makes clear the target of his argument by saying that the thesis of the five essays in this part of the book is "that the antimulticulturalist, anti-affirmative action, antifeminist, antigay, antiethnic studies backlash has proceeded in just the manner I have described [i.e., by claiming its definitions of terms to be absolute], and it is the effort of these chapters to deprive the backlashers of a vocabulary to which no one has an exclusive claim."[48] Interestingly, later in his introduction he seems to shift the target. Speaking of the vocabulary such as free speech, fairness, and merit, he says, "That vocabulary is by and large the vocabulary of liberalism, and it is the structure of liberal thought that is my target in every one of these essays."[49] Liberalism had seen the conflict between different ideologies that has occurred, and sought to find ways to reduce the conflict by producing neutral procedural mechanisms.

---

[45]Ibid., pp. 7-8.
[46]Ibid., p. 9.
[47]Ibid., p. 10.
[48]Ibid., p. 11.
[49]Ibid., p. 16.

Fish is speaking of what we generally term modernism, and sees a contradiction between "a strong acknowledgment of the unavailability of a transcendent perspective of the kind provided by traditional Christianity" on the one hand and on the other hand a faith "in the capacity of partial (in two senses) human intelligences to put aside their partialities and hew to a standard that transcends them."[50] It is popular to introduce the idea of the marketplace of ideas, where ideas may compete freely, and those that are most soundly based on fact or reality will emerge as victorious. This very idea, however, is itself ideologically colored, for the boundaries of the discourse are defined by reference to ideological presuppositions. "Reason" is appealed to as the neutral arbiter of disputes. This idea of a neutral judge is highly appealing, and seems a possibility as long as one remains on the level of abstraction. Whenever the discussion moves to concrete specific cases, however, "the imperative to Reason takes the form of giving *reasons*, and there is a huge and fatal disparity between the claim of Reason to be independent of ideology and the pedigree of any of the reasons you might think to give. This is so because the reasons you think to give will always be a function of the personal and institutional history that has brought you to a moment of dispute."[51]

The interpretive turn. Fish claims that a major change has taken place in what he terms "the *intellectual* configuration of scholarly inquiry." This "interpretive turn" involves a reversal of the traditional understanding of the relationship of language to its object. The usual conception had been that objects are logically prior, and that language serves the purpose of describing them. The newer version is that "language has been promoted to a constitutive role and declared by theorists of various stripes . . . to bring facts into being rather than simply report on them."[52] Thus, if a literary critic understands the categories available to him or her to be lyric, drama, epic, and novel, then he or she will see something identified as a literary work as one of these, and the details of such a work will be seen in light of what this person thinks to be appropriate to that category. Similarly, if one has as categories of historical description such concepts as progress, decline, consolidation, and dispersion, then "historical inquiry will *produce* events that display those characteristics rather than the very different characteristics that might emerge in the wake of an alternative descriptive vocabulary."[53]

Part of Fish's argument is historical: "The revolution, if that is the word,

---

[50]Ibid.
[51]Ibid., pp. 17-18.
[52]Ibid., p. 56.
[53]Ibid., p. 57.

has succeeded and passed through several stages of revision." Again, "if there is now no vigorous discussion of deconstruction in the academy, it is because its lessons have been absorbed and its formulations—the irreducibility of difference, the priority of the signifier over the signified, the social construction of the self—have been canonized."[54] This is an accomplished fact. It is apparent that Fish is not simply discussing literary criticism, and that this is a much more inclusive phenomenon: "if poststructuralism has given way to postmodernism as the new all-purpose term, it is because the implications of the first term are now being extended far beyond the realm of aesthetics and philosophy to the very texture of everyday life."[55] The revolution, whatever one may call it, now seems to be of such proportions that its theoretical basis is functioning much like the metanarratives and worldviews of an earlier period.

Analytical Summary

1. Texts do not have literal normative meanings that are objectively present within the texts themselves.

2. The meaning of a text is that which it has within a given interpretive community.

3. Consequently, the reader is not free to give any individual meaning to a text, but is constrained by the community's interpretation. There is not an infinite number of possible interpretations of a text.

4. Perceiving and interpreting are not two separate stages in a process. The community supplies the very categories of perception itself.

5. The terms *objective* and *subjective* are not helpful, since they suggest a distinction between the interpreter and the object interpreted.

6. Disputes cannot be resolved by appeal to the facts, but are the means by which the facts are settled. Reasons do not confirm one's faith; they are extensions of one's faith.

7. Our judgments about ethical issues are historically conditioned.

---

[54]Ibid.
[55]Ibid.

part 3

---

evaluating postmodernism

10

positive evaluation of postmodernism

Postmodernism has a number of values, which can be beneficial if we see and appreciate them. In doing so, however, we must first distinguish types of postmodernism, or more correctly, differing themes or strands that can be found within a given postmodern author. These, then, in turn, give rise to differing interpretations of that author's thought. For want of better terminology, we may call these the conservative and the more radical varieties or interpretations of postmodernism. For example, Derrida may be interpreted as saying merely that there is always an element of the contradictory within any scheme of thought, that there is always both positive and negative evidence for a particular idea, and that we therefore should hold our views with a certain degree of tentativity. On the other hand, there are times when he seems to be saying something much more radical, as that there are alternative logics, and that something may be both true and untrue—apparently even at the same time and in the same respect. Very different understandings and estimations of Derrida's thought can be formulated, depending on which of these strands one emphasizes.

It is important, however, to keep both in mind, and to remember that one cannot assume, especially with a deconstructionist, that if he holds a particular tenet, he may not also hold its contradictory. So one president, in recommending for tenure an "evangelical deconstructionist" on his faculty, said in response to criticisms by the board of trustees of that school, "But he says x." To this president, unacquainted with deconstruction, that settled the question of whether the professor in question believed not-x, which unfortunately he also affirmed. Much of what follows in this chapter rests on a more conservative reading of these postmodernists. Whether this interpretation can be maintained will have to be considered in a subsequent chapter.

This is not to say that the postmodernist is, by virtue of calling attention to these issues, necessarily immune from criticism on their basis. Most of us have greater facility for seeing a problem in someone else than in recognizing it in ourselves, but that does not mitigate the value of insights we may have. Insights are valid, unless they rest on a denial of themselves. This means that, in the final analysis, we may learn from the failures of postmodernists as well as from their successes.

The Conditioned Nature of Knowledge

The deconstructionists, following the lead of the sociologists of knowledge, have correctly pointed out the influence of time, place, and culture on our perception of the true and on our conclusions. The degree of such influence, and the response to this fact, will of course be an issue for debate.

One rather easily identified version of this is the way the very choice of issues to address is affected by time and place. If one examines the statements of faith drawn up by theological conservatives during the fundamentalist-modernist controversy, one will note the general absence of references to Jesus' humanity. This was not because the framers of those affirmations of faith did not believe in his humanity, but because that was not under dispute. The argument sometimes advanced that "the church has never taken a stand on that" because that issue has not been settled by a council or a creed, rests on the fact that, in most of those cases, there was no delineation because the issue was not in dispute.

James Orr, in his *Progress of Dogma*, pointed out that different doctrines came in for attention at different times in the history of the church.[1] Even the choice of topics for discussion is a function of time. There was little debate over the method and process of the origin of humans until the publication of Darwin's *Origin of Species* and other subsequent similar works. The inerrancy of Scripture supplanted the sequence of events connected with the second coming as a major topic for debate, just as the latter had earlier replaced the virgin birth as a primary topic.

This also suggests, however, that the point in time may affect not only the primacy of topics addressed, but the orientation to them. Who, for example, can claim that his or her view of the doctrine of justification, of interpretation of the book of Romans, has not been influenced by the fact that

---

[1]James Orr, *The Progress of Dogma* (Grand Rapids, Mich.: Eerdmans, n.d.), pp. 20-32.

Martin Luther lived and wrote his commentary on Romans?

Location geographically, culturally, and socioeconomically also has an effect on our understanding. My doctoral mentor, a Canadian, remarked in class one day that his son was receiving in an American school a different understanding of the American Revolution than what he had been given in a Canadian school. A more contemporary example is the great difference between white Americans and African Americans in their reaction to the O. J. Simpson murder trial verdict. Numerous similar influences could be noted. The Sermon on the Mount and Paul's teaching in Romans 13 might be read quite differently by someone oppressed by a totalitarian regime than by a Christian in a high elected position in American government.

The Effect of Presuppositional Differences

Unfortunately, what happens when we are unaware of our own presuppositions is that we also are unaware that they color our understanding of what we perceive. Consequently, we unconsciously read them into the biblical text, or into other writings. We filter those writings through our own interpretational grid.

One place where this becomes particularly influential is in the evaluation of another view. For years I have taught my students that in a critical paper, "I disagree" is not a satisfactory criticism. When I receive a paper with such a comment on it, I usually write a snide comment like, "So you and he disagree. Who's right, you or he?" A fair amount of criticism is made from the perspective of the critic, assuming as criteria for evaluation, the critic's view. To the extent that the thinker being criticized does not accept that view or portion of it being employed, that is not a valid criticism. Such criticism is merely an expression of difference. Valid criticism uses either criteria that the person being criticized would accept, or some other, universal criteria, which all such views must fulfill.

Of course, what usually happens in these situations is that we do not recognize that these are presuppositions. They appear to us to be simply the way things are. Some careful identification of our own presuppositions will need to be made if we are to engage in this sort of activity. This is particularly a problem for persons working within a strong tradition. Sometimes criticisms of Lutheran theologians by Reformed theologians boils down to something like, "This is not truly Reformed." That, however, begs the question of the truth of the Reformed system.

This means that we also must evaluate scholarly contributions in light of the author's intention. The first rule of writing book reviews is "Read the book," and its first subrule is "And be sure to include the preface in your reading." Much of the distortion that takes place in interpreting the thought of others stems from saying, in effect, "If he was trying to do this, then what he has done falls short," when the thinker being examined may not have had any such intention in mind, and probably told the reader or hearer so. It could, of course, be contended that the writer should have dealt with this topic, or should have attempted to fulfill this goal, but that is quite another matter, and it must be argued, not merely asserted. We cannot require adherence to our agenda unless we are prepared to defend the inevitability of that agenda. To fail to do so will make us appear absurd.

More subtle is the unconscious use of our own position to interpret another person's thought while not entering fully into her or his presuppositions. The thoughts of the other are filtered through our presuppositional grid. The result, to the extent that the presuppositions are inconsistent, is that internal contradiction is found in the other's thought. Actually, there may not be internal contradiction, but rather, the contradiction exists between the other's thought and what the other would hold if she or he were we.

Countless examples of this could be given. My master's thesis dealt with an article by a philosopher analyzing the thought of Plato. He found two major concepts in Plato that he felt were self-contradictory, one of which was the self-predication conception. This concept holds that the forms are predicated of themselves, that is, that the form of whiteness is white, that the form of humanity is a human being, and so on. This concept, however, assumes an Aristotelian subject and attribute scheme that is foreign to Plato, as properly understood. The thrust of the argument was that Plato was not a very good Aristotelian, which I am sure would not have bothered Plato in the slightest.[2] A similar instance can be found in the recent dispute between Thomas Morris and William Mann over the doctrine of divine simplicity.[3] Morris analyses Mann's property instance concept through basically Aristotelian property-attribute categories, whereas the property instance idea works perfectly well, without internal contradiction, on Platonic categories. If we are going to argue in this fashion, we must be prepared to defend our right to use such criteria, that is, to defend our own position as true.

Another form of this problem is the fallacy of the suppressed premise. Frequently an argument proceeds by using premises that are themselves the conclusion of another argument. The person advancing the argument

---

[2]Millard J. Erickson, "Platonic Forms and Self-Predication: A Critical Examination of Gregory Vlastos' Interpretation of the Third Man Argument in the *Parmenides*" (master's thesis, University of Chicago, June 1958).

[3]William E. Mann, "Divine Simplicity," *Religious Studies* 18, no. 4 (1982): 451-71, esp. 465-68; Thomas V. Morris, "On God and Mann: A View of Divine Simplicity," *Religious Studies* 21, no. 3 (1985): 299-318.

does not recognize this, however. He may think that this is the only possible position on this issue. What is happening here is that presuppositions are creeping in unnoticed. This will not do, if the deconstructionists are right, however. An argument may proceed something like this:

All A is B.

Therefore, all A is C.

For the argument to be valid, however, the suppressed premise, "All B is C," must be true. Here what typically happens is that this is not even recognized as a premise. The assumption is made that all B is C, or is not recognized as being an assumption because of course everyone knows that B equals C. That may or may not be the case, however. An argument containing a suppressed and therefore unrecognized premise is an enthymeme. These must be carefully guarded against. Unless the statement "Some B is not C" (the contradictory of "All B is C") is somehow internally contradictory or absurd, the conclusion does not follow, at least not without further argumentation.

This awareness of unnoticed presuppositions may help protect us from some unreflective and even premature commitments. Without suggesting that I approve of the activities of Dr. Jack Kevorkian, I note that many evangelical Christians have made knee-jerk reactions to the issue of assisted suicide, without asking whether there are different species of self-willed death. Are the following morally generic forms of self-willed death: voluntarily sacrificing one's own life for the good of others; bringing about one's death where there was no prospect of immediate death otherwise and no great physical suffering; and altering the conditions of one's death but not altering significantly its time? I am not sure whether they are, or whether there may be morally relevant differences, but we cannot simply short-circuit the reasoning process and be morally or intellectually responsible.

We should be willing to allow ourselves to feel the full force of the postmodernists' contention. This includes the contention that there are alternative logics. Perhaps what seems to us to adhere so obviously to the principles of logic is simply the conditioned view we have acquired. Perhaps it is simply a particular type of logic of a particular variety of Western thought. There may be different ways of reasoning, and there may be different ways of perceiving the world. Ernst Cassirer, for example, tells of certain non-Western persons, who could navigate a river with great precision, but who could not describe the course of the river, and if asked to make a drawing of it, did not seem to understand what was being asked. They had a concrete understanding of space, but not an abstract conception of it.[4] Perhaps

---

[4]Ernst Cassirer, *An Essay on Man: An Introduction to a Philosophy of Human Culture* (Garden City, N.Y.: Doubleday, 1944), pp. 44-46.

this is the case with our traditional logic as well. Is it possible to function with a quite different logic, and to do so without assuming the logic to which it is supposed to be the alternative? That is a question that must be examined carefully and at great length.

The Limitations on Foundationalism

The postmodernists have correctly discerned the problematic status of foundationalism, as usually conceived. By that I mean the approach that attempts to begin with some absolute and indubitable starting point, and to proceed from that point to its conclusions. Whether theoretically or practically, this does not work in a postmodern age, where some do not accept that starting point, or to put it differently, do not make that presupposition. What may appear to some to be self-evident truths, or what an earlier epistemology considered intuitive truths, are not accepted as such by large numbers of persons today.

Frequently in the past, theologians who were foundationalists have used this approach as a means for developing a natural theology, a rational demonstration of God's existence through certain rational proofs. These were believed to be so objective that any rational person who was willing to expend the effort to examine the evidence would come to the conclusion that God does indeed exist. The cogency of such arguments is under serious question, to say the least, at the present time.

It appears to me that some form of presuppositionalism would be a more effective strategy of communication, and a more appropriate way of forming our own convictions. Some form of "soft foundationalism" will need to be developed as we seek to find common ground for communication. This task must be undertaken. Thus far, most postmoderns, with the possible exception of Richard Rorty, have not really asked how we can communicate with one another at all.

The Negative Within

The deconstructionists, especially Derrida, exercise their craft by finding within every view or system the elements of its own contradiction. These are identified and isolated, thus causing each system to be its own criticism, as it were. Rather than a complete and consistent system, each view is to some extent self-destructive. This is how Derrida examines the concept of *khōra* in Plato's thought, for example.

Here is an important insight. Seldom is our understanding so clear and the material so consistent that a system can be constructed with no internal problems. The temptation, of course, is to smooth over or ignore or suppress the contradictory elements. Yet to do so is not true intellectual honesty.

This suggests that we need to recognize the contradictory elements and the problematic considerations in the realm that our theory is attempting to account for. Further, we must acknowledge frankly the presence of such factors, and our own inability, currently at least, to dispose of them. This means that we will not be able to give absolute and incontrovertible proofs of our theories. What we need to do instead is to present some sort of probability case for our claims. This should therefore cause us to hold our views with a certain amount of tentativity, rather than dogmatism. It should also contribute to a somewhat more secure type of view, since it cannot be shattered by a single piece of negative evidence.

This means that when evidence is marshaled, what will probably need to be done is to cite both the supportive and the contradictory evidences. To do so will create a greater credibility than will the claim that the evidence is universally supportive. At a professional society meeting several years ago I listened to a debate on a rather controversial subject. The data being examined with respect to the thesis being debated was a collection of texts from classical sources. The interesting (and frustrating) thing about the debate was that each of the two scholars contended that every single one of the passages supported his view. I found myself amazed and skeptical about the methodology. I wished I had heard something like this from one or both of the debaters: "Twenty-four of these cases support my view; four are ambiguous; two of them, quite frankly, appear to contradict my thesis." I would have had much more respect for the scholar, and much less skepticism about his position and his case. It seems unlikely that either view was that unambiguously supported by the data, and quite obvious that both could not be so supported.

This suggests that our views should be held with a measure of tentativity, and with an openness to change them. On a disputed view, I must marshal all of the evidence on both sides, and make some sort of estimation of the relative strength of those two sets of considerations. If in my judgment 60 percent of the evidence is on one side and 40 percent on the other side, I must adopt the former view. I should, however, continue to hold that in tension with the considerations on the other side, continue to examine the evidence, and reassess from time to time the relative strength of the two. And, should the balance of the evidence shift, I must be prepared to change my conviction on that issue. Similarly, the degree of conviction with which I hold a position should be proportional to the degree of its evidential support. A view that is supported by 95 percent of the evidence will be held with greater certainty than one that has only 65 percent of the data supporting it.

In practice, this may not be what actually happens. Once a conclusion is adopted, the mind may slam firmly shut, and the conclusion is held as if 100 percent of the evidence supports it, and to justify that, every contrary evidence is refuted, by whatever contrived means is necessary. Nothing can pry such a mind open again.

This also suggests a particular philosophy of education. There are various ways to present what we consider to be the correct view on a particular subject. One is simply to give only that view, introducing alternatives strictly as positions to be refuted and rejected. A second approach is to give all of the options without endorsing any one, and simply leave the students to make their own choice. The third, which would seem to be most consonant with this insight, is to present each legitimate option as objectively and fairly as possible, giving the major arguments its advocates advance, and then indicate which one we personally favor, and why.

I regularly remind my students that one of the crucial issues in any dialogue is who gets to set the terms. I have always been impressed that whenever any high-level political summit takes place, the aides on both sides spend considerable time discussing the seating arrangements at the table. Where one sits has a considerable bearing on the effect of the contribution. This is an insight that even King Arthur, long ago, recognized and settled by having a round table, although that did not resolve the issue of who sat closer to the king than did others. Similarly, choosing which end of the field to defend at what part of the game may be more important than whether to begin the game on offense or on defense, at least when the game is not being played in a domed stadium. The definitions of terms or the form in which the question is to be discussed goes a long way toward determining the success of one side or the other in the discussion. An example is the classification sometimes used of persons as warm or cold. I ask my students whom they think selected those terms, a member of the former category or of the latter. The answer is quite obvious, for *warm* is a moderate term and *cold* is an extreme term. The effect might be considerably different if the issues were set as hot and cool. The ideal combination would be a warm heart with a cool head. Quite different would be a cold heart with a hot head. The truth, as the postmodernists have pointed out, sometimes is influenced by the definition of terms.

For Christians, and in particular conservative or evangelical Christians, the doctrine of original sin makes this concern even larger.[5] This doctrine,

---

[5]Interestingly, Stanley Fish says that "original sin would seem to be the only relevant model" for the explanation of disagreement of interpretation, for those who hold that the meaning of the text is determinate (*Is There a Text in This Class?* [Cambridge, Mass.: Harvard University Press, 1980], p. 338).

which says that all of us are by nature inclined to sin, means that we naturally tend to favor ourselves and to see things in a way that is biased in our own favor. This is not a popular doctrine, and probably never has been or will be. It is amazing to me that in spite of the evil and tragedy we witnessed in the twentieth century, the belief in the inherent goodness of humans seems to persist and prosper. G. K. Chesterton once remarked that "certain new theologians dispute original sin, which is the only part of Christian theology which can really be proved."[6]

An interesting expression of this empirical discovery of the fact of original sin is found in Langdon Gilkey's book *Shantung Compound.* Gilkey had grown up in a liberal Christian environment, and his father was dean of Rockefeller Chapel at the University of Chicago. As an undergraduate, Gilkey attended Yale University, and experienced the graciousness and generosity of his peers and their families. He mentions having been frequently invited home by his classmates and enjoying their generous hospitality. During World War II he was imprisoned in a Japanese prisoner of war camp in China. There he was in charge of assigning housing to the prisoners. He recounts the lengths to which prisoners, including the Christian missionaries, went to seek a more favorable allotment of space. Some even moved their beds a fraction of an inch during the night. He says that he came to realize that whereas persons are generous when there is abundance or at least adequacy of the necessities of life, they become quite different in the face of a shortage. His former estimate of human nature had been based on observing them in the former circumstances, but now he had discovered what he called "ordinary human cussedness."[7] He had actually discovered original sin, although he would not have used the term. Anyone who has been in a situation of assigning offices or parking places, even to Christians, can testify to a similar experience.

At this point a somewhat similar procedure to that of the postmodernists may be followed, but for a different reason. The modernists had a very individualistic approach to knowledge, which was not adequate for reasons such as we have described above, and postmodernism is correct in its critique of this approach. If our own perspective is limited by its own conditioning, then we dare not expose ourselves only to our own view or to that of others who hold it. The reason, for those of us who hold to the objectivity of truth, is not because truth is plural, so that differing and even conflicting views may both or all be true. Rather, it is to gather from other cultures and times insights that our own may lack, to reduce the element of subjectivity in our

---

[6]G. K. Chesterton, *Orthodoxy* (Garden City, N.Y.: Doubleday, 1959), p. 15.
[7]Langdon Gilkey, *Shantung Compound* (New York: Harper & Row, 1966), pp. 89-90.

own thinking. Multiculturalism is important, not because all cultures are equally acceptable and true for their own group, but because no one culture has the entire truth.

The Use of Knowledge as Power

The postmodernists have correctly pointed out that truth can be manipulated as a means of achieving one's ends. While the particular areas that Foucault appeals to are overgeneralized, there is nonetheless adequate evidence that such manipulation does take place. It can be seen in numerous areas.

1. Politics. "Spin doctoring" has become a household word. It is the technique of stating or interpreting facts and events in the most favorable possible way. Thus the actions and words of members of one's own party are interpreted as favorably as possible, and negative considerations are ignored or underemphasized, or even so explained in such a way that they are made to appear positive. One's opponent, on the other hand, is so described as to maximize the negatives. Each party is quick to take the credit for good news, and to attempt to pin the blame for negative developments in the economy or in world politics on the opposition. Data are carefully selected in order to accomplish these goals.

The furor over President Bill Clinton and his testimony regarding the Monica Lewinsky affair was very instructive. Clinton, a Yale Law School graduate and former attorney general of the state of Arkansas, meticulously worded his responses to the original inquiry. Using a very carefully narrowed and nuanced definition of sexual relations, he was able to reply that he had not had sexual relations with Ms. Lewinsky. So tortured was this distinction that even the Senate minority leader of the president's own party called on him to desist from such legalistic hairsplitting.

The basis on which political activity functions is also instructive, and fits the general pattern that Foucault, in particular, has outlined. Politics is grounded on a series of tradeoffs of favors. I vote for your bill because you have voted for mine in the past, or because I expect you to vote my way in the future. Lobbyists expect support for bills they favor, and in return contribute heavily to the reelection campaign of the candidates who support them. It is the old system of mutual and reciprocal back-scratching. This can also enter into Christian activities as well. Faculty members may vote for a motion or a program, not because on principle they agree with it, but because they owe someone a vote or will need their vote. These considerations generally relate to one's own self-interest. There was a time when pastors were recommended to posts because they were the best qualified for that position. If, however, the basis of recommendation is because of an "old boy network," then political considerations have triumphed. Whenever it is difficult to understand how someone whose credentials are unimpressive obtained a particular position, this may be an indication that politics has been at work.

On one occasion, the chapel speaker at a seminary where I taught was a Lutheran clergyman, who in one election had been the Republican nominee for the United States Senate, running (unsuccessfully) against Hubert Humphrey. In the informal discussion time that followed his presentation, one student asked, "How, as a Christian, can you be involved in something as dirty as politics?" Without hesitation, the clergyman replied, "Unless the Baptist Church is very different from the Lutheran Church, you have more politics in your church than in the Democratic and Republican parties combined."

This is true, not only in terms of church, but also of educational institutions. We need to remember, however, about the basis of political activity, of trading of favors, that this is the second lowest level in Leonard Kohlberg's analysis of moral development. This, in other words, is immature behavior, morally.

This will help explain why the legal code sometimes appears to be illogical. The Internal Revenue Service personal income tax code, for example, extends particular favorable treatment to some groups, while not extending it to what would seem to be equally deserving groups, in terms of the reasons underlying the provision. These are generally known as "tax incentives" when they favor us and "tax loopholes" or "tax giveaways" when they favor others but not us. The reason is that the law has not been formulated on the basis of logical consistency, but rather, in terms of responsiveness to the pressures of certain groups, to which key legislators owed favors.

2. Euphemistic descriptions. One way this is done is by referring to an act by certain of its consequences, rather than by a description of the act itself. So, for example, in the situation ethics controversy in the 1960s (a phenomenon that is still very much with us), Frau Bergmeier's act of committing adultery so that she would become pregnant and be released from a prison camp was described as "sacrificial adultery" and as "reuniting her family."[8] This practice can be carried to great lengths. So Al Capone, the most notorious criminal of the prohibition era, expressed dismay: "I have spent the best years of my life giving people the lighter pleasures, helping them have a good time, and all I get is abuse, the existence of a hunted man."[9]

---

[8] Joseph Fletcher, *Situation Ethics* (Philadelphia: Westminster Press, 1964), pp. 164-65.
[9] Dale Carnegie, *How to Win Friends and Influence People* (New York: Simon & Schuster, 1936), p. 21.

The opposite practice—of omitting mention of the consequences and labeling an act simply by the barest physical action—is also misleading. To describe the murder of a person by shooting as "he bent the index finger of his right hand," without mentioning that the finger was positioned on the trigger of a loaded revolver aimed point blank at someone's head, is true but incomplete.

3. Biased research. The same tendencies can be seen in the actions of business corporations. A particularly striking version of this is the alliance of tobacco companies. Because absolute proof is not possible in scientific inductive studies, the tobacco executives argue that the connection between smoking (and especially, secondary smoke) and lung cancer has not been conclusively established. They commission their own studies to produce contradictory evidence. Although perhaps less clear and dramatic, other corporations in other fields of business do the same thing.

4. Book cooking. The technique that is popularly known as "cooking the books" arranges financial reports to appear more favorable than would otherwise be the case. Certain unusual sources of income are included and compared with a previous year that does not contain such income, or certain expenses are written off or placed in different cost centers. During the time of earnings reports, it is sometimes amazing to observe how many corporations report earnings per share one cent higher than that anticipated by analysts! Money is "co-opted" from one cost center to be used for another, but not necessarily identified as such.

5. Other statistical manipulation. Not only financial books can be cooked, however. The same thing can be done with other types of statistics. This can be seen in the differing estimates of the number of persons present and involved in demonstrations. Similarly, there was a dispute in the United States Congress over the basis on which the year 2000 census should be taken. One party maintained that in the traditional canvassing method, certain groups of persons (who happen to be more favorable to their party) tend not to get counted, in some cases because they have no permanent residence address. Since congressional seats are apportioned on the basis of population, this party is penalized by the customary method of counting. They favored instead a sampling technique, which the other party contended would unfairly penalize them. This is a struggle over whose facts or whose truth will be deemed official.

Unfortunately, Christian institutions are not exempt from such practices. Joel Gregory, in his fascinating book *Too Great a Temptation*, reports a practice of padding attendance statistics. Since numerical growth is an important consideration, the statistics must increase, and so they do. Higher figures are reported whether attendance increases or not. In the case Gregory is recounting, eventually the discrepancy between the number of worshipers reported and those actually present becomes so great as to be obvious to any careful observer. Presumably, when a change of senior pastors takes place, the counter is reset.[10] George Barna's research suggests that this may not be a unique case.[11] Selective reporting can again be utilized here. A statement such as "Enrollment in our nursing department increased by 50 percent over last year" may be technically correct, but may in some cases be translatable as "This is one department in which enrollment did not decline."

6. *Subtle qualifiers.* This points up the importance of noticing carefully the qualifying terms in statements. These are introduced in order to preserve the technical truthfulness of the statements. The adjectives and adverbs in a statement may thus be as important as (or more important than) the nouns and verbs, for these are the qualifiers, together with the comparatives. One cold war era joke described a dual track meet between the United States and the Soviet Union, which the United States team won. According to the story, however, Pravda reported, "U.S.S.R. places second in track meet; U.S.A. finishes next to last." The statements were true but misleading.

Such incidents do occur in actual life, and here again, Christian institutions are not above reproach. One denominational official wrote in the denomination's official publication that "we have reduced the amount of our interest-bearing indebtedness by x dollars." Many pastors and laypersons, reading that optimistic report, were encouraged. One pastor who had served on the governing board of the denomination pointed out that the statement should be read carefully: "the amount of *interest-bearing* indebtedness." The correct translation of that statement was, "We are borrowing money from our own trust funds, and (unlike the federal government) we don't pay ourselves interest."

7. *News editing.* Editing of news is a necessary activity for a newspaper, since almost invariably more material is gathered than can be published. At that point, however, subjective factors can enter in such a way as to skew the overall impression. A small quotation, taken out of its context, can be made to represent a speaker as saying the exact opposite of that person's overall position. The stories selected, their length, and the prominence of their placement, all are additional forms of managing the news, and thus of managing the truth.

---

[10]See Joel Gregory, *Too Great a Temptation: The Seductive Power of America's Super Church* (Fort Worth, Tex.: Summit, 1994), pp. 203-6.

[11]George Barna, *Today's Pastors: A Revealing Look at What Pastors Are Saying About Themselves, Their Peers and the Pressures They Face* (Ventura, Calif.: Regal, 1993), p. 78.

8. Use of innuendo. One way truth is used manipulatively is by the innuendo of what is not said, or by making a true statement that is ambiguous, but from which unusual inferences may be made. An old and humorous example is a ship's first mate who sometimes drank while on duty. The captain repeatedly warned him that if the first mate did not change his behavior, he, the captain, would enter the fact of the first mate's intoxication in the ship's log. Finally, when on one occasion the mate was drunk, the captain wrote in the log, "The first mate was drunk tonight." When the first mate realized what had been done, he pled with the captain to remove the notation, for he realized that when the ship's owner read that in the log, he would fire the first mate. The captain refused, pointing out that once something was entered in the log, it could not be removed. When he finally became convinced that he could do nothing to help his own situation, the first mate resolved to obtain an element of revenge on the captain. The next time that he had the command, he wrote in the ship's log: "The captain was sober tonight!" In one institution, the head of the organization distributed a memo to the entire community, to the effect that he had placed one of the employees on leave of absence, and asking the members of that Christian community to pray for the employee and his wife, "as they seek to work out their problems." Readers were left to surmise the worst, although neither the employee nor his wife was experiencing any moral, doctrinal, or domestic problems.

9. Benign (or not so benign) neglect. It is not only by not stating differing perspectives, but educational institutions can in effect silence a particular dissenting view simply by assuring that no representatives of that view are present on the faculty. In the psychology department of a state university where I had a minor, there was no official exclusion of views such as Gestalt theory, psychoanalysis, and so on. There simply were no department members who held those views. Every professor there was a behaviorist. This can also be done by omitting mention of significant works, or by only recommending only certain books. This is actually a subtle and effective form of censorship.

This also means that any sort of political correctness must be avoided and resisted, insofar as that means the deliberate suppression of the right of a divergent view to be aired. This is quite different from a situation where such views are presented or allowed to be presented, but rebutted. Even situations in which a speaker is shouted down, so that his or her assertions cannot be heard, are instances of this type of thing. In such situations, "truth" is being manipulated, because the power is present to prevent dissent from being heard.

10. Use of unfair rhetoric. It is worth noting that certain types of rhetoric appear to be inherently unfair. As a rather general illustration, one of the most unfair things one can say to one's dialogue partner is, "You are being defensive." What sort of response can the other make to such a charge? Contesting the charge of being defensive simply demonstrates how true that is. On the other hand, not responding is an apparent admission of the truth of the charge. There are, of course, forms of response that can avoid the dilemma, but they are not immediately obvious. This may be something like the old question, "Have you stopped beating your wife?"

Some media give a particularly unfair advantage, or facilitate the use of power to control belief and opinion, and thus ultimately, the truth, at least functionally. A periodical that presents one side of an issue without also presenting the other side or even acknowledging that such an alternative exists has a special advantage. There may, of course, be forms of recourse, such as letters to the editor, but if "the journal [newspaper, magazine, etc.] reserves the right to select and to edit letters received," there is no assurance that the contrary voice will be heard, and with any effectiveness. An editorial may exercise an unusual degree of influence. What does one do who disagrees, who writes a letter to the editor, but whose letter is not published? Does one take out an ad in the paper, rebutting the editorial? Even if one can afford it, in all likelihood the paper has a pre-announced policy of reserving the right to reject any advertisements it chooses to. Does one then start an alternative newspaper? This is hardly practical for most persons.

Certain forms of communication are particularly difficult to respond to. The cartoon, for example, really cannot be replied to, at least not without making oneself appear ridiculous. If the cartoon does not clearly identify the persons being criticized, this is particularly the case. Movies or television often are similarly insulated. When, for example, CBS picked out of context Vice President Dan Quayle's comment about Murphy Brown and built an entire episode around it, ridiculing Quayle, what avenue of response was available to him, without either appearing ridiculous or seeming to suppress free speech? Note, however, that the very form of presentation of the case served to suppress a free and fair engagement of the different viewpoints. What was done was in effect a type of ad hominem argument. We must realize that next only to the government, the media have the greatest potential for controlling the truth, or engaging in use of knowledge as a means of power.

Other forms of presentation allow a satire without opportunity for response. Comic strips are a particularly appropriate version of this. The author of "Doonesbury," for example, regularly engages in satires of various public figures which actually constitute criticism, yet remains invulnerable to any accounting regarding accuracy of the statements.

The Necessity of a Hermeneutic of Suspicion

These postmodernists are correct as well in urging a hermeneutic of suspicion. Without becoming cynical, we will want to ask whether the person making the statement has any vested interest in the matter. If so, we need to scrutinize very carefully both the statement and its supporting evidence. A piece of sales literature for a product being considered should be regarded somewhat differently than the results published by an independent testing laboratory of their evaluation of the product.

It might be useful to develop a "credibility quotient" for each source attended to. This would be in part a function of this vested interest issue just mentioned. It would also, however, be calculated on the basis of the person's or organization's previous record. A person regularly given to exaggeration might be assigned a credibility quotient of 50 percent. The same might be appropriate for someone who would not intentionally deceive, but is not himself sufficient skeptical about the pronouncement of others whom he then cites, or who is not meticulously careful about verifying facts. On the other hand, there are persons who, because of carefulness or modesty, regularly understate matters. Such persons have a credibility quotient exceeding 100 percent. Their statements would have to be multiplied by more than one, their claims and estimates increased.

Whether we realize it or not, others are assigning credibility quotients to us and our organizations. I would propose that we strive to merit credibility quotients of at least 100 percent. One way to do this is to apply a hermeneutic of suspicion to our own beliefs and utterances. That means, practically, that I must realize that I will be more susceptible to believing statements that agree with my beliefs than those that contradict them. To be objective, I must therefore demand more evidence for the former type than I do for the latter, and more than I think ought to be necessary. This is because I am very tied to my own viewpoint.

A further step in this direction will be deliberate exposure to differing viewpoints, and to persons who come from such differing perspectives and differing cultures. It is helpful to study the thought of scholars from a very different time period than our own. The same is true of different cultures. We only really become aware of our presuppositions when they are challenged. In this respect, presuppositions are like grammar. The average person who knows only one language, frequently English, tends to be unaware of grammar. This is not grammar; it is simply the way the language is. When such a person begins study of a different language, however, he or she frequently becomes aware of grammar for the first time, and then recognizes grammar within his or her native language.

The Role of Community

There is value in the postmodern emphasis on community versus individuality. All of us are influenced by the conditioning effect of our background and circumstances, which exert a strong influence on our understanding of facts and events. One of the checks on this is the influence of a larger community on our individual biases. Note, however, that we are here referring to the effect of that community on our understanding of something that does exist, independent of our perception of it. This is where our use of the role of community will differ from that of most postmodernists. When we only expose ourselves to our own thoughts about things, those thoughts increasingly take on the status of self-evidence. It is only as we share our perspectives with others that they are able to point out considerations that we have overlooked or underestimated. For the Christian, this takes on a different dimension. Part of traditional Christian belief is that the Holy Spirit indwells all believers, and that he leads the group collectively toward an understanding of the truth. Thus, as Paul put it, no part of the body (the church) can afford to disregard or depreciate any other part of the body (1 Cor 12:12-26).

Yet, if the insights regarding the conditioning effects of our environment are accurate, the greatest benefit of community will come through being part of a diverse community. In other words, the community is a group of those who have not been exposed to identical conditioning. This means that beyond the most natural communities that we might fall into by circumstance, there will be a need for seeking some sort of community that comprises persons of a different gender, age, socioeconomic group, cultural and ethnic background, and so on.

In speaking of community we are not speaking of a mere collection of persons. There are such assemblages that come together to witness or participate in a certain event, such as a dramatic or musical presentation or an athletic contest. It may even be a matter of the viewership of a particular television program. During the time they are together, they experience a sort of common experience, although their perception of it and their interpretation of it may vary considerably from one person to another. When the event is over and the crowd departs, there is very little if any real communion or interchange between those who were together. What distinguishes a community from a group or a crowd is the presence of some sort of ongoing commitment to the group. Thus, in a community, members recognize that differences remain and that they have an opportunity to influence one another. With some types of communities there is always the possibility of withdrawal if one finds significant differences with some or most members of the group, and transferring to another group more in agreement with oneself. In such situations, however, there is not really community. The objectifying effect of the community on the individual, which Fish speaks of, is largely dissipated.

The Value of Narrative

Finally, we should observe the appropriateness of the emphasis on narrative. For still a fairly large percentage of the world's population, oral rather than written communication is the primary and most effective means of communication. And for such persons, discursive or logically structured presentations are not necessarily the most effective form for that oral presentation to follow. These people find stories to be much more manageable, and more easily remembered, for there is a natural basis of cohesiveness: the plot or story line. In primarily oral societies, it is not uncommon to find storytellers who can recite from memory for days at a time, without any sort of manuscript or notes. It is also disconcerting for the storyteller who attempts to abbreviate or modify the story in some other way, to have the listeners, who may have heard the story several times, correct him. The story should be told as they have heard it and learned it, for that form has come to take on a significance of its own.

What must of course be considered are the proper functions and the improper functions of narrative, or the limits beyond which its utility declines. Is narrative a matter of communicating and elucidating information that could be placed in propositional form, is it the hermeneutical key to understanding the realities of life, or does it have a heuristic, so that the very act of dealing with narrative enables us to discover truths? These are issues that we will need to pursue further, in a later chapter.

For the Christian believer, there may be instructive and helpful elements within postmodernism, which may at times be prophetic in nature, in the biblical sense of prophecy. Postmodernists may have exposed the vulnerability or fallibility of some of our reasoning and our actions. Just as God used unbelieving nations and kings as a means of purifying his people and calling them back to him, so we should ask ourselves at what points the contentions of postmodernism are on target, and use these insights to bring us closer to the truth.

11

negative evaluation
of postmodernism

The evaluation of postmodernism encounters a dual difficulty. On the one hand, this is not a monolithic movement. Thus, criticisms that apply to one postmodern thinker do not necessarily apply to another, or at least not to the same degree. Beyond that, however, there are even variations within the thought of a given thinker. The thought of both Derrida and Foucault contains a more conservative and a more radical strain. A given criticism will apply to one strain, but not to the other.

This internal diversity poses problems for the thinker himself. Superficially it appears to be an advantage, for the rhetorical strength of the radical statements is accompanied by the ability to dodge criticism by pointing out that one has said something quite different than this. Actually, however, it is also perhaps a larger liability than an asset. For to the extent that one attends to the more radical statements, the difficulties with those statements can be attacked. If, however, one turns to the more conservative statements, deconstruction turns out to be rather trivial, not saying something unique, but rather what a number of other positions have also enunciated. Interestingly, those who have made these similar statements claim disagreement with persons like Derrida and Foucault.[1] Thus, the dilemma is triviality or vulnerability.

---

[1] John M. Ellis, *Against Deconstruction* (Princeton, N.J.: Princeton University Press, 1989), pp. 39-44, 66; Michael Fischer, *Does Deconstruction Make Any Difference? Poststructuralism and the Defense of Poetry in Modern Criticism* (Bloomington: Indiana University Press, 1985), pp. 58-59.

In a criticism of this type, the very criteria employed will frequently be disputed. In particular, postmoderns generally contend that the criticisms leveled against them assume the very modernism that they would dispute. Another frequent response is that the critic simply does not understand the position being criticized. It is therefore essential that we at least consider the question of what criteria are to be employed. To some extent, these criteria are given their justification in the next two chapters, but I will indicate briefly here something of what I am using, and why.

In a situation like this, some appeal must be made to pragmatic considerations. If dialogue and communication of ideas is deemed to be a good, then that which hinders this is negative. If the functioning of humans in some communal way with a maximum of harmony and productivity and the welfare of the largest number is a good, then whatever militates against this is a negative.

In light of this, one criterion that would seem to be appropriate is that of consistency. By that I mean that the meaning of any term or expression should remain constant unless some indication has been given that a shift of meaning is involved. This is essential if communication is to take place. For if a word can mean both one thing and its contradiction, then one has no way of knowing what really is meant, for nothing is excluded by it.

Another element of this principle of consistency is that ad hoc exceptions should not be made to an enunciated principle. This is not to say that there are not exempting factors, which cause a rule not to apply. Thus, the rule, "All A is X," can have as a subsidiary rule, or a qualifying statement, "Except instances of A_e." That is legitimate, for then the rule is preserved whole. What is not legitimate is to say, "All A is X, except this A," but without specifying a basis for making an exception to the rule. Again the problem becomes that without such specification, the rule becomes useless. How do I know whether this A is to be treated as X? If that A is not, why should this A not also?

Specifically, the problem of autoreferentiality must be faced. By that I mean that a theory must be able to account for itself. If it applies criteria to other views that it fails to apply to itself, or that it does not satisfy itself, that undercuts the seriousness with which the theory can be regarded.

We will see that one major problem with postmodernism is its ability to maintain its position consistently. Postmodernists may, of course, respond by asserting that the principle of consistency is simply a modern conception, and that to require it of postmodernism is in effect insisting on the correctness of modernism. I would contend, however, that this is not the case. Consistency is not restricted to modernism. It is a requisite for any communication to take place. Postmodernists may simply remain silent, and it is possible that there are many more postmodernists than we generally realize, and that many of them are simply unrecognizable because they do not identify themselves. It is, however, those who do that are my concern in this book.

There is yet another dimension of this problem. Postmodernism contends that logic and reason are just types of rhetoric, means used to convince by appeal to emotion, or something similar. The problem, however, is that this really cannot be believed. If we ask ourselves whether to believe this assertion, we realize that we do not have to. For, as Hugo Maynell says of these claims, "If they are sound, and we accept them because we think that they are so, we are thereby committed to the view that logic and reason are means of establishing truth. But if they are mere rhetoric, then we have no business to be convinced by them."[2]

Problems of Logical Consistency

The practice of deconstruction. A first concern deals with the practice of deconstruction, as found in Derrida's thought. For Derrida, one major element in deconstruction is, as we saw, autodeconstruction. He believes that he finds within systems of thought contrary elements, or what is sometimes referred to as alterity, which have been ignored or suppressed, in order to formulate a system of thought. Deconstruction consists in part in identifying and restoring these elements to their proper places. As such, it presumably is applicable to everything.

What about deconstruction itself, however, considered not just as a method, but as the underlying philosophy on which that method is based? Should not deconstruction be subject to its own criteria? This is the question of autoreferentiality. Here, interestingly, Derrida demurs: "Justice in itself, if such a thing exists, outside or beyond law, is not deconstructible. No more than deconstruction itself, if such a thing exists. Deconstruction is justice."[3]

Interestingly, now, we have an exception to the principle of deconstruction, namely, deconstruction itself, which he here equates with justice. Why, however, is this not extended to justice? Caputo offers an answer: "Justice is not deconstructible. After all, not everything is deconstructible, or there would be no point to deconstruction."[4]

---

[2]Hugo Maynell, "Archdeconstruction and Postpostmodernism," *Heythrop Journal* 36, no. 2 (1995): 133.
[3]Jacques Derrida, "Force of Law: The Mystical Foundation of Authority," in *Deconstruction and the Possibility of Justice*, ed. Drucilla Cornell, Michel Rosenfeld, and David Gray Carlson (New York: Routledge, 1992), pp. 14-15.
[4]John D. Caputo, in *Deconstruction in a Nutshell: A Conversation with Jacques Derrida* (New York: Fordham University Press, 1997), pp. 131-32.

But perhaps this is just that point, that there is no point to deconstruction, or that there need not be. Why must it be pursued? Perhaps it should be discarded. But Derrida and Caputo seem to be making deconstruction something of a good in itself, the ultimate good or the ultimate presupposition. This, however, begins to sound as if deconstruction/justice is inherently or intrinsically good. It is difficult to see how this avoids the problem of logocentrism or transcendental signification.

Ironically, this very claim to exemption from deconstruction requires the deconstruction of deconstruction. I pointed out that Derrida employed the principle of autodeconstruction, of finding contrary elements or alterity within a philosophy. If, however, deconstruction maintains that everything must be deconstructed, except justice and deconstruction itself, then we have within the theory a contradictory element, an element of alterity. Thus, if deconstruction is not to be turned on itself, it must be, for this alterity calls for deconstruction.

What, however, is the status of justice in this scheme of things? Derrida is quite clear, as is Caputo, his commentator, that justice cannot be deconstructed. It is the one undeconstructible entity. Why should justice have this privileged status, however? Does this not give the impression that it is somehow a transcendental signified, and that this is a case of a metaphysic of presence? Derrida is quite insistent both that this is not a transcendental signified and that justice is not deconstructible, but it is not clear on what basis he can make such assertions together. Nor is any satisfactory justification given for treating justice this way.

Further, Derrida insists that the judge must create justice, rather than calculating or discovering it. On what basis does he act justly, however? What is the epistemology of this act? When we trust that the judge has acted justly, in what are we placing our trust? Is this a sort of final given, so that whatever the judge decides is thereby justice, or is it appropriate to question the justice of the judge's actions? If it is the former, it would seem to be the case that a new sort of authoritarianism has been introduced. And what is to be done to or said to the person who questions the judge, either as to whether this decree is just, or more fundamentally, whether justice has this final and undeconstructible status? If justice cannot be verified or validated by something more basic or more ultimate, what sort of reply can be made, to convince such a person? It would seem this will lead us to some sort of power action.

The options are three. One is the passive approach of saying, in effect, "You differ, and that is your privilege. We simply come to different conclusions on this matter." The second approach would be to offer some argument in support of the sanctity of justice, establishing it by appeal to something more ultimate. Derrida has rejected that option, however. If one is to do more than merely leave the discussion with an agreement to disagree, and a witness to one's own convictions, some form of power exertion seems to be called for. It would involve a dogmatic assertion of one's own opinion. One may choose to stop the deconstruction process short of applying it to justice and to deconstruction, but that would be a rather arbitrary decision and action, unless some justification is given for it. If one claims that these are exceptions to the principles of deconstruction, then can one reject the assertion of someone who would also claim similar exceptional status for another viewpoint, or another value?

If Derrida is sincere about rejecting intrinsicalism, then is it possible to say that justice as such has any identifiable nature? Perhaps this is what Caputo means when he says that everything is to be deconstructed, but that justice is not a *thing*. Then, justice is not a nominative, or even an adjective, so that one could speak of a particular decision by a judge as being a just decision. Rather, it is adverbial in nature. We then would apply justice, not to the outcome of the judge's decision, but to his action in so deciding. We would say that the judge acted justly. It appears that what Derrida is saying is that it is the action of judge, the nature of his deciding, rather than what he decides, that is the locus of justice. This would seem to be supported by his contention that the judge must not decide in a prefabricated fashion, by consulting the legal code.

Foucault also encounters the problem, particularly in connection with his discussion of history. When pressed about his writing of fictional history, he says:

> The question that I won't succeed in answering here but have been asking myself from the beginning is roughly the following: What is history, given there is continually being produced within it a separation of true and false? By that I mean four things. First, in what sense is the production and transformation of the true/false division characteristic and decisive for our historicity? Second, in what specific ways has this relation operated in "Western" societies that produce scientific knowledge whose forms are perpetually changing and whose values are posited as universal? Third, what historical knowledge is possible of a history that itself produces the true/false distinction on which such knowledge depends? Fourth, isn't the most general of political problems the problem of truth? How can one analyze the connection between ways of distinguishing true and false and ways of governing oneself and others? The search for a new foundation for each of these practices, in itself and relative to the other, the will to discover a different way of governing oneself through a different way of dividing up true and false—this what I would call "political *spiritualité.*"[5]

---

[5]Michel Foucault, "Questions of Method," in *After Philosophy: End or Transformation?* ed. Kenneth Baynes, James Bohman, and Thomas McCarthy (Cambridge: MIT Press, 1987), p. 112.

Foucault, however, as so often, simply indicates that this is on his agenda, an agenda which he never completed.

Fish cannot avoid this problem, either. It is interesting to observe inductively Fish's conception of the second-level discourse that makes up his writing. It is presented as if it is a correct description of the way things are, and as if there is some neutral arena in which evidence could be evaluated. He offers considerable argumentation, for example, of his contention that SAT scores do not measure native intelligence, but are strongly affected by such factors as cultural background.[6] He uses such language as "the fact that,"[7] "the inescapable conclusion was that,"[8] "as a matter of *fact*,"[9] "Nor is it the case that,"[10] and "the truth is that."[11] He reacts quite defensively to the charges of "McCarthyism" brought against his own department, claiming that this does not fit the facts: "This general finding can be further substantiated by the facts about the English department at Duke, which has been offered by Mr. D'Souza and others as the very symbol of what has gone wrong; I say flatly that there is no relationship whatsoever between the media characterization of that department and the reality of its everyday life, and I am prepared to back up that statement with massive documentation."[12] The tone, and without some sort of disclaimer, quite possibly also the substance, of his argument, strongly resembles the type of approach he considers untenable.

The role of power. Foucault has made much of the way power has been exercised in history. Here again we find the same sort of dual or internally contradictory themes as in Derrida. In Foucault's case, however, the form is somewhat different. If all knowledge is based on power or is constituted by it, then must we not ask the same question of Foucault's thought? Is it not simply an attempt to exercise power as well? Is this not simply an attempt to nullify the power of institutions? And is not his urging of persons to reject the versions of truths that have been presented them by such institutional sources simply a disguised attempt to establish his own authority? Why should his view of these matters be accepted as preferable to any alternative? If his contention is somehow exempt from such scrutiny, then may there not be other views of which this is true as well? Actually, his state-

---

[6]Stanley Fish, *There's No Such Thing as Free Speech, and It's a Good Thing, Too* (New York: Oxford University Press, 1994), pp. 63-64.

[7]Ibid., p. 64.

[8]Ibid., p. 65.

[9]Ibid., p. 71.

[10]Ibid., p. 72.

[11]Ibid.

[12]Ibid., pp. 71-72.

ments about the aim of disrupting neat systems seem more directed at getting his way and getting his view accepted, than at attaining a true and fair outcome.

Ostensibly, postmodernism is concerned with justice, with making certain that those in power do not use their power to enforce their views on others. Many postmodernists do not practice this concern themselves, however. Rather than encouraging free expression of all viewpoints, they sometimes seem intent on enforcing conformity. Anyone who has experienced the intolerance of political correctness knows what this means. The efforts to shout a person down, to cut off another to prevent her or him from expressing her or his views, are examples of this. And the efforts to obtain, not equal treatment for oneself, but superior treatment, are further examples.

Some have charged that the very claim of relativism is itself a form of exercise of power, or an attempt at retention of it. It is when those in dominance find viable challenges to that power being raised, that they emphasize relative values, or find reality unknowable. Sarah Lennox contends that the hesitation about the knowability of reality is merely an inversion of Western arrogance.[13] Similarly, Sandra Harding claims that, "historically, relativism appears as an intellectual possibility, and as a 'problem,' only for dominating groups at the point where the hegemony (the universality) of their views is being challenged. [Relativism] is fundamentally a sexist response that attempts to preserve the legitimacy of androcentric claims in the face of contrary evidence."[14]

This tendency surfaces in Foucault's use of fictive history. There is, as I noted in an earlier chapter, a certain amount of dispute over whether Foucault is doing history or philosophy. His historical analyses purport to be arguments seeking to establish his thesis that power is used to oppress by showing how it actually has been thus used in the past. As such, its force depends on these things having actually happened. When pressed about the accuracy of some of his details, however, he responds by contending that there is and must be a "fictive" dimension, in which a creative element enters. We must seriously ask, however, what is the status of such fictionalizing? How is it done, and how is it to be evaluated, or why should it be accepted? This appears to be exactly the type of activity he has described as

---

[13]Sarah Lennox, "Anthropology and the Politics of Deconstruction" (paper presented at the ninth annual conference of the National Women's Studies Association, Atlanta, Ga., June 1987).

[14]Sandra Harding, "Introduction: Is There a Feminist Method?" in *Feminism and Methodology,* ed. Sandra Harding (Bloomington: Indiana University Press, 1987), pp. 1-14, esp. p. 10.

the use of power to produce knowledge. Many of the things we have been given to believe, by politicians and others, are actually creations or hoaxes, even though they may have been what we wanted to hear, and were made more plausible by those wishes. Truth is manufactured, just as it was in the novel *1984*. Why, however, should we accept Foucault's fiction, rather than some alternative fiction? It appears that this is an instance of Foucault attempting to create the history by his own writing. It is his method of getting his view accepted. But if the power analysis is a means of deconstructing other views, then it must also be done with his.

We must ask, however, whether there is some connection between the teachings of postmodernism and these tendencies. I believe there is not only an empirical coincidence of these factors, but a logical connection. The reason is that when there is no belief in the intrinsic (or metaphysical) value of certain actions or beliefs, then there is nothing beyond various human interests to which to appeal. Consequently, discussion becomes a means of obtaining a hearing for one's own concerns, and some of the means of doing so that have traditionally been considered illegitimate are no longer so.

The problem can be seen when the question is asked, how are differences of opinion to be adjudicated? The more traditional way has been by persuasion, by offering arguments to show that one view is more adequately supported by the relevant considerations than is another. Derrida rejects that approach. But that seems to lead us to the idea of a view being accepted merely because of the force with which its advocate advances it. And that leads to one form or another of a shouting match.

Historical conditioning. One primary argument employed by these postmodernists is that all views are historically conditioned. They are held, and take the particular form they do, because of their historical situation, rather than because they somehow more adequately reflect reality than do competitive views. We must ask, however, if this argument does not and must not also apply to these postmodern conceptions as well. Proponents of postmodernism hold certain ideas because of historical conditioning. So, for example, the insistence on the exercise of one's own freedom and the criticism of any use of power that seems to encroach on that freedom is actually a reflection of the existentialist mood of our times.

Another place where this conditioning can be seen is the treatment that is to be made of the conflicting elements within a given philosophy. There are several possible ways of dealing with such conflict. One would be to seek to find ways of harmonizing disparate elements, ways of interpreting them so that they do not actually conflict with one another. The other, apparently that followed by Derrida, is to look for contradictions within a given thought system. We must then ask, however, why this is done. Ordinarily, attempts are made, in dealing with any body of material, to find coherence or agreement among its constituent elements. Here, however, preference seems to be given to the idea of contradiction. This is a presupposition that guides the inquiry and the treatment. As such, it seems to be a derivation from Kierkegaard (whose thought Derrida admires) and other existentialists. If this is the case, however, it is also potentially in need of being deconstructed. It would seem here that Derrida's view is also historically conditioned, drawing not on objective considerations, but bringing to the deconstruction of other views a criterion that grows out of its own situation in the intellectual scene, temporally and geographically.

This same dynamic seems to be at work in Derrida's preference for writing over speaking. One of the reasons for preferring writing, in fact, perhaps the most important reason, is that it frees up the symbol for the free play of words, whereas speech restricts the meaning. There is a preference for fluidity of meaning that reflects this same discontinuity assumption.

Historical conditioning has the same nullifying effect on deconstruction as it has on other schemes of thought. Do the deconstructionists claim that their own views are exempt from this feature of their theory? If so, why? And why should such exemption not be claimed by other views as well? We should notice that they are here facing the same problem that the sociology of knowledge faced regarding its principles. As I noted in chapter 4, the sociologists of knowledge refused to carry through on their theory, and offered very inadequate reasons for this failure. The postmodernists have a similar problem. Again, one cannot develop a theory and insist on its applicability to all views other than itself.

Yet we should ask further whether this conditioning is as significant as the postmodernists want to make it. Does the fact that a particular situation conduces to a particular conclusion invalidate that conclusion? Is it not simply an explanation of how a given conclusion came to be adopted, rather than a criterion of its validity? As Alvin Plantinga says, "Had Einstein been born in the eighteenth century, he would not have believed special relativity; nothing follows about special relativity."[15]

The role of philosophy. There is strong objection, especially by Derrida, to the imperialistic role sometimes played by philosophy. On that model, philosophy weighs truth claims and pronounces what is correct. It also lays the ground rules and maps the terrain for several disciplines of thought. It claims to build an all-inclusive scheme, which explains all of reality. Thus, it claims for itself a superior role and view. We must ask, however, what phi-

---

[15]Alvin Plantinga, *Warranted Christian Belief* (New York: Oxford University Press, 2000), p. 428.

losophy's role is on the models being proposed to us. It is certainly not the superior perspective in a positive sense of ruling on truth or determining right and wrong. It does, however, claim to be the discipline that deconstructs views, all of which are subject to its scrutiny and ruling. In a negative sense, philosophy is the universal arbiter. Thus, philosophy still maintains an imperialistic role, be that good or bad.

Alternative logic. One of the most radical and most interesting claims is Derrida's claim that he is not using the traditional logic, but a different or alternative logic. That becomes part of the basis for rejecting the more conventional views. Certainly, if this is truly the case, we have indeed a radical development here, a radical departure from the more traditional approach.

What, then, is this alternative logic? The answer is not so clear. On the one hand, it appears that this logic is very close to the Hegelian dialectic, where two antithetical theses are gathered up into a synthesis in which both elements are at least in part preserved. Derrida himself speaks of its "almost absolute proximity to Hegel," yet in the final stage breaks with Hegel. The most noted statement is Derrida's "It is thus not simply false to say that Mallarmé is a Platonist or a Hegelian. But it is above all not true. And vice versa."[16] Without further explanation, it is difficult to determine what sort of logic is functioning here. Barbara Johnson proposes that the very word *destruction* symbolizes this alternative logic, since it is neither construction nor deconstruction.[17] This she asserts to undermine the either-or logic of construction-destruction. This may not necessarily be the case, however. Construction and destruction may actually be contraries, not contradictories. It may be that deconstruction is a contradictory both of construction and of deconstruction. If this is the case, it is not necessarily a different logic, but a different set of data being analyzed under the traditional logic. What remains is a lack of clarity regarding what is being affirmed. It appears that the claim of an alternative logic is being advanced as a reason why objections to Derrida's position are not damaging, and need not be taken seriously.

Whether he is speaking of logic in the narrow sense, or the broader and more general sense of discourse or method, not only is Derrida unable to carry on his discussion without the use of the logic he is rejecting, but he recognizes and acknowledges this problem. So he says, "We have no language—no syntax and no lexicon—which is foreign to this history; we can

---

[16]Jacques Derrida, *Dissemination*, trans. Barbara Johnson (Chicago: University of Chicago Press, 1981), p. 207.

[17]Barbara Johnson, "Nothing Fails Like Success," in *A World of Difference* (Baltimore: Johns Hopkins University Press, 1987), pp. 12-13.

pronounce not a single destructive proposition which has not already had to slip into the form, the logic, and the implicit postulates of precisely what it seeks to contest." He goes on to say of the attempt to reject the idea of a transcendental signified that "one must reject even the concept and word 'sign' itself—which is precisely what cannot be done."[18] If this is the case, and Derrida's comments are to be taken at face value, then the claim to an alternative logic may be adjudged to be either unintelligible or not genuine and sincere. In any event, it is impossible to consider it a serious element in the deconstructionist position. Although given in a different context, Johnson's comment on Derrida is telling here as well: "Derrida thus finds himself in the uncomfortable position of attempting to account for an error by means of tools derived from that very error. For it is not possible to show that the belief in truth is an error without implicitly believing in the notion of Truth."[19]

The locus of meaning. There seems to be one deep and inherent dilemma at the heart of deconstruction. On the one hand, when criticized, the deconstructionist frequently complains that logical objections cannot be brought against the view, because they presuppose the very traditional logic that deconstruction rejects. The very idea that a logical analysis of deconstruction could be made, and that it could be summarized in a series of logical theses, is rejected. There is something ineffable about deconstruction. On the other hand, however, deconstructionists frequently complain that their ideas have been misunderstood or misrepresented. Thus, for example, John Searle wrote an eight-page review of Derrida's thought.[20] Derrida wrote a response in the same journal, which reached ninety-three pages in length. In this response, he frequently and in rather great detail contended that Searle had misunderstood what he, Derrida, really was saying.[21] This evoked a variety of reactions from deconstructionists. Some were embarrassed at this response, which seemed to slip back into a nondeconstructionist mode, while others seemed to second Derrida's contentions.[22]

This same phenomenon can be found in Fish's work. He uses the incident that is the central exhibit of his book *Is There a Text in This Class?* to argue that the meaning of a sentence is given it by an interpretive commu-

---

[18]Jacques Derrida, *Writing and Difference* (Chicago: University of Chicago Press, 1978), pp. 280-81.
[19]Barbara Johnson, "Translator's Introduction," in Derrida, *Dissemination,* p. x.
[20]John R. Searle, "Reiterating the Differences: A Reply to Derrida," in *Glyph* (Baltimore: Johns Hopkins University Press, 1977), 1:198-208.
[21]Jacques Derrida, "Limited, Inc., abc . . .," in *Glyph* (Baltimore: Johns Hopkins University Press, 1977), 2:162-254.
[22]Fischer, *Does Deconstruction Make Any Difference?* pp. 40-41.

nity. Actually, there is another interpretation that fits the incident better. At one point, the difference of understanding between the student and professor over the meaning of her question ceased: when she indicated the meaning she intended. It could be argued that words have objective meanings, which of course have been assigned by the practitioners of the language in which they appear. In a sense, these are almost different words, although they are spelled and pronounced the same. The speaker had selected which of these to use, and her selection and intention governed the question of meaning here.

Logical and Rhetorical Difficulties

Speech and writing. One key point in Derrida's argument is the contention of the priority of writing over speech. By this he does not mean a temporal priority, that writing comes into existence before spoken language, but rather a logical priority, that it is more basic than speech. In so doing, however, he seems to ignore a number of crucial considerations that argue the opposite. One is the fact that in the learning process, children learn to speak before they learn to write. Another is the fact that there are many people, and even entire language groups, who have a spoken language but not writing. Yet another is the fact of nonverbal communication, which according to some communication specialists may actually comprise as much as 70 percent of communication. There are elements in spoken speech, such as tone, emphasis, and pitch, which cannot readily be communicated in writing, except imperfectly through such roundabout means as saying, "raises inflection on last syllable" or "lifts eyebrows."

Derrida does not comment on such considerations, but Jonathan Culler, one of the clearer proponents of deconstruction, does raise these objections (although he does not answer them). Further, however, is the rhetorical form of the argument Derrida uses in claiming this priority for writing over speech. He begins with a triad: language, writing and speaking, in which language is divided into speaking and writing. At some point, however, he moves to a more inclusive conception of writing, as comprising "graphic" and "phonic" writing. What he has done here, however, is to redefine writing, or rather to reassign the term, so that this latter triad—writing-graphic-phonic—is roughly equivalent to the earlier triad—language-writing-speech. This, however, is to engage in stipulative definition, in which, in terms of the original triad, what he has done is not to show the priority of writing over speech, but of language over speech, and presumably over writing as well. As such, this becomes merely assertion, without support. This type of shift of meaning, without notice of what is being done, contributes to the difficulty of understanding Derrida's thought.

Caricature of opposing positions. It is interesting to notice the nature of the argument that is advanced, especially by Derrida, but also, to a considerable extent, by Foucault. Basically they state the position being opposed in the most extreme and naive or primitive form. Thus, for instance, basically a commonsense realism is set up as the standard or accepted view, or a crudely referential theory of language. The problems with such a view are set forth, something that is not too difficult to do. Then, however, the alternative, deconstruction is presented. Relatively little positive argument is given for this position, the assumption being that disproving the traditional view entails the establishment of this alternative, deconstruction. Logically, however, this does not follow unless these are the only two options and one must choose one over the other. There may be several additional options, and indeed such have been offered, as John Ellis points out. He also observes that what Derrida opposes is actually a caricature of the viable current options.[23] And the most cogent arguments for a view of the general type being opposed are overlooked or disregarded.

Choice of terminology. A further problem centers on the choice of terminology for the concepts being discussed. The deconstructionists, especially Derrida, use distinctive terms. In some cases, the concepts being represented by the terms are fairly common, but they are usually designated by quite different terms. So, for example, the attack on the reference theory of meaning is instead identified as dealing with the "metaphysics of presence." In Ellis's judgment, the purpose of this difference of terminology is to make it appear that this is a new set of issues, and that a relatively novel and creative solution is being advanced. Thus it does not seem strange that Derrida does not come to grips with the extensive discussion of the issues that has already taken place. So, for example, in discussing what is essentially the issue of authorial intent (what Wimsatt and Beardsley term the "intentional fallacy") Derrida instead speaks of "the death of the author." Instead of stating that there is no final interpretation of a text, Derrida says that "all interpretation is misinterpretation." Similar language, sometimes emotive in nature, is used to characterize the views of those who oppose his ideas. Instead of critical bias or individual temperament, Derrida writes of "desire," "blindness," and "fatigue."[24]

Derrida also sometimes resorts to the use of hyperbole to make his point more emphatically. Thus in underscoring the priority of speaking over writing, he refers to "the ethnocentrism which everywhere and always, had controlled the concept of writing."[25] Apart from the inaccuracy of the statement,

---

[23]Ellis, *Against Deconstruction*, p. 38.
[24]Ibid., pp. 140-43.
[25]Jacques Derrida, *Of Grammatology* (Baltimore: Johns Hopkins University Press, 1976), p. 3.

and of his interpretation of Saussure's role in relationship to the issue, he has stated this in such a universal and absolute fashion that only a single contrary instance would be necessary to disprove it.

Obscurity. There is the problem of the obscurity with which deconstructionists, especially Derrida, but also Foucault, write. If one has not been able to experience this problem fully, the following sample may serve to illustrate it. Speaking of the process of dissemination or *différance*, Derrida says:

> Not that it opens onto an inexhaustible wealth of meaning or the transcendence of a semantic excess. By means of this angle, this fold, this doubled fold of an undecidable, a mark marks both the marked and the mark, the re-marked site of the mark. The writing which, at this moment, re-marks itself (something completely other than a representation of itself) can no longer be counted on the list of themes (it is not a theme, and can in no case become one); it must be subtracted from (hollow) and added to (relief) the list. The hollow is the relief, but the lack and the surplus can never be stabilized in the plenitude of a form or an equation, in the stationary correspondence of a symmetry or a homology. . . . This work always has this theoretical result among others: a criticism concerned only with content (that is, a thematic criticism, be it philosophical, sociological, or psychoanalytic style, that takes the theme—manifest or hidden, full or empty—as the substance of the text, as its object or as its illustrated truth) can no more measure itself against certain texts (or rather the structure of certain textual scenes) than can a purely formalist criticism which would be interested only in the code, the pure play of signifiers, the technical manipulation of a text-object, thereby overlooking the genetic effects or the ("historical," if you will) inscription of the text read and of the new test this criticism writes.[26]

A number of explanations of this obscurity have been given. Barbara Johnson, out of her experience of translating Derrida, indicates several varieties: (1) Syntax, in which "ambiguity is rampant. Parentheses go on for pages. A sentence beginning on p. 319 does not end until p. 323, having embraced two pages of Un Coup de dès and a long quotation from Robert Greer Cohn. Punctuation arrests without necessarily clarifying." (2) Allusions. Frequently Derrida alludes to some source without identifying that source. (3) Fading in and out. Johnson believes that it is as if borders of the material had to signal the active disconnection from the logos. (4) Multiple coherences. The unit of coherence is not always the word, sentence, paragraph, or essay. "Different threads of Dissemination are woven together through the bindings of grammar (the future perfect), 'theme' (stones, columns, folds, caves, beds, textiles, seeds, etc.), letters (or, d, i), anagrammati-

---

[26]Derrida, *Positions*, pp. 46-47.

cal plays (graft/graph, semen/semantics, lit/lire), etc." (5) Nonbinary logic, which I have noted above. It appears that this is part of the process of deconstruction of Western metaphysics, which is based on the either-or of the standard laws of logic.[27]

Another translator, Alan Bass, suggests two additional reasons for the obscurity: Derrida often refers back to some of his previous writings and anticipates others that are to come, but without explaining what he is doing; and Derrida uses the classical terminology of philosophy but gives the terms new meaning, again without indicating what he is doing.[28]

Similarly, Foucault sometimes goes on in lengthy, involved sentences, in which reference and syntax are far from clear. One of his sentences, for example, is 185 words in length.[29]

Is a complaint about stylistic problems such as these really a valid criticism, however? Bear in mind that these postmodernists frequently object that they have been misunderstood, even at times conveying the impression that only those who embrace their view can understand it. Yet even their translators, who basically accept their view, take note of the obscurity. If communication with those of differing views is desired, then effort must be made by both parties to understand the other, and to make their own views as understandable to the other as possible. These are highly trained thinkers, who should be able to communicate with a degree of clarity.[30] It is almost as if the obscurity is deliberate, in order to procure immunity from criticism. Anyone who writes in an abstruse style such as the one postmodernists often employ has, however, forfeited some degree of the right to complain of being misunderstood. If such a reply is to be employed, some concerted effort should be made to clarify what is being said.

Practical Difficulties

Subjective reactions. There also appear to be practical difficulties. One is the tendency to lapse into very subjective responses. Foucault ostensibly rejects

---

[27] Johnson, "Translator's Introduction," in Derrida, *Dissemination*, pp. xvi-xvii.

[28] Alan Bass, "Translator's Preface," in Derrida, *Writing and Difference*, p. xiv.

[29] Michel Foucault, *Madness and Civilization: A History of Insanity in the Age of Reason* (New York: Vintage, 1973), pp. 275-76.

[30] Samuel Wheeler, an analytic philosopher, tentatively offers a criterion of analytic philosophy as clear writing, but notes that this criterion is relative to one's training. He tells of giving Derrida a piece of analytic philosophy which Wheeler thought to be a model of clarity, and Derrida responded that he had tried to read it but could not understand what was going on. By contrast, Derrida considered Heidegger very clear. Wheeler comments: "So: You are an analytic philosopher if you think Krinke writes clearly; you are a continental philosopher if you think Heidegger writes clearly" (Samuel C. Wheeler III, *Deconstruction as Analytic Philosophy* [Stanford, Calif.: Stanford University Press, 2000], p. 2).

such a practice when he writes, "If I open a book and see that the author is accusing an adversary of 'infantile leftism,' I shut it again right away. That's not my way of doing things; I don't belong to the world of people who do things that way."[31] Yet earlier he had written, "In France, certain half-witted 'commentators,' persist in labeling me a 'structuralist.' I have been unable to get it into their tiny minds that I have used none of the methods, concepts, or key terms that characterize structural analysis."[32] Similarly, Derrida says, "Every week I receive critical commentaries and studies on deconstruction which operate on the assumption that what they call 'post-structuralism' amounts to saying that there is nothing beyond language, that we are submerged in words—and other stupidities of that sort."[33] Fish concludes his discussion of "how to recognize a poem when you see one" by saying of Meyer Abrams's view of interpretation, "There is something of the police state in Abrams's vision, complete with posted rules and boundaries, watchdogs to enforce them, procedures for identifying their violators as criminals."[34] The difficulty with such subjective reactions and vocabulary is that this does not contribute to effective discussion between dialogue partners. Instead of being able to deal with the issues as they are, emotions become too prominent. Dialogues can turn into feuds.

Breakdown of academic and scholarly standards. Beyond that, there seems to be some breakdown of standards of any kind for scholarship. One example of this type is found in the Vincennes branch of the University of Paris, of which Foucault was one of the founding faculty members. Students did not attend class, and in some cases received credit for the course simply by slipping under the door of the professor's office a statement that they had completed the assignments and thus deserved credit. This, however, is a logical outcome of a situation in which truth does not necessarily exist as something independent of the knower, waiting to be discovered.

The problem with the insistence on indeterminacy is that it also is accompanied by a rejection of traditional standards of evaluation. In fact, there is a sense that the application of any restrictions on possible meaning is a repressive function of the institution. So, for example, Spivak speaks of

---

[31]Michel Foucault, "Polemics, Politics, and Problemizations: An Interview with Michel Foucault," in *The Foucault Reader*, ed. Paul Rabinow (New York: Pantheon, 1984), p. 381.

[32]Michel Foucault, *The Order of Things: An Archaeology of the Human Sciences* (New York: Vintage, 1973), p. xiv. As I pointed out in chapter seven, this statement about his relationship to structuralism is in contradiction to his own statement elsewhere.

[33]Richard Kearney, *Dialogue with Contemporary Continental Thinkers: The Phenomenological Heritage* (Manchester: Manchester University Press, 1984), p. 123.

[34]Stanley Fish, *Is There a Text in This Class? The Authority of Interpretive Communities* (Cambridge, Mass.: Harvard University Press, 1980), p. 337.

deconstruction as "a way out of the closure of knowledge. By inaugurating the open-ended indefiniteness of textuality—by thus 'placing it above the abyss' (mettre en abime) as the French expression would have it—it shows us the lure of the abyss as freedom." Spivak sees such an approach as a free fall, intoxicating us with "the prospect of never hitting bottom."[35]

There is something that prevents this free fall, however, namely, the academic profession. The standards that are used in grading papers, in evaluating articles, in determining promotions, are seen as restrictive, and as another manifestation of the rules that govern and repress society in general. So Derrida says that the writer has liberties that the teacher is not allowed to have. He speaks of a "feminist leader" who criticized him and "used the most academic criteriology against me, demanded 'proof,' and so on."[36] He says, "This operation [superimposing one text on another] would never be considered legitimate on the part of a teacher, who must give his references and tell what he's talking about, giving it its recognizable title."[37] These authorities "demand an author, an I capable of organizing a narrative sequence, of remembering and telling the truth: 'exactly what happened,' 'recounting facts that he remembers,' in other words saying 'I' (I am the same as the one to whom these things happened and so on, and thereby assuring the unity or identity of narratee or reader, and so on)."[38]

This is not to say that the standards of academic quality held in the past are infallible and cannot be replaced. What seems to be lacking, however, is a positive alternative benchmark of scholarly quality, stated and defended. The difficulty, furthermore, is that when the very idea of definite standards of evaluation, and of fixed meaning, is undermined, the academic enterprise becomes transformed into a political one. Rather than attempting to argue for an interpretation on the basis of some discernable characteristics of the text, what is done is essentially a manipulative endeavor.

Beyond that, however, the value of education, at least in departments of English, becomes questionable. If there is not truth toward which study and analysis takes us, then each person creates the truth. And in this situation, more than one student has already concluded that there is no point in taking a course from a professor, if the teacher's opinion of the meaning of a writing is no more accurate or authoritative than is the student's.

Societal applicability. We must also ask whether the proposals the decon-

---

[35]Gayatri Chakravorty Spivak, "Translator's Preface," in Jacques Derrida, *Of Grammatology* (Baltimore: Johns Hopkins University Press, 1976), p. lxxvii.

[36]Jacques Derrida, in *Deconstruction and Criticism,* ed. Harold Bloom et al. (New York: Seabury, 1979), pp. 166-67.

[37]Ibid., pp. 84-85.

[38]Ibid., p. 98.

structionists are making can be applied, particularly on a societal level. Foucault has proposed a type of anarchy, in which attempts to impose beliefs and practices by use of power are opposed and resisted. Will this work on a societal basis, however? What kind of society would we have if every individual felt free to reject laws and practices that he or she felt were unfair? It would seem that for society to function at all requires the necessary subjugation of individual desires and impulses. If everyone simply acts on his or her own impulses, in defiance of any sort of restriction, chaos would be the result.

One dramatic instance is that of Foucault's final sickness and death. His friends urged him to be careful and cautious in his behavior in the San Francisco gay community. This he declined to do, since it was contrary to his very approach to life, and he contracted the HIV virus, which ultimately caused his death. In this case, reality made its presence known emphatically and dramatically.

Another one of the most serious problems, however, concerns whether the agenda of deconstruction really can be carried through. Derrida finally admits that it is impossible to reject the logocentric approach without actually having to reassume or reaffirm that very approach.[39] This is surely a serious basic problem, that is not really answered here. We merely note that if this is the case, then how can one take seriously the whole approach that rejects logocentrism?

Ethical effects. Another very serious consideration is the ethical impact of postmodernism on society. The problems of our current society, with young people killing one another, and numerous other atrocities, have been well documented and need no repetition here.[40] While it is not possible to attach exact causal connections, the transition to a postmodern culture has certainly been accompanied by disastrous effects.

Postmodernism has come under criticism by women and minorities. Their criticism is directed to the apparent relativizing of moral values. It appears to them that, just when they are coming into a position to become equal participants in the benefits that white males have so long enjoyed, the moral values that argued for equality and nondiscrimination are being removed, tending to undercut their demands. Nancy Hartsock, for example, thinks it curious that the argument that verbal constructs do not really correspond to reality in some direct way has arisen just at the time that women and non-Western people have begun to speak of the injustices in the world, and to express their concerns.[41] Specifically, the charge is made that the

---

[39]Derrida, *Writing and Difference*, pp. 280-81.

[40]For a more vivid description of the current situation, see Thomas C. Oden, *Requiem: A Lament in Three Movements* (Nashville: Abingdon, 1995), pp. 116-18.

[41]Nancy Hartsock, "Rethinking Modernism," *Cultural Critique* 7 (fall 1987): 187-206.

rejection of metanarratives by Lyotard and others works against the cause of social justice for these undergroups.

There have been a considerable number of such criticisms. One comes from Nancy Fraser and Linda Nicholson. Speaking of their concern about male domination, they argue postmodernism has negated some of the major critiques that they would raise against it. They say, for example:

> Then, we submit, it would be apparent that many of the genres rejected by postmodernists are necessary for social criticism. For a phenomenon as pervasive and multifaceted as male dominance simply cannot be adequately grasped with the meagre critical resources to which they would limit us. On the contrary, effective criticism of this phenomenon requires an array of different methods and genres. It requires as a minimum large narratives about changes in social organization and ideology, empirical and social-theoretical analyses of macrostructures and hermeneutical and institutional analyses of cultural production, historically and culturally specific sociologies of genders. The list could go on.[42]

Rorty, as we have seen, is optimistic about continuing to do ethics without any sort of metaphysical basis, and in the face of relativism or irony. Others are not so sanguine, however. Foucault acknowledges that he has not been able to do much in terms of constructive dealing with problems. In connection with what was termed the "anesthetizing effect" of his *Discipline and Punish* on social workers in prisons, he responds that he realizes that he has not succeeded in overturning certain conditions, and that his "project is far from being of comparable scope." His hope is that he has simply been of some assistance in wearing down certain self-evident understandings. He says, "I hardly feel capable of attempting much more than that [the negative task]. If only what I have tried to say might somehow, to some degree, not remain altogether foreign to some such real effects. . . . And yet I realize how much all this can remain precarious, how easily it can all lapse back into somnolence."[43]

Derrida also does not attempt to give much ethical guidance. He speaks of the importance of justice, and of the judge creating justice, but has little to say about the content of justice. In fact, the attempt to give content in some invariable way to justice is contrary to his very program. In the case of both Foucault and Derrida, what they tend to say is that they have not yet been able to develop that type of thing, but appear to be holding out hope that

---

[42]Nancy Fraser and Linda Nicholson, "Social Criticism Without Philosophy: An Encounter Between Feminism and Postmodernism," in *Postmodernism: A Reader*, ed. Thomas Docherty (New York: Columbia University Press, 1993), p. 421.

[43]Foucault, "Questions of Method," p. 112.

such will emerge sometime, somehow. In practice, however, this seems to be a virtual disengagement from the ethical task.

We have noted the objections of feminists. Others have also attacked post-modernism for its indifference or ineffectiveness. Todd Gitlin, for example, criticizes postmodernism for its dismissal of political engagement and sub-stituting of a view that "beholds the world blankly, with a knowingness that dissolves feeling and commitment into irony. . . . Old verities crumbled, but new ones have not settled in. Self-regarding irony and blankness are a way of staving off anxieties, rages, terrors, and hungers that have been kicked up but cannot find resolution."[44]

There is some historical evidence that similar situations in the past have produced disabling effects, allowing situations of injustice to occur. For example, David Hirsch has documented the way in which Hitler took advan-tage of the relativism and nihilism in the intellectual world at his time and place, to advance a theory that justified his horrible acts.[45] Hugo Maynell, who argues that there are real norms of truth and right, comments: "What are we to say against any atrocity, say in the former Yugoslavia, unless we acknowledge that there are real moral norms which such atrocities vio-late."[46]

The Practicality of Neopragmatism

A number of serious problems attaching specifically to Richard Rorty's view deserve separate attention. It is apparent that Rorty thinks that cruelty should be avoided or minimized, and together with this such factors as humiliation. Conversely, kindness is to be promoted. If these are things that we should do, then it would seem to be appropriate to use such terms as to say that these are wrong and right, respectively.

The status of ethical judgments. When we ask, however, why we should avoid the former and maximize the latter, the usual answer is something such as that these are inherently contrary to or favorable to the nature of humans. Something intrinsic in the nature of certain acts and something intrinsic in human nature makes them desirable or undesirable. Rorty does not follow that approach, however. His answer is not that there is some intrinsic quality to these actions or to human nature that makes humiliation contrary to the welfare of humans, but that it simply is the case that humans have a common susceptibility to humiliation that animals do not have.

---

[44]Todd Gitlin, "Hip-Deep in Post-Modernism," *New York Times Book Review,* November 6, 1988, pp. 35-36.

[45]David H. Hirsch, *The Deconstruction of Literature: Criticism After Auschwitz* (Hanover, N.H.: University Press of New England, 1991).

[46]Maynell, "Archdeconstruction and Postpostmodernism," p. 134.

If, however, we press the question of why we should avoid humiliation of persons, it seems to be that this is painful, and presumably, humans do not like pain. And if we ask why we should not allow pain to come to humans other than ourselves, presumably the answer must be that this is the common agreement of our community or our culture. The problem, however, comes when we find a society that does not oppose pain or cruelty, or humiliation. What do we do in that situation? The usual answer here would be that reasons are to be given, to argue that the kindness is preferable or superior to cruelty. That is not the approach that Rorty will follow, however. He will not offer reasons in the usual sense. What he will do instead is to offer paraphrases, restating the issues in such a way that they can be seen differently. He would suggest, "Try thinking of it this way." And presumably, if a given community thinks a certain way, then that way of thinking is truth for them.

There have been communities, however, where values opposite to those Rorty advocates have been espoused. One of the most conspicuous of these was World War II Nazi Germany. To be sure, many ordinary German citizens did not know the full extent of the Nazi atrocities, but the disappearance of Jews from the society was quite widely known. Suppose, then, that Germany had won the war—something that could have happened. Then the values of cruelty (at least toward the Jews) would have been the official view of that community, which would have been considerably enlarged. Would cruelty then have been right? Rorty replies that the aim in discourse is to widen the circle of consensus as widely as possible, to bring as many persons into agreement as possible. What his position ignores, however, is the fact that some persons are more equal than others. There are some persons, in positions of influence or power, whose opinion on a subject is much more important than that of others. Thus, if the Nazi leaders espoused cruelty and had the power to enforce their views, it did not really matter what the average person felt.

The problem for Rorty in this situation is this: Would he be willing to say that for that community, cruelty was not wrong? Or would he insist that because all humans find cruelty unpleasant, it is therefore wrong in that context as well? It seems that he wants to make this pair of qualities (cruelty-kindness) some sort of universal. This is a question that he does not really seem to answer.

The nature of communities. A further problem relates to the matter of communities. Rorty indicates that communities are contingent, just like the world, self and language. That, in theory, allows for and perhaps even conduces to, the idea of plurality of communities. There is nothing inherently good about a particular community; it is whatever one chooses. The problem, however, is that plurality of communities may not be workable in our time, and after all, it is workability that is the measure of "objectivity." We now live in a world where isolationism, of the old variety, simply is not workable. Several nations already possess the ability to bring about widespread destruction of life and property with a single attack, and several more will soon have that capacity. Nations represent different communities, often with rather different values. When conflict reaches a sufficiently high level, the result is war. Although communities are all contingent, community is not. In the face of this problem, that we must in some sense function as a world community, how does one go about settling disputes, where there is no truth of an objective nature? How does one go about formulating a unity in which there really is a world community?

Private irony and public liberalism. One common objection to the view Rorty is advocating is that without the support of a metaphysical basis for the values he is promoting, such as kindness, the split he is advocating between private irony and public liberalism will not work. Society will dissolve. His reply to this is that the same sort of warning was expressed about the decline of religious faith. Without a belief in reward or punishment after this life, liberal societies would be weakened, according to that objection. In reality, however, that has not happened. Instead of concern for some future reward, the focus was shifted to social rewards, so that the hope for paradise became instead transmuted into the hope for one's grandchildren. Something similar should be expected in this case.

We must inquire about this analogy, however. What has happened in the case of the decline of religious faith is that the support religious faith formerly offered for values has been replaced by another type of support. It is as if a post supporting a roof has been replaced by a different kind of post. Now, however, what Rorty is suggesting is the removal of that substitute post, but without proposing anything to take its place. The parallel to the loss of religious faith seems not to be an appropriate one. Nor is this the whole of the situation. With the deterioration in conventional morality, the rise of crime, the indifference to the morality of public officials so long as the economy is prospering, some would argue that the loss of religious faith has had serious consequences, that we are not just getting along fine without that faith. This is, of course, a controversial assertion, but the point is that the correctness of the first part of the analogy (that the loss of religious faith has not harmed morality) is debatable.

In the case of Rorty himself, there may be some lag between his private irony and his public liberalism. In other words, his early worldview was Trotskyite. Accompanying that was a certain moral agenda, which he summarizes by saying that "the point of being human was to spend one's life fighting social injustice." He later came to abandon the private belief in the system of thought that undergirded this ethical agenda, but the practice persisted, probably based on a conditioned response, or something of that type. This is not uncommon, even among intellectuals. C. S. Lewis tells of his atheistic tutor, a onetime Presbyterian, who still wore a different and somewhat more respectable suit when he worked in his garden on Sundays than he wore for gardening on the other days of the week.[47] That Rorty is able to maintain his public liberalism is not the real test of the situation he describes. That test will come when a generation is present that has never believed in that metaphysic, or any other.

Vagueness and evasiveness. There is considerable vagueness about much of what Rorty asserts, which is a bit disconcerting. He suggests that "our purposes would be best served by" giving up the older view of truth; that such a view "is not helpful"; that we "see how we get on" if we abandon that view. He characterizes his method as using metaphors and paraphrases to "make the vocabulary in which the objections are phrased look bad"; he acknowledges that "anything could be made to look bad . . . by being redescribed." Objections to his view, such as that it is relativism, "should not be answered, but rather evaded" and "brushed aside." The problem is that he really does not give enough content to these expressions to enable us to understand them or to evaluate them. What does it mean to say that something is not helpful? How does one judge that something looks bad? It appears that Rorty is again on the horns of a dilemma. On the one hand, if he gives more concrete content to these expressions or criteria, he is in danger of falling back into the dreaded intrinsicalism. On the other hand, without doing so, the proposals become so nebulous as not to be helpful.

Note the nature of the criticism I am bringing to bear here. I am not claiming at this point that Rorty has not argued adequately for his position. Rather, my complaint is that it is not sufficiently clear exactly what he is proposing. The former criticism would be brushed aside with the comment that it simply assumes the older view of truth. The latter criterion, clarity or sufficient explanation to enable understanding, would seem not to be restricted to a given ideology, however. Rather, clarity is a more general quality, desirable for any conception that seeks broader acceptance. One wonders why Rorty does not clarify or specify further. The suspicion lingers that the problem is the dilemma of unintelligibility or vulnerability to criticism.

Neopragmatism and autoreferentiality. There is a broader problem, which

---

[47]C. S. Lewis, *Surprised by Joy: The Shape of My Early Life* (New York: Harcourt Brace Jovanovich, 1955), p. 139.

applies to all pragmatisms, in varying degrees. Truth is that which works out, which has beneficial consequences. Two questions must be put to this assertion, however. One is the question of the grounds for accepting this view. A correspondence view of truth is often advanced as being the theory that itself is true, in the sense of being the one that most adequately "fits the facts." It is justified in terms of its own criteria. What of the pragmatic theory of truth? Is it justified in terms of itself? Is it the theory that itself works out better than others? This is what Rorty seems to be advocating, which is why he is so sensitive to the charge that ethics cannot be conducted on such a basis. It also, however, thrusts a burden of responsibility on him. He would say that to insist that a theory be "proven" represents a fall back into intrinsicalism, but that is not what is being called for here. If he is advocating his theory as something to be accepted and put into practice, then presumably its own workability needs to be shown.

Beyond that, however, workability presumes a value judgment of sorts, which in turn assumes some values. Apparently such value judgments as the positive value of kindness and the negative value of cruelty lie at the basis of his program. He suggests that we deal with the question, "What humiliates?" rather than asking, "Why should I avoid humiliating?" The latter assumes the old intrinsicalist view. Suppose, however, that we rephrase the question somewhat, to say, "Should I avoid humiliating?" Here, the possible answers would seem to be, "Yes," "No," or "Yes, because. . ." The first two answers, however, smack of authoritarianism. Rorty says that "The metaphysician wants to bolster the wish to be kind with arguments, whereas the ironist simply wants to improve the chances of being kind." It is not completely clear what the answer would be to the person who says, "But I don't want to be kind."

If the upshot of this objection is that measuring the truth of an assertion by whether it works assumes some unexamined and unjustified values, there is another problem with pragmatism as well. How broad is the measure of workability, and in particular, over how long a period of time must it be measured? Some ideas, methods and devices that work out well over the short term do not do so over a longer term. Jumping from an aircraft without a parachute may be very practical for a period of time. It increases the thrill of the fall. At some point, however, the practicality of a parachute becomes apparent, if not to the person making the leap, certainly at least to others observing the end of the fall.

Rorty's method and rhetoric deserve special attention. His apparent endorsement of Freud's interpretation proposes that what leads persons to certain views is not reasons so much as causes. We believe what we do because of some influence in our earlier life, or perhaps because of some scrambling of the neurons in the brain, rather than because we have gotten a closer approximation to reality. If this is the case, the role of persuasion is not to provide better and more cogent or persuasive reasons, but to introduce factors (as causative or influencing considerations) that will affect the person. This would include such activities as rephrasing or paraphrasing statements. One must ask, however, whether such activities and their effects do not in some sense involve restating one's opponent's position in the most unfavorable light. This begins to approximate manipulation, in which we get people to act the way we want them to. As such, it has more in common with brainwashing than with what we usually think of as ethical persuasion. Note, however, that in the final analysis Rorty does not seem to be able to escape totally the more objectivistic way of thinking. When he suggests that there are no objective criteria for evaluating views, he seems to be contending that this really is the case. In other words, in practice Rorty seems to have to slip back into something not too different from what he denounces in theory.

The other disturbing feature of Rorty's rhetoric is the way he handles any objections. These are almost uniformly disposed of by saying that they presuppose the very view he is opposing, namely, the metaphysical view of intrinsic values and truths. That, of course, would be begging the question. There is, further, no neutral or objective criterion, by which differing views could be scrutinized and evaluated. We must ask, however, what it is in common between the two views that enables them to communicate with one another. This is a question that does not seem to be asked, but to fail to do so calls into question the entire endeavor in which Rorty is engaged. Insofar as he does address the question, his response seems to be that of the "passing theory," but that is at such a general and elementary level that it hardly seems adequate for more abstract and sophisticated discussion.

We have examined certain of the positive features of postmodernism, as well as a large number of problems attaching to it. It is my judgment that the negatives considerably outweigh the positives, and that the positive contributions of postmodernism can be retained by less radical positions, which also avoid most of its difficulties. It is irresponsible to criticize or reject a view without offering a better alternative. It is to that task that we turn in the chapters that follow.

part 4

beyond postmodernism

12

the nature of truth

We have seen that one of the strong emphases of postmodernism is the conception that all understanding is conditioned historically and culturally, and that moral principles are grounded in communities rather than in the nature of things. Postmodernism challenges the idea that our beliefs are true, in the sense of being in agreement with an objective world. The challenge comes in two forms in postmodernism. One is that what we perceive and how we judge it is, if not determined, at least strongly influenced, by the culture of which we are a part. Rather than seeing things as they are, our judgments are the result of material that has been filtered through our cultural apparatus.[1] In this respect, this is an extension of part of Immanuel Kant's discussion of the distinction between the noumenal and phenomenal worlds.

The other criticism is that knowledge, rather than being the source of power, is actually a product of it. Knowledge is the result of what those who have power determine that it be. By suppressing contrary voices, the powerful make sure that the truth is that which favors them. Knowledge is thus only the product of Nietzsche's will to power.[2]

---

[1] Richard Rorty, *Contingency, Irony, and Solidarity* (Cambridge: Cambridge University Press, 1989), pp. 3-6.
[2] Michel Foucault, "Truth and Power," in *Power/Knowledge*, ed. Colin Gordon (New York: Pantheon, 1980), p. 133; *Discipline and Punish: The Birth of the Prison* (New York: Vintage, 1979), pp. 27-28.

What all of this means is that knowledge does not have a sterilized character, that there is no neutral area into which disputants may enter to settle their debate by appeal to objective data. Truth must be seen in a different fashion. In particular, postmodernism rejects epistemological realism, a correspondence view of truth, a referential understanding of language and foundationalism in epistemology. In the place of correspondence to reality, postmodernism often substitutes one of two options. One alternative is a coherence view of truth, the idea that the test of truth is to be found by taking our ideas as a whole, not atomistically, and checking the coherence of the set of propositions. The other option is the use of a pragmatic view of truth, namely, the idea that truth is that which works, or enables us to make progress toward mutually agreed-on goals.

The problem can be seen when non-postmodernists attempt to engage postmodernists in discussion, and especially, to offer criticism of postmodernism. The most frequent response is that there is no neutral basis of discussion, no common arena into which one can enter. The other is to dismiss all criticisms as based on the discredited views of modernism. Whether labeling that opposing view as logocentrism, metaphysics of presence, foundationalism, commonsense realism, or some other epithet, these strategies seem to imply that discussion can proceed only by accepting the postmodern conception. That, however, seems to call for surrender before the battle can be fought. Is there a better way of approaching the problem?

Those outside this movement have given a variety of responses to it, which tend to fall into two general types. On the one hand, some draw on the general tenor of the movement and attempt to integrate their thought with it, while ignoring or arbitrarily rejecting some of the more extreme elements, which appear to conflict with their ideology.[3] In so doing, they create an ultimately unstable condition, the discussion of which goes beyond the limitations of this book. On the other hand, a number of conservatives have simply rejected postmodernism, subjecting it to several criticisms.[4]

The problem with many of these latter responses is that postmodernists have deflected them as being modern in nature, based on the outlook that postmodernists reject. In some cases, the postmodern response is that the objectors simply do not understand what has been said. Not only can one not understand postmodernism from a modern perspective, there is no neutral perspective, outside either of these orientations, from which an objective judgment can be made.

---

[3]Stanley Grenz, *A Primer on Postmodernism* (Grand Rapids, Mich.: Eerdmans, 1996).
[4]David Wells, *No Place for Truth: Or Whatever Happened to Evangelical Theology?* (Grand Rapids, Mich.: Eerdmans, 1993).

Complicating the picture, however, is the fact that certain problems within postmodernism have been becoming increasingly evident. One of these is the problem of autoreferentiality: postmodernism's failure to apply its tenets to its own view. This shows itself in the insistence that deconstruction itself cannot be deconstructed, and that whereas all laws must be deconstructed in the name of justice, justice is the one thing that cannot be deconstructed.[5] Closely related to this problem is the inability to practice consistently the rejection of certain factors, such as logocentrism or authorial intent.

This then raises the question of what sort of paradigm we are to utilize when comparing and contrasting paradigms, or what view of truth underlies our discussion of views of truth. Another way of putting this point is, how do persons who hold different paradigms communicate with one another? There would seem to be three logical possibilities: (1) our discussion of post-modernism must itself be a postmodern discussion; (2) our discussion of postmodernism can be done from a modernist perspective; (3) there is some neutral perspective, which is not limited to either modernism or postmod-ernism, from which this discussion may be carried on.

If one facet of the problem is the difficulty of refuting postmodernism from outside it, the other is the difficulty postmodernists find in critiquing more traditional views. Derrida indicates that all thought shows historical conditioning. There is no transcendental truth, no God's-eye view of things. Foucault similarly indicates that all knowledge is mitigated by the exercise of power. Rorty rejects the idea of any foundationalism that is able to con-struct a system on the basis of neutral factors. Derrida, however, is the one who faces frankly the question of the status of what he has written:

> This circle is unique. It describes the form of the relation between the history of metaphysics and the destruction of the history of metaphysics. We have no language—no syntax and no lexicon—which is foreign to this history; we can pronounce not a single destructive proposition which has not already had to slip into the form, the logic and the implicit postulations of precisely what it seeks to contest.[6]

Similarly, in *Grammatology* he indicates that he does not intend to reject the concepts of sign and signification, but only their closure: "Of course, it is not a question of 'rejecting' these notions; they are necessary and, at least at present, nothing is conceivable for us without them."[7]

---

[5] Jacques Derrida, in *Deconstruction in a Nutshell: A Conversation with Jacques Derrida*, ed. John D. Caputo (New York: Fordham University Press, 1997), pp. 16-17.

[6] Jacques Derrida, *Writing and Difference* (Chicago: University of Chicago Press, 1978), pp. 280-81.

[7] Jacques Derrida, *Of Grammatology* (Baltimore: Johns Hopkins University Press, 1976), p. 13.

On either basis, then, the need for attempting to define the locus and language of dialogue is apparent, if communication is to take place.

The Nature of Truth

I would propose that on a pre-reflective level, or in actual practice, virtually all sane persons function with what I would term a "primitive correspondence" view of truth. By this I mean an understanding of truth as a quality of statements that correctly represent the "state of affairs" being referred to. This is true, in actual practice, of postmodernists as well as modernists. I offer the following examples in support of this contention:

1. William James, one of the fathers of modern pragmatism, offered a preliminary definition of truth as follows: "Truth, as any dictionary will tell you, is a property of certain of our ideas. It means their 'agreement,' as falsity means their disagreement, with 'reality.' Pragmatists and intellectualists both accept this definition as a matter of course. They begin to quarrel only after the question is raised as to what may precisely be meant by the term 'agreement,' and what by the term 'reality,' when reality is taken as something for our ideas to agree with."[8]

2. Alan White's article on "Coherence Theory of Truth" in the *Encyclopedia of Philosophy* gives a similar interpretation. He says that "what the coherence theory really does is to give the criteria for the truth and falsity of a priori, or analytic, statements."[9] He then goes on to criticize the coherence theory.

> It confuses the reasons, or criteria, for calling a statement true or false with the meaning of "truth" or "falsity." As far as the criteria of truth are concerned, we can say only of a priori, or analytic, statements that they are true because they cohere with each other, and only of empirical statements that they are true because of what the world is like; however, as far as the meaning of truth is concerned, we can say of any kind of statement that it is true if it corresponds to the facts. Thus, as well as saying that a true a priori statement coheres with other statements in the system, we can also say that it corresponds to the a priori facts.[10]

3. Derrida also works with a conception of truth as some sort of accurate representation of the state of affairs. This can be seen most clearly in his ninety-three-page response to William Searle's eleven-page critique of his

---

[8]William James, "Pragmatism's Conception of Truth," in *"Pragmatism," and Four Essays from "The Meaning of Truth"* (New York: Meridian, 1955), p. 132.
[9]Alan R. White, "Coherence Theory of Truth," in *The Encyclopedia of Philosophy*, ed. Paul Edwards (New York: Macmillan, 1967), 2:132.
[10]Ibid., 2:133.

view. The thrust which he repeated, over and over again, was that Searle had misunderstood what he, Derrida, was saying.[11] This appears to be a claim that Searle's representation of what Derrida said was not what Derrida really meant. This, however, becomes a question of the fit of an interpretation with what it claims to state.

4. Rorty defines truth in terms of how it works out, what the results are. Does he carry this view of truth to apply it to itself, however? Does he hold that the view that truth is what works out itself works out, or does he contend that the evaluation of that working out is indeed measured by whether certain results are of a certain nature? That is to say, that this course of action does indeed result in less humiliation, or in better health, or whatever? It appears that he also is consulting some state of affairs that the theory describes.

5. The example that forms the centerpiece of Stanley Fish's *Is There a Text in This Class?* is revealing. A student came to one of Fish's colleagues at the end of the first day of class and asked him, "Is there a text in this class?" Without hesitating, the teacher replied, "Yes; it's the *Norton Anthology of Literature.*" The student then said, "No, No. I mean in this class do we believe in poems and things, or is it just us?" Fish's explanation of what happened is that meaning does not exist independently of interpretive communities. The incident forms one evidence for the theory he is advancing.[12]

Note, however, that there is another explanation, which I believe is more adequate than Fish's. Although having the same linguistic makeup and sound, these are in a sense different words, or at least different definitions of the same linguistic symbols. These different meanings have different referents. One may detect these by looking them up in a dictionary. It suggests that the context is frequently the indication of which of these meanings is involved in a given instance.

There is another feature of Fish's illustration that he does not bring out, however. The correction of the professor's understanding of the student's question came when the student who had spoken those words explained what she meant. Then the meaning became readily apparent. A given word may have several meanings, but what identifies which particular meaning is to be understood in a given case is the speaker's intention. To suggest that it is the interpretive community that gives the meaning is to beg the question.

From these brief illustrations of how several leading postmodernists actu-

---

[11]Jacques Derrida, "Limited, Inc., abc . . . ," in *Glyph* (Baltimore: Johns Hopkins University Press, 1977), 2:162-254.

[12]Stanley Fish, *Is There a Text in This Class? The Authority of Interpretive Communities* (Cambridge, Mass.: Harvard University Press, 1980), p. 305.

ally function, it is now possible to offer several tentative observations regarding postmodernism and its presentation of its views. We will see that in practice these postmodernists fit our general thesis regarding the nature of truth.

1. Postmodernists present their views not simply as an expression of their own feelings, but apparently with the expectation that others will understand and accept them.

2. Postmodernists seem to hold that their views are in some ways superior or preferable to alternative views.

3. Postmodernists believe that there are correct and incorrect interpretations of what they have said, and that this distinction transcends personal or group subjective reactions.

Beyond these theoretical considerations, however, on the practical level of ordinary human discussion, in everyday human social and business dealings, truth is thought of as the way things are. If, for example, I come to the checkout counter at the supermarket or the discount store and have a dispute with the checkout person about how many of a certain item I have, the appeal is settled by counting. It makes no difference whether my contention that I have three of that item is as consistent as the employee's contention that I have four. It also is not a question of whether three "works out" better than does four, because while that might be the case for me, it probably is not better for the store. If I am stopped by a police officer who claims to have clocked me on his radar device at a speed in excess of the speed limit, there is an assumption that some state of affairs exists both for me and for him that we are trying to understand.

Similarly, our entire court system, as well as that in other cultures, is premised on the determination of the pertinent facts. I would also contend that measured on pragmatic criteria, only some type of correspondence view is practical, even for postmodern philosophers and theologians, when they are functioning *qua* human being. I have in mind here the type of thing that Dallas Willard has referred to in saying that even the most subjective and relative postmodernist becomes strangely objective when such issues as faculty benefits are at stake. As Hugo Maynell puts it, "Not only does everyone else assume in effect that what I have called rationality is the best means to believing truly and acting well; deconstructionists and postmodernists do so themselves, the moment they leave their desks."[13] He goes on to illustrate this with how a postmodernist functions when he wants to know the balance in his bank account, or his uncle's birthday.

---

[13]Hugo Maynell, "Archdeconstruction and Postpostmodernism," *Heythrop Journal* 36, no. 2 (1995): 133.

I am arguing that the different theories of truth are not actually so much differing views of the *nature* of truth as they are differing *tests* of truth. They differ, in other words, as to whether the mark or sign or test of truth is primarily consistency, agreement with experience, or practical implications. It is not a question of definition of truth, but rather of justification or of warrant, depending on one's philosophical orientation.

What I am really attempting to obtain here is a view of truth that would be neither distinctively modern nor postmodern. It would take into account the insights of the modern period as well as those of the postmodern, rather than simply retreating into a premodern orientation, as if these subsequent movements and periods had never occurred. Thus, in a genuine sense, what I am seeking is a "postpostmodern" view of truth. Actually, I am proposing a perennialist view of truth, one that is assumed throughout premodern, modern and postmodern periods, but am attempting to give it a uniquely postpostmodern orientation.

In using this term, I wish to acknowledge a prior use in print of this term by Maynell.[14] Although I arrived at this term independently of his use of it, and may have been using it before he did, he has used it in print previously, and there may be others who have been using the term as well. There is a great deal of similarity between his use of the term and the way I am employing it here. While not yet prepared to use *postmodern* in the past tense, I agree with Maynell that postmodernism, as usually identified, must be, can be and is being transcended. This is said without attempting in any sense to contend that a postpostmodern view is superior to postmodernism because it follows and replaces it and that what follows is superior to what precedes. Indeed, postpostmodernism readopts, in a somewhat modified fashion, some of what postmodernism rejected.

I also want to call attention to the preliminary and nascent character of my proposal. This is really only a sketch of the direction in which I believe we will need to move, not a fully worked out version of that. Much hard work, preferably done in collaboration, is needed to flesh out these theses. I would consequently term the subtitle of this chapter, "*Toward* a postpostmodern view of truth."[15]

Interparadigmal Communication

With these preliminary matters in mind, then, let us begin by noticing what

---

[14]Ibid., pp. 125-39.

[15]For a thorough treatment of the biblical view of truth and its contrast with the postmodern view, see Douglas Groothuis, *Truth Decay* (Downers Grove, Ill.: InterVarsity Press, 2000), pp. 60-110.

happens when various persons disagree with one another. Certain propositions on each side are asserted, and (at least some of) those on the other side
are rejected. How are we to interpret this disagreement? Several possibilities
exist.

1. The discussants are not actually talking about the same thing. They
may both be right, but be passing by each other in their conversation. This
was the case in William James' famous example of the debate over whether
the man goes around the squirrel on the side of the tree.[16] If one means by
"goes around" that one is successively to the north, then to the west, then to
the south, and finally to the east of the squirrel, then the man does indeed
"go around" the squirrel. If, however, "goes around" means to be first on the
side facing the squirrel's stomach, then on the side facing his left side, next
on the side facing his back, and finally on the side facing his right side, then
the man does not go around the squirrel. As anyone who has ever tried to
observe a squirrel on a tree knows, as the man moves around the tree the
squirrel does also, thus always keeping his stomach side toward the man, or
keeping the tree between the man and himself. In any discussion it may be
the case that the disputants are not actually talking about the same thing.
They may both be right.

2. The discussants are talking about the same thing, but are misunderstanding one another. They may actually be in agreement without realizing
it, perhaps because of difference of terminology, or they may disagree, but
not on a different point than they think. They may misunderstand what the
other is saying. Or one may understand the other and the basis of their disagreement, but the other does not.

3. There is a plurality of truth. On this basis, both parties are right, both
have the truth, for there is more than one truth. Even though they may contradict each other, neither is wrong. This is, of course, a radical solution, and
is the one that postmodernism frequently appears to be advocating.

4. There is a genuine disagreement here. There is one truth, and the two
disputants disagree as to what that is. Here the problem is to determine
what is true, and to have a theory as to what truth is, and how one arrives at
and recognizes that truth. There are several possible indications that the two
parties believe that what separates them is a difference of "states of affairs."
One is if at least one claims to have been misunderstood, thus suggesting
that there is a true and a false interpretation of what is said. Another is if
one attempts to refute the other's position, suggesting that the contradictory
of the true view is false. A further indication is if they attempt to persuade

---

[16]William James, "What Pragmatism Means," in *"Pragmatism," and Four Essays from "The Meaning of Truth"* (New York: Meridian, 1955), pp. 41-42.

one another. This implies that communication across different communities is possible.

How can such communication take place when there is a claim that a totally different paradigm is involved? Here it may be helpful to us to observe what takes place when two persons, neither of whom understands the other person's language, try to communicate. If there is a translator, who knows both languages, that solves the problem, but let us assume that no such translator is available. There is no one who can move from one language to the other. The usual situation is for one to speak the other person's language, to move from his own to the other person's linguistic territory, but that also is not possible here. The alternative is for the person to continue to speak his own language, a language different from that which the other person understands, but that will be of no avail. We must ask, therefore, whether there is some sort of universal language, which is not the language of either of these persons, into which they may enter and converse on this neutral ground. While English functions this way in much of the world, English is not a neutral language. It is simply one language that is the second language of a large number of persons. Despite efforts to create an artificial language, such as Esperanto, there is no such language, functionally.

One other possibility remains, which is generally utilized by people in such situations who really must communicate. They endeavor to learn each other's language by beginning in an elementary fashion, pointing to some object for which then each gives her or his own word. Gradually they begin to learn how the other refers to such, and extend this to more and more areas of communication. What is happening here must be examined carefully, however. The means by which they learn each other's language is by entering into a common area, at the prelinguistic level. While the two persons have different words for what an English speaker would call a dog, both have the concept of dog, and it is this common concept that becomes the link between the different words for dog in the two languages.

5. There is, of course, one other explanation. That is that the disagreement is not really about factual matters, about states of affairs, but that the dispute is about power, about who will force the other to submit to his or her direction. On this analysis, the discussion is not attempting to persuade the person with respect to belief, but rather represents a manipulation of the other person, an attempt to bring about conformity to one's wishes. This happens in politics. It is not necessarily that one party convinces the other of its view, but rather that they manage to muster more votes, by whatever means, and thus pass a law to which the other party must submit. Unless there is some common language of communication, persuasion would seem to have to give way to something of this type.

What we may have here are differing tests of truth, but perhaps not as sharply different views of truth. Indeed, they may all assume that truth is a correct description of a state of affairs, which may be assessed by correspondence with certain data, coherence of the tenets, or pragmatic implications. I suggest that clarity has been lost in the discussions because of excessive focus on certain issues. One of these is the concept of "objects." Epistemologies have been discussed in terms of whether the idea or the language fits with certain objects of knowledge. The difficulties of finding any sort of exact correspondence have clouded the whole question of our knowledge. A second problem has been too strong a focus on universal theories or metanarratives. The difficulties involved in trying to formulate inclusive explanations have tended to override the concern about whether specific statements can be justified. Finally, too much has been made of hard foundationalism. The idea that knowledge can be based on certain indubitable starting points is not too difficult to undercut. That does not, however, settle the question of whether there does not need to be some basis for the assertions that are made, some basis in a "reality" accessible to both parties in the discussion.

This is not to say that there are not differing perspectives on matters, which are affected by our historical situation, our unique position in the world. This, however, does not alter the fact that all of these discussions seem to assume that there is some common state of affairs, however general or specific that may be, about which the various parties differ. What seems to have happened here is that epistemological considerations ("we cannot know this exactly") have been metamorphized into ontological considerations ("there is no common state of affairs to be discussed").

Let us take this issue a step further. Suppose that you and another person are sitting together at a table. The only item on the table is what appears to you to be a blue book. The other person touches it and says, "Blue book." Then a few minutes later, nothing in the situation having changed, he says, again obviously referring to this same object, "Green ring." What are the possibilities of interpretation of this situation?

1. There is another sense in which the blue book is "green ring." For example, that may be the title of the book, rather than a description of its appearance or nature. In other words, "green ring" is being predicated of the object in a different way than "blue book" is.

2. The book may contain a reference to a green ring. Thus, what is being referred to is something internal to the book as book, part of the story it recounts.

3. The other person is referring to a feature of the blue book that you had not previously noticed, or at least had not been previously mentioned. The

book may, for example, be ringed in green.

4. The other person is hallucinating, seeing a green ring that is not there.

5. You are hallucinating, failing to see something that has now appeared, or failing to observe the transformation of the book into a ring.

6. The other person is now speaking a different language, one in which "green ring" means what "blue book" means in English (the way *Gift* means in German what *poison* means in English).

I would propose that a good general principle in interpreting situations like this is to utilize the least radical explanation that will adequately account for the phenomena. This is a negative application of the law of parsimony. Our aim, after all, is to keep the discussion going. This is like saying that if I have a gangrenous toe, while the surgeon could save my life by amputating at the hip, the knee, or the ankle, simply removing the toe would accomplish the same results with fewer unfortunate and unnecessary side effects.

Reducing One's Own Conditionedness

If the postmodernists are correct in their contention of the conditioning influence on our beliefs of the social and historical setting in which we find ourselves (and I believe they are), then what are we to do about it? One option is simply to say that this is how things are, and that the subjective factors of our situation are inescapable. We must simply agree to disagree. While that sounds good in theory, in practice postmodernists proceed to argue with those who differ with them, contending that their view is more correct or more deserving of adoption. It would appear to me that if we are to have genuine dialogue, and if we are to come closer to the truth, we must work at reducing the inevitable subjectivity as much as possible.

How should I go about attempting to narrow the influence of these conditioning factors? As a first step, one must practice the ancient great philosophers' dictum, "Know thyself." This is not because, as Plato believed, the truth is innate as a result of the soul's contact with it in an earlier life, but because it will enable us to become aware of those factors, formerly and presently external to us but now so internalized that they are part of who we are, and affect how we perceive matters. I strongly recommend that each academic write his or her autobiography in some detail, not with the aim of publishing it, but of contributing to self-understanding. One needs to scrutinize the details of one's life, asking how these bear on outlook and presuppositions. How does the fact of one's ethnicity, the nature of upbringing, sexual identity (or as it is often termed now, "gender," suggesting that human beings are parts of speech), age, the experiences of life, affect one's outlook?

To take an example from a nontheological realm, I grew up in a very poor farm family. We did not have electricity until I was in high school. Some years my father could not make any payment on the principal of the mortgage on our farm, instead paying only the interest. Poor as my family was, I remember well the disdain with which my parents looked on those who were on "relief," as welfare was termed in those days. Living on a farm there was little opportunity to find gainful employment to provide savings for college. When I left for college the total my parents were able to give me was $50, the same as each of my siblings received. Although tuition was much less then than it is now, financial aid and scholarships were also much more limited.

I worked my way through college and seminary at a variety of jobs, from answering the telephone at night in a funeral home, to assembling Sunday newspapers all Saturday night, to back-breaking factory work. I recall going from door to door down a business street near the college, seeking part-time employment. As a college freshman, I regularly took the end slice of bread in the college cafeteria because it cost one cent, rather than the two cents that the regular slices cost. Knowing this about my background helps me understand that I will have a natural bias toward a conservative view of matters economic and political. It also, incidentally, helps me understand why I have sometimes been accused of being "frugal." This is the sort of autobiographical analysis I recommend as part of the self-understanding process. Although at times painful, it is essential if we are to reduce the conditioning effect of our environment and circumstances.

The other major effort that will help narrow the circle of subjectivity is genuine interaction with others, preferably of a different cultural background than ours. This should have two beneficial effects. It should help make us aware of the particular perspective from which we think and speak. It should also enable us to enter into the other person's perspective, in such a way as to understand better how they think, and why they think that way. Hopefully, these two influences would not only work on me, but upon my dialogue partner.

This dialogue can be carried on in several ways. One, and probably the most effective, is direct personal encounter and dialogue. Here there can be responses to the questions we have and to the tenets we advance. That may not always be practical, however. Some of the most helpful dialogue partners we might wish to engage are removed from us, either in distance or in time. Reading their works may be the most practical form of encounter we can practice.

Communication and Culture

What I have been trying to argue in this chapter is that differing paradigms may not really differ so much in the understanding of the nature of truth. At least, this is the case if representatives of the two are actually advancing their views as something that the other ought to accept, if they offer arguments in support of their view and criticisms of the other's view. They are assuming some common realm of consideration within which these views are more or less adequate, and a similar conception of the nature of truth. Where they differ is in the perspective from which they view this evidence, the selection of the evidence, or the interpretation of the evidence. It is these differences to which we must give attention.

The problem is not simply in the differing perspectives on the object of discussion. It is also the differing perspectives on what each of the persons in the dialogue is saying. Each has an internal understanding of his or her own perspective, but an external understanding of the other's perspective.

To make this more specific, let us suppose that two persons, a and b, are discussing a common object, Q. We will then have two factors:

Qa The object Q, as a understands it.

Qb The object Q as b understands it.

Now, however, the problem becomes more complex:

Qaa a's understanding of Q, as a understands his own understanding.

Qbb b's understanding of Q, as b understands her own understanding.

Qab a's understanding of Q, as b understands a's understanding.

Qba b's understanding of Q, as a understands b's understanding.

It is important to see that not only our understanding of the object, but our understanding of the respective understandings of the object, is conditioned. It is at this level that much misunderstanding takes place. Postmodernism has emphasized this insight, although it is not the exclusive possession of postmodernism, and I sought to deal with that in chapter ten, the positive evaluation of postmodernism.

Perhaps an illustration will make clearer the point I am seeking to make. Suppose two persons, one an American and the other a German, are discussing the temperature of the water in a given container. Both being bilingual, each speaks his native language in the discussion. Is the water that the American would call *hot water* what the German would term *heisses Wasser*, or not? On the surface of things, it should be fairly easy to resolve the issue. The English term *hot* and the German term *heiss* (uninflected form) are dictionary synonyms, as are *water* and *Wasser*, and the common derivation is fairly obvious.

In this case, however, we have a problem, because like many synonyms, these are not exact synonyms. While the German has the set of categories (*heiss, warm, kühl* and *kalt*), and the American has the set of categories (*hot, warm, cool* and *cold*), the dividing line (or transitional range) between *warm* and *heiss* is several degrees higher for the German than that between *warm* and *hot* is for the American. In the judgment of the American, one could bathe safely in *hot water*, whereas the German would fear being scalded in *heisses Wasser*. The difference is not simply in their preference in temperature. Let us suppose that the two have not both tested the temperature of the water. The German reports that *das Wasser ist heiss*, whereupon the American would interpret him as saying that *the water is hot* and might consequently scald himself. In terms of the categories above, the problem is the difference between Qaa and Qab.

What can be done to alleviate the communication and understanding problem I have described? It would appear that great effort must be exerted to enter into the other person's perspective, or to adopt the other person's presuppositions. It will be a matter of trying to actually see things from the other person's standpoint. That, in turn, requires suspension of judgment, and a considerable amount of listening and questioning, rather than speaking or thinking about what we are going to say next.

What I am saying is that in terms of the set of explanations offered on pages 238-39 above, we are trying to narrow the possibilities. Disregarding the fifth explanation, we are attempting to reduce 1 and 2, so that only 3 and 4 remain. If we are successful in identifying genuine differences, there is then the possibility of making genuine progress toward resolving them.

We have been told for some time that there are major cultural differences that prevent or at least seriously hamper our attempts to communicate across cultures. Because of the different perspectives, it simply is not possible to see what the other person sees, or to see it in the same way. It appears that this may have been overstated. In some cases, the conception of what the other person holds has been misunderstood or exaggerated. I think of a native of India, who reported that one American professor told him, "You simply do not understand the Eastern mind." Imagine an American in effect telling an Indian that he, the American, understood the Eastern mind better than the Indian did.

More extensive is the account of the experience of an American theology professor, Paul Griffiths, in learning to interact with Buddhists. He had studied the languages necessary to read the writings of first-millennium Indian Buddhist writers. He says of those texts:

> I immediately felt a great sense of familiarity, of recognition. Here was a philosophical tradition I could recognise, feel at home with, understand. Here was a tradition for which virtually all of the philosophical questions which had troubled me and my tradition—questions about knowledge, truth, personal identity, language and reference—were also burning issues. Here, I felt, was a tradition which also placed great stress upon the probative significance of valid

arguments with true premises, a tradition which, at the end of its arguments, likes to write (in Sanskrit), *siddham etat* (that's proved), the Sanskrit equivalent of QED.[17]

Contrary to the idea that a twentieth-century Western analytic philosopher and a fifth-century Indian Buddhist philosopher have such radically different views of the nature of philosophy and reason that they cannot communicate, Griffiths contends that their "understandings of what it is to do philosophy are substantially the same."[18] Beyond that, he says, "it just isn't clear that as a matter of fact the criteria for rationality and truth are so different from culture to culture. I would argue that, as far as Indian Buddhism and Anglo-American analytical philosophy are concerned, they are close to identical."[19] He believes that what has prevented such crosscultural dialogue is what he terms "philosophical apartheid." On the contrary, he believes that it is possible for Western twentieth-century philosophers and Buddhists, even from a much earlier time, to engage in fruitful philosophical argument. The reason this is possible is "because the norms of rationality and truth are substantially identical in both cultures; what counts as a good argument in one counts as a good argument in another."[20]

Improving the Quality of Dialogue

If there is to be progress in such discussions, certain ground rules will need to be followed. While some postmodernists may declare that these are simply calls for concessions to the modern orientation, they are essential if communication is to take place and if it is to be effective. That this is the case can be seen by the disdain postmodernists themselves express toward deviations from these guidelines, while in some cases practicing such deviations themselves. The argument for these guidelines is pragmatic. They are intended to facilitate communication. They are designed to make sure that discussions between those of differing paradigms are true arguments, in the academic sense of the word, rather than quarrels. For if they become the latter, they are in reality power struggles, which on a societal basis generate increasing conflict, and in extreme cases, even violence.

   1. Care must be used in the choice of language. Expressions such as "that

---

[17]Paul J. Griffiths, "Philosophizing Across Cultures: Or, How to Argue with a Buddhist," *Criterion* 26, no. 1 (1987): 11. For a more complete treatment of this subject see his *An Apologetic for Apologetics: A Study in the Logic of Interreligious Dialogue* (Maryknoll, N.Y.: Orbis, 1991).

[18]Griffiths, "Philosophizing Across Cultures," p. 11.

[19]Ibid., p. 13.

[20]Ibid., p. 14.

is stupid" or "that is ridiculous"[21] must be avoided. These do not actually further the discussion at all. They may serve to put off the disputant, but nothing is really gained toward understanding the issues. Similarly, labeling must be avoided. The use of expressions like "the myth of . . ." and "the . . . fallacy," unless they relate to widely recognized genuine fallacies, are not helpful and may be cases of trying to co-opt the high ground. Beyond that, however, it is almost always possible to assign some sort of label to a given view, such as that it is "dualistic" or "monistic," or that it is "rationalist," or "irrationalist," or "scholastic," or something of the type. One can either be accused of circularity or of incoherence. In each case, there are definite forms of each term that are merely descriptive, but usually a wide variety of views are included under the general nomenclature. Consider, for example, Lovejoy's thirteen pragmatisms,[22] or Brightman's five types of idealism.[23] What often happens rhetorically is that because of the wide range of semantic reference, the term may carry negative connotations because of one of the possible references, which, if there is no further specification, will tend to attach to any application of the word. As we shall see in the next chapter, that is a common occurrence in references to foundationalism.

2. We must divest ourselves of the idea that the most recent is therefore superior. This idea of progress has been a prominent feature of modernism. Yet it also is still found in much postmodernism, perhaps indicating that postmodernism has not broken as free from its modernist precursors as might be thought. In fact, the very name, *post*modern, has the connotation of transcending what has gone before. We must similarly reject any such moves as, "No one believes that anymore." These represent a type of rhetorical power play, seeking to short-circuit the discussion process in such a way as to settle the matter by fiat. An idea cannot be assumed to be either good or bad because it is new or different. Its value must be assessed on its own terms. It is impressive, however, to notice how many times such a move is made. Thomas Oden has suggested that a sort of moratorium be declared on words like "new," which is frequently used as a synonym for good.[24]

What is actually happening here is what is sometimes called "chronological snobbery." This is the idea of the inherent superiority of the present to

---

[21]Jacques Derrida, in Richard Kearney, *Dialogues with Contemporary Continental Thinkers* (Manchester: Manchester University Press, 1984), pp. 123-24.

[22]Arthur O. Lovejoy, "The Thirteen Pragmatisms," *Journal of Philosophy* 5 (1908): 6-12, 29-39.

[23]Edgar Sheffield Brightman, "The Definition of Idealism," *Journal of Philosophy* 30 (1933): 429-35.

[24]Thomas C. Oden, *After Modernity . . . What? Agenda for Theology* (Grand Rapids, Mich.: Zondervan, 1990), p. 42.

anything that has gone before. It is rather widespread. It derives much of its force from the fact that in technology this is true. The assumption is that this is a universal principle, a sort of metanarrative, as it were. That must be challenged. An idea is good because it has qualities that commend it, not because it is old or new.

This problem of chronological snobbery goes beyond simply considering itself superior to any predecessor, however. Advocates of a new view often believe that it has some sort of status of finality, that it will not be succeeded by any other view. While seldom enunciated in this fashion, this belief is often implicitly present nonetheless. While other views have replaced those that have preceded them, and this view has surpassed all of its predecessors, there is no real consideration of the logical possibility that this view will also succumb to something else. Modernism, by its very name, appeared to be what is now, and by definition could scarcely be replaced. With respect to postmodernism, that terminology seems to claim yet a further finality. Everything after modernism is, by definition, postmodern. Perhaps, however, we need to think in terms of postpostmodernism. The idea that not only is our view superior to what has gone before, but is also the ultimate belief should be termed "chronocentrism." Just as ethnocentrism assumes the superiority of the speaker's (or writer's) culture, so chronocentrism assumes the superiority of the speaker's time.

3. Great care must be exercised to treat differing viewpoints fairly. It is tempting to give only one side of an argument, to state a view one differs with and immediately refute it, or to cite poor examples of the other view. This type of approach simply will not do in a postpostmodern age. It will only guarantee that disagreement and even discord will prevail.

4. Any sort of ad hominem arguments must be avoided. This is not to say that it is not in order to call attention to inconsistency between a given thinker's theory and practice, but any irrelevant personal suggestions must be avoided. I have in mind here something like George Lindbeck's statement regarding the cognitivist view of doctrine, that it is held primarily by the persons among whom the sects especially recruit, and that only persons "who combine unusual insecurity with naivete can easily manage to do this" [accept sets of objectively and immutably true propositions].[25]

5. Discussants must freely and honestly acknowledge their views, and state their meaning openly. While this may seem strange, I am convinced that it will be increasingly important. Until about 1995, I had only once encountered a situation where political pressure was brought to bear to

---

[25]George Lindbeck, *The Nature of Doctrine: Religion and Theology in a Postliberal Age* (Philadelphia: Westminster Press, 1984), p. 16.

affect the conclusions of a piece of scholarly research in which I and two others were engaged. More recently, however, I have found obstacles to research. Access was blocked to material that would document the view of a particular person. On another occasion, efforts have been made to discourage me from publishing the results of research. In another case, a professor was surprised to find that a student was familiar with his view because he had consulted the library's copy of the professor's dissertation, which the professor in question did not realize the library possessed. Immediately after the class, the professor went to the library and checked out his own dissertation, thus making it inaccessible for the remainder of the semester. Thus far, the evidence is only anecdotal, but in an age in which scholarly conclusions are regarded as both the cause and the result of political considerations, we may expect more of this. We must ourselves demonstrate the integrity to be willing to state our beliefs openly.

6. The practice of "dipolar alternation" must be rejected. By this I mean the practice of stating contradictory positions on a given issue. When criticized for holding A the person shifts to position B, and loudly protests, "But I said 'B.'" This of course is true, but the person also said "A." On the other hand, when criticized for holding B, the reply is, "But I hold to A." The problem with this is that a person can be allowed to hold both, but cannot then also claim that his view and its contradictory are not both true.

7. There must be clear discussion of the terms involved and their denotation. The practice of retaining a term, but changing its definition may seem easier than arguing for a differing viewpoint, but in the long run it will only contribute to confusion. One of my graduate philosophy professors, Eliseo Vivas of Northwestern University, used to speak of what he called "the infinite coefficient of elasticity of words," in that they can be stretched and stretched to cover ever wider circles of meaning, but without breaking.

8. Accurate information must be used in academic argumentation. The use of "fictive" work in history must be decried. It is one thing to say that our understanding of history is affected by the situation in which we find ourselves. It is quite another thing to say that history can be imaginatively created in order to make it fit our biases. We must make certain that persons know that we may well be mistaken about some factual matter, since we are fallible human beings, but that they can be assured that we have very thoroughly sought to verify the accuracy of our statements, and that we would most assuredly not deliberately concoct our data.

We may need to exercise diligence in our use of secondary sources. This means that we will need to check for typographical errors that may have crept in. Beyond that, however, we will want to need to be as diligent in going back to original languages as we would with the biblical text. Just as personal interpretation can enter into translations from Greek and Hebrew, so they can also creep into renditions of French and German.

9. In a postmodern age, it will be necessary to practice a hermeneutic of suspicion with respect to qualifiers and intensifiers. "Clintonism" has been identified with such presidential statements as, "I was never alone in a hotel with that woman"—a statement technically correct, since there were other persons in the building, but not necessarily in the same room with Clinton and the woman in question. We need to be alert to similar statements in discussions.

10. The introduction of irrelevant considerations needs to be excluded. If, as in the Clinton impeachment trial, an objection is raised such as, "This is just a personal dispute," or "x has a personal vendetta against y, and this is part of it," we must reply with something like this: "Even if that were the case, what bearing does that consideration have on the issue of whether the criticism is accurate?"

Common Logic

I further want to argue that all beliefs and all assertions assume certain common logical considerations. Even Derrida, Foucault and Rorty do not really believe that contradictories can both be true. Certainly, they do not believe that their views and the views they are attempting to refute are equally true. Even if they were to assert that "it is the case that two contradictories can both be true," they would not also accept the statement that "it is not the case that two contradictories can both be true." By affirming the former, they intend to reject the latter. If this is not the case, then all meaningful communication breaks down. Disagreements based on ambiguities of terms or qualities, or imprecision of perception and measurement, do not alter this fact. Even postmodernists cannot assimilate the liar's paradox, which in the case of the American Philosophical Association assumes the form of a T-shirt, on the front of which is the statement, "The sentence on the back of this shirt is false," and the back of which bears the statement, "The sentence on the front of this shirt is true."

I sometimes say to someone who is advancing what he or she considers to be a postmodern view of truth something like this: "I agree with you completely; and you are totally wrong." If I say this, then by deduction, what I am saying is, "I believe this, but I know that my belief is wrong." Apart from wish-fulfillment, and short of some sort of mental illness, it simply is not humanly possible to believe something that one regards as false. One may, of course, deny on one level what one knows on another level to be true, such as the denial that goes on in the case of death of a loved one, or one's own serious and perhaps fatal illness. One who contends that it is not just psychologically but also logically possible to believe what one considers to be false must give an account of just what belief means in such a setting.

It is interesting to note that those who have sought to defend Derrida's new logic find it necessary to do so by distinguishing it from traditional logic, and that this very move of necessity utilizes the very logic to which it is supposed to be an alternative. John Ellis points this out in his report of the discussion of Barbara Johnson's significant paper, "Nothing Fails Like Success."

> Jerry Aline Flieger ("The Art of Being Taken by Surprise," *SCE Reports* 8, Fall 1980), one of a number who received Johnson's paper favorably, asserted that the "old" logic that deconstruction replaced was the logic of "binary oppositions," i.e., contrasts of opposing terms. But in an amusing contradiction immediately following this, she decided that the way to "pin down the 'unclear' logic of deconstruction" was to proceed by distinguishing it from traditional logic: "the clearest distinction between traditionalist and deconstructive logic resides in . . ." (p. 57). In other words, binary logic is needed to characterize deconstructive logic. This example, like many others, leads to the thought that these claims for an "other" logic have often been too lightly made without being adequately thought through.[26]

Even the anthropological data sometimes appealed to do not count against the contention I am working with here, that the basic laws of logic, namely, the law of identity, the law of contradiction, and the law of excluded middle, are presupposed in all dialogue. Lévy-Bruhl, for example, speaks of mythical thought as "prelogical," and contends that we cannot approach the examination of such cultural practices applying our laws of logic. Even the law of contradiction, together with all the other logical laws, becomes invalid.[27] Yet Cassirer says, "But that all primitive mentality necessarily is prelogical or mystical seems to be in contradiction with our anthropological and ethnological evidence. We find many spheres of primitive life and culture that show the well-known features of our own cultural life. As long as we assume an absolute heterogeneity between our own logic and that of the primitive mind, as long as we think them specifically different from and radically opposed to each other, we can scarcely account for this fact."[28]

---

[26] John Ellis, *Against Deconstruction* (Princeton, N.J.: Princeton University Press, 1989), pp. 8-9 n. 3.

[27] Lucien Lévy-Bruhl, *How Natives Think*, trans. Lilian A. Clare (New York: Washington Square, 1966); *Primitive Mentality*, trans. Lilian A. Clare (New York: Macmillan, 1923); *The "Soul" of the Primitive*, trans. Lilian A. Clare (London : Allen & Unwin, 1966).

[28] Ernst Cassirer, *An Essay on Man: An Introduction to a Philosophy of Human Culture* (Garden City, N.Y.: Doubleday, 1944), p. 107.

Postmodernists sometimes assert that this sort of logic is a characteristic of the modern period and of modernism as an ideology. My contention is that it is not simply a uniquely modern conception. It is a conception that the premodern period also shared. And, beyond that, I am arguing that even postmoderns, to the degree that they advocate their view, also must work with that logic. Although Derrida in particular has contended that there is an alternative logic, his failure to give that logic any concrete and understandable content renders his assertion unimpressive. Even that contention requires the logic that it would replace, as we noted in the quotations from Derrida. It may well be that we find paradoxes at times, but even the ability to identify a paradox assumes the laws of logic.

If this is indeed the case, then we must raise the question of whether we are responsible for and must believe the logical implications of the things that we believe. Suppose, for example, that a person believes that a particular object is a right angle triangle, on a surface of zero curvature, and that the lengths of the two sides adjoining the right angle are three and four feet. Is that person also then committed to the belief that the length of the other side is five feet? Since the Pythagorean Theorem says that the square of the hypotenuse of a right angle triangle is equal to the squares of the other two sides, is the person free to deny that in the triangle in question, the other side is five feet in length?

To be sure, the laws of logic are notoriously difficult to enforce. Frequently, someone who says something like, "You can't push the law of contradiction that far," actually means, "I don't want to accept the conclusions to which my beliefs should lead me." Yet I would contend that the person who holds the former is also logically committed to the latter. To put it differently, that person holds implicitly to the latter, or has this as an implicit belief. This is the case, because in other areas of life, in commonplace circumstances, the person believes in and abides by these logical laws. What we must do is to think through the implications of our beliefs and help others to do the same with respect to their views.

In this chapter I have argued that discussion and debate, even when claimed to extend across paradigms, presupposes a common view of truth and logic. In the next chapter we will investigate different ways of assessing the truth of specific claims.

13

assessing the truth

Another question that must be asked concerns the criteria or tests for truth. Postmodernists are virtually unanimous in their opinion that foundationalism, which characterized modernism, must be rejected. In its place, they generally substitute a coherentist or pragmatic approach.

Foundationalism
In light of the considerable amount of discussion about foundationalism, a definition is needed. In general, classical foundationalism contended that in the knowing process there are certain unshakable starting points. These are not justified by any other propositions. They are simply immediately justified. They possess a character such that they are indubitable (they cannot be doubted) and incorrigible (it is not possible to be mistaken about them). In the rationalist form of foundationalism, such as that of Descartes, such a foundation is known rationally, or by pure thought, while for an empiricist like Locke, the foundation is sense data. These foundations serve as justification for other beliefs, which are then mediately justified.

Much of the discussion of foundationalism, and especially, much postmodernist criticism, has been directed at a model of classical foundationalism, with Descartes being the most frequently selected representative. In some ways that approach has yielded a relatively easy target. When foundationalism is said to be dead, this is what is usually meant by foundationalism. However, a comparatively large number of foundationalisms have been presented since about 1975 that differ in significant ways from the classical versions of foundationalism. These make more modest claims about their effectiveness. Triplett comments, "It is not clear that the standard arguments against foundationalism will work against these newer, more modest theories. Indeed, these theories were by and large designed with the purpose of overcoming standard objections."[1] These distinctions must be noted, if the discussion of foundationalism is to be accurate.

William Alston speaks of two types of foundationalism,[2] while Triplett has a much more elaborate morphology. He classifies varieties of foundationalism on the basis of two issues, their "specifications of the nature of basic propositions" and "accounts of the relation between basic and nonbasic propositions." Within each of these two major categories there are subgroupings, with two or more varieties of each, leading to no fewer than twenty labels for foundationalist views.[3] One of the most sustained critiques of classical foundationalism, Reformed epistemology, constructs its own type of foundationalism. Thus it is extremely important to identify the exact character of the foundationalism we are discussing.

Not only postmodernists but also most philosophers have, in the past quarter-century, asserted or assumed that foundationalism, having been refuted, is dead. Frequently the objection has been accompanied by something of a moral tone: "Suddenly 'anti-foundationalist' is a good thing to be," said Simpson,[4] and Levi pronounced that "opposition to foundationalism ought to be the philosophical equivalent of resistance to sin."[5] Triplett's comment here is well taken: "At this point in time, however, we have to deal not with a single foundationalist theory but with a variety of related theories." His further comment is a helpful caution: "Whether the arguments that have been made against foundationalism are successful against all theories that might be appropriately described as foundational remains to be seen."[6]

Triplett gives a more general characterization of foundationalism:

EF1: There are basic propositions.

EF2: Any justified empirical proposition is either basic or derives its justification, at least in part, from the fact that it stands in an appropriate rela-

---

[1]Tim Triplett, "Recent Work on Foundationalism," *American Philosophical Quarterly* 27, no. 2 (1990): 93.

[2]William Alston, "Two Types of Foundationalism," *Journal of Philosophy* 73, no. 7 (1976): 165-85.

[3]Triplett, "Recent Work on Foundationalism," p. 97.

[4]Evan Simpson, "Introduction: Colloquimur, ergo sumus," in *Anti-Foundationalism and Practical Reasoning*, ed. E. Simpson (Edmonton: Academic Printing & Publishing, 1987), p. 2.

[5]Isaac Levi, "Edification According to Rorty," *Canadian Journal of Philosophy* 11 (1981): 590.

[6]Triplett, "Recent Work on Foundationalism," p. 96.

tion to propositions which are basic.[7] This means, simply, that there are propositions that form starting points. They are not justified by derivation from any other propositions. These are called basic, and are justified by that status. There are other justified propositions that derive their justification from "standing in an appropriate relationship to basic propositions."

Note that this definition does not specify the nature of the basic propositions—whether renditions of sense experience or logical a prioris, whether indubitable in some sense or not. This means that in theory a large variety of views can be classified as foundationalisms. In fact, the concept of foundationalism becomes so expanded that even ostensive anti-foundationalists are classified as foundationalists of a type. With respect to his category of context dependence of basic propositions Triplett has a class termed "contextual foundationalism." A subcategory of this group maintains that what function as basic propositions vary with different cultural, historical, or scientific conditions. This sociocultural form of contextual foundationalism includes the later Wittgenstein, Quine and Sellars, none of whom identified themselves as foundationalists. Even Rorty falls into this group: "Although his metaphilosophical conclusions imply the rejection of *any* positive theory of knowledge, Rorty's specific comments on and criticisms of traditional theories of knowledge seem to imply one sort of Contextual Foundationalist account, according to which basic propositions are whatever fundamental assumptions remain accepted and unchallenged in a given social or even conversational context."[8]

One problem that has beset most forms of hard foundationalism is the epistemic regress problem. This is the question of how we justify some item of belief or knowledge, and then, how we justify the justifier.[9] If I say that I believe *j*, and then am asked why, my answer is that I believe *j* because of *k*. The further question may then be pressed, however, as to why I consider *k* to be adequate justification for *j*. For example, if I assert that there is a yellow table in the room, I may be asked why I believe this and would probably give some answer such as, "because I see it there," or "I am having a sensory perception of it." Suppose, however, that I am asked, "How do you know that your sensory perception is accurate?" I may give some further justification for this belief, but then I am faced with justifying that justification and so am involved in a vicious infinite regress.

A further problem raised by Plantinga is that foundationalism does not fulfill its own criterion. In order to be rational, on the foundationalist view, a

---

[7]Ibid.

[8]Ibid., p. 101.

[9]This is what Alston calls "iterative foundationalism" in "Two Types of Foundationalism."

belief must be either foundational—self-evident, evident to the senses, or incorrigible; or derivative—inferred by logical principles from the foundational or properly basic beliefs. Now the question, according to Plantinga, is whether classical foundationalism is rational. Which of the two criteria of rationality does the contention that these are the criteria of rationality fulfill? It would appear that it does not meet either of these. In other words, foundationalism is self-referentially inconsistent.[10]

There is a further problem with foundationalism, according to Plantinga. Many common beliefs of ordinary life, on which we base our living, are clearly justified beliefs, yet are excluded by the criteria of classical foundationalism. These are matters that are not evident to the senses, self-evident, or incorrigible. That being the case, they must be justified by a demonstration of their relationship to foundational or properly basic beliefs. No one, however, has ever produced such demonstration. Plantinga says, "Consider all those propositions that entail, say, that there are enduring physical objects, or that there are persons distinct from myself, or that the world has existed for more than five minutes: none of these propositions, I think, is more probable than not with respect to what is self-evident or incorrigible for me; at any rate no one has given good reason to think any of them is."[11] The first objection does indicate the problem of epistemic regress. One must stop the process of justification at some point, but where and why? This is the dilemma that faces any epistemology.

Coherentism

In light of these problems, large numbers of philosophers have turned to other forms of justification. While some of them have embraced pragmatic criteria, most have adopted coherentism. The major difference between coherentism and foundationalism is how their propositions are related to one another in terms of their justification. In foundationalism there is a monodirectional justification. Basic or foundational beliefs justify the derived beliefs, but not vice versa. In coherentism, however, the relationship is more complex. There really are no basic propositions. All propositions, even those about sensory experience, must be justified by relationship to other propositions within the epistemic system. Justification of a proposition is sought, not by showing the relationship to certain epistemologically privileged propositions, termed basic or foundational, but by showing the

---

[10]Alvin Plantinga, "Reason and Belief in God," in *Faith and Rationality*, ed. Alvin Plantinga and Nicholas Wolterstorff (Notre Dame, Ind.: University of Notre Dame Press, 1983), pp. 60-61.

[11]Ibid., pp. 59-60.

coherence of any proposition with the other propositions in the system.

There is, for this approach, a problem of epistemic regress as well, but it is a different type of regress than that encountered by foundationalism. Here the problem is that we are caught in a regress in a vicious circle. If *m* is justified by *n*, and *n* is justified by *o*, and *o* is justified by *q*, and *q* is justified by *m*, then it appears that *m* is justified by itself. In most cases, of course, the circle is considerably larger than this, so that the direct circularity is not quite so obvious. Further, a number of coherentisms in effect say that each proposition is justified by each of the others, thus constituting a more holistic approach.

There are versions of coherentism that escape the major effect of this form of the regress problem, and they are best termed *holistic coherentism*. The central conception of coherentism with respect to justification is that a belief is justified by its coherence with one's other beliefs. The unit of coherence theoretically varies with the size of the set of beliefs one holds, since it may involve all of one's other beliefs. Some of these, of course, may be closer to the belief at issue and thus may be more significant for producing coherence with it. While such a definition of coherence would apply to circular views of justification, it does not cover holistic forms of coherence, which are nonlinear. That is to say, justification for a given belief does not necessarily emerge from a direct inferential line running to it from propositions that serve as premises for it, which in turn are related by a similar direct inferential line to other premises, until there is a return to the original proposition as a premise. Audi expresses a moderate version of holistic coherence as follows:

> For any *S* and any *t*, if *S* has any justified beliefs at *t*, then at *t*, (1) they are each justified by virtue of their coherence with one or more others of *S*'s beliefs; and (2) they would remain justified even if (other things remaining equal) any justification they derive from sources other than coherence were eliminated.[12]

On this model, coherence is not necessarily a straight-line type of relationship to another (justified) belief or proposition. It is a question of the relationship between this belief and potentially a large number of propositions, conceivably even all the beliefs one holds. It avoids the problem of the regress by drawing a distinction not ordinarily found in foundationalism. It contends that the epistemic chain terminates in a belief that is *psychologically direct* but *epistemically indirect*. The last link in the process is as belief,

---

[12]Robert Audi, *The Structure of Justification* (Cambridge: Cambridge University Press, 1993), p. 138.

direct, since it is noninferential. As knowledge, however, it is indirect, not simply in the usual sense that it is inferential, but in a broader sense. This belief "constitutes knowledge only by virtue of receiving support from other knowledge or belief."[13] It is not inferred from other elements of knowledge, but its status as knowledge depends on its coherence with one's other beliefs, many of which are, presumably, knowledge themselves. As Audi puts it, "It is thus knowledge *through*, though not by inference from, other knowledge—or at least through justified beliefs; hence it is epistemically indirect and thus non-foundational."[14]

This type of holistic coherentism fits within one of Triplett's varieties of foundationalism, namely, psychological foundationalism, for it holds that if we have any beliefs at all, we have some that are direct or non-inferential. Nonetheless, it denies epistemological foundationalism, since it rejects the idea that for there to be knowledge at all, some of it must be epistemically direct.

Fallibilist Foundationalism

The question then is whether there is any form of foundationalism that retains the epistemic directness of knowledge, but at the same time pre-serves the values found in holistic coherentism. A moderate or fallibilistic type of foundationalism is the best candidate for such a role. The term *falli-bilist* means that a justified belief, even a foundational one, can be found to be false. Further, in this type of foundationalism, the superstructural beliefs are not necessarily related to the foundational beliefs through a deductive relationship. Rather, they may be inductively justified by foundational beliefs. Thus, unless they are necessary truths, they may be false even if the foundational beliefs are true. Just as one's foundational beliefs may be falli-ble, so may one's inferences, so that the superstructural or derived beliefs are fallible.

Moreover, a fallibilist foundationalism must allow for discovering error, both in the foundational and the superstructural beliefs. Foundational beliefs may be found to conflict with other, justified foundational beliefs, or with superstructure beliefs that are sufficiently well supported to be consid-ered justified. This latter variety might, for example, be the case where one superstructure belief conflicts with another superstructure belief that is deductively inferentially derived from or implied by a justified foundational belief.

This means that the foundations, while necessary, need not be absolute.

---

[13]Ibid., p. 140.
[14]Ibid.

Audi puts it this way: "it requires epistemic unmoved movers, but not unmovable movers. Solid ground is enough, even if bedrock is better. There are also different kinds of bedrock, and not all of them have the invulnerability apparently belonging to beliefs of luminously self-evident truths of logic."[15] While this analysis applies primarily to justification, it also means that foundationalism with respect to knowledge can be fallibilistic, for the grounds for one's knowledge are not indefeasible. Perceptual grounds can be overridden, for example. One can fail or cease to know a proposition, not because it is false or discovered to be so, but because one ceases to be justified in believing it.

How, then, does this type of modest foundationalism relate to coherentism? One obvious point of relationship is negative in nature. Incoherence or contradiction may serve to defeat justified, even directly justified and hence foundational, belief. An example would be the defeat of a memorial belief, such as remembering an oak tree growing in a certain spot, but being unable to find sensory evidence that such a tree ever grew there.

Second, however, although not attributing its truth to coherence, a fallibilist foundationalism can employ the principle of independence. This is one of a whole set of principles coherentists commonly utilize. This is the principle that "the larger the number of independent mutually coherent factors one believes to support the truth of a proposition, the better one's justification for believing it (other things being equal)."[16] Thus, the greater the confirmatory effect of more than one sense, or of sense and memory, or of sense and self-evidence, the stronger the justification. Therefore, while the role of coherence in this type of fallibilist foundationalism is restricted, it is a significant one.

What then is the difference between a fallibilist foundationalism and a holistic coherentism? It is not that the latter allows a place for or appeals to coherence and the former does not. Nor is it even, in Audi's judgment, a question of whether coherence is necessary to justification. Rather, it is a question of whether coherence is a basic source of it and is a sufficient basis for justification.[17]

The Justification of Worldviews

Worldviews are broad, inclusive explanatory schemes. They are understandings of the world and of life, on the basis of which we function. We may begin by asking why it is that any of us comes to hold the view of life and

---

[15]Ibid., p. 134.
[16]Ibid., p. 136.
[17]Ibid., p. 162.

the world that we have. Initially, it should be observed, probably few people adopt the understanding that they have because of primarily intellectual reasons. In all likelihood, we receive our beliefs and values from our parents, or those who nurture and teach us. This is the correct insight of which postmodernism has reminded us. At some point we come either to adopt them as genuinely our own, or reject them in favor of a different set. This transition may take place in any of several ways. It may be through an intellectual process of concluding that our previous beliefs are or are not cogent. It may be, and frequently is, the case that the decision is made for existential reasons. As Kierkegaard pointed out in his *Stages on Life's Way,* the move from one life-orientation to another is frequently a leap, in which one is driven by boredom or frustration to another way of life.[18] This may take place in a traumatic or a more gradual fashion. It may simply be a sense that a given way of life is not satisfying to us, or that it is not something that we can live out consistently. However the conviction comes about, it is something of a step into uncharted territory.

Those who retain an earlier commitment may do so out of a sense of satisfaction with that view of things. This is an essential for any viable understanding of the world and life. All of us are humans first. We must be able to live life and live it with a certain degree of satisfaction. Kierkegaard ridicules the philosopher who builds a huge intellectual edifice, but then lives in a little shack outside of it.[19] A view that one may hold as an intellectual but must discard as a human being is seriously deficient.

At this point it may seem that we are basically adopting Richard Rorty's neopragmatism. Three important qualifications must be made to the use of the pragmatic test for justification of beliefs, however. The first is that we are here not talking about simply an isolated conception, but rather a grand or inclusive understanding. Second, we are talking about whether an idea works, not over a brief span of time, but measured on a long-term perspective. We have noted earlier that jumping from an airplane without a parachute may work out very well for a time, increasing the exhilaration of the experience. Near the end of the jump, however, or as soon as one thinks about the conclusion of the experience, the practicality of such a parachute-free endeavor is seriously challenged. A philosophy of life that not only enables one to live successfully and satisfyingly but also to face death and whatever may lie beyond it is to be preferred to one that supplies intense but brief satisfaction.

---

[18]Søren Kierkegaard, *Stages on Life's Way* (Princeton, N.J.: Princeton University Press, 1940); *Either-Or: A Fragment of Life* (Princeton, N.J.: Princeton University Press, 1944).

[19]*The Journals of Søren Kierkegaard: A Selection,* ed. and trans. Alexander Dru (Oxford: Oxford University Press, 1938), p. 156 (#583).

The third qualification is that this criterion cannot serve alone. While a grand illusion might be very gratifying for a time, and perhaps even throughout life, we would generally judge that to be less than the most complete fulfillment of what life was intended to be. Frequently mentally ill persons, at least those whose illness is sufficiently serious to be identified as psychosis, have gone into their condition to avoid the painful experience of reality. In their condition they may be much happier than they were when fully aware of reality. Yet, society usually judges this to be an undesirable condition, if for no other reason than that a society made up entirely of such persons could not survive and function effectively. Therefore, we must apply additional tests to a conception to help assure its truth. The pragmatic test works because those ideas and actions that fit the way things are work out better, in the long run, than those that do not. Thus, the pragmatic test depends on correspondence.

Earlier we examined foundationalism and observed that there are many forms of current foundationalism that are not vulnerable to the criticisms usually directed against classical foundationalism. We also observed that some of these more modest foundationalisms not only are not antithetical to coherence measures of truth, but actually agree with coherence at many points. The Christian theism we are proposing involves a foundationalism of this more modest sort. There are certain basic propositions in terms of which other derived propositions are justified. Yet the secondary propositions are not simply derived deductively from the basic beliefs. Rather, the relationship may in some cases be more nearly that of induction.

This type of foundationalism is not the absolute type found in classical foundationalism such as that of Descartes, however. Rather, this is a fallibilist foundationalism. That is to say, this view recognizes the possibility of error and misinterpretation in the knowing process. While it is one thing to say that we have absolute truth, it is another thing to say that we know and understand it absolutely. It is further quite another matter to contend that we have absolute certainty that we are in the truth. There is a full recognition that in the knowing process we are affected by the conditioning that postmodernism has described so vividly. We have no absolute assurance that our sensations exactly represent the objects that we are perceiving.

What we are proposing here is something that could probably be best classified as critical realism, although without fully endorsing all that has been denoted by that term. Fundamentally, the realist movement in the twentieth century arose largely as a reaction against the idealism of the nineteenth century. According to that view, material objects cannot exist independently of knowing minds. To a large extent that idealism bases this view on what has come to be called the "ego-centric predicament." This is the contention that it is never possible to know objects just as they are—Kant's *Dinge an Sich*. Rather, we always know them in connection with our consciousness of them. Even if we could discover that they exist even when they are not known, or what they are like when not known, that very discovery would be an act of human consciousness. In Kant's version of the problem, we simply cannot bypass the knowing apparatus to make some sort of direct contact with the object of knowledge. Realism, on the other hand, argues that from the fact that we never know anything independently of our consciousness it does not follow that such objects do not exist independently of that consciousness. And, if the idealist argument succeeds with respect to physical objects, it must also succeed with respect to other persons and thus leads us to an untenable solipsism.

I am not certain that the egocentric predicament can be dismissed quite this easily. Solipsism is indeed quite tenable and irrefutable. The fact that others within my consciousness seem to have the same conception of me that I have of them does not establish their existence independent of me. It may be that I am simply having an idea of a person, and that this idea includes the element that said person has an idea of me. Thus, the initial refutation of idealism is no more cogent than Johnson's refutation of Berkeley by kicking a stone. What is more pertinent, in my judgment, is that no one really lives on this idealistic basis. It is a theory that no one lives out, at least no one who attempts to contend for it.

This early realism began to become a revival of Common Sense Realism, not unlike that of Thomas Reid. Indeed, G. E. Moore's refutation of idealism in some ways constituted a commonsense view of perception. His defense was mounted largely in terms of the certainty of simple perceptual judgments such as, "This is a hand." He offered two arguments. First, the denial of such statements leads to inconsistency in belief and behavior. Second, the grounds for the denial of such views involve propositions that are themselves less certain than the propositions they deny.[20] The remaining problem, however, was to account for error and difference of understanding. How can two persons have a somewhat different perception of the same object? For example, two persons, looking at an object from different places, seem to "see" something different. One, looking directly down on it, sees a circle, while the other, removed a distance from it horizontally, reports seeing an ellipse. Perspective realism and theories of appearing contend that the perception is taking place from different perspectives, and that each person, if occupying the perspective of the other, would have the same sensory

---

[20]George Edward Moore, "A Defense of Common Sense," and "Proof of an External World," in *Philosophical Papers* (New York: Macmillan, 1959), pp. 32-59, 127-50.

experience that the other has.[21] Indirect or dualist realism accounts for the problem by distinguishing between the external material objects that are the causes and ultimate objects of perceiving, and the mental effects produced in the perceiver by those objects. This was the form of realism that Descartes and Locke had held. This, however, has been criticized both on the grounds that it cannot escape the egocentric predicament, and that it is ultimately circular. It appears to have transferred the usual understanding of perception from outside to inside the person.

Considerations such as these led to the rise of critical realism in the early twentieth century. Critical realists have proceeded by a closer examination of the perceptual process. They contend that while perception involves an intuition or direct awareness of the external object, it is much more than that. Even perception involves a type of judgment. This is not a two-step process, in which we first perceive a spherical green blob of sense data, and then interpret it as being a bush. Rather, we perceive it as a bush.[22]

If, however, this complex perceptive or interpretive process can vary depending on the circumstances of the person, in what sense can we rely on sensory experience? There are, according to critical realism, a number of ways this can be checked. One is the use of different senses, so what one sees is also confirmed by what one feels. Another is comparing the evidence of different persons, different perceivers of the object. This can best be accomplished by each attempting to view matters from the other's perspective. In the context of the physical perception we are discussing here, it involves the person who sees an ellipse moving to the position occupied by the person who reports seeing a circle, and verifying that under those circumstances each sees what the other has seen under that circumstance.[23]

This process has to be carried further than critical realists have traditionally carried it, however. For the problem is not simply one of physical variations in the perceptual process. The postmodernists contend that the conditioning is social and cultural in nature; it cannot be reduced to simple

---

[21] Evander Bradley McGilvary et al., *Toward a Perspective Realism*, ed. Albert P. Ramsperger (La Salle, Ill.: Open Court, 1956). For theories of appearing, see Roderick M. Chisholm, "The Theory of Appearing," in *Philosophical Analysis: A Collection of Essays*, ed. Max Black (Englewood, N.J.: Prentice-Hall, 1950), pp. 97-112.

[22] Rodney J. Hirst, "Realism," in *The Encyclopedia of Philosophy*, ed. Paul Edwards (New York: Macmillan, 1967), 7:82.

[23] For discussions of critical realism, see Durant Drake et al., *Essays in Critical Realism* (New York: Gordian, 1968); Arthur O. Lovejoy, *The Revolt Against Dualism* (Chicago: Open Court, 1930); Rodney J. Hirst, *The Problems of Perception* (New York: Humanities, 1959). For a recent discussion of realism and its alternative, see Panayot Butchvarow, "Metaphysical Realism," in *Cambridge Dictionary of Philosophy*, ed. Robert Audi (New York: Cambridge University Press, 1995), pp. 488-89.

physical factors, such as that I feel this object to be hot because I have just taken my hand off a block of ice. What must consequently be done, I have argued earlier, is some intensive self-examination, to determine the social influences that bear on my perception and conception. One way of doing this, I have suggested, is writing an intellectual autobiography. Another is intentional interaction with persons of a different background, preferably a radically different background, than mine. The difference in viewpoints should alert us to possible conditioning effects on each of us.

It may seem strange that we have taken so much space to discuss realism, since idealism is not really a viable option for many people in our time. What should be noted, however, is that, as Rorty has pointed out, the same issues are present, in a different form than they were a century earlier, when realism's opponent was idealism.[24] Now, the challenge to realism is from antirealism, or antirepresentationalism. In a sense this plays the role that idealism played a hundred years earlier.

In the final analysis, a critical realism is justified on basically pragmatic grounds. This may seem strange, in light of Rorty's claim to neopragmatism. One may interpret Rorty as simply saying that we cannot have certainty about the objects of reference, but that he is not denying such. Yet, he proceeds on the basis of realism, or at least of representationalism. As we have argued in an earlier critical chapter, on a practical level, Rorty cannot escape acting as if his words represent something beyond themselves, if he is to advocate his theory. To say something works one must check the actual outcome against reality. So on a secondary level (reference to the theory), he is in effect forced to deny what he affirms on the primary level, in the theory itself. What we are contending here is that whether a realistic view is correct, its assumption seems to enable us to communicate, and to make progress toward the refining of our understanding of the world.

Given this understanding of the nature of the basic or foundational propositions, the superstructure of the knowledge is justified by its relationship to these foundations. This relationship is not necessarily an exclusively deductive one, however. On such a model, all derived propositions would be obtained from the foundations by direct inference. There are at least two other types of justificatory relationships. In these, the enumerative induction version consists of making a series of observations, whereupon one arrives at a probable conclusion. The explanatory induction version consists of those statements that arise as means of explaining or making clear the foundational statements. Those statements are justified by way of providing

---

[24]Richard Rorty, "Introduction," in *Objectivity, Relativism, and Truth* (Cambridge: Cambridge University Press, 1991), p. 2.

the best explanation of the foundational propositions. In either of these, however, the relationship of the derivative statements to the foundational statements is at least partly that of induction, rather than deduction.

We have noted the postmodern emphasis upon the historical conditioning of all human thought. Everyone's thoughts and beliefs are derived from a definite situation in life and the world, and all of reality and all of history is viewed from that particular perspective. We now need to ask how we can assess truth in light of reality, and how discussion and debate can go on between representatives of differing perspectives.

We have identified our epistemological position as critical realism. In other words, while we have no absolute way of establishing the existence of objects external to ourselves, or of being certain that our ideas of those objects correspond exactly to them, we can find ways of cross-checking our understanding, in such a way that we can communicate with one another. We may need to qualify that further, by terming it "perspectival critical realism." That means that although we may view reality from different perspectives, there is a common reality there to which we are relating and of which we are speaking.

Critical Realism and Dialogue

It has sometimes been assumed that perspectivalism must inevitably lead to some sort of relativism, in which perhaps each party is speaking of a totally different reality. Donald Davidson has considered this issue in his well-known essay, "On the Very Idea of a Conceptual Scheme."[25] He maintains that to see that two conceptual schemes are different requires at least understanding the other scheme well enough to recognize that it is different. If it were utterly unique, then it could not be known. Thus, it is important to distinguish between what we might term subjective relativism and objective relativism. In this case, critical realism is the same as objective relativism. There is one reality, even though there may be quite different perspectives on it.

How, then, can there be communication between different perspectives, and how can there be tests of the truth of a belief, held from a particular perspective? Here an illustration from the realm of physical perception may help. Let us suppose that there are two persons, discussing the shape of a particular object. Each of them can see only one surface of the object, which is a large rectangular solid, oriented in a north-south direction, and measuring forty feet in length, twenty feet in width, and twenty feet in height. A is

---

[25]Donald Davidson, "On the Very Idea of a Conceptual Scheme," *Proceedings and Addresses of the American Philosophical Association* 47 (November 1974): 5-20.

to the west of the object, facing it from some distance, and is so restrained that he cannot see anything but the surface facing him. For practical purposes, the object is two-dimensional, a rectangle, the length of which is twice its height. B, on the other hand, is to the south of the object, but with the same limitations that A had from the perspective of the west. To B, the object will also be two-dimensional, but will appear to be a square.

Now suppose each can communicate with the other, but cannot move from his own position to that of the other person. One of two things might result. First, they might simply disagree, each thinking he is right, because of course he knows what he sees. This would be the paradigm on which much discussion must be understood, where there is no resolution of the difference because there is no realization that the other person is working from a different perspective.

There is another possibility. The two might begin to become really serious and reflective in their dialogue. Each insists that he must believe his eyes and that he sees this particular object. Perhaps they are not in actual proximity to one another, but are communicating by wireless telephone. They are observing an object, but from their perspective, can only see its one side. Suppose, further, that the two know each other quite well and are convinced both of the observational skill and the integrity of the partner. They might then conclude that each is having a veridical experience. They would then seek an explanation that would integrate the two statements that have been justified by virtue of derivation from sensory experience. From the testimonies of both, they might project the idea that both are right, and that the object is actually a rectangular solid. They would thus get beyond the impasse of the five men and the elephant, each of whom extrapolated from a part of the elephant (e.g., the side or the tusk) that the whole elephant was like this (e.g., a wall or a spear). Here each would be applying the additional test of coherence to what he has established by a foundational test. The same, of course, could be done if a single person were first to view one side and then the other.

Now let us modify our case somewhat. Suppose that while A sees only the one side of the object, the long side, B has a rather different perspective. He is at a greater height, say, for example, a height of forty feet. He is now able to see something that A does not. From his perspective, there is information that A simply does not have from his perspective. Now, the debate is not whether the object is a square or a rectangle; it is whether it is a rectangle or a rectangular solid. How can this difference be adjudicated? In the former case, each person could move into the perspective of the other and could see why the other's belief makes perfectly good sense. Each would be able to say, "I can understand why you see it this way. If I were you, I would agree." They might, however, not realize that they are speaking of the same object, and might not be able put their minds together and realize that the object is a rectangular solid. They might simply agree, "A sees a rectangle and B sees a square."

From the superior vantage point that B has in the second example, however, he does not simply see something different than A sees. He sees more than A sees, he has superior observation. Now suppose that each were to make a transition to the other's perspective. B would understand why A does not conclude as B does, but when A moves to B's perspective, he would presumably agree with B, that is, would see that B's judgment is correct.

This is how, on the theory of critical realism, dialogue should take place, and how truth, or a closer approximation to the truth, can be arrived at. It is a matter of true statements either being foundational, in the sense of being sensory, or being derivable from such foundational statements, by either deduction or induction. It is also a matter of coherence of these statements with others that either are themselves foundational or legitimately derived from foundational beliefs.

A further look needs to be taken at the nature of this dialogue. What we have called for is for each of the dialogue partners to look at matters from the other's perspective. These perspectives differ not spatially but in terms of social and historical conditioning. This means an actual stepping into the other's place. How can this be done, however?

How can those who would discuss and even debate different worldviews engage in dialogue? If each simply presents arguments from his perspective, they will seem very persuasive to him and to those who agree with him, but will not appear so to someone who views reality from a different perspective. Something more than this must be done. To the degree possible, each discussant must enter into the other person's presuppositions, try to view the world from the other person's perspective, try to see reality as the other does, and thus try to understand why the other person's understanding seems to make so much sense to him.

This requires a genuine sense of empathy. What will be required here is what linguist Kenneth Pike described as emic, rather than etic, understanding. While these terms have been given many definitions, we are here using them as follows. An emic perspective or approach is an understanding of reality from within the worldview of those who participate in that reality or behavior. It involves seeing what they see from where they see it, feeling what they feel as they feel it. The emic then is participant-relative, while the etic is observer-relative.[26]

---

[26]See *Emics and Etics: The Insider/Outsider Debate*, ed. Thomas N. Headland, Kenneth L. Pike, and Marvin Harris (Newbury Park, Calif.: Sage, 1990).

The two partners in the dialogue must, as it were, invite each other to accept, provisionally, their view. They must be prepared to set aside their own way of thinking and seeing; they must listen, respectfully and attentively, to what the other has to say. They must really attempt to understand why the other's viewpoint makes sense to him. This will probably involve the two, in turn, looking together, first from one's perspective, and then from that of the other, without interrupting, disputing or attempting to offer one's own better explanation.

Will this not, however, simply lead to a stalemate, in which each sees that the other's view makes sense to the other, but returns to his own perspective and remains within it? Is it not the case that from perspective A, view A makes more sense, and from perspective B, view B makes more sense, but that it is impossible to view the whole from a perspective-free viewpoint? If one view is true, or more true than the other, however, there should be some basis for pointing this out to the other, some point of superiority that can be noted.

Christianity and Justification

We must now ask what, in this context, the Christian worldview offers in its support. Here we must take full cognizance of the insights I have offered regarding critical realism. An approach called natural theology has often operated on the assumption that the Christian worldview, or at least elements of it, could be demonstrated to any reasonable person willing to consider it on his or her own terms. The approach I take here will follow a somewhat different procedure. I attempt to take full account of the postmodern insight that all knowing is done from an individual's particular perspective.[27]

In keeping with the procedure we have outlined above, this approach calls for the Christian believer to invite his or her non-Christian dialogue partner to try to look at the world from within the Christian life and world view. This means entering so empathetically into the Christian perspective as to be able to understand, at least to some extent, the Christian view of things. It means asking the nonbeliever to consider the possibility of the

---

[27]What follows is not intended to be either a complete epistemology or a complete apologetic. It is only a sketch of each. The next two chapters will fill out somewhat two areas of pertinence of the Christian view. My approach does not fit exactly any of the traditional classifications of apologetic methods, having most in common with the presuppositional and the cumulative case methods. Interestingly, a recent comparative presentation of five different approaches reveals that they have a great deal in common and a great deal of overlap with one another. See Steven B. Cowan, ed., *Five Views on Apologetics* (Grand Rapids, Mich.: Zondervan, 2000).

truth of the Christian teaching, as found in the Holy Scriptures. This may seem to some to involve a type of circularity, presupposing the very thing that one is attempting to establish as true, namely, the existence of the Christian God. Instead, it is more a matter of considering the hypothesis that Christianity is true. In this respect, the endeavor is not greatly different from what is regularly done in evaluating scientific hypotheses. In a sense, Christians have an additional foundational basis, beyond what most persons have. For the Christian, one foundation from which beliefs are drawn and in relationship to which they are justified, is whether they are taught within the books of canonical Scripture, believed to be specially revealed truth from God.[28] While such a hypothetical or provisional faith cannot be exercised entirely, of course, particularly without the supernatural work of the Holy Spirit, we may inquire regarding the type of evidence that could be seen in support of the truth of Christianity.

Believing and committed Christians do not, in most cases, come to that conviction as a result of a thorough examination of all the rational and empirical evidence for the existence of God. They have had what they understand as an encounter with God through Jesus Christ, an experience of God that they believe to be a direct contact with him. It involved such vividness and created such satisfaction that they experienced it as reality.

This belief took place within a context. Whether explicitly or implicitly, the believer's understanding of God and the means of approach to him was that found in the Bible. As the Christian matures and studies more fully the content of that Bible, he or she develops a more comprehensive outlook on life. This is an interpretation of reality that enables the person to make sense of that manifold.

It should be pointed out that this worldview is derived in large part from the Bible, which claims to be a communication from God of truths about himself not otherwise discoverable from examination of the universe. Yet, having said that, there are tests to which this comprehensive understanding may be assessed as to its truth value.

Pragmatic value. The first dimension is the pragmatic test. We observed earlier that Christians generally find comfort and peace in their faith. We might term this the pragmatic dimension of our faith, or the life-view aspect of the life and world view. For the Christian, there is a sense of being right with the universe, of having obtained cosmic forgiveness, that is, not simply

---

[28]We are not here restricting our understanding of supernatural revelation to information or, as it is sometimes termed, "propositional revelation" alone. What God reveals is himself, but he does so at least in part by revealing truths about himself, or revealing himself in such a way that propositions can be derived from the revelation.

the forgiveness of individual wrongs that other humans can give, but the forgiveness of wrong against the very structure of the moral universe. There is the sense of being able to trust oneself to the care of an all-wise, all-powerful and all-loving Father (Mt 10:26-31). There is a sense of value, of being of infinite worth. This comes not from a sense of our own achievements, but from knowing that the almighty God has created us in his likeness (Gen 1:26-27; 9:6) and has given his only Son to redeem us. There is a sense of importance, of being able to contribute to the fulfillment of God's eternal plans, in which each of us is a part (Rom 12:3-8; 1 Cor 12:1-31). There is the knowledge that beyond this life there is an eternity of life for us, with the Lord (1 Thess 4:15-17).[29]

Logical consistency and coherence. Further, the Christian worldview satisfies the logical test of consistency and coherence. This is both a negative and a positive test. Negatively, this means that the central conceptions of the Christian faith do not contradict one another. While there are ideas that stretch our understanding and sometimes have to be called mysteries, they are not contradictions. For example, the doctrine of the Trinity claims that God is one and that he is three, but not that he is one and three at the same time, in the same respect.[30] The doctrine of the incarnation declares that Jesus is both divine and human, but is one person. It does not claim that his humanity and deity involve possessing contradictory attributes simultaneously, and in the same respect.[31]

Beyond that, however, the Christian worldview is not simply free of internal conflicts; there is positive coherence among its elements. For example, the understanding of God, humanity, the person of Christ, and other doctrines, all come together in a beautifully harmonious fashion in the doctrine of divine atonement. There is a harmony and mutual implication that conveys an aesthetic quality to the worldview. As we shall observe later, there is also coherence between the Christian worldview and other truths, established independently.

This coherence means that justification of the Christian life and world view is holistic. It may not be possible to validate each detail of the Christian belief in a direct fashion. For example, not every historical detail can be

---

[29]For a treatment of a number of these issues on a popular level, see my *Does It Matter if God Exists? Understanding Who God Is and What He Does for Us* (Grand Rapids, Mich.: Baker, 1996).

[30]This issue is discussed at greater length in Millard J. Erickson, *God in Three Persons: A Contemporary Interpretation of the Trinity* (Grand Rapids, Mich.: Baker, 1995).

[31]For a more complete treatment of this issue, see Millard J. Erickson, *The Word Became Flesh: A Contemporary Incarnational Christology* (Grand Rapids, Mich.: Baker, 1991); Thomas Morris, *The Logic of God Incarnate* (Ithaca, N.Y.: Cornell University Press, 1986).

tested, in part because some of the necessary data have been destroyed. Rather, the individual elements of the faith are justified by being part of the whole, and the whole is, overall, seen to have validity.

Concrete factuality. The Christian worldview differs from some other religions in being more than just a system of thought and a way of living. It is not just a philosophy. It involves concrete historical occurrences. It makes the claim that God has actually entered into human history. While many of these historical occurrences are difficult to verify directly, others have excellent corroboration. Historical science and archaeology offer considerable support for the claims of historicity at those points where the worldview is tied specifically to historical events. The progress of these sciences in the twentieth century moved away from the rather skeptical views of an earlier period to where a high degree of confidence in the records that we now have seems justified.

The supernatural. A fourth area of consideration is the presence of the supernatural within Christianity. The fulfillment of prophecies, sometimes quite detailed, and given long before the occurrences, argues for a knowledge that transcends human limitations. The miracles within Christianity, once considered an embarrassment to believers, now argue for the presence of supernatural activity. The supreme miracle, the resurrection of Jesus Christ from the dead, carries the sort of attestation that would ordinarily bring widespread and unquestioning acceptance, if it were not for the anti-supernatural biases of many persons.[32]

Metaphysical intelligibility. The Christian worldview is more than simply specific historical facts, however. It is genuinely a world and life view, a metanarrative, which gives an explanation that ties together the whole of reality and experience. One of these phenomena that it ties together is ethical experience. Each human has a moral sense of oughtness, or a sense that there is a definite difference between right and wrong. The existence of psychopaths and sociopaths is no defeater of this contention, any more than the existence of persons missing one or more limbs, perhaps even from birth, genuinely contradicts the rule that humans have two arms and two legs. This moral impulse is something more than merely the sense that doing right will be more expedient for a person than will doing wrong.[33] This fits well with the Christian contention that we are made in the image of God, and that each person has the law of God written on his or her heart. It also gives justifica-

---

[32]The literature on supernatural Christian evidences is extensive. For a recent defense of the resurrection of Jesus, see Wolfhart Pannenberg, *Systematic Theology* (Grand Rapids, Mich.: Eerdmans, 1994), 2:343-63.

[33]See, e.g., C. S. Lewis, *Mere Christianity* (New York: Macmillan, 1960), pp. 17-39; Edward J. Carnell, *Christian Commitment: An Apologetic* (New York: Macmillan, 1957), pp. 80-116.

tion for ethical judgments, even by the minority, for it says that right and wrong are not merely the product of the judgment of human communities, but come from the will, and ultimately the nature, of God himself.

The Christian worldview also enables us to make greater sense of the amazing order, and the highly improbable chance occurrence of conditions that are favorable to the existence of life and to the development of humans. For example, Roger Penrose of Oxford University has calculated at one chance in $10^{10(123)}$ the odds of the conditions of low entropy present in the Big Bang occurring.[34] Other highly improbable events are involved in the arrival of the complexity of our present world. The Christian contends that this did not all happen by chance plus motion plus time. Rather, the Christian explanation is that an intelligent God has brought it all to pass. Here the claim is that Christianity gives a better explanation of these phenomena than does any alternative explanation. It is worth noting that some of the major competitors to the Christian worldview have fallen on hard times. Dialectical materialism, the worldview behind communism, is extinct except for a few places like Cuba, North Korea, and some university campuses. Naturalism has become a victim of the rejection of Enlightenment rationalism. Even naturalistic evolution has come under increasing attack.[35]

Note that this is not an argument in the style of the theistic arguments. There, one began with the data of experience, and sought to derive from those an explanation, which was in the form of a theistic view. Then it ordinarily was necessary to offer a second proof, namely, that the god established by the proofs was the God of Christianity. We grant that it may not be possible to derive this answer from the problems. Rather, we are claiming that Christianity supplies a proposed answer and we are able to see how this fits the problems and answers the unanswered questions.

An analogy may help to clarify the difference between this approach, with its emphasis on revelation, and that which would begin with natural theology. Suppose one were given a combination lock, but not the combination to it. One might attempt, by a process of trial and error, to find the combination. Given a sufficient amount of time and effort, one would eventually discover the correct combination, but with a lock with forty numbers, there are sixty-four thousand possible combinations, so that effort might take a considerable amount of time. On the other hand, suppose that one were given a combination and told that it is the correct combination. If indeed that were the case,

---

[34]Roger Penrose, *The Emperor's New Mind* (New York: Oxford University Press, 1989), pp. 339-44.

[35]E.g., Phillip E. Johnson, *Defeating Darwinism by Opening Minds* (Downers Grove, Ill.: InterVarsity Press, 1997).

one could verify it very quickly. What we are claiming here is that the Christian worldview is not a human discovery. It is something that God has revealed, and its fit with the data of experience can be seen by one who is willing to enter sympathetically into the Christian perspective. Like the person who sees the rectangular solid from a higher perspective, and thus can see its three dimensions, the Christian is confident that because she or he indeed does have the higher perspective, which God has revealed, the cogency of the Christian faith can be seen by those within it. As we shall see in the next chapter, even Rorty concedes the possibility of such a theistically based worldview.

14

---

the christian story
as metanarrative

In general, postmodernism is sharply critical of all-inclusive explanations or metanarratives. One major objection to metanarratives is that they are used as means of oppression, that is, of suppression of the contrary voices that some might raise in contrast to the dominant view. Does it necessarily follow that this must be the case, however? The fact that this use is frequently made of metanarrative does not mean that repression must invariably happen. This would particularly be the case for views that can account for the presence of contrary motifs, and that give such contradictions the right of expression and then respond rationally. How does the Christian story fit within this context?

My first contention is that the biblical story constitutes the one genuine metanarrative. By that we mean that the kingdom of God and all that is entailed in that concept is a comprehensive explanation of all that exists and occurs. In the nature of metanarratives, although there may be considerable overlap among competing metanarratives, in the final analysis only one can be true.

The Possibility of a Metanarrative
One distinctive feature of postmodernism is the rather clear and universal rejection of metanarratives. In light of this objection, we must consider carefully whether the idea of a metanarrative is even possible. There are several distinct objections, or aspects of the objection, each of which must be exam-

ined and responded to if a Christian metanarrative is to be advanced.

1. It is not possible to construct a metanarrative anymore, simply because it is no longer possible for anyone to possess all knowledge.[1] On this argument, metanarratives could be constructed in the past, when the fund of knowledge was relatively small. Then there could be universal geniuses, like Aristotle and Leibnitz, but that time is past. With information exploding, it simply is no longer conceivable that anyone could have the knowledge necessary to construct such a synoptic vision.

It is obvious that in the form in which the objection is presented, it is essentially true. The knowledge possessed by humans in the twentieth century not merely increased—it increased exponentially. No single human can know in detail all of the fields of knowledge that exist. Not only has there been increase in the knowledge of each field, but the number of fields of knowledge has increased. Yet this in itself need not be an insurmountable problem. For in a sense, we are closer to understanding our universe and our history than we have ever been. While no one person possesses all knowledge, with the increasing specialization that exists in scholarship, teams of scholars can collectively know much larger bodies of knowledge than ever were known previously. While no one can know all of this, what is needed and possible is someone with a sufficient understanding of each field to be able to serve as the coordinator of the knowledge of each of the others, so that their knowledge is a coordinated whole. This was what gave rise to the idea of universities, which today actually are in many cases "pluriversities." And with increasingly powerful computers, the storage and correlation of such data in huge databases is also increasingly a reality.

Yet, this objection has not really been overcome. For the synoptic vision required by the one who would coordinate the specialists' knowledge, and the ability of such specialists to understand each other's concepts well enough to be able to interact effectively, are very difficult achievements. Further, even our knowledge at any given stage of development of human thought is less than complete. Thus, the metanarrative that currently appears most adequate, and therefore is considered true, might well be overturned at some point in the future, as additional information becomes available.

A further response, however, is particularly appropriate to the type of metanarrative we are proposing. Even though no finite human being, or even any combination of them, can possibly know all that there is to be known and thus construct a genuine metanarrative, such knowledge would

---

[1]Richard Rorty, "Trotsky and the Wild Orchids," in *Wild Orchids and Trotsky: Messages from American Universities*, ed. Mark Edmundson (New York: Penguin, 1993), p. 23.

be possible to an infinite being, whose mind can discover, comprehend, and combine all truth. If that infinite being is actually the creator or source of all truth, then such a metanarrative would be even more possible. And it is just this that we are proposing with the concept of the Christian story. Christianity contends that an infinite, all-knowing, all-powerful God exists, and that he is the one who has created all that is, and is in control of all that happens. Thus, the kingdom of God is his story, the narrative of what he has done, is doing, and will do. The Christian metanarrative is not a human discovery and construction. It has been divinely revealed. And because God's knowledge is unlimited, such a metanarrative is a possibility for him.

2. A second objection is closely related to the first. It is that a metanarrative necessarily must involve the whole span of history, including what is yet to come. Without this knowledge, a surprising turn of history might occur, in which something completely unexpected comes to pass, thus totally disrupting the holoscopic vision that had been formed. And humans are notoriously incapable of knowing and predicting the future. We are able to do quite well in some areas of natural science. Astronomy is a prime example, where astronomers can predict with considerable accuracy the time of return of a given planet. In other areas, such as geology, predicting the exact time of a volcanic eruption or of an earthquake is actually quite problematic.

With respect to human behavior, however, knowledge of the future is especially problematic. History often takes unforeseen turns. How many persons, for example, were able to anticipate the radical political changes that took place in Eastern Europe in the late 1980s? And one commentator has referred to economics as the science that made astrology respectable. In January 1999, fifty-four leading U.S. economists were polled for their judgment of where interest rates, both short-term (six months) and long-term (thirty years), would be six months later. The number of these economists who correctly forecast short-term rates was one, while the number who correctly forecast long-term rates was also one, and these were not the same person! Similarly, polls of expert economists over the past forty years have, of the six recessions during that time, correctly predicted zero![2] Prescience in human beings is a very limited attribute.

What makes the Christian metanarrative unusual is that it is revealed to us by a God who knows the entire future, whether it involves events that he directly causes, those brought about indirectly through natural laws, or the actions of free moral agents. While the doctrine of exhaustive definite divine foreknowledge is currently under considerable debate, even among evangel-

---

[2]*Investech Research Market Analyst* 99, no. 9 (1999): 7-8.

icals, this would seem to be essential to the type of metanarrative we are discussing. The presence of such foreknowledge, demonstrated especially with respect to prophecy, will be a part of the latter portion of this section of the chapter.

3. Another objection is that metanarratives, by their very nature, lead to oppression.[3] Because they are totalizing in character, metanarratives cannot tolerate contrary views, and therefore suppress any opposition. They cannot coexist with a plurality of views, for their view is all-inclusive. In point of fact, says this objection, metanarratives have historically been used as means of oppression, whether they be political metanarratives, such as Nazism or communism, or religious views, such as Christianity.

There is, of course, a strong measure of historical truth in this contention. Realistically, it must be acknowledged that not only political movements but also Christianity have indeed functioned in the fashion alleged. Luther's attitude toward the peasants and Anabaptists and Calvin's treatment of Servetus are examples often cited. Yet, a closer examination of the nature of Jesus' teachings (e.g., Lk 6:27) will reveal that this is not necessarily the case, and indeed, that intolerance and persecution of those who differ is antithetical to the real nature of the Christian metanarrative.

There is another aspect to this charge, however. If metanarratives are the cause of the difficulty, then, by application of the principle of difference in inductive logic, where there is not a metanarrative, there should not be oppression, at least not of this type. When, however, we extend this line of inquiry, an interesting result emerges. For even petit narratives frequently are employed in an oppressive fashion. Although in theory postmodernism tolerates plurality of views, in practice various petit narratives compete for a position of preeminence, and those that achieve it do not always extend complete freedom of expression and equal rights to competing petit narratives. An outstanding example of this is of course political correctness, which tolerates no differences. What we may, of course, be encountering here is a tendency of petit narratives not to remain that, but to become metanarratives themselves. In any event, since oppression is not found exclusively in metanarratives, we face the possibility that the cause of such oppression is not metanarratives per se, but some other factor, which may or may not be an invariable accompaniment of metanarratives, but which is not restricted to such.

4. A further reason for the impossibility of any metanarrative is that all

---

[3]Michel Foucault, "Revolutionary Action: 'Until Now,'" in *Language, Counter-Memory, Practice: Selected Essays and Interviews,* ed. Donald F. Bouchard (Ithaca, N.Y.: Cornell University Press, 1977), p. 219.

metanarratives contain contradictory elements, and thus autodeconstruct. Derrida especially argues this point.[4] Because there are always contradictory elements, the construction of a metanarrative proceeds by suppressing those elements, that alterity. Thus, the subjugation of such contrary voices is, in effect, a form of oppression.

This is a problem with which any attempted metanarrative must contend. For if it contains genuinely contradictory elements, then it cannot really be a metanarrative. Yet, the problem may not be as obvious or as conclusive as Derrida would have us believe. For in the interpretation of any data being considered by a system, there are several possible ways of handling the material. We may proceed on the assumption that there is a basic unity, and attempt to integrate the various elements with one another. Or, we may look for those ways in which the different elements diverge from one another. Depending on the orientation used, rather different results will emerge. It appears that postmodernists like Derrida are doing the latter. But that becomes a matter of imposing one's predispositions on the material under study.

5. A fifth objection to metanarratives is not so much another objection as such, but rather a motivating reason lying behind the objection. It was the twentieth-century preference for the atomistic and aversion to the holoscopic, or inclusive truth. In part, this was the result of the information explosion mentioned earlier, but it has almost been a temperamental matter of preference. The twentieth century in philosophy, for example, has been referred to as the "age of analysis," as contrasted to earlier periods that were synthetic in their orientation.[5] This led to each subdiscipline of philosophy becoming one step removed from any sort of normative judgments, so that ethics became metaethics, metaphysics became the analysis of metaphysical terms, and so on. Similarly, behavioristic psychology eschewed any sort of comprehensive theory of personality, and sought to modify specific behaviors.

Note, however, that this aversion to inclusive views is a characteristic of the twentieth century, and as such is a phenomenon of late modernism. If the preceding analysis is correct, then the postmodern objection to metanarratives is itself a continuation and extension of modernism, or may be what Thomas Oden has called "ultramodernism." Yet, in a number of areas, a pendular swing back toward a more inclusive endeavor has begun. Note, for

---

[4]Jacques Derrida, in *Deconstruction in a Nutshell: A Conversation with Jacques Derrida*, ed. John D. Caputo (New York: Fordham University Press, 1997), p. 9.
[5]Morton White, ed., *The Age of Analysis: Twentieth Century Philosophers* (New York: New American Library, 1955).

example, the type of metaphysical work being done by Christian philosophers such as Alvin Plantinga, which, though largely analytic in nature, is
nonetheless much more normative and constructive than the type of analytic philosophy we have just described.

Is this type of theistically based metanarrative a possibility? An interesting hint emerges in Rorty's autobiographical sketch, quoted earlier. It bears
quoting again. Describing his experience as a philosophy student at the University of Chicago and his failure to achieve a satisfactory inclusive worldview, he says:

> As I tried to figure out what had gone wrong, I gradually decided that the
> whole idea of holding reality and justice in a single vision had been a mis-
> take—that a pursuit of such a vision had been precisely what led Plato astray.
> More specifically, I decided that only religion—only a nonargumentative faith
> in a surrogate parent who, unlike any real parent, embodied love, power, and
> justice in equal measure—could do the trick Plato wanted done. Since I
> couldn't imagine becoming religious, and indeed had gotten more and more
> raucously secularist, I decided that the hope of getting a single vision by
> becoming a philosopher had been a self-deceptive atheist's way out. So I
> decided to write a book about what intellectual life would be like if one could
> manage to give up the Platonic attempt to hold reality and justice in a single
> vision.[6]

Rorty seems to be saying that there would be one way of working out such
an inclusive view, namely, a frankly theistic view. His reason for not going
in that direction was that he simply was not open to becoming religious. In
effect, the comment is, "It can be done, but I had lost interest." Yet his comment does open the door, even on his intellectual terms at that point in his
life, for the type of endeavor we are proposing.

The Necessity of Metanarrative

But if the objections to metanarrative are not compelling, is there positive
argument for the necessity of metanarrative? Here my contention is that
even those who object to metanarratives involve themselves in some such
metanarrative as well. While this is not compelling, it does at least raise for
us serious questions regarding the possibility of avoiding metanarratives
completely.

What I will point out in the postmodernists I cite here are by no means
comprehensive or fully worked out explicit metanarratives. Rather, they are
indications of implicit or partially developed metanarratives. In this respect,
the phenomenon is a parallel to Reginald Fuller's reference to ontic ele-

---

[6]Rorty, "Trotsky and the Wild Orchids," pp. 41-42.

ments of Christology, versus the ontological.[7] What we do have are indications that a more comprehensive view lies behind some of the contentions made by the postmodernists. They may not be enunciated with the completeness of an explicit metanarrative, but they function as metanarratives do.

Richard Rorty. This can be seen the most clearly in Rorty. A clue is found in his autobiographical statement, where he states that at age twelve he concluded that he "knew that the point of being human was to spend one's life fighting social injustice."[8] This sounds very much like a world and life view. Whether he uses the term or not, he seems to speak of the very essence of humanity. Further, he repeatedly speaks of his concern for liberal values. His discussion of humiliation is especially illuminating. He contends that what binds the ironist to the rest of society is a common susceptibility to a particular type of pain that the animals do not share, namely, humiliation. He insists that instead of asking, "Why should I avoid humiliating?" one should ask, "What humiliates?"[9] This, however, as we pointed out in the chapter on negative criticism, fails to deal with the question, "Should I avoid humiliating?" Rorty seems to assume the answer to that question, rather than justifying it. He recognizes that irony in philosophy has not helped liberalism, but claims that the reason is that something is expected of irony that it cannot supply, namely, a justification for avoiding cruelty. If that expectation were eliminated, the problem would also be eliminated.[10] We should observe about Rorty's advocacy of avoidance of evil that he does not appear to be advocating it merely for a segment of society. This seems to be present wherever humanity is present. His liberalism, a liberal humanism, is his metanarrative, in a modest sense of that word.

Jacques Derrida. In Jacques Derrida, there is not so clear an indication of the existence of a metanarrative, but it is nonetheless present. It can be seen by examining his concept of justice. This, he says, is the underlying basis or motivation for his effort to deconstruct the law: "But justice is not the law. Justice is what gives us the impulse, the drive, or the movement to improve the law, that is to deconstruct the law. Without a call for justice we would not have any interest in deconstructing the law. That is why I said that the condition of possibility of deconstruction is a call for justice. Justice is not reducible to the law, to a given system of legal structures. That means that

[7]Reginald H. Fuller, *The Foundations of New Testament Christology* (New York: Scribner, 1965), pp. 248-49.
[8]Rorty, "Trotsky and the Wild Orchids," p. 35.
[9]Richard Rorty, "Private Irony and Liberal Hope," in *Contingency, Irony, and Solidarity* (Cambridge: Cambridge University Press, 1989), p. 91.
[10]Ibid., p. 94.

justice is always unequal to itself. It is non-coincident with itself."[11] This appears to be the unquestionable value he is seeking to pursue. Its privileged status, almost like Plato's Idea of the Good, means that the seemingly universal practice of deconstruction stops short of justice itself: "Justice in itself, if such a thing exists, outside or beyond law, is not deconstructible. No more than deconstruction itself, if such a thing exists. Deconstruction is justice."[12] Deconstruction, then, which Derrida proposes to apply to so many factors within our society, is for the purpose of achieving justice, although that is not something that can ever be completely attained. Here we have a metanarrative of sorts, the idea that justice must be sought after, and that it utilizes the method of deconstruction to achieve that goal.

Michel Foucault. Finally, we may note the presence of a metanarrative in the thought of Foucault. Here it could probably best be identified as the will-to-power, or the importance of the political. He insists at great length that power, including that of knowledge, has been used to suppress the divergent factors in society. He is especially opposed to any sort of universalizing theory. He believes that changes will take place, not by proposing a better theory, but by the use of political means. A new politics of truth must be developed: "The essential political problem for the intellectual is not to criticize the ideological contents supposedly linked to science, or to ensure that his own scientific practice is accompanied by a correct ideology, but that of ascertaining the possibility of constituting a new politics of truth. The problem is not changing people's consciousnesses—or what's in their heads—but the political, economic, institutional régime of the production of truth."[13]

Whether he realizes it or not, however, Foucault has just proposed a new theory, about the nature and role of power and the means to altering the structures of society. He claims not to be advancing a general theory: "Reject all theory and all forms of general discourse. This need for theory is still part of the system we reject." Yet there is another basis on which to oppose the system, namely, actual experiences: "It is possible that the rough outline of a future society is supplied by the recent experiences with drugs, sex, communes, other forms of consciousness, and other forms of individuality."[14] This is a type of epistemology, which says that there is greater

[11]Derrida, in *Deconstruction in a Nutshell*, pp. 16-17.
[12]Jacques Derrida, in *Deconstruction and the Possibility of Justice*, ed. David Gray Carlson, Drucilla Cornell, and Michel Rosenfeld (New York: Routledge, 1992), pp. 14-15.
[13]Jacques Derrida, "Truth and Power," in *Power/Knowledge*, ed. Colin Gordon (New York: Pantheon, 1980), p. 133.
[14]Ibid., p. 231.

authenticity to these types of experiences than there is to the general theories of a more abstract or intellectual fashion.

It is difficult to characterize accurately or completely the type of metanarrative found within the thought of these different thinkers. A clue can be found, however, in the influence of Marxism on the thought of each of these men. What unites them is a type of liberal ideology, which includes a strong emphasis on the goodness of human beings, particular in their unhampered freedom. This is a scheme of values with an implicit ideology.

The Nature and Role of Narrative

It is important that we recognize that metanarratives are not necessarily written in narrative form. The concept is that of inclusiveness, whether that takes narrative form or not. Thus, for instance, the recounting of an historical event or movement may be expressed by rehearsing the series of happenings, or it may be done in more analytical form. To some extent, however, all historical references require some narrative element within them.

Two major problems, however, beset the use of the narrative form for conveying truth. One of these is that the efficacy of a narrative depends on its credibility, by which is meant that it either must be true to the facts of a given incident, or at least be true to what could have been an actual historical event. In other words, it must not be contrary to what could have occurred. It is interesting to note the extensive use of narrative as a communicational device by Jesus, which might be a clue to us as to the value of narration for communication. Recently a Generation Xer objected to one of my sermons on the basis that I told too many stories. I probably failed him by not asking him to apply that criterion to Jesus' teaching. Jesus' parables were essentially narratives, and they need not have actually occurred to be effective. In the account in Luke 7:36-50, it is not important whether the parable of the two debtors and the forgiving creditor actually happened. It is true, but not in the same sense as the account of the Pharisee, Jesus, and the sinful woman. What is necessary, however, is that it possess credibility, that is, that it fit the realm of possibility. Its message depends on this realism.

A former colleague tells a story that illustrates this requirement. It involves a French soldier in Napoleon's army, who had lost an arm in battle. When Napoleon toured the hospital where the soldier was being treated, he stopped at this man's bed, asked his story, and praised him for his sacrifice. Upon hearing this, the soldier stood to his feet, saluted, and replied, "For you and for France, my Emperor, I would gladly give my other arm as well," then took his sword and cut off his other arm. The story strikes one immediately with the power of the man's dedication. Very quickly, however, the unreality of the situation dawns upon one with the question, "How does a one-armed man cut off his arm?"

There is another problem with narrative. For it to serve effectively as a means of communication of truth, it must be interpreted. Jesus accompanied his parables with an interpretation, which, we should note, was not in parabolic form. Without that, the parables would be opaque, and for many of his hearers actually were because of the numerous different interpretations they could bear. This happens constantly in our own experience, without our realizing it. The impact of any event depends on our perceiving it as having a particular meaning. When we see a person performing an action, for example, our judgment of what that action really is depends on a judgment, frequently unconscious, based on our experience, as to what is really occurring.

A dramatic instance of this occurred several years ago on the Bayshore Freeway south of San Francisco. A mother was driving with her young daughter, who was carrying in a bottle a bug she had found. The mother, who was deathly afraid of insects, had warned her daughter to be careful not to let the bug escape, but nonetheless, the daughter after a time said, "Mommy, I think the bug got away." Shortly thereafter, the mother, feeling a strange discomfort in her right shoe, realized that she had found the bug. At the first opportunity she pulled the car onto the shoulder, jumped out and began stamping her foot, trying to kill the bug by what resembled a convulsive seizure. Another motorist, seeing the woman in what he recognized from experience to be a seizure, pulled over as well, ran to the woman, threw her to the ground, and held her tongue, to prevent her from swallowing it. As the woman struggled to free herself from the man, who had to administer increasing force, a police car happened along. The two officers, amazed that a man would attempt to rape a woman alongside a busy freeway, quickly pulled their car over, ran to the woman, and pulled her attacker off her. Only after a considerable time was the misunderstanding resolved to the satisfaction of all parties. The woman got into her car to drive off, whereupon her frightened daughter, who had observed all the activity, said, "Mommy, it's all right. I found the bug still in the bottle." Either we are given an interpretation of an event or we supply it ourselves, and our interpretation may very well be inaccurate.

The necessity of interpreted narrative came home to me forcibly about a decade ago when I attended a Kabuki theater in Tokyo. My host was a former student of mine who pastors a church in the Tokyo area. I was given a small radio receiver and earphone, on which I could hear an English interpretation. During the intermission I met a German couple, who were also using the English translation device, the only one available, and who were delighted to find someone whose knowledge of German was better than their knowledge of English. Although my host did not understand what I was saying as I explained the first act to the Germans, he observed that I seemed to have understood the play very well, and we compared our understanding. To both my amazement and that of Pastor Nakazawa, it became apparent that I had a better grasp of what had happened in the first act than did he. He understood every word spoken by the actors, but my English translation, which did not translate word for word but only summarized what was being said, included the narrator's interpretation of the actors' speeches and actions.

The Christian Metanarrative

Having said all that we have, how shall we understand the kingdom of God as a metanarrative? What is there about it that commends it to us? A brief sketch of that metanarrative is first in order.

In the beginning, God. Before anything else was, there has always been one supreme being, God. Existing as three persons who nonetheless constitute a perfect unity, this God was sufficient within himself. He lacked nothing for his satisfaction or joy. His nature being essential love, as unselfish concern for the other, his triune nature enabled his love to be fulfilled within himself, needing no external object. Yet, in his outgoing, altruistic nature, he chose to bring into existence finite entities. He created a physical universe, together with light and energy. He constituted it with certain natural laws, which produced a regularity of action. Beyond that, he furnished the physical universe, populating it with plants and animals. He furnished his presence, the place called heaven, with spiritual beings, angels, who worshiped and served him. And he created human beings, capable of knowing and obeying him, to dwell on his earth. And when he completed this creation, he looked upon it and pronounced his perfect judgment, "It is good."

Initially, God's plan for humanity proceeded smoothly. The first man and his companion, the woman, were happy to obey God and have fellowship with him. They accepted their responsibility of naming and governing the creatures. They were satisfied to be his children. Then, however, a disruption of this perfect relationship occurred. At some unspecified time, but apparently after the completion of the rest of the universe but before this human disobedience, a rebellion had taken place within God's angelic forces, led by one of their number who aspired to be equal with God. Those who had participated in this unsuccessful coup were cast out of heaven, and from that time have lived, not to obey, but to oppose, the causes of God.

It was not that some small element of sin existed that infected and contaminated otherwise pure beings. Rather, when they used their freedom in a way contrary to its intended purposes, a relationship was broken and became twisted and perverse. Not as a new substance, but as a distorted relationship, sin became a genuine reality in the world. And one of the efforts of this supreme demon, Satan, was to pervert the rest of God's perfect creation, beginning at the very pinnacle, with humans. So it was that he planted the seeds of sin in the mind of the first woman, Eve, creating doubt about the correctness of God's statement and leading her to eat the fruit of the one forbidden tree, in violation of God's prohibition. Eve soon encouraged her husband to do the same, and he quickly followed.

When this happened, however, severe disruptions occurred throughout the entire creation. Nature, which had been the servant of the humans, now at times became their enemy. Evils such as disease and death, which had previously been only potential, now became realities. Humans became enemies of other humans, and treated them with cruelty and exploitation. The human beings' natural tendency came to be to focus on their own wants and desires, at the expense either of God or of other humans. At one point the wickedness became so repugnant to God that he resolved to send a flood, which destroyed all except a few righteous people, Noah and his family, as well as the animals he had brought into the ark, the great boat God had commanded Noah to build for his deliverance.

Out of this rapidly growing human race, God selected one person, Abraham, and made a unique agreement with him. Abraham and his descendants were to be God's special covenant people, those who would have a unique relationship with him. He gave them a particular land to be their home. He delivered them from bondage to another people, the Egyptians, and brought them back to that sacred land, giving them victory over the people who occupied it. Again, however, his people turned from him, following false gods instead, and God allowed them to be taken off into captivity. Even then, he remained true to his promise, and delivered them from that captivity, to return to the promised land.

The nature of the spiritual economy that God had created was that sin, as a violation of God's law and the relationship with him, brought liability to punishment. To die without having been forgiven and restored by God was to be subject to eternal death, which meant endless separation from the God for fellowship with whom one had been created. No human being could offer anything to God to negate this punishment. God, however, decided in eternity that when this point came he would do for humans what they could not do for themselves. And so the triune God determined that one of him, God the Son, would, without ceasing to be divine, add humanity to his deity and be born into the human race. This he did, being born in Nazareth as Jesus, the son of a virgin, Mary. He lived a life of perfect holiness and obedi-

ence to the Father. Then, in an act of perfect self-sacrifice, he died an undeserved death, thereby taking on himself all the guilt of all humans who had
ever lived or ever will live. Any human who voluntarily acknowledges to
God his or her own sin, turns from and accepts this sacrificial provision, is
immediately forgiven, granted eternal life, restored to fellowship with the
Father, and welcomed into the church universal.

This kingdom is present wherever persons voluntarily and genuinely
give their allegiance to God. It is only incomplete during the earthly life of
any given individual, and within the human race, only a portion actually
make God the king of their lives. Someday, however, it will be complete,
when Christ returns and brings all things into submission to himself.

There are several salient features of this narrative that contribute to
assessing its value. In keeping with the insights of speech-act theory, the
expression *happy* is probably preferable to the narrower idea of *true*, since it
applies to the effectiveness of a wider variety of material.

Universality. The first of these happy characteristics of narrative is its universality. Although this topic will be developed at greater length in a subsequent chapter, we may note here that God is the Creator of all things and of
all humans, and is the one who is directing all things to his intended purposes. He will ultimately reconcile all things to himself. This involves the
redemption not only of the human race, but of the entire creation. Every
person, whether from a joyfully chosen discipleship or from a forcefully created submission, will acknowledge that Jesus Christ is Lord (Phil 2:9-11).

This universality may not at first appear to be a positive, from the standpoint of postmodernism, which reacts against all-inclusive stories as being
the means of oppression. Actually, a closer examination may reveal the
opposite. For in Derrida's version of deconstruction, what he is actually
claiming is autodeconstruction, that is, the idea that every narrative contains within itself elements that contradict the major theme, thus causing its
own deconstruction. As we have seen, he applies this to all philosophies,
such as the element of *khōra* in Plato's thought. Presumably, a narrative that
did not contain any contradictory elements would be undeconstructible. Yet
the one philosophy that cannot be deconstructed is deconstruction, and the
one element that is impervious to such activity is justice. Ironically, however, that very claim to exception is what makes deconstruction vulnerable
to deconstruction. For it contains within itself the very contradiction that is
the target of deconstruction: it proposes that everything is deconstructible;
yet also contains the claim that there is something that is not deconstructible. So it would appear that if it were possible, an inclusive consistency or coherence would be a positive from the standpoint of
deconstruction. The strong aversion to all-inclusiveness, at least on the theo-

retical level, appears to be of the nature of presupposition, or even of disposition.

Realism. Some metanarratives suffer from being unable to account for the complexity of human experience and history. So, for example, one of the most common and pervasive beliefs is the essential goodness of humanity. This is a recurrent or perennial philosophy that has managed to survive such seemingly strong contradictory developments as two World Wars and a great economic depression in the twentieth century alone, as well as continued warfare, so that on average one year out of twenty in recorded human history, worldwide peace breaks out. While this philosophy describes well the positive aspect of humanity, it has real difficulty with the negative components of our experience. Conversely, very pessimistic views convey a good explanation of the negative side of history, but without accounting for the genuine goodness to be found regularly in human beings.

It is here that the Christian doctrine of humanity is especially relevant. For according to that doctrine, humans were originally created by God in his own image and as the highest of his earthly creatures. They alone had the capacity to obey him freely and genuinely. In this image, the capacity for knowledge of God, for knowledge of self, for interaction with other selves, and for self-transcendence in space and time are wonderful possibilities. In the role of steward of God's creation, the human displays wonderful powers of creativity. Yet, the biblical narrative also tells of the fall, of the universal fact of sin, of the tendency of humans to use the image of God in negative, cruel, and destructive ways. While these are seemingly contradictory facets of human nature and thus of human history, they harmonize well within the biblical account of humanity, created and fallen. The Christian metanarrative displays the quality of realism that we described earlier.

We have already observed that pure narrative, unless it includes a certain amount of interpretation, either by the narrator or by the characters in the narration, or supplied by the experience of the recipient, will have certain limitations. In this connection, it is worth noting that although there is considerable talk about "narrative theology," that really is something of a misnomer for much that bears that title. Rather than being narrative theology, much of it could more accurately be referred to as "theology of narrative." Its content deals with narrative truth, but the theology itself is not written in the form of narrative. This does point out, however, that the content and the form need not match each other. We are familiar with the fact that a sermon of a rather discursive type can be preached on a narrative passage. It need not itself be a story or a narrative. Conversely, a narrative sermon may be preached on a passage that is not essentially narrative in nature, as Eugene

Lowry has reminded us.[15] Ideally, a narrative passage would be dealt with in a narrative sermon, but unless the sermon went beyond simply repeating the narrative of the passage, it would not truly be a sermon, but rather, merely a Scripture reading or a storytelling.

Consequently we should also note that the metanarrative of Scripture is not restricted to the material that takes the literary form of narrative. By that we mean that narrative cannot be made the inclusive category for characterizing Scripture. While much of it is narrative in nature, much of it cannot be termed that except by a most extreme stretch of the meaning of narrative. The historical books are primarily narrative of course, as well as the prophetic material, which is narrative given before the event rather than after or contemporaneous with it. Yet, much of the poetical material is not narrative in form, an admission that even the "biblical theology movement" had to admit, and the same would have to be said of most of the epistolary material.[16]

Resolution. A final positive or happy quality of the Christian narrative is its ability to bring the narrative to a satisfactory resolution. This may seem superfluous to a thoroughly modern or at least postmodern person, since much contemporary drama does not have to make sense of things. In the long run, however, we cannot live sanely and happily on the basis of narratives that leave us with major puzzles or problems. Here it is that the Christian metanarrative shows its special strength. Cyclical views have a tendency to lead to despair of the value of life and history, and even nirvana is a somewhat resigned approach to the meaning of history. Christianity, however, proposes that there will be actual resolution of the puzzle, including the serious problem of evil.

This may seem strange, since the problem of evil is one of Christianity's perpetual problems. By that is meant the intellectual problem of how a perfectly good and omnipotent God can allow evil to persist in this world. Yet this, in a sense, is the problem of the problem of evil, how to explain its presence, rather than the problem of evil, namely, how to eliminate evil. As Jürgen Moltmann has pointed out, one solution to the problem of evil is not how to explain evil, or explain it away, but to eliminate evil, thus removing the necessity of explaining it.[17] Christianity has many themes for alleviating the reality of evil, such as God's assumption of the effects of sin himself, in the incarnation. Yet its greatest contribution to the resolution of the problem

---

[15]Eugene L. Lowry, *The Homiletical Plot* (Atlanta: John Knox Press, 1980).

[16]G. Ernest Wright, *God Who Acts: Biblical Theology as Recital* (London: SCM Press, 1952), p. 103; James Barr, "The Interpretation of Scripture. II. Revelation Through History in the Old Testament and Modern Theology," *Interpretation* 17 (1963): 196.

[17]Jürgen Moltmann, "Hope and History," *Theology Today* 25 (1972): 384-85.

is the eschatological dimension, according to which, beyond this life there will be a great judgment in which justice will be administered and all evil and pain will be eliminated. The drama in which good and evil have been in conflict for so long will come to a satisfactory resolution.

Although many human schemes have offered the solution to human ills, whether by economic, educational, or scientific means, they have all sooner or later proved ineffective, the most recent being communism. And although Christianity seems at times not to have made much progress in the world, it is true as Chesterton has said, "The Christian ideal has not been tried and found wanting. It has been found difficult; and left untried."[18] And the promise is that there will be a supernaturally introduced consummation, in which all things are reconciled unto the Lord (Col 1:20).

---

[18]G. K. Chesterton, *What's Wrong with the World* (New York: Cassell, 1910), p. 39.

15

the kingdom of god
as ultimate community

Much discussion in postmodernism has concerned the role of community. In this chapter I argue that the biblical concept of the kingdom of God is especially relevant to those contemporary concerns. As such, this discussion will be quite different from most treatments of the kingdom of God. That is to say, it will not be an extended treatment of the biblical teaching about the kingdom of God. That omission is not because of ignorance of the discussions that continue over the exact meaning of that expression. Conservative Christians have done relatively better with these intramural questions than in relating it outside Christian circles. Rather, since systematic theology also works at relating its concepts to contemporary issues and problems, and because more is still undone in this latter area than in the former, I will especially be asking how this important and even central biblical concept relates to some of the issues raised by postmodernism. I should identify my understanding of the kingdom more closely with the idea of *reign*, as developed especially by George Eldon Ladd, than with the idea of *realm*.[1]

The Concept of Community in Postmodernism

Objection to the idea of kingdom. There is an immediate problem, however, in using the concept of kingdom today, at least in Western democratic coun-

---

[1]George E. Ladd, *Crucial Questions About the Kingdom* (Grand Rapids, Mich.: Eerdmans, 1952), pp. 77-98.

tries. Even in some Christian circles, terms like *king* and *Lord* have been deleted from songs, and less offending terms substituted for them. Some of the old-time liberals disliked the term and even suggested substituting the idea of the democracy of God.[2] For Western minds the problem with the idea of king is that it carries the connotation of arbitrary and absolute power. In the language of contemporary liberation theology, it smacks of hierarchy, in which humans are subjugated to an external power.

Some of this objection stems from the individualism that is so common in our time. Each individual is free to formulate his or her own beliefs, and to make his or her own choices. While this may seem to be contradicted by the postmodern emphasis on community, that is not actually the case. For to some extent, the idea of community is really only individuality on a somewhat larger basis, a collective manifestation of individualism, as it were. The individuals within the community have exercised their own freedom in choosing to be part of that community, and reserve the right to withdraw if they choose. Note the tendency in our society away from any sort of long-term commitments. Note also, the combination of libertarian understanding of freedom with an emphasis on community.

This objection may also derive from an implicit or explicit naturalism in many cases. Here, the idea is that all truth is within the system of nature; that there is nothing outside or beyond or above nature that defines what is truth. Here again, postmodernism, with its inherent pluralism, seems to deny this contention, for there is openness to the supernatural, and indeed, to several different varieties of it. Yet, there is still a limitation on the possible supernaturalisms, for the only really valid options are gods that humans can in some sense control. Even the idea of the responsive God of openness theology is essentially a God who has chosen not to violate human freedom.

Some of this is the egalitarianism that has increasingly become dominant in our culture. By this I have in mind not the idea that everyone should have equal opportunity, but that their actual status should be equalized. In a realm most familiar to academics, this is reflected in what is commonly referred to as "grade inflation," which actually has the effect of being "grade equalization." Until someone institutes a higher grade than "A," which I actually expect will happen sometime soon, the tendency is to conclude that everyone is a good student.[3] It can also be seen in the popularity of talk shows, where everyone can share an opinion, regardless of knowledge or

---

[2]Even a self-identified evangelical, Gregory A. Boyd, says, "The cosmos is, by divine choice, more of a democracy than it is a monarchy" (*God at War: The Bible & Spiritual Conflict* [Downers Grove, Ill.: InterVarsity Press, 1997], p. 58).
[3]The grade of A+ is in some places becoming quite widely used, so that students may have a grade point average of more than 4.0.

insight on the subject, and it is basically treated as equal to the judgment of experts, who have devoted a life to study and reflection on the matter. In such an atmosphere, the idea that God is the all-knowing, final authority on all matters seems strangely foreign.[4]

What is at stake here is not the precise term *kingdom of God*, but the concept of God's authority, his right to create and determine what is to occur, his right to decide the fortunes and destiny of humans. I would contend that this is of the very essence of the Christian faith. It is a matter of whether we will, in Philip Watson's words, "Let God Be God."[5] For if our Christian faith does not include the idea of a being superior to us, who has created us and to whom we owe all that we have and are, then it has been so modified as to be scarcely recognizable as what it has been identified with throughout the years of its history. As J. G. Machen said of liberalism, these views that eliminate the idea of the supremacy of God may be true, but they are not Christianity.[6]

The nature of authority. We must ask, however, whether this objection to the idea of God's kingship is a valid one. It may be helpful here to ask about the nature of authority or power. The objection to divine authority frequently seems to assume that it is power against the subjects, used to subjugate their best interests. That need not be the case, however. Frequently power over is power for, not power against, the person. One of the most common illustrations of this is drawn from the realm of sports, where the coach may in some cases have almost absolute power over the athletes under his or her leadership. The same, however, can also be said in realms such as music, where stringent control of the student or performer is exercised by the instructor or director. The military drill sergeant has similarly total control over the recruits placed under his command.

An outstanding example of benevolent power, or power for, is the gymnast, Mary Lou Retton and her coach, Bela Karolyi. During the several months of his coaching her prior to the 1984 Olympics, Karolyi had virtually total control over every area of Retton's life. He determined what she would

---

[4]This is also accompanied by "title inflation," in which academic officers receive elevated designations without the usual increase of responsibility. The title *provost*, formerly reserved for an academic officer who presided over several schools within a university, is now in some cases applied to the dean of a single school. Departments become schools, with a dean rather than a chairperson. A chancellor was once the head of a university system with many campuses, such as the University of California. More recently, it has come to represent what was formerly denominated *president emeritus*.

[5]Philip Watson, *Let God Be God: An Interpretation of the Theology of Martin Luther* (Philadelphia: Muhlenberg, 1923).

[6]J. Gresham Machen, *Christianity or Liberalism* (Grand Rapids, Mich.: Eerdmans, 1923), pp. 7-8.

eat and when, when she would go to bed, and the length and content of her practice sessions. He constantly monitored how she performed each gymnastic event, instructing her how to do each of these, and requiring total obedience. What he did was not for Mary Lou's harm, however, but for her good, so that she might develop her skills to the highest possible level of excellence that her physical capabilities permitted.[7] Similarly, the music instructor or director does not exercise her control in order to oppress those under her command, but for their good, that they might produce the highest quality music possible. And, difficult though it may be for military veterans to believe, the drill sergeant has in mind the welfare of the recruits, not only that they might be able to inflict the maximum amount of damage on the enemy, but also so that they might preserve their lives and health.

It can be shown from Scripture that this is the nature of the rule that constitutes the kingdom of God. When God established a kingdom in Israel, although the people demanded it for the wrong reason, it was God's intention and desire that the king would rule over the people for their good. When Adam and Eve were placed over the creation as God's vicegerents, it was with the intention that they would develop it to its full potential. God's rule is also directly spoken of in terms of this benevolent concern. So he says, for example, "'For I know the plans I have for you,' declares the LORD, 'plans to prosper you and not to harm you, plans to give you hope and a future'" (Jer 29:11). Jesus also speaks of the relationship between himself and his disciples, referring to them not as his servants or slaves, but as his friends (Jn 15:15). One of the dimensions usually associated with the type of dominion objected to is the arbitrariness, in which the monarch does as he pleases, without feeling obligated to inform his subjects of his plans or the rationale behind them. Here, however, Jesus points out what is confirmed in many other places in Scripture: that God has informed us of a great deal about his plans, more, in fact, than we are able to understand at any given point.

The necessity of community. Actually, the successful functioning of any group of people in a society requires the subjugation of some individual desires and wills. This is an absolute necessity, without which society would be in a state of chaos. The response to this is usually that it is the will of the whole, but that may be only a bare majority, or even a mere plurality, of the whole. Jesse Ventura was elected by a plurality of the votes in the gubernatorial election in Minnesota in November 1998, but although a majority of

---

[7]For an extended treatment and application of this case, see Rebecca Pentz, "Can Jesus Save Women?" in *Encountering Jesus: A Debate on Christology*, ed. Stephen Davis (Philadelphia: Westminster Press, 1988), pp. 77-91, 101-9.

the eligible voters in Minnesota did not vote for him, they still became subject to his actions as governor.

Beyond that, however, much of the power exercised in our society is wielded by persons who were not elected or selected by the people, the bureaucrats who make and carry out the actual policy. Sometimes this power is exercised in rather arbitrary, unfair, and oppressive fashion, much as any monarch would. The congressional hearings on the Internal Revenue Service, for instance, revealed the lengths to which agents had gone in some cases to intimidate and harass citizens, whose servants they are, in theory. The word *service* in the name of the agency was often forgotten, with the exception of the man who wrote to the IRS, saying, "Dear Internal Revenue Service. I wish to thank you for the service you have performed on my behalf over the years. However, I find that I am no longer in need of your services, and therefore request that you remove my name from your files." The Internal Revenue Service is not the only governmental agency that can be arbitrary and oppressive.

If, then, the problem is unwillingness to submit oneself to any external authority, there will be difficulty with any type of organization of society. If, however, the problem lies with a supernatural authority, then it would seem that the problem lies more with the one raising the objection, than with the Christian understanding of God.

We have noted that postmodernism does not necessarily object to the supernatural as such, at least in theory. Its problem lies rather with the absoluteness that attaches to a God who claims to be the only true god. Thus, while taking into account the insights of postmodernism as well as the issues it raises, what we must do is go beyond postmodernism. We must work toward a postpostmodernism, not simply ignoring the phenomenon of postmodernism, and reverting to a prepostmodernism, but also not merely halting with postmodernism. We must transcend postmodernism, in part by not tying ourselves too closely to the ideology of any given period.

Community and interpretation. One problem postmodernism has faced is the danger of subjectivism and individualism in interpretation of texts. Since in most forms of postmodernism there is no universal or transcendent grounding of meaning, or even an inherent or intrinsic meaning of the text, the danger is that each individual will find his or her own meaning for the text. Then, discussions of the meaning of the text become focused more on the person than on the text itself. In effect, everyone's meaning would be valid, but only for the person holding it. Conflict could well be the result.

The customary check on this is to introduce the role of the community. Here the meaning of the text is what the community's conventions have established. So, rather than being the individual's private meaning, the interpretation has a measure of greater extensiveness, provided by the group. This seems to avoid the problems of individualism just referred to.

Communities and conflict. Actually, however, the problem is not solved, but simply transferred and enlarged. For the same problem of potential conflict can occur at the level of the group or the community. When two communities have differing interpretations of the text, the same problem of subjectivity is present. In this case, the group is simply a larger version of the individual, with the same limitations. While it may not be a matter of individuality, there is the same problem of autonomy. For this reason, among others, the Roman Catholic Church has insisted on interpretation being given by the Church, and especially by the pope as the earthly head of that church.

Community, however, we need to observe, is not simply a matter of the immediate community of which we are a part, in the sense of coming in direct contact. It may include a widely diversified collection of individuals. In those groups that stress their historical heritage, there is a sense of the ongoing life of a body that persists through many years and centuries of time. And for those groups that find as their uniting focus a particular ideology, this community may have great geographical and cultural extent.

In saying what we have, we are of course taking a position on several disputed issues about the kingdom of God, if we are equating it with the community of which we here speak. One of the great disputes within Christianity in the first half of the twentieth century concerned whether the kingdom was present or future. In general, more liberal theologies regarded the kingdom as present, whose expansion could be largely promoted by human effort. Their social gospel was a means by which this kingdom was to be instituted, as society was transformed through educational, political, and economic means, so that increasingly God's will was done and the ideal conditions spoken of in Scripture regarding the future were realized. Fundamentalism, on the other hand, increasingly made the kingdom a matter of the future, especially in connection with a millennium that Christ would establish at his return to earth. As the dispute between the two theological parties proceeded, the division became ever greater on this issue of the status of the kingdom.

The Kingdom of God and Universality

Temporal. Let us now consider how the kingdom of God fits our concerns. If our community needs to be universal, this means that it must also extend to other time periods. This seems paradoxical in a postmodern age, for postmodernism, together with most recent thought, has a reduced regard for the past and for the value of history. Yet the value of history, or in other words, continuity with past elements of the human community, is helpful, if not indeed essential, to the successful functioning of the human community in the present. For as George Santayana so eloquently put it, "Progress, far from consisting in change, depends on retentiveness. . . . Those who cannot remember the past are condemned to repeat it."[8] Without the experience of those who have preceded us, we have only the wisdom we currently possess or can acquire, which typically lacks the objectivity of self-criticism. With the experience of those who have gone before, we are able to see our ideas in a much larger framework in our own cultural setting. We may well discover that some of the novel ideas we have discovered are not so unprecedented as we had thought. And we can benefit from the evaluation that has been given to them experientially.

Of course, we need to be conscious of the question of the applicability of those past insights to present situations. Observations about the superiority of horse and buggy transportation over the novelty of the automobile that would not last, made in 1900 when there were only a few thousand cars in use, have to be evaluated in their context. Yet, in numerous areas the lessons of history may be perennial in nature, and knowing them may spare us from making those same mistakes anew.

An example drawn from a nontheological realm may be helpful. In 1999 and the years immediately preceding, stock market commentators were divided between two views of economics: what might be termed the historicist view and the "new era" view. The former group contended that by all the traditional historical measures of stock valuation, such as price-earnings, price-dividend, and price-book value, the market was grossly overvalued. It was not only overvalued, but much more overvalued than ever before in recorded history. Further, said this conventional wisdom, in such situations in the past, the risk of decline has been much greater than the prospect of advance. At some point, these measures of value will return to more normal levels, and if history repeats itself, will drop to below the norm before resuming their upward climb.

The other school of thought, the "new era" economists, insisted that the traditional measures of value no longer apply, for we were in a period quite different from past conditions. In a time of low inflation and relatively low interest rates, the premium of earnings over fixed income securities is not so large. Further, we have moved from the industrial era into the information era. In a time of vast internet economic activity, there will be rapid economic growth.

---

[8]George Santayana, *The Life of Reason or the Phases of Human Progress,* 2nd ed. (New York: Charles Scribner's Sons, 1936), 1:284; one vol. rev. ed. (New York: Charles Scribner's Sons, 1953), p. 82.

Was such new era thinking correct? Alan Greenspan, chairman of the federal reserve board, evidently did not think so. After his famous "irrational exuberance statement," he said, "Regrettably, history is strewn with visions of such 'new eras' that, in the end, have proven to be a mirage."[9] Two years later he repeated this thought: "I do not say we are in a new era, because I have experienced far too many alleged new eras in my lifetime that have come and gone."[10] Greenspan's comments suggest that the idea of a new era is not unprecedented. Let us hear some expressions of the new era concept:

> We are in a period of the most wonderful progress in science and invention, especially as applied to communication and transportation, this or any other country has ever known. It is obviously our present great fortune to live in what, in the light of history, will be recognized as a golden age of American industry.[11]

Here is another:

> Now, of course, the crucial weaknesses of such periods—price inflation, heavy inventories, over-extension of commercial credit—are totally absent. The security market seems to be suffering only an attack of stock indigestion. There is additional reassurance in the fact that, should business show any further signs of fatigue, the banking system is in a good position now to administer any needed credit tonic from its excellent Reserve supply.[12]

Contrary voices can of course be found, such as the following:

> For five years, at least, American business has been in the grip of an apocalyptic, holy-rolling exaltation over the unparalleled prosperity of the 'new era' upon which we, or it, or somebody has entered. Discussions of economic conditions in the press, on the platform, and by public officials have carried us into a cloudland of fantasy where all appraisal of present and future accomplishment is suffused with the vague implication that a North American millennium is imminent. Clear, critical, realistic and rational recognition of current problems and perplexities is rare.[13]

My purpose in giving you these quotations is not to try to settle the "new era" versus "bubble" debate. That purpose may become clearer when noting the dates of those four statements. They are respectively, from *Forbes* magazine of June 15, 1929, four and one half months before the stock market crash; *Business Week* of October 19, 1929, a week before the crash; and *Busi-*

---

[9]Alan Greenspan, February 26, 1997.
[10]Alan Greenspan, May 6, 1999.
[11]"Stock Values Anticipate Golden Age," *Forbes,* June 15, 1929.
[12]"Business Outlook," *Business Week,* October 19, 1929.
[13]"The New Era-tionality," *Business Week,* September 7, 1929.

ness Week of September 7, 1929, four days after the final top had been reached. My point is that those who speak of a new era are in many cases unaware that there have been new era claims in the past, and should at least consider the lessons learned earlier. To put it differently, this time the future may be different than it has been in the past. There have, however, been other times when persons thought the future was to be different from the past, when it turned out not to be the case. In other words, if it really *is* different this time, there needs to be some justification for that belief, other than merely the belief itself.[14]

Now what does all of this have to do with the topic at hand? Apart from the fact that systematic theology does not function in isolation from other disciplines, including the social sciences, there is a reminder here that the human community possesses a historical breadth whose wisdom should not be neglected. Theological parallels exist in abundance. It is not uncommon for Christians, in times of great moral deterioration in society, to believe that the Lord's second coming must be near. The assumption is that this period is one of such moral degradation that things are worse than ever before. It is instructive, however, to discover that in the Gay 90s and the Roaring 20s Christians often felt the same, and probably with good justification. For that matter, the moral conditions in Rome in the early centuries of Christianity were hardly ideal. That the Lord's return *may* be at hand is not the issue; that it *must* be, is.

A striking example of failure to function in this connection with the Christian community can be found in the Millerites, the followers of William Miller. Miller became convinced that the Lord's return was to occur in 1843. When that failed to happen, Miller's followers became disillusioned, and that disillusionment became even more intense a year later when the recalculation by one of their leaders, Samuel S. Snow, also proved incorrect. Earlier forms of chiliasm would have given them and us a similar lesson.

With respect to doctrine, knowledge of the experience of the earlier population of the Christian community can be of great help to us. I used to lecture on Arianism, whereupon my teaching assistant and a friend would knock at the classroom door, dressed in dark suits, and ask to come in and speak to us. Then, the two men distributed copies of the *Watchtower* and presented the beliefs of Jehovah's Witnesses. The parallel between these views and the Arian views the students had just heard could not be overlooked. The judgment of the church community and of history upon Arian-

---

[14]The dispute was to some extent settled in favor of the traditional analysts versus the new era or new economy theorists in the year 2000, when the Nasdaq declined by approximately one half, and many of the new-economy dot-com stocks became dot-bombs.

ism should be a valuable guide to us in evaluating contemporary Jehovah's Witness teaching. The same might be said about some forms of oneness Pentecostalism, with respect to the church community's judgment on modalistic monarchianism. Evangelicals have not been especially enthusiastic about or well-versed in the study of patristics. The recent project led by Thomas Oden, however, to reissue early church commentaries is a reminder that the church must utilize its entire community.

This is not merely a matter of studying intellectually what the church has believed in the past, or how it has expressed it. There is a value in experiencing what the earlier part of the community experienced. I love to go to historic spots and try to imagine what the persons felt who stood there many years ago. For example, at the Gettysburg battlefield I stood where General Robert E. Lee stood as he saw his defeated troops returning from that fateful last day of the battle. I have stood outside the doors of the Cathedral in Wittenberg and tried to feel what Martin Luther was experiencing when he nailed the ninety-five theses to the door almost five centuries ago. And sometime soon I plan to engage in two experiences. I will don a backpack and walk from my cousin's farm to the Grass Lake Cemetery eleven miles away, to simulate the experience of my grandfather and grandmother who made that trip on foot each Sunday for five years, carrying their infant daughters, my mother and my aunt, to attend a church of their convictions. On some January day I plan to borrow a power ice augur, go out to Rush Lake, cut through the ice, and thrust my bare arm into the water. I want to simulate in a small way the experience of the thirty-two new converts in my home church in 1876 and the fifty-four in 1878 who, converted during January prayer week, unwilling to wait until spring and lacking an indoor baptistry, were immersed there, after cutting through two to three foot thick ice. Only then can I begin to understand what doctrinal conviction has meant in the church community of which I am a part.

The kingdom of God must also encompass those who will be part of it in the future and they are as significant as any other. We can gain some understanding of the place of the future community by our study of the activities depicted in Scripture of that future activity. I have in mind here particularly, the descriptions of future worship and service that we find in prophetic Scripture.

One problem that immediately comes to mind is that we do not currently know who will be part of the future community, or what their lives will be like. Most of them do not even exist as of yet. This problem would be alleviated, however, if one member of that community were already alive, and had indeed experienced the future. It is here that the doctrine of God, especially as enunciated by the theologians of hope, is particularly important.

The traditional view of God is that he knows the future in its entirety, including every action of every individual who will ever inhabit it. The current dispute over the open view of God[15] means that if we adopt the view of God's limited foreknowledge, the future dimension of the kingdom of God becomes comparatively irrelevant to us.

Global. The expansion of the community temporally may be among those who are in the same cultural stream as we are. Beyond that, however, since Christianity is a faith for all persons, it must extend to those of different geographical and cultural situations than ours. To use the terminology currently popular, it must be understood as truly global. One great benefit of the transportation and communication revolution is the global consciousness that has developed. Here it must be quite frankly pointed out that much of what passes for postmodernism is remarkably Western, and thus ethnocentric.[16] This is not to say that the third world does not display any characteristics of postmodernism, but rather that what we frequently here set up as something of a paradigm is rather provincially based on French thought and experience, or on American pragmatism. Yet the world is not simply Western, or North American, or European, although in doing our theology we have tended to function as if that were the case. Recently I read an interview with a scholar who had just published a new history of Christian thought. In the interview he stated that when he writes the revised edition of it in twenty years, he expects that it will include third world theologians. The voices of Kazoh Kitamori, Leonardo Boff, Ken Gnanakan, Miroslav Volf, and a host of others cry out that this book either is already at least thirty years out of date, or it should be entitled *The Story of European and North American White Male Christian Theology.*

If we are to benefit from the cultural richness and breadth that characterizes the kingdom of God, we must deliberately seek to encompass all segments of the community. I deliberately involve myself in a theological study group of worldwide Christians, in part because I want a check on my own ethnocentrism. This is not to say that the Africans or the Asians are free of such influences themselves. I frequently find that their objections to some biblical interpretations as "Western" actually reflect their own cultural conditioning. That does not mitigate the fact, however, that we all need each other's insights. I have frequently cited the case of the Japanese pastor and

---

[15]See, e.g., Clark Pinnock, Richard Rice, John Sanders, William Hasker, and David Basinger, *The Openness of God: A Biblical Challenge to the Traditional Understanding of God* (Downers Grove, Ill.: InterVarsity Press, 1994).

[16]Rey Chow, "Rereading Mandarin Ducks and Butterflies: A Response to the 'Postmodern' Condition," in *Postmodernism: A Reader,* ed. Thomas Docherty (New York: Columbia University Press, 1993), pp. 471-89.

theologian who told an American theologian, "Your understanding of the priesthood of the believer is based more upon the United States Constitution than it is upon the New Testament." Was he correct, or was his own view perhaps derived from the influence of Japanese society and its political structure? I do not know, but the very question in itself is a crucial one.

A type of ideological imperialism has been possible because much of the theological work was done in Europe and North America, just as was true of philosophy. With the explosive growth of the third world segment of the Christian community, however, that will and must change. I propose that the Christian community is in a unique position to be able to break down the barriers formed by national and cultural communities. I think of the time, in 1987, that my wife and I, with a group of ninety-two tourists from twenty-six different countries crossed the border from Jordan to Israel at the Allenby Bridge. As the Israeli immigration agents checked our passports from a variety of nations, they became increasingly puzzled, for they had never encountered a group like this before. Here were Soviets and Americans, as well as citizens of many other diverse nations, traveling together, who obviously were friends. The Israelis were completely dumbfounded. What they failed to realize was that we were members of a much larger community, whose significance far exceeded geographical or political differences. I think of the time we worshiped with a congregation in Beijing, where we understood not a word of the music or the message, but where the sense of solidarity with the Chinese believers was powerful, so much so that our Chinese non-Christian guide told us that she felt very alone at that moment. The kingdom of God offers a type of community that has the potential for overcoming the dangerous divisiveness in our world.

Socioeconomic. Beyond this, however, the kingdom of God is inclusive in terms of socioeconomic classes. Again, this is an area where postmodernism has not always excelled. Although ostensibly a protest against oppression, it has reflected a peculiarly middle-class orientation. This is seen in some of its literary activities, which seem to be related to the type of intellectual and personal problems that comfortable or even affluent middle-class persons experience. It is much less conscious of the problems of crime, drug addiction, suicide, divorce, and other issues that the ordinary person faces. Peter Hodgson's comments on Mark Taylor's deconstructive theology are pertinent. While Hodgson's words may be unduly severe here, bordering on ad hominem, they do make the point eloquently:

> Taylor's god, it appears to me, is for those who don't need a real God—a God who saves from sin and death and the oppressive powers—because they already have all that life can offer; this is a god for those who have the leisure

and economic resources to engage in an endless play of words, to spend themselves unreservedly in the carnival of life, to engage in solipsistic play primarily to avoid boredom and attain a certain aesthetic and erotic pleasure.
Taylor's god is a god for the children of privilege, not the children of poverty; a
god for the oppressors, not the oppressed (although of course he wants to do
away with all the structures of domination); a god for the pleasant lawns of
ivied colleges, not for the weeds and mud of the basic ecclesial communities; a
god for the upwardly mobile, not for the underside of history.[17]

I will always be thankful for the rural near poverty in which I grew up, and
for the experience of serving an inner-city, multiracial congregation as my
first pastorate in Chicago. Engaging in my doctoral studies while serving
that parish was an excellent experience in integrating the theoretical and
the practical, but also in enabling me to realize that it is not only the highly
educated and middle classes who have theological insight. I have learned
much about theology and about life from people like Lenora and Tyrone,
whose complexion is very different from mine, and whose cultural and
social background is also quite unlike mine. I think of a young African-
American businessman, new to the church that I was serving as interim pastor, who listened to a long discussion of a potential pastoral candidate, in
which objection was several times raised to another candidate on the basis
that a particular current staff member did not favor him or would not work
well with him. Finally, unable to contain himself any longer, he expressed a
significant insight: "I keep hearing, 'Harry, Harry, Harry,' when I should be
hearing 'The Lord, the Lord, the Lord.'" Those present of a different culture
were reluctant to express what came naturally to this minority person.

Educational level. Nor is theological insight limited to those of a particular
educational level of attainment. We must divest ourselves of our twentieth-
century version of Plato's philosopher-king conception, that only highly
trained theologians can do theology correctly. To be sure, some unsophisti-
cated theology only expresses past errors, long ago considered and rejected
by the church. Yet we should not overlook what Helmut Thielicke has
termed "the theological instinct of the children of God," describing the frus-
trated pietist, who did not know intellectually how to refute Rudolf Bultmann's demythologization, but sensed intuitively that something was
seriously wrong with it.[18]

Postmodernism has reminded us, correctly, that we are not purely cogni-
tive or rational creatures. Experience plays a major part in our understand-

---

[17]Peter C. Hodgson, review of *Erring, Religious Studies Review* 12, nos. 3-4 (1986): 257-58.
[18]Helmut Thielicke, *A Little Exercise for Young Theologians* (Grand Rapids, Mich.: Eerdmans,
   1962), pp. 25-26.

ing and our beliefs. From the perspective of evangelical Christianity, this means that the content of revelation is a deliverance wholly from God, but that the understanding of the revelation is affected and can be assisted by our experience of God's actual working in our lives. But what the kingdom of God says to us is that it is not merely the experience of individual Christians, or of an elite segment of the church, but of the entire, universal community, that helps us understand and apply that truth.

Gender. Finally, the community of God is, as we say in our time, gender-inclusive. That ought to be a reminder to us that not all insights into the Christian faith, or more broadly, into the meaning of life, come from males. The alternative would be for males to develop more fully their feminine side. By that I do not mean that they should become effeminate, but that the more typically feminine dimensions, such as empathy, need to be developed. For there is no question that we tend to view issues and value considerations as a result of certain natural tendencies or qualities of our own. Thus, a more "macho" conception of the ideal of the sanctified Christian may emerge from a study by a male theologian, who will tend to be more aware of passages that seem to encourage aggressiveness and firmness, versus those that stress gentleness and understanding.

At the very least, then, this means that male theologians also need to be in dialogue with women. In our experience, is it the case that none of those who show the best theological understanding are women? Or that none of those who can effectively articulate their views verbally are women? That none of the best analytical thinkers are women? That none of the best writers are women? That none of the best teachers are women? If we can find instances of women who possess each of the separate gifts necessary for being a theologian, then perhaps the church needs to rethink some of the traditional stances with respect to the office.

Communities and the Formulation of Values and Understanding

We need now to look more closely at the nature of community and how its values and understandings are formed. The ideal usually thought of is a voluntary community, in which each person freely chooses to be part of the community, and each person exercises a free and equal part in the decision-making that takes place. In practice, however, this is not exactly the case. Some persons, in the very nature of things, have a greater influence in the formation of the beliefs, values, and practices of the group than do others. They either are elected or otherwise chosen for positions of particular influence, or they are more influential and persuasive than others, or they simply are more assertive than others. There is no question that in American society some persons exercise a more significant role than others. Those who are more economically advantaged, for example, receive a greater advantage with respect to justice, if for no other reason than that they can obtain more skilled legal representation. Even within churches of a congregational form of church government, some members exercise more influence than others, whether that is good in a given case or not.

Need of information. In general, those communities that are better informed formulate superior views with respect to their values. This does not, of course, assume that virtue and morality follow directly from possession of correct information, but it does suggest that those communities that function the best will be those whose decisions are made based on correct information. For example, a community where the decisions are made based on correct knowledge of matters of public health will probably possess better health than will one that is less well informed, especially if the former has the resources to enact its policies based on that knowledge.

One major difficulty for communities is of course their lack of complete knowledge. We still experience the serious effects of cancer, for example, because society's knowledge of the causes and the cures of cancer is limited. With respect to solving society's problems, our knowledge is far behind the information we have about the physical and biological environment. Attempts to govern the economies of individual societies and of the world community are based on the discipline of economics. That discipline, however, is far from a science. As we noted in chapter fourteen, because economics is a trend-following rather than trend-predicting discipline, economists' record in predicting the future has been very poor.

Need of moral or spiritual strength. Even when there is adequate knowledge of the variables to be dealt with, limited economic resources often make impossible or impractical the implementation of cures that are available. More serious than either the lack of knowledge or the lack of material resources to implement the consequences of that knowledge is the lack of moral or spiritual strength to carry out the best course of action. For example, the problems caused by the use of alcohol as a beverage are now quite widely known. Whether alcoholism, driving under the influence, family disruptions, effects upon personal health, or any of a number of other social ills, one would ordinarily think that where such problems with the use of a substance are known, the usual procedure would be to outlaw it. That, however, was tried in the United States on an earlier occasion, and the law was repealed. Although we today probably know much more about the adverse effects of alcohol than we did during the prohibition era, it is extremely unlikely that prohibition would again be chosen by society. And even when it was in force, criminal practices grew up to help fill the vacuum created by the absence of legally obtainable alcoholic beverages.

God as the leader of the community. What is remarkable about the community known as the kingdom of God is its leader. God, the head of the Kingdom of God, is a person of infinite knowledge. Nothing is unknown to him, including the future actions of all persons, good and evil. Thus, his plans, decisions, and actions are based on perfect awareness of all the factors, including the implications and consequences of any of these actions. Further, he is a being of infinite goodness, devoid of malice or selfishness. Because he possesses, by right of creation, everything that is, he has no greed. Possessing all power and knowledge, he is not jealous or insecure. He espouses the highest values, including glorification of the highest being in the universe, and the welfare of his creatures, whom he loves with a perfect love. Possessing all power, he is able to bring about infinitely wise and good ends.

This sort of unilateral power may seem repulsive to a postmodern age that stresses human autonomy so strongly. Yet, as we noted earlier, God's power should not be thought of as power against but as power for, power used wisely for the ultimate welfare of the person. The objection to divine authority often comes down to little more than insistence on the right to will one's own self-destruction. Just as children who insist on their own way will often do themselves considerable harm that would not be the case if they followed the directions of a wise parent, so the unwillingness to submit to divine wisdom leads to lesser ultimate well-being and happiness than could otherwise be the case.

Increasingly, human societies throughout the world are organized on a democratic basis. What we think of as a democracy is actually a rather inefficient and ineffective form of organizing a community. The decisions made by the general populace are in many cases unwise, and are the result of a canceling of various special interests. A dictatorship, or at least an oligarchy, is a much more efficient form of society. The problem is that dictators are often neither wise nor benevolent, and use their power for their own benefit. Indeed, when Israel insisted upon having a human king, Jehovah warned them of this very danger (1 Sam 8:7-19). If, however, this sole head of the society were both perfectly knowledgeable and completely loving and pure in his motives and actions, then this would constitute the perfect society.[19]

It should be noted, however, that this king does not exercise his power independently and abstractly. The view of God in relationship to persons is

---

[19]Interestingly, with all of the emphasis upon community, the degree of strength of commitment to one's chosen community seems considerably less than in earlier time periods. Note, for example, the ease with which persons move from one church to another, or even from one marriage and family to another.

not primarily what we would call coercion. The picture rather is of one who works in and through human personalities, so that action is both that of God and of the person involved. This is seen most clearly in Paul's statement in Philippians 2:12-13: "work out your salvation with fear and trembling, for it is God who works in you to will and to act according to his good purpose." This suggests that God exercises his leadership by rational persuasion, setting forth the truth, and bringing about belief and action in accordance with his will.

But if the kingdom of God is truly to be community, must there not be a sense in which the king's beliefs and values become genuinely those of all the members of the community, rather than being imposed from without? Two observations here are especially pertinent. The first is that God is not simply external to the human race. In the person of Jesus of Nazareth the triune God entered into the human race, becoming genuinely one of us (Phil 2:5-8; Heb 4:14-16).

The second relevant observation is that the kingdom of God is wider than simply human members. If the kingdom refers to God's rule rather than a realm, then it includes both superhuman (angels and demons) and subhuman (inanimate and animate creatures) elements. In the former realm, the good angels already obey God's will, and the evil angels or demons will some day become subject in the same way as will rebellious humans. In the latter realm, God's will is already being obeyed. Inanimate nature obeys God's will mechanically, following the laws of physics implanted within it. The animate creation obeys God's will instinctively, again following his dictates without conscious awareness of doing so.

Final universal agreement. The final pertinent observation is that there will indeed come to be universal agreement. The passage that has played such an important part in this discussion is applicable at this point as well. In Philippians 2:10-11, Paul speaks of every knee bowing and every tongue confessing that Jesus Christ is Lord, to the glory of the Father. This involves everyone in heaven and on earth and under the earth, apparently referring to all persons, whether the regenerate or the rejecting. The reference to "at the name of Jesus" also suggests not coercion, but recognition of who Jesus is. For that will be a time of great manifestation of the truth, so obvious as to be undeniable. And at that point all will recognize the truth of the Christian metanarrative, some to their great joy at the confirmation of what they have believed and on the basis of which they have lived, and others with great anguish at the recognition, too late, of the truth of what they have rejected and even opposed. Truly, Jesus will reconcile all things to himself (Eph 2:16; Col 1:20), but for some the reconciliation will be a sad and bitter one.

16

making the transition
to postpostmodernism

We come now to the question of how we relate to postmodernism
and postmodernists. Here Christians must ask themselves, from the standpoint of their commitment to historic Christianity, just how closely the formulation and expression of a doctrinal view should be aligned to the views
and the spirit of postmodernism. This is a perennial question, which in this
case must be asked in relationship to this particular ideology that is so
strongly with us. In a sense, the issues are no different than they have been
for the church in any other period of its existence, but the particular form of
expression involved is different from that of any earlier period.

There is an unchanging and timeless quality to Christianity, which is at
least partly doctrinal. This appears in any number of passages, in both the
Old Testament and the New Testament. For example, when God appears to
Moses and identifies himself as Yahweh, he not only says that he is the Lord,
the God of Moses' fathers, of Abraham, Isaac, and Jacob, but adds, "This is
my name forever, the name by which I am to be remembered from generation to generation" (Ex 3:15). Who and what he had been in the past he was
now, and would be forever. He does not change. The same idea is expressed
with respect to his character, when he says to the people of Israel through
Malachi, "I the LORD do not change. So you, O descendants of Jacob, are not
destroyed" (Mal 3:6). The point is that being patient and merciful, God does
not destroy them. His nature has not changed, so they can count on him to
be as he has been in the past.

This emphasis on the permanence of the Christian faith is expressed especially in relationship to the person of Jesus Christ, the very center of Christian belief and commitment. In Hebrews 13, the writer exhorts his (or her) readers to be faithful and not to covet wealth, and part of the basis for this encouragement is that God has said, "Never will I leave you; never will I forsake you" (v. 5), a statement reminiscent of Jesus' promise at the time of the Great Commission: "And surely I am with you always, to the very end of the age" (Mt 28:20). Then, however, the writer clinches the argument by saying, "Jesus Christ is the same yesterday and today and forever" (Heb. 13:8). He[1] follows this by saying, "Do not be carried away by all kinds of strange teachings" (Heb. 13:9). Because Jesus is unchanging, they should not accept novel doctrines. There is a finality to Jesus Christ's work, which means it need never be improved on, revised, or updated. This idea is repeated numerous times. Unlike human priests, who must offer repeated sacrifices, both for their own sins and those of the people, "He sacrificed for their sins once for all when he offered himself" (Heb 7:27). Similar emphasis on the permanence of Christ's redemption can be found in Romans 6:10; Hebrews 9:12, 26; 10:10; 1 Peter 3:18; Jude 3, 25. Even the expression, "the faith" (Jude 3; 1 Tim 1:19; Tit 1:13), is a technical term, referring to a body of teachings. So it is clear that certain doctrines are permanent, are part of the Christian religion, and are of such an indispensable nature that if they are given up, Christianity itself is lost.

Yet having said that, we recognize that Christianity's pertinence to human need throughout all periods of time is because this permanent nature of Christianity relates to a permanent or abiding quality of human nature as well. Thus, the human need for forgiveness, and the human inability to atone for one's own sin, means that Christianity will always be relevant to humanity. There are, however, specific human needs that arise in connection with particular historical situations, and as such, call for very specific cures or applications. A better way of putting this may be to say that different aspects of the human predicament emerge more forcefully at some times than at others. Further, the particularized forms that the universal or perennial needs take at different times may vary considerably in their appearance. Thus, some degree of timeliness or contemporaneity is needed for the Christian message.

The way this contemporizing is done may vary greatly in different theologies. Some maintain that no tailoring of the Christian message to a particu-

---

[1]The masculine is used here simply because all of the biblical writers whose identity we know were males. This should not be construed as a judgment about the identity, or even the gender, of the author of the book of Hebrews.

lar time is necessary. All that is necessary is to proclaim the lasting message in the same form. The Holy Spirit will apply this to the specific situation and need of different persons. No contextualization is really needed by the one who is proclaiming the message. Thus, the form of proclamation may take a somewhat stereotypical nature. This is in a sense a non-dialogical proclamation. There is only one pole, that of the authoritative message, and the receptor in a sense makes no difference to the style of the proclamation. There is no dialectic or real dialogue between the source and the receptor. A second strategy insists on preserving the content or the substance of, in this case, theology, but contends that its form of expression may be adapted, or contextualized, to the situation. These are what William Hordern termed "translators," although in the evangelical form, the body of what is to be retained but translated is somewhat more extensive than that of some of the translators of whom Hordern wrote.[2] Finally, there are those whom Hordern calls transformers, who hold that not only the form of expression but also to some extent, the content, of the message, must be modified if necessary to communicate with the contemporary world. Thus, some elements of the message that do not fit the current milieu are either to be de-emphasized or even deleted if necessary.[3]

The approach I am advocating in this work seeks to adapt to a given context by expressing itself in such a way as to be understandable by those in that situation. It will not, however, try to make itself acceptable, at least not without a radical change on the part of unbelievers. This is because there seem to be two possible types of scandal or hindrance to people believing the gospel and becoming followers of Jesus Christ. One is the offense of the messenger, which may come from failure to communicate as well as one might, or even from just plain personal offensiveness by the communicator. There is, however, a legitimate and ineradicable element of offense in the gospel, a dimension of it that will always be offensive to the non-Christian, and to remove this is to cause Christianity to cease to be Christianity. Paul was referring to this when he spoke of God's wisdom being foolishness to humans, and said, "but we preach Christ crucified: a stumbling block to Jews and foolishness to Gentiles" (1 Cor 1:23). Our goal is to make sure that we do not eliminate the normal and necessarily and inherent scandal of the gospel, while avoiding the unnecessary obstacles of poor representation by the messenger.

If our intention is to gain a hearing for our message, without in the pro-

---

[2]William E. Hordern, *New Directions in Theology Today*, vol. 1, *Introduction* (Philadelphia: Westminster Press, 1966), pp. 146-48.
[3]Ibid., pp. 142-46.

cess compromising that message, what can we do to be alert to the possibility of excessive concession to the spirit of the times? One warning sign is a strong adoption of the terminology of the day, although that in itself is not decisive. We must look closely into the meaning involved, to make certain that it is indeed biblical meaning. Still, because expressions, clichés, and "buzz words" often function as signals evoking certain emotions but not requiring understanding, heavy adoption of the contemporary terminology may indicate a failure to press for retention of the timeless message.

On the other hand, such concession may actually be indicated by a desire to retain the traditional terminology, but with such modification or even stretch of the semantic range that the customary meaning may have been evacuated. An example is Rudolf Bultmann's redefinition of the term *resurrection*. In his usage, resurrection is not something that happens to physical bodies, but to psyches. It is existential, not literal. So resurrection for the disciples did not mean that Jesus had literally come back to life, but that he was still alive in their hearts and their faith. Their belief in their own resurrection did not mean that they expected their bodies to be raised from the dead, but that their faith, dashed by the death of Jesus, had returned, and that they again had hope.[4] William Lane Craig comments regarding this concept, "Only a Bultmannian would think to ask, 'But was his body still in the grave?'"[5] We have referred earlier to the expression "the infinite coefficient of elasticity of words." According to this concept, you can stretch the meaning of words almost indefinitely, so they mean something quite different from what they were ordinarily understood to mean, without their breaking. When this is done, however, the words cease to have any real meaning, becoming merely affective signals.

At different times within its history, the church has found itself facing a specific type of ideology, and has frequently employed that ideology to give its expression of itself. For example, the church fathers, particularly the Alexandrians, made extensive use of Platonic and Neo-Platonic philosophy in the formulation of their doctrinal system. By the time of Thomas Aquinas, Aristotle's philosophy was beginning to come into its own, and Thomas used it heavily to structure his theology. Much nineteenth-century liberal theology drew on idealism, whether the absolute idealism of Hegel, or the more personalistic idealism of a Leibnitz or Lotze, while some conservative theologians adopted the Common Sense Realism of the Scottish philosopher

---

[4]Rudolf Bultmann, "New Testament and Mythology," in *Kerygma and Myth: A Theological Debate,* ed. Hans Werner Bartsch (London: SPCK, 1953), pp. 38-43.
[5]William Lane Craig, *Assessing the New Testament Evidence for the Historicity of the Resurrection of Jesus* (Lewiston, N.Y.: Edwin Mellen, 1989), p. 91.

Thomas Reid. In the twentieth century, probably the most utilized philosophy was existentialism, especially that of Søren Kierkegaard, as seen in the
thought of Rudolf Bultmann, Paul Tillich, Reinhold Niebuhr, and Emil Brunner, but also, to an extent he did not recognize or acknowledge, even in the
theology of Karl Barth. Although Barth saw this existentialism in his early
thought and sought to purge it from his theology,[6] it still remained, in more
muted form, in his later work.

Although the charge that evangelicalism has thoroughly accepted and
adopted the ideology known as modernism has been overstated, as we shall
see, there is nonetheless considerable truth in this charge. This happened in
several ways. Evangelicals as a rule did not simply accept the conclusions of
modernism regarding naturalism, or at least a tendency toward that. This
was the route that many liberals, who were trying to "modernize" the Christian faith, traveled. Two other types of response were more typical of evangelicals. One was basically to adopt modernism's methodology, but to use it
to come to different conclusions than did secular modernists. This was an
attempt to construct a better modernism than that which often presented
itself. Some varieties of natural theology were of this type, constructing, on
the basis of human reason, at least some portions of a Christian theology.
The other approach was to use the method of modernism to refute modernism. In either of these cases, evangelicalism was allowing modernism to set
the agenda or the ground rules of intellectual discussion. It was, in other
words, basically conceding that modernism was correct in its framing of the
debate.

It can be seen in Harold Lindsell's view of biblical inerrancy as set forth
in *Battle for the Bible.* Because he held that a Bible inspired by a perfect,
omniscient God must be completely perfect and accurate in all its affirmations, Lindsell adopted a view of language that called for maximum speci-
ficity of reference. So he went to great lengths to harmonize the Gospel
accounts regarding the number of times that the cock crowed and the
number of distinct denials of Jesus that Peter uttered.[7] Similarly, because
2 Chronicles 4:2 speaks of a cast metal sea that is ten cubits from rim to
rim and has a circumference of thirty cubits, Lindsell had a problem. Since
the circumference of a circle is pi times the diameter, inerrancy should
require that the circumference be 31.4159 cubits. Lindsell's solution was to
conclude that the diameter must be to the outside edges, but that the cir-

---

[6]Thomas Forsyth Torrance, *Karl Barth: An Introduction to His Early Theology, 1910-1931*
(London: SCM Press, 1962), p. 134; *Karl Barth: Church Dogmatics* 1/1, trans. G. T. Thom-
son (Edinburgh: T & T Clark, 1936), author's foreword, pp. ix-x.
[7]Harold Lindsell, *The Battle for the Bible* (Grand Rapids, Mich.: Zondervan, 1976), pp. 165-
67.

cumference was measured on the inside of the sea.[8]

The adoption of modernism can also be seen in some varieties of evangelical interpretation. Commendably desiring to curtail the subjectivity of interpretation that some more liberal hermeneutics allows, these evangelicals have strongly emphasized the authorial intent, and relied on rather mechanical means of determining that intent. In so doing, however, they have neglected some biblical teachings that would in some ways modify such an approach. Some other evangelical hermeneutics have accepted wholeheartedly the hermeneutic of E. D. Hirsch. Because Hirsch is a literature professor who does not believe in any special illuminating work by the Holy Spirit, the meaning is that which can be found by various principles of interpretation.[9] So in some evangelicals' hermeneutics, the Holy Spirit plays little or no direct part in illuminating the meaning of the biblical text.[10] The result is that an essentially modern system has caused the neglect or muting of one aspect of the traditional doctrine of original sin, and of the doctrine of the internal witness of the Holy Spirit, of which the Reformers made so much, and interpretation has become a rather mechanical process.[11]

Some critics of evangelicalism have gone so far as to claim that twentieth-century evangelicalism was essentially modern. This charge has been especially leveled against Carl F. H. Henry, by persons such as Hans Frei.[12] In some ways, this is a surprising claim, since in one of his earliest writings Henry critiqued the modern mind.[13] A more promising hypothesis would be that Henry utilizes modern methodology and modern presuppositions to criticize the customary modern conclusions. Yet, one evaluation of Henry's thought has argued that on the normal criteria of modernity, Henry is not a modernist.[14]

If there has sometimes been a tendency to identify too closely and uncritically with modern thought, then we should also learn from those mistakes and take care not to make the same mistake with respect to postmodernism, that is, of too closely identifying with it in our desire to be contemporary

---

[8]Ibid., pp. 174-76.

[9]E. D. Hirsch Jr., *Validity in Interpretation* (New Haven, Conn.: Yale University Press, 1967).

[10]E.g., Robert H. Stein, *Playing by the Rules: A Basic Guide to Interpreting the Bible* (Grand Rapids, Mich.: Baker, 1994), pp. 65-71.

[11]For an alternative view, see Bernard Ramm, *The Witness of the Spirit* (Grand Rapids, Mich.: Eerdmans, 1960).

[12]Hans Frei, *Types of Christian Theology,* ed. George Hunsinger and William C. Placher (New Haven, Conn.: Yale University Press, 1992), pp. 23-25.

[13]Carl F. H. Henry, *Remaking the Modern Mind* (Grand Rapids, Mich.: Eerdmans, 1946).

[14]Chad Owen Brand, "Is Carl Henry a Modernist? Rationalism and Foundationalism in Post-War Evangelical Theology," *Trinity Journal* 20, no. 1 (1999): 3-21.

and relevant. This would come through accepting postmodernism's definitions of terms and allowing it to set the terms of the discussion. At times
postmodernism seems to function somewhat like Microsoft. One joke about
Microsoft is that if Microsoft built toasters, they would be cumbersome toasters that were prone to jam, but that eventually Microsoft would come to
dominate the market, whereby it would establish the standards for toasters,
and even claim that it invented toast. So postmodernism often gives the
impression that its analysis of the situation and its criteria of acceptability
are in some sense absolute and final. Yet we must recognize that postmodernism, like modernism before it, does not have the final word.

To be effective commentators on the cultural and intellectual scene, but
beyond that, to influence that scene, we must be able to read the times.
Indeed, Jesus criticized those who seemed to be able to read the signs of the
weather, but not the signs of the times. When the Pharisees and Sadducees
came to him and asked for a sign from heaven, he replied, "When evening
comes, you say, 'It will be fair weather, for the sky is red,' and in the morning,
'Today it will be stormy, for the sky is red and overcast.' You know how to interpret the appearance of the sky, but you cannot interpret the signs of the times"
(Mt 16:2-3). Similarly, as his disciples we should be able to discern the signs of
the times. Jesus was concerned not only with reading the signs of the times
that were then, but also of the times that were to come. If we only understand
what is currently happening, and not what will occur, we will always be in the
unenviable position of being behind, of attempting to catch up.

Customarily there is some overlap of eras. There are no bells that ring,
signaling the end of one era and the beginning of the next. At any given
time there are ideas that are waning and even dying, ideas that are in the
ascendancy, and some that are just coming into being. So one can find
examples of premodernism, modernism, and postmodernism coexisting.
Those who represent the dominant school of thought tend to regard contradictory ideas or movements as reversions to an earlier set of ideas, rather
than as new challenges and instances of what will eventually displace the
currently regnant view, which is what some of them are. Thus, in a period
in which postmodernism is strong and is perhaps the primary ideology,
early elements of a postpostmodernism may well be visible.

Unfortunately, evangelicalism has often been a step behind in its understanding of the intellectual and social milieu. Thus it is often reactive, rather
than proactive. Evangelicals often use the insights and arguments of a generation earlier, even though those who held them then may have abandoned
them. Some of what is presented to evangelical audiences as fresh and new
will not appear that way to those who have a broader familiarity with intellectual history.

This causes me to fear that some evangelicals may well make the same sort of mistake with respect to postmodernism that some evangelicals made in relationship to modernism. We will get postmodernism figured out and formulate our answers to its questions about the time the general culture stops asking those questions and moves on to something else.

What I am proposing here is that evangelicals need to be in the vanguard of thought. Rather than merely relating to postmodernism, evangelicals must understand that postmodernism is simply another stop along the way, not the final destination. We must be preparing for the postpostmodern era, and even helping to bring it about, while realizing that it, or actually probably several varieties of postpostmodern life and thought, will not be the terminus of the process either.

This is not to minimize the legitimate, and in some cases, valuable insights of postmodernism, of which we need to be aware and which we should take into account in formulating our own theology and our strategy for relating to culture. Some of these will themselves need to be discarded. Just as church coffeehouses gave way to bus ministries and then to seeker-sensitive worship services, the means of relating to postmodernism must be held to rather loosely. If Christianity is in the final analysis an unchanging message about an unchanging God, then if we must err it will be better to err on the side of emphasizing the timeless elements rather than becoming too closely correlated with any given era or philosophy. Yet some of these insights are simply too helpful to be ignored in our time.

It is, of course, important to recognize that there have always been persons who have been "postmodern" in any period of time. That is to say that there have always been some persons that were more intuitive than discursive in their approach to reality. Similarly, there will always be people who are more objective or "scientific" in their thinking, even in a postmodern age. What is characteristic of postmodernity is the tendency of the former to become more nearly normative for the age.

Relating to the Characteristics of Postmodernism

Humans not entirely rational. One insight that needs to be observed and utilized is that people, to a large extent, are not purely rational in their behavior. This can be observed in any number of areas, such as attire and fashion, but perhaps nowhere more dramatically than in the performance of the stock market during the latter stages of the long bull market which began in 1982. As more and more persons of limited experience entered the market, "fundamentalists," those who base their evaluations on such objective factors as the ratio of price to earnings, price to dividend payments, and price to book value, have become confounded. For on such criteria, the bull market by 1999 was not only more overvalued than at any previous time, but actually extremely more overvalued than it had ever been before.

Yet when questioned about their knowledge of the workings and pricing of the stock market, many investors who have made large amounts of money revealed a profound lack of understanding. Their belief that they will continue to receive annual returns of 20 percent and more lay alongside belief that somehow the preservation of their capital is guaranteed by the U.S. government, or lack of understanding that bond prices decline when interest rates go up. They believed prices would go up, simply because they have gone up, even though historical figures indicated that periods of similar valuational levels are times of extraordinary likelihood of stock market decline. The characterization of stock market behavior as "irrational exuberance" by the chairman of the Federal Reserve Board subjected him to considerable amounts of ridicule, especially by the host of a popular money and investing program on public television. Systems of investing based on astrology have become fairly popular, although there is no scientific basis for believing in a connection between the alignment of planets and the level of the market.

This stock market example suggests that in our presentation of the Christian message we must not expect that the response will be based entirely or even primarily on logical and rational considerations. The assumption that if one can present a closely reasoned argument people will be persuaded may not be as valid in a postmodern age as it was in an earlier time. It may be necessary to work harder at making ideas emotionally attractive than at making them logically compelling. In so doing, it will be necessary to take great pains to avoid manipulating people. We must constantly ask ourselves how legitimate it is to use arguments that one knows not to be valid, to convince people who think they are.

The nature of personal knowledge. A correct insight, significant not only for a postmodern period but also more broadly, concerns the nature of personal knowledge. During the years that I was a seminary administrator, where much of my responsibility related to assessing people, I came increasingly to trust my intuitions about persons. Although I sought for objective confirmation of those intuitions, and even sought to devise simulated situations to see how persons would react, I found that those initial impressions generally proved reliable. There is a very real sense in which, on the level of interpersonal relationships, communication takes place that cannot necessarily be analyzed in logical categories, but is genuine nonetheless. This is what Edward John Carnell referred to as "the third way of knowing," and it deserves increased attention, especially in a postmodern age.[15]

---

[15]Edward J. Carnell, *Christian Commitment: An Apologetic* (New York: Macmillan, 1957).

Again I want to point out the importance of objective checks on these subjective ways of knowing. The perversion of this approach can be seen most dramatically in matters of ethics, where a philosophy expressed by Debbie Boone in the theme song of the movie *You Light Up My Life* as "how can it be wrong when it feels so right?" has led to all sorts of distortions. It is possible to have hallucinations that seem very real, under certain circumstances. If I receive a hard blow on the head I may hear a ringing sound, even though no sound waves corresponding to this sound exist in the world external to my head. What has happened is that a stimulus has affected certain nerve centers directly, bypassing the usual auditory apparatus. Some people have mastered the philosophy summarized by one cynic as, "Sincerity is what counts. You learn to fake that, and you will really succeed." Our intuitions about them may not always be reliable.

Internal impressions, devoid of external sensory references, may also be unreliable, as any pilot can testify. One of the exercises student pilots are assigned, and any pilot is usually asked to perform in a biennial flight review, required to retain the right to exercise the privileges of the pilot certificate, is "unusual attitude recoveries." The pilot wears a hood, which prevents her or him from seeing outside the cockpit. The instructor then takes the controls, instructs the pilot to look at the floor, so that the pilot cannot even see the flight instruments, puts the plane into an unusual attitude, such as a climbing turn to the right or a diving turn to the left, then tells the pilot, "You've got the plane." Based solely on the instruments, the pilot must quickly assess the situation and return the plane to straight and level flight, without overcompensating so as to induce a stall or similar predicament. Those who have experienced such a situation will testify that it simply is not possible, on the basis of one's visceral feelings, to determine the actual orientation of the plane. This was brought home dramatically by the crash of John F. Kennedy Jr. on July 16, 1999. What probably happened was that he simply came to a point of literally not being able to tell which way was up, and he and his passengers paid with their lives.

Yet, having said this, we will want to relate to postmodern people in ways to which they are more likely to respond. One of these is the insight that the one-size-fits-all approach that the church has sometimes utilized in evangelism and in apologetics may need to be abandoned in favor of more personalized approaches. We will need to "incarnate" the truth in our behavior. Ironically, while people respond to interest in themselves as persons, they also want to preserve their own sense of distance, so that they may remain somewhat anonymous. Some successful ministries have allowed people to retain this degree of anonymity. But communicating that we are interested in them for their own sake, and that there is authenticity to our lives and words, will be very important, and this takes time.[16]

Imagination and creativity. The role of imagination and creativity in presenting the Christian message is also important. Much of our preaching and teaching is bland. It presents ideas in forms that are familiar to people, so they assume they understand what is being said, and tune out. Imagination will enable us to see things in a fresh way, and if incorporated into our presentation, may enable our hearers and readers to grasp them in a fresh way as well. In this respect, persons who have grown up always having television have been handicapped, for television leaves little to the imagination. In an earlier period, of radio drama, one could only "see" the characters and events in one's imagination. We need to recapture something of that imaginative power if we are to minister effectively in a media-driven age. I am not sure whether imagination can be developed, but there can be no harm in observing regularly the efforts of those who possess unusual imaginative powers. I strongly recommend regular reading of such comic strips as "The Far Side," "Close to Home," "Strange Brew," and the business-oriented "Bottom Liners," or the sports-focused "In the Stands." Those who do not have access to these comic strips in their local daily newspaper can also find them at the appropriate websites.

Reading and listening to writers and speakers who possess such imagination can also be a spur to our own creativity. I recall watching a television program on the life of Theodore Roosevelt. When the topic was the 1912 election campaign in which Roosevelt ran as a third-party candidate, commentators were describing the contrasting styles of Roosevelt and Woodrow Wilson (Taft, the incumbent president and the Republican nominee, was scarcely a factor). Roosevelt was described as fiery, and Wilson as professorial. Then the professor describing them referred to Roosevelt as "hot" and Wilson as "cool." Real communication took place, however, when he said, "If they were musical instruments, Wilson would be a violin, and Roosevelt would be a ukelele." The cultivation and use of imagery, analogy, metaphor, and parables should be helpful in communicating in a postmodern age.

The order of movement in presentation. The order of movement in our presentations is also important. Traditionally, we have assumed that people move from the rational to the emotional, and our ministry has proceeded on that basis. We have sought to demonstrate truths logically, assuming that people will then feel emotionally what they know to be true. Actually, we probably should proceed by helping people first to feel the emotional impact before seeing the rational considerations. In a way, this is what old time

---

[16]For an example of personalized apologetics, see David K. Clark, *Dialogical Apologetics: A Person-Centered Approach to Christian Defense* (Grand Rapids, Mich.: Baker, 1993).

"hell-fire" preaching evangelists were seeking: to enable people to feel the serious consequences of belief or the lack thereof. Strangely, such preaching is now roundly criticized by persons who themselves function on a similarly non-rational basis. Apart from the fact that logical consistency is not a highly valued quality for such people, it appears that the objection is not primarily to the method, but to the content of the message.

Subtlety and indirectness. One way this effect can be created is through a certain type of subtlety. Rather than a very direct approach in which we state our thesis overtly and immediately, we may want to engage in the practice of what I term, "sneaking up on people with the truth." This is an indirect approach in which the person feels the emotional impact before seeing the full logical implications. A prime example of this is the way the prophet Nathan dealt with King David, after David had committed adultery with Bathsheba and arranged the death of her husband Uriah, which was tantamount to murder (2 Sam 12:1-14). If Nathan had gone to David and asked, "What do you think, King David, of a king who has numerous wives and concubines, and yet takes the one wife of another man, and then engages in murder to cover it up?" he might have paid with his life, but more important, would not have persuaded David. David might well have reacted angrily and defensively, pointing out that he was under unusual stress because of the conditions of war, and that Bathsheba had unwittingly placed temptation in his way by appearing unclothed on her roof in his full sight.

Instead, Nathan used a parable, which enabled David to feel the injustice of the situation without recognizing its full application. He told a story of a rich man who had many sheep, but instead of slaughtering one of them to feed his family, he took the only lamb of a poor neighbor, a lamb that was a virtual pet of the family. David became incensed on hearing the story, and declared, "the man who did this should die." Only then did Nathan point out that the story was not actually about a man and a sheep, but about David, Bathsheba, and Uriah. Jesus also utilized this method, especially in his parabolic teaching. Notice, for example, the parable of the good Samaritan (Lk 10:25-37) or of the two debtors (Lk 7:36-50).

The value of narrative. We also learn from postmodernism the value of narrative as a means of delivering the message. We are here speaking of the communicational role of narrative, rather than the hermeneutic or the heuristic functions, which postmodernism sometimes attributes to narrative. With all of narrative's limitations, which we addressed in an earlier chapter, it still is a very useful communicational device when properly employed and with proper qualifications. Here we must be prepared to vary the style or the form of communication without altering the substance or the content of that communication. We must, conversely, be able to avoid identifying one style of preaching as the "biblical" way. Bruce Shelley and Marshall Shelley have identified a certain traditional preaching style as "preaching as a statement."[17] This was often the classical form of exposition, or sometimes of evangelism. A definite proposition or thesis is set forth and rational (biblical) evidences, logically structured, are advanced in support of the thesis. Major points have subpoints, each with its appropriate backing. The order of organization was sometimes a verse-by-verse commentary, but more frequently followed the pattern established by classical rhetoric, going back to Basil, the two Gregories, John Chrysostom, Ambrose, and Augustine.[18] This was appropriate and effective for audiences for whom scientific models were considered the best form of organization, with logistic or straight-line reasoning.

Today this is ineffective for many of our contemporaries. The ability to follow long and involved logical arguments has been negatively impacted by the mass media. Thus, attention spans become limited to following "sound bites." So preaching as a statement has in many places given way to what Shelley and Shelley call "preaching on a slant." Here the aim is not so much intellectual as affective. The effort is made, not to supply information and to persuade, as to massage the feeling tone.[19] What Timothy Warren of Dallas Seminary proposes instead of either of these is what he calls "preaching in stereo."[20] This pays heed not merely to the pole of the message, as does preaching as a statement, or to the pole of the hearer, as does preaching on a slant, but to both. It gives roughly equal attention to both the source and the reception. To borrow an analogy from hunting, it is concerned not merely with loading the gun with ammunition or with aiming the gun, but with both.

In part this means that narrative will need to be employed to a greater extent than in the past. There will be an element of drama, of a story line, of an unfolding plot. What holds the attention of a reader of a mystery story is uncertainty about the outcome. That uncertainty is largely lost in most preaching and Bible teaching to audiences who are familiar with the Scriptures. In preaching as a statement, one of the slogans was, "Tell 'em what you're gonna tell 'em; tell 'em; tell 'em what you told 'em." When the thesis or proposition is presented at the very beginning, the element of suspense is

---

[17]Bruce L. Shelley and Marshall Shelley, *The Consumer Church: Can Evangelicals Win the World Without Losing Their Souls?* (Downers Grove, Ill.: InterVarsity Press, 1992), pp. 191-92.

[18]Charles Dargan, *A History of Preaching* (New York: Hodder & Stoughton, 1905), 1:65.

[19]Shelley and Shelley, *Consumer Church,* pp. 192-98.

[20]Timothy Warren, "Preaching the Cross to a Postmodern World," *Ministry,* May 1999, pp. 19-20.

immediately dissipated. An alternative to this is inductive preaching, where the thesis is not presented initially, but emerges gradually during the unfolding of the sermon, perhaps only becoming explicit at the very end.[21] The listener is engaged in discovering the central thrust of the message. Often this is done with a narrative, but a narrative in which the identity of the characters may not be revealed initially, and the Scripture passage is not read until that identity has been established. Some traditional preachers have criticized the use of narrative and drama in preaching as not being truly biblical preaching. It would be instructive, however, to apply such criteria to the evaluation of Jesus' preaching, especially his parabolic preaching and teaching. Perhaps this is a more biblical type of preaching than some of that done on the basis of classical rhetorical theory.

Drama in delivery. The delivery of the message should also employ the dramatic factor. This may be done by the use of a dramatic presentation, such as a skit, prior to the message, paralleling the theme of the biblical exposition, but placing it in a contemporary setting. Or a dramatic production of this type may be inserted into the sermon itself. The speaker may give what is partially or entirely a dramatic sermon, portraying or impersonating one or more characters from the plot, and interpreting the action by commenting, or by sharing the character's thinking during the action. Rather than being frozen into one position behind the pulpit, the preacher, thanks to the use of cordless microphones, is able to incorporate motion into the delivery, moving about, confronting members of the audience face to face, and so on. The speaker's position on the platform may signal different viewpoints or different characters.

Indications of Postpostmodernism's Inception
We have suggested earlier that we must be thinking in terms of postpostmodernism, and seeking to bring it to reality. At any given time one can find representatives of several different ideologies coexisting simultaneously. In the late twentieth century, there were postmodernists, modernists, and even premodernists simultaneously, even within American society. While one philosophy is in severe decline and even virtual eclipse, another is in ascendancy and yet another is beginning to rise. While some postmodernists seem to think that the final period and the final ideology have been reached, postmodernism is also an historical phenomenon, conditioned by its situation in time and culture. Since every ideology up until the present time has eventually been displaced, it should not be surprising if this one is also. Because social and intellectual change took place much more rapidly

---

[21]See Fred Craddock, *Overhearing the Gospel* (Nashville: Abingdon, 1978).

in the late twentieth century than it had previously, postmodernism may have a shorter life span than modernism had. Further, certain contradictory elements within postmodernism make it inherently unstable, and it might therefore fade more rapidly. While postmodernism is still the dominant ideology of our day, there are indications that it has passed its peak, or at least that the rate of its growth has declined, and that there are some early signs of the rise of a postpostmodernism. A number of these need to be noted.

Movement toward more conservative ethical values. The first is the straws in the wind indicating a move toward more conservative ethical values, including sexual ethics. The percentage of college freshmen supporting legalized abortion dropped from 65 percent in 1990 to 51 percent in 1999. In a 1996 poll, the age group with the largest percentage who agreed that "abortion is the same thing as murdering a child" was the eighteen- to twenty-nine-year-old group, with 56 percent agreeing.[22] While some of this conservative shift undoubtedly is a result of the fears created by AIDS, some of it apparently is a reaction against the end results of the sexual revolution. Even Hugh Hefner has been quoted as saying, "There were excesses in the sexual revolution." The rate of abortions has also begun to decline.

There is also indication of a backlash of sorts coming out of the personal scandals of the Clinton presidency. While a rather high percentage of persons still say that they would not want their children to grow up to be like Bill Clinton, the prospect of a change in the White House from anything associated with the Clinton capers seemed in the 2000 presidential election to be appealing to the American electorate. Perhaps the spectacle of the morality of soap operas being manifested in the Oval Office has caused people to say, "Enough is enough!"

The reaction to some of the violence in American society also seems to be calling for a view of morality that sounds strangely objective in nature. While there had been a number of school shootings (Jonesboro, Arkansas; Salem, Oregon) none had produced quite the forceful reaction that the incident at Columbine High School in Littleton, Colorado, on April 20, 1999, evoked. There seems to be a sense that something is radically wrong with our society, and that the problem is moral and spiritual in nature. Even calls for a return to voluntary prayer and posting of the ten commandments in the public schools are being heard more frequently.

Other cultural changes. There are other, more diverse indications of shift. Two articles appearing in the same issue of *U.S. News and World Report* are instructive. One dealt with Reformed Judaism, and the overwhelming adop-

---

[22]Frederica Mathewes-Green, "The Abortion Debate Is Over," *Christianity Today* 43, no. 14 (1999): 86.

tion by the Central Conference of American Rabbis of a "Statement of Principles," which Jeffery L. Sheler refers to as "a historic move back to the future." This statement, although nonbinding, encourages the learning of Hebrew, the making of aliyah (moving permanently to Israel), the following of mitzvot (sacred obligations). Although specific obligations, such as keeping a kosher home and wearing a prayer shawl and yarmulke, were omitted, the framers of the document say that this is exactly what is implied by the statement. Predictably, some reform Jews see this as a selling out of the principles of their movement. Rabbi Robert Selzer, a professor of Jewish history at Hunter College of the City University of New York, warned that these changes "may be part of the global trend toward a rightwing, conservative religiosity" and risk "turning Reform Judaism into Conservative Judaism Lite."[23]

An article on art in that same issue is also exceedingly interesting. In 1975 Tom Wolfe had "declared that the emperor of modern art had no clothes."[24] According to the *U.S. News* article, "In the drive toward an art that is less tired and more expansionist in its representation of human experience, contemporary artists have exploded traditional ideas such as the primacy of painting—while embracing such charmingly old-fashioned notions as beauty, texture, and figuration."[25] Conceptualism had elaborated what a number of earlier artists had already asserted: art is whatever the artist does. In the late 1970s and early 1980s, however, a number of artists, including such former conceptualists as Sigmar Polke, David Salle, and Baldessari began making more traditional art objects, including even paintings. The article comments, "More to the point, their new work seemed to build, at least in part, from traditional aesthetic criteria."[26] Tolson then poses the question "Are beauty, representation, and craftsmanship returning, then? Yes," he says, "but with a difference. That difference is not postmodern irony, but a more heartfelt fusion of seeming opposites: figuration and abstraction; tradition and antitradition; heroic individualism and group-solidarity collectivism; paintinglike photography and photographylike painting; perspectival depth and a deliberate flatness."[27] While not a pure break with the modern period, or what Thomas Oden would probably term ultramodernism, this is clearly a move back toward an earlier, representationist understanding of art, and toward linear perspective. Although some will

---

[23]Jeffery L. Sheler, "The Reformed Reform," *U.S. News and World Report*, June 7, 1999, p. 56.

[24]Tom Wolfe, *The Painted Word* (New York : Farrar, Straus & Giroux, 1975).

[25]Jay Tolson, "What's After Modern?" *U.S. News and World Report*, June 7, 1999, p. 50.

[26]Ibid., p. 51.

[27]Ibid., pp. 51-52.

surely object that this is simply the revival of a persistent premodernism, it is worth noting that a number of the persons leading this shift are former conceptualists.

Other trends appear to be building. The "retro" phenomenon, in which clothing, automobiles, watches, and so on, that imitate an earlier period, may have significance here. The sensational success of the New Beetle from Volkswagen may be an indication of this trend. The New Beetle is not simply the return to the old beetle, with all of its eccentricities. It resembles the old Beetle in appearance, but from an engineering standpoint is totally different. Chrysler's PT Cruiser, which represents a return to the 1930s, proved so popular initially that some dealers were selling them for $10,000 over list price. The reactions, even by Stanley Fish, to *Dutch,* Morris's biography of Ronald Reagan, written in a somewhat postmodern form, are also instructive. Even an increase in the sale of business suits may indicate a return to more traditional practices. The developments in the stock market in 2000 also point out the hazard of less rational approaches to investing. While the Federal Reserve Board chairman decried "irrational exuberance" in the markets, the rise, especially in high tech stocks, continued, in many cases divorced from traditional measures of value. A decline of more than two-thirds in the value of Nasdaq, and of more than 99 percent of the value of some dot-com stocks, however, was a harsh encounter with reality. It seems paradoxical to say that the boom in investing in technology was not rational, since high tech includes the most scientific segments of our culture. The confidence in that high tech segment, however, was not based on rational considerations.

For some time it has been apparent that postmodernism contains two rather contradictory elements, and particularly there is a more conservative and a more radical variety of deconstruction. Some recent developments have revealed that the synthesis of these two is beginning to dissolve. We have referred earlier to John Searle's criticism of Derrida's thought and Derrida's extended response to it.[28] This response in turn evoked two contrasting reactions among Derrida's followers. Some were embarrassed by the response, feeling that Derrida had denied the very principles of deconstruction, and had in effect returned to a pre-postmodern stance, while others endorsed what he had said.[29] As this synthesis continues to unravel, however, deconstruction will either have to be modified or will decline. As John

---

[28]John Searle, "Reiterating the Differences: A Reply to Derrida," in *Glyph* (Baltimore: Johns Hopkins University Press, 1977), 1:198-208; Jacques Derrida, "Limited, Inc., abc . . .," in *Glyph* (Baltimore: Johns Hopkins University Press, 1977), 2:162-254.

[29]Michael Fisher, *Does Deconstruction Make Any Difference? Poststructuralism and the Defense of Poetry in Modern Criticism* (Bloomington: Indiana University Press, 1985), pp. 41-42.

Ellis declares, deconstruction is on the horns of a dilemma: either it must become more objective, and thus lose its distinctiveness, or it must more consistently reject authorial intent and objectivity of meaning, in which case it forfeits its right to assert its own view.[30]

Defections from deconstruction. The problems that some deconstructionists are beginning to see and acknowledge within their movement will have to be resolved at some point. Barbara Johnson, one of Derrida's translators and herself a deconstructionist, sees clearly the problem that Derrida faces: "Derrida thus finds himself in the uncomfortable position of attempting to account for an error by means of tools derived from that very error. For it is not possible to show that the belief in truth is an error without implicitly believing in the notion of Truth."[31]

Persons as astute as Johnson will not continue to hold such paradoxes forever. Sooner or later the discomfort experienced by Derrida in that predicament will have to be resolved, if not by Derrida, then by Johnson. We should not find the idea of deconstruction's decline and replacement surprising. Every ideology up until this time has eventually declined and many have even passed off the scene; there is no reason to believe that postmodernism will be any different. In this case, the expected life span will probably be even shorter than those of preceding movements, as we have noted above.

Defections can be expected. One of these appears to be Harold Bloom, of the Yale School of interpretation. In his earlier writings, Bloom was associated with deconstruction, although Geoffrey Hartman, in the preface to a 1979 symposium by a group of deconstructionists, refers to Bloom and himself as "barely deconstructionists."[32] In his essay in that volume Bloom shows some reservation about deconstruction, noting that "Deconstructionist criticism refuses to situate itself in its own historical dilemma, and so by a charming paradox it falls victim to a genealogy to which evidently it must remain blind."[33] Yet he comes down fairly strongly on the side of deconstruction. He asserts that "Language, in relation to poetry, can be conceived in two valid ways, as I have learned, slowly and reluctantly. Either one can believe in a magical theory of all language, as the Kabbalists, many poets, and Walter Benjamin did, or else one must yield to a thoroughgoing linguis-

---

[30]John M. Ellis, *Against Deconstruction* (Princeton, N.J.: Princeton University Press, 1989), p. 66.

[31]Barbara Johnson, "Translator's Introduction," in Jacques Derrida, *Dissemination* (Chicago: University of Chicago Press, 1981), p. x.

[32]Geoffrey H. Hartman, "Preface," in *Deconstruction and Criticism*, ed. Harold Bloom, Paul de Man, Jacques Derrida, Geoffrey H. Hartman and J. Hillis Miller (New York: Continuum, 1979), p. ix.

[33]Harold Bloom, "The Breaking of Form," in *Deconstruction and Criticism*, pp. 12-13.

tic nihilism, which in its most refined form is the mode now called Decon-struction."[34] He speaks of a meeting of distinguished professors, in which each confessed his belief in real presence of the literary text, its existence independent of their devotion to it and its priority over them. He then goes on to say, "I only know a text, any text, because I know a reading of it, someone else's reading, my own reading, a composite reading." He denies being able to know *Lycidas* by Milton. He says, "Words, even if we take them as magic, refer only to other words, to the end of it. Words will not interpret themselves, and common rules for interpreting words will never exist."[35]Yet he has prefaced these statements by saying, "When I observe that there are no texts, only interpretations, I am not yielding to extreme subjectivism, nor am I necessarily expounding any particular theory of textuality."[36]

Note, however, some fifteen years later, the tone of Bloom's "Elegaic Conclusion" to *The Western Canon*. He traces his academic history by saying, "I began my teaching career nearly forty years ago in an academic context dominated by the ideas of T. S. Eliot; ideas that roused me to fury, and against which I fought as vigorously as I could. Finding myself now surrounded by professors of hip-hop; by clones of Gallic-Germanic theory; by ideologues of gender and of various sexual persuasions; by multiculturalists unlimited, I realize that the Balkanization of literary studies is irreversible."[37] His jeremiad against the deterioration of what currently passes for literature and literary criticism is so strongly reminiscent of Allan Bloom's *Closing of the American Mind*[38] that one almost wonders which Bloom one is reading. He says, "I have been against, in turn, the neo-Christian New Criticism of T. S. Eliot and his academic followers; the deconstruction of Paul de Man and his clones; the current rampages of New Left and Old Right on the supposed inequities, and even more dubious moralities, of the literary Canon."[39] He states, "Precisely why students of literature have become amateur political scientists, uninformed sociologists, incompetent anthropologists, mediocre philosophers, and overdetermined cultural historians, while a puzzling matter, is not beyond all conjecture. They resent literature, or are

---

[34]Ibid., p. 4.

[35]Ibid., pp. 8-9.

[36]Ibid., p. 7.

[37]Harold Bloom, *The Western Canon: The Books and Schools of the Ages* (New York: Harcourt Brace, 1994), p. 517.

[38]Allan Bloom, *The Closing of the American Mind: How Higher Education Has Failed Democracy and Impoverished the Souls of Today's Students* (New York: Simon & Schuster, 1987).

[39]Bloom, *Western Canon*, p. 520.

ashamed of it, or are just not all that fond of reading it."[40] His comment is informative: "Either there were aesthetic values, or there are only the over-determinations of race, class, and gender. You must choose, for if you believe that all value ascribed to poems or plays or novels and stories is only a mystification in the service of the ruling class, then why should you read at all rather than go forth to serve the desperate needs of the exploited classes?"[41] Bloom is not returning to some view of absolute objective mean-ing of texts, but if he was "barely a deconstructionist" in 1979, he scarcely can be considered one in 1994. It appears that what has happened to Bloom is that he has seen the lengths to which the principles of deconstruction can lead, and has reacted against it. I would anticipate further defections of this type in the future.

Means of Accelerating the Transition

If, however, one is convinced that postmodernism is a mistaken and waning ideology, which is being and will be replaced by a postpostmodernism, what can be done to help bring about that postpostmodern belief? Here it would seem to me that we must find ways to help accelerate people's personal his-tory, to enable them to move into the future quickly enough to be affected by it. Most people do not see far enough down the road ahead for it to make any difference. The situation is somewhat like the predicament of the liter-ally near-sighted person. The optical condition prevents him or her from seeing anything that is very far away. If the person is to see that object, one of two things must be done: either the functional eyesight of the person must be improved, as through the use of corrective lenses or by laser sur-gery or the like, or the object must be brought closer to the person (or the person brought closer to the object). What we will want to do with the post-modernist is to push him or her to the logical and existential conclusions of his or her view, to bring the implications closer to home. Some people can-not be converted from their way of thinking to another view simply because they have not lived long enough to have put their philosophy to the test of workability. We must help them move through those experiences. I suggest several techniques for assisting postmoderns to see the difficulties of post-modernism.

Reality simulation. We must find ways to simulate reality that has not yet been experienced. There are mechanical devices that can help create a vir-tual reality. The Olympic Center in Lillehamer, Norway, has a bobsled simu-lator that enables one to feel something of the emotions of riding an actual

---

[40]Ibid., p. 521.
[41]Ibid., p. 522.

bobsled. Automobile simulators have also been developed. In aviation, much instrument flight training is done on simulators, and the airlines have large, complex, expensive simulators that are extremely realistic. Medical simulators have been developed to enable medical students to practice their skills without the presence of a live patient.

I am not proposing the idea of virtual reality simulators for theologians, but am suggesting the creation of experiences that would emulate the outcome of postmodernism. There is a website that has a "fright simulator," to help persons experience certain economic crises.[42] I am advocating something similar here.

Case studies. Law schools have long used this method for teaching law, and business schools often do likewise. Although postmodernism does not yet have a long history, there have been enough precursors with sufficient resemblance to postmodernism for them to provide adequate case studies. And even postmodernism can provide us some examples. The experience with academic quality in the new Vincennes campus of the University of Paris, which Foucault helped to found, might be instructive for us.

Depriving postmodernism of undeserved possibilities. We must help "starve off" the postmodernist from some of the undeserved possibilities. By that I mean that many postmodernists are living on borrowed capital, existing by drawing on resources that their own views deny. We must help to call in the loan. In many cases I have felt that such persons do not believe too little, but rather, too much. They believe something that they have no right to believe, given their other beliefs. What we are to do here is to be better postmodernists, more thoroughgoing postmodernists, and then help other thinkers become that also.

Breaking down the distinction between the theoretical and the practical. Another way of putting this is to close the gap between one's official and unofficial philosophy. The former is what one professes to believe; the latter is what one reveals by actions to be what he or she actually believes. Tracing out the practical implications of one's belief or finding the presuppositions of one's actions should manifest the problems that exist.

Attaining a greater degree of objectivity. Postmodernism's insight is correct, that our historical situation and conditioning introduces a certain amount of subjectivity into all that we perceive and think. Since it is presumably impossible to "get outside our own skins," how can this subjectivity be reduced?

For example, if we understand that our interpretation of the Bible is affected by our philosophical presuppositions, we might decide that we are

---

[42] < www.fundadvice.com/simulator/index.html >.

going to use the Bible to formulate our presuppositions, thus avoiding the problem of distortion from external presuppositions. Here, however, we encounter a problem. For even the attempt to determine what presuppositions the biblical revelation provides is affected by our own antecedent presuppositions. We tend to find there what we bring with us to the study of the Scripture. Is there any escape from this quandary?

I believe help is available. We seem to be involved in a circular pattern here, since the Bible is to supply our philosophical conceptions, but our discerning of those within the Bible is itself affected by our antecedent philosophy. I propose that while a complete breakout of the circle may not be possible, its effect may be reduced by converting the circle into a spiral, and then narrowing that spiral. In other words, a series of incremental changes will be necessary. We should seek to discern whether the Bible gives us a metaphysic, then check against it our own conceptions, correcting them to fit, then repeating the exegesis, again matching the results to our philosophy, and continuing in this process. It is like adjusting an automobile compass. One does not attempt to eliminate the entire directional error in one step. Rather, one successively heads the car in each of the four primary directions, each time removing one half of the remaining compass error.

Something similar can be done with our philosophical assumptions. Unfortunately, this is generally not done, nor its need even acknowledged. What is frequently done is to point out how our opponents' philosophical views have distorted their understanding of Scripture, but not to ask what our own presuppositions may be, proceeding instead as if our own reading of the Scripture is simply the way it is, and our own outlook neutral and philosophically sterilized. Numerous examples of this type can be given. Thus, Jack Rogers argues that the philosophy behind the Old Princeton view of biblical inspiration was the Scottish Common Sense Realism of Thomas Reid, but never inquires about his own presuppositions.[43] John A. T. Robinson attributes the dualistic view of human nature to Greek thought, but does not suggest that he might be working with any presuppositions of his own.[44] The openness of God theologians attribute the distortion in Christian theology of the (biblical) open picture to the influence of God to the fusion of classical Greek thought with the biblical Hebraic view, but never raise the

---

[43]Jack Rogers, "The Church Doctrine of Biblical Authority," in *Biblical Authority*, ed. Jack Rogers (Waco, Tex.: Word, 1977), pp. 39-40. Rogers does identify his view in a general way with Platonism and the contrasting view with Aristotelianism, but never gets as specific about his view as he does in labeling the Princeton view Common Sense Realism. See also Jack Rogers and Donald McKim, *The Authority and Interpretation of the Bible: An Historical Approach* (San Francisco: Harper & Row, 1979).

[44]John A. T. Robinson, *The Body: A Study in Pauline Theology* (London: SCM Press, 1952).

possibility of any conditioning influence on their own ideas.[45]

Globalization. What claims to be postmodernism is actually frequently quite Euro-American, and male, Anglo, and middle class as well. As such, it is actually crypto-modern. As we have argued in the chapter on community, postpostmodernism must become genuinely and validly global, as one means of increasing its self-criticism and objectivity.

In this final chapter I have contended is that it is possible to relate to postmoderns by taking into account some of the ways in which they think and listen. Because there is a permanent element to Christianity, we cannot relate it too closely to postmodernism, which like all the ideologies that have preceded it will also be supplanted. Indications are appearing that the extremes of postmodernism are beginning to bring about a reaction, which we may call postpostmodernism. There are certain steps and actions we can take to help accelerate this transition, making a greater entrée to biblical Christianity, while at the same time seeking to assure that we are not merely tying the message to the form of a particular previous period.

---

[45]Clark Pinnock, Richard Rice, John Sanders, William Hasker, and David Basinger, *The Openness of God: A Biblical Challenge to the Traditional Understanding of God* (Downers Grove, Ill.: InterVarsity Press, 1994), pp. 59-76, 103, 129-33.

Name Index

Subject Index

Scripture Index